Mobilizing the Russian Nation

Despite the enormous literature that exists on the Russian revolution and its origins, very little is known about the ways in which ordinary Russians thought about and experienced the First World War. Melissa Kirschke Stockdale presents the first comprehensive study of the ways in which the Great War affected Russian notions of national identity and citizenship. The book examines the patriotic and nationalist organizations that emerged during the war, the role of the Russian Orthodox Church, the press, and the intelligentsia in mobilizing Russian society, the war's impact on conceptions of citizenship, and the new, democratized ideas of Russian nationhood that appeared as a result both of the war and of the 1917 revolution. Russia's war experience is revealed as a process that helped consolidate in the Russian population a sense of membership in a great national community, rather than being a test of patriotism that they failed.

MELISSA K. STOCKDALE is a Brian and Sandra O'Brien Presidential Professor and Professor of History at the University of Oklahoma, specializing in modern Russian history. Her previous publications include *Paul Miliukov and the Quest for a Liberal Russia, 1880–1918* (1997) and, with Murray Frame, Boris Kolonitskii, and Steven G. Marks, *Russian Culture in War and Revolution, 1914–1922* (2014).

Studies in the Social and Cultural History of Modern Warfare

General Editor
Jay Winter, *Yale University*

Advisory Editors
David Blight, *Yale University*
Richard Bosworth, *University of Western Australia*
Peter Fritzsche, *University of Illinois, Urbana-Champaign*
Carol Gluck, *Columbia University*
Benedict Kiernan, *Yale University*
Antoine Prost, *Université de Paris-Sorbonne*
Robert Wohl, *University of California, Los Angeles*

In recent years the field of modern history has been enriched by the exploration of two parallel histories. These are the social and cultural history of armed conflict, and the impact of military events on social and cultural history.

Studies in the Social and Cultural History of Modern Warfare presents the fruits of this growing area of research, reflecting both the colonization of military history by cultural historians and the reciprocal interest of military historians in social and cultural history, to the benefit of both. The series offers the latest scholarship in European and non-European events from the 1850s to the present day.

This is book 45 in the series, and a full list of titles in the series can be found at: www.cambridge.org/modernwarfare

Mobilizing the Russian Nation: Patriotism and Citizenship in the First World War

Melissa Kirschke Stockdale
University of Oklahoma

CAMBRIDGE
UNIVERSITY PRESS

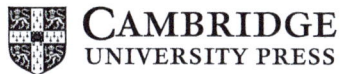

CAMBRIDGE
UNIVERSITY PRESS

University Printing House, Cambridge CB2 8BS, United Kingdom

Cambridge University Press is part of the University of Cambridge.

It furthers the University's mission by disseminating knowledge in the pursuit of education, learning and research at the highest international levels of excellence.

www.cambridge.org
Information on this title: www.cambridge.org/9781107093867

© Melissa Kirschke Stockdale 2016

This publication is in copyright. Subject to statutory exception and to the provisions of relevant collective licensing agreements, no reproduction of any part may take place without the written permission of Cambridge University Press.

First published 2016

Printed in the United Kingdom by Clays, St Ives plc

A catalogue record for this publication is available from the British Library

Library of Congress Cataloguing in Publication data
Names: Stockdale, Melissa Kirschke, author.
Title: Mobilizing the Russian nation : patriotism and citizenship in the First World War / Melissa Kirschke Stockdale, University of Oklahoma.
Description: New York : Cambridge University Press, 2016. | Series: Studies in the social and cultural history of modern warfare ; 45 | Includes bibliographical references and index.
Identifiers: LCCN 2015045377| ISBN 9781107093867 (Hardback) | ISBN 9781107474857 (Paperback)
Subjects: LCSH: World War, 1914-1918–Social aspects–Russia. | World War, 1914-1918–Political aspects–Russia. | War and society–Russia–History–20th century. | Industrial mobilization–Russia–History–20th century. | Patriotism–Russia–History–20th century. | World War, 1914-1918–Russia.
Classification: LCC DK264.8 .S76 2016 | DDC 940.3/47–dc23 LC record available at http://lccn.loc.gov/2015045377

ISBN 978-1-107-09386-7 Hardback

Cambridge University Press has no responsibility for the persistence or accuracy of URLs for external or third-party internet websites referred to in this publication, and does not guarantee that any content on such websites is, or will remain, accurate or appropriate.

Contents

List of Figures		*page* vi
Acknowledgments		x
Note on Usage and Translation		xiii
Chronology		xiv
Introduction	Mobilizing a Nation: Patriotism and Citizenship in Russia's Great War, 1914–1918	1
1	A Sacred Union: Patriotic Narratives and the Language of Inclusion	15
2	National Mobilization: Government, Propaganda, and the Press	45
3	"On the Altar of the Fatherland": The Orthodox Church and the Language of Sacrifice	75
4	"All for the War!": War Relief and the Language of Citizenship	106
5	United in Gratitude: Honoring Soldiers and Defining the Nation	140
6	Fantasies of Treason: Sorting Out Membership in the Russian National Community	166
7	"For Freedom and the Fatherland": Shaping Citizens in Revolutionary 1917	213
	Conclusion	247
	Select Bibliography	261
	Index	277

Figures

1.1 On July 20, 1914, a diverse crowd of approximately 250,000 people gathered on Palace Square to see Tsar Nicholas II, following Germany's declaration of war. Photo courtesy of Bettmann/Corbis. *page* 19
1.2 Nicholas and Alexandra being greeted by throngs at the Kremlin in Moscow, August 1914. Photo reproduced from *Letopis' voiny*, courtesy of Harvard University. 20
1.3 Some 20,000 people joined a patriotic demonstration in Moscow in front of the statue of Kuz'ma Minin and Prince Dmitrii Pozharskii, July 1914. Photo reproduced from *Letopis' voiny*, courtesy of Harvard University. 28
1.4 A wartime session of the State Duma; in July 1914, the Duma symbolized the people's patriotic transcendence of political, national, and religious differences. Photograph courtesy of Bettmann/Corbis. 29
2.1 "German atrocities at Kalisz," 1914; depictions of a barbaric enemy were one means of promoting internal unity. Political Poster Collection, #RU/SU 374, courtesy of Hoover Institution Library & Archives, Stanford University. 50
2.2 A symbolic map of Russia and Europe, from 1915; mass editions of maps of Russia and the theaters of war were distributed throughout the war. Political Poster Collection, #RU/SU 780A, courtesy of Hoover Institution Library & Archives, Stanford University. 64
2.3 The slogan of this 1916 poster tells the viewer that buying into the war loan is "patriotic and profitable." Its depiction of a handsome young worker making munitions conveys the all-class nature of the sacred union. Political Poster Collection, #RU/SU 1226, courtesy of Hoover Institution Library & Archives, Stanford University. 65

List of Figures vii

2.4 The legend of this 1916 war loan poster reads "Our cities, villages, and churches await liberation ..." Political Poster Collection, #RU/SU 1241, courtesy of Hoover Institution Library & Archives, Stanford University. 67
2.5 A *lubok*-style poster depicting the feat of heroic Cossack Koz'ma Kriuchkov, the first recipient of the St. George Cross for valor in the Great War. Political Poster Collection, #RU/SU 83, courtesy of Hoover Institution Library & Archives, Stanford University. 68
3.1 Crowds praying in front of Kazan Cathedral in Petrograd on the All-Russian Day of Prayer, July 8, 1915. Reproduced from *Letopis' voiny*, RP9.L6255, Houghton Library, Harvard University. 83
3.2 "News from the War." Peasants listen attentively as a young man reads aloud from a newspaper; secular and religious authorities were particularly concerned to keep rural Russians connected to the war effort. Drawing by N. Bogdanov-Bel'skii, from the popular illustrated magazine *Niva*. 84
3.3 "A Sign of the August Victory." The image of the Mother of God and Christ Child appearing to Russian troops in 1914, prior to their success in Galicia, reinforces portrayal of the conflict as a "holy war." Political Poster Collection, #RU/SU 357, courtesy of Hoover Institution Library & Archives, Stanford University. 90
4.1 A map of the Russian empire in 1914; networks of war-relief organizations came into being across the country. Courtesy of the Drawing Office, School of Geography, Earth and Environmental Sciences, University of Birmingham. 111
4.2 A 1914 poster, "Moscow Aids the Wounded," 1914, depicts how a caring and compassionate community looks after the country's defenders. Political Poster Collection, #RU/SU 763, courtesy of Hoover Institution Library & Archives, Stanford University. 117
4.3 This poster, "War and the Press," advertises a fundraising exhibit organized in 1914 by the Union of Cities; with 630 member towns, it constituted one of the largest war-relief networks. Political Poster Collection, #RU/SU 862, courtesy of Hoover Institution Library & Archives, Stanford University. 127

List of Figures

4.4 A poster depicting the heroic feat of Sister of Mercy Rimma Ivanovna during battle, in 1915; inspiring images of Sisters of Mercy were ubiquitous in wartime Russia. Political Poster Collection, #RU/SU 353, courtesy of Hoover Institution Library & Archives, Stanford University.   132

4.5 This 1916 calendar, passed out by a rural credit cooperative, features drawings of rural people aiding the war effort in a variety of ways, including making boots for the army and sending gifts to soldiers. Political Poster Collection, #RU/SU 1091, courtesy of Hoover Institution Library & Archives, Stanford University.   135

5.1 "Dear Unexpected Guest." This poster conveys the esteem given the country's defenders, depicting a soldier being wounded, cared for in a hospital, and awarded a St. George Cross for valor, then returning home to the surprise and delight of his peasant family. Political Poster Collection, #RU/SU 684, courtesy of Hoover Institution Library & Archives, Stanford University.   151

5.2 Crowds gather in Petrograd for the formal launch of the St. George Cavaliers traveling exhibition, July 1916, one of the more innovative wartime efforts to celebrate the country's heroes. From *Letopis' voiny*, courtesy of Harvard University.   152

6.1 A symbolic rendering of the rapprochement of the two Slavic "sisters," Russia and Poland. Political Poster Collection, #RU/SU 854, courtesy of Hoover Institution Library & Archives, Stanford University.   174

6.2 "Down with the German Yoke!" Headlines on this 1914 poster trumpet "The Secrets of German Intrigues" and "German Provocations in Poland." Political Poster Collection, #RU/SU 1123, courtesy of Hoover Institution Library & Archives, Stanford University.   196

6.3 "A Letter Home." An artist's rendering of a widely reproduced photograph. Millions of letters passed between the front and home front during the war, attentively monitored by military censors. Political Poster Collection, #RU/SU 338, courtesy of Hoover Institution Library & Archives, Stanford University.   209

7.1 Russian soldiers take an oath of loyalty to the country and its new government in March 1917; their original oath pledged loyalty to the person of the tsar. Photo courtesy of Bettmann/Corbis.   215

7.2 Blinded veterans, led by a Sister of Mercy, demonstrate in support of continuing the war until victory, Petrograd, 1917; the great majority of soldiers did not share their sentiments. Photo courtesy of Bettmann/Corbis. 218

7.3 This poster for the 1917 liberty loan, by artist Boris Kustodiev, links continuing the war with defense of Russia's newly won freedoms. Political Poster Collection, #RU/SU 1225, courtesy of Hoover Institution Library & Archives, Stanford University 228

7.4 Mariia "Yashka" Bochkareva and soldiers of the first Women's Battalion of Death. In revolutionary 1917, "soldier-citizens" included as many as 6,000 women volunteers. From the Winifred Ramplee-Smith Collection, courtesy of the Hoover Institution Library & Archives, Stanford University. 237

Acknowledgments

It is truly a pleasure to acknowledge the abundant support and encouragement I have received for this project over the years. Funding was critical, making possible eight research trips to Russia as well as visits to collections in the United States, rights for and production of images, and much-valued time off for writing. I would like to thank the National Endowment for the Humanities, the American Philosophical Society, the International Research and Exchange Board, the Fulbright–Hayes Program, the Kennan Institute, and the College of Arts and Sciences and the Research Council of the University of Oklahoma. I am also grateful for funding received through my Presidential Professorship at the University of Oklahoma, made possible by the generous endowment of Brian and Sandra O'Brien, and the Kinney–Sugg Outstanding Professor Award, thanks to the kind gift of Sandy Kinney and Mike Sugg.

I am particularly grateful for my year in residence as a Wilson Scholar, at the Woodrow Wilson International Center for Scholars in Washington, DC. This remarkable program not only provides time and space for writing, but folds participants into a stimulating, congenial, and supportive group of scholars, staff, and librarians. I thank Blair Ruble, Will Pomeranz, and Christian Ostermann; staffers Kim Connor, Lucy Jilka (now at the State Department), Liz Malinkin, the late Edmita Bulota, and Lindsay Collins; and my research assistant, Madeleine Bachuretz. The terrific scholars from whom I learned so much – and whose company I so enjoyed – include Martin Dimitrov, Boris Lanin, Philippa Strum, Oleksandr Merezhko, Bruce Parrott, Charles Maier, Liudmila Pravikova, Susan Carruthers, David Greenberg, Mel Leffler, and Evgenii Tsimbaev.

Research is possible only thanks to the expertise and aid of archivists and librarians. I sincerely thank Laurie Scrivener, Molly Murphy, and the interlibrary loan staff at the University of Oklahoma; archivists Carol Leadenham, Jani Vishnu, and Stephanie Stewart at the Hoover Institution; Tanya Chebotarev, Curator of the Bakhmeteff Archive of Columbia University; the archivists of the State Archive of the Russian

Acknowledgments

Federation (Gosudarstvennyi arkhiv Rossiiskoi federatsii, GARF), and especially Nina Abdulatovna, head of the Reading Room, who has helped me countless times over the years; the librarians of Widener Library of Harvard University; the archivists and staff of the Russian State Military History Archive (Rossiiskii gosudarstvennyi voenno-istoricheskii arkhiv, RGVIA); the archivists and staff of the Russian State History Archive (Rossiiskii gosudarstvennyi istoricheskii arkhiv, RGIA); Janet Spikes, Dagne Gizaw, and Michelle Kamalich, librarians of the Wilson Center; the staff of the Slavic Division at the New York Public Library (sadly, a division that no longer exists); the librarians of the Russian National Library, particularly those of the wonderful "Gazetnyi zal" on the Fontanka; and the librarians of the Russian State Library, in Moscow, especially the amazing staff of the Military History Division.

Colleagues and friends have discussed with me Russian history, the First World War, nationalism, gender, and a host of other absorbing topics for many years, informing me, challenging me, pointing me toward sources, helping me refine ideas (and ditch a few along the way). In addition to the many colleagues – too numerous to list – who have commented on papers I have delivered at various scholarly conferences and workshops, I sincerely thank Brad Bradley, Kathy Brosnan, Jane Burbank, Laurie Burnham, Roger Chickering, Jennifer Davis Cline, Chris Ely, Cathy Ann Frierson, Rob Griswold, Nicky Gullace, Gary Hamburg, Pat Herlihy, Peter Holquist, Jill Irvine, Emily Johnson, David Levy, Norihito Naganawa, Colonel Brian Newberry, Josh Piker, Aleksandr Polunov, William Rosenberg, Tom Schwartz, Marsha Seifert, Alex Semyonov, Valentin Shelokhaev, Pavel Shcherbinin, Laurie Stoff, David Stone, Anastasia Tumanova, David Wrobel, and Oleg Zimarin. My superb colleagues on the editorial board of "Russia's Great War and Revolution" have been an unfailing source of inspiration, expertise, and just plain fun: I particularly thank Adele Lindenmeyr, David McDonald, Tony Heywood, John Steinberg, and, of course, the incomparable "Team Culture."

I am especially indebted to the friends and colleagues who took the time to read and thoughtfully comment on chapters, or the two articles that became parts of chapters, greatly improving them in the process: Laurie Burnham, Murray Frame, Cathy Ann Frierson, Sandie Holguin, Cathy Kelley, Boris Kolonitskii, Judy Lewis, Adele Lindenmeyr, Steve Marks, Bob Rundstrom, Dan Snell, Linda Reese, Aviel Roshwald, Ted Weeks, Christine Worobec, and the anonymous readers for the *American Historical Review*. Equally, I thank the scholars who read the typescript for Cambridge University Press and offered detailed suggestions for its improvement, including Mark von Hagen and Karen Petrone, as well as the reviewer who remains anonymous. Over the many years of this project I benefited in innumerable ways from the erudition and encouragement of the late Abbott "Tom" Gleason, my mentor and treasured friend. I greatly appreciate the support and expert advice of my editors at Cambridge, Michael Watson, Rosalyn Scott, and Claire Sissen, and copy-editor Karen Anderson Howes, as well as their patience with a number of missed deadlines.

Part of chapter five was first published as "'United in Gratitude': Honoring Soldiers and Defining the Nation in Russia's Great War," *Kritika, New Series, vol 7, no. 3* (Summer 2006): 459–85; part of chapter seven was first published as "'My Death for the Motherland is Happiness': Women, Patriotism, and Solidering in Russia's Great War, 1914–1917," *American Historical Review vol 109, no. 1* (February 2004): 78–116. I gratefully acknowledge Slavica Publishers and Oxford University Press, respectively, for permission to republish this material.

Finally, there are the people who offered love, friendship, and encouragement, including critical support during two battles with breast cancer: I absolutely could not have completed this project without you. In addition to beloved friends named above, I thank Martha Skeeters, Amy "Arie" Storer, Andrea Zizzi, Jana Hutchins Brewer, Shmuel Galai, and my wonderful extended family. Above all, I thank my son, Nic Stockdale, my sister, Amy Helene Kirschke, and my mom, Jane Elizabeth Bruce, who make life good and for whom I am so grateful: I lovingly dedicate this book to you.

Note on Usage and Translation

I have used the Library of Congress transliteration system in this book, without diacritical marks. Proper names are also rendered according to this system, though not consistently: familiar names such as Nicholas II appear in their usual English form. Non-Russian names of citizens of the Russian empire are given in Russianized form – thus General Ianushkevich, not Januszkewicz – except in citations and bibliography, where the author's name is rendered as it was published. Place names are especially tricky, since some have changed – sometimes multiple times – since 1914. For the most part, I use today's place names – Helsinki, for example, instead of Helsingfors – for the convenience of nonspecialists.

Until February 1, 1918 (when the Soviet regime changed the Russian calendar), Russia used the Julian calendar, which lagged behind the Western, Gregorian calendar by thirteen days in the twentieth century; this means that the outbreak of the First World War in Russia was on July 19, 1914, rather than August 1. Because my texts often invoke these, I have given dates prior to 1918 in the "old style."

All translations, unless otherwise noted, are my own.

Chronology

1914

July 4–13	Massive political strikes in St. Petersburg.
July 16/17	General mobilization declared.
July 19	Germany declares war on Russia.
July 20	Nicholas issues manifesto on war, greets crowd on Senate Square.
July 26	One-day special session of the legistlative chambers.
August	Formation of Union of Zemstvos and Union of Cities.
August 1	Manifesto promising autonomy to Poland.
August 19	St. Petersburg renamed Petrograd.
September 16	Prohibition extended for duration of war.
November 5	Bolshevik Duma deputies arrested on treason charges.

1915

January 27–29	Three-day special session of legislative chambers.
February–December	Decrees limiting property ownership in Russia by enemy aliens.
March 18	Miasoedev espionage scandal breaks.
April 18	Germans begin breakthrough of Russian lines at Gorlice, which will become the "Great Retreat."
May 27–29	Anti-German riots in Moscow.
July 19	Legislative chambers reconvene (first anniversary of war).
August 4	De facto abolition of Jewish Pale of Settlement.

August 22	Creation and program of Duma's Progressive Bloc announced; Nicholas II decides to assume supreme command of army.
September 3	Unexpected prorogation of legislative chambers; more moderate ministers are replaced with conservatives in Council of Ministers.

1916

January 20	Goremykin removed as premier; replaced by Shtiurmer.
February 9	Legislative chambers reconvened, remain in session until summer recess.
March 5	Announcement of fifth internal war loan, launch of massive publicity campaign.
Spring	Provisioning problems and inflation becoming dominant topic in press.
May 22	Brusilov offensive opens, enjoys initial success.
June 19	State Duma passes "peasant bill."
Summer	Massive uprisings over labor requisitions in Kazakhstan and Central Asia.
October–January 1917	Isolated mutinies in some frontline units.
November 1	Legislative chambers reconvene; Miliukov's "stupidity or treason" speech.
December 16/17	Murder of Rasputin.

1917

February 23	Beginning of massive bread riots, protests, and strikes in Petrograd.
February 26	Closure of Duma announced; troops ordered to fire on crowds.
February 27	Troops of Petrograd garrison go over to strikers; ministers arrested; Soviet of Soldiers' and Workers' Deputies and Temporary Committee of Duma formed.
March 2/3	Nicholas II abdicates.

March 3	Announcement of creation of Provisional Government, to govern until a constituent assembly can be elected and convened; Duma is not reconvened.
May 5	Formation of coalition Provisional Government, following antigovernment protests concerning war aims; socialists join government.
June 10	Ukrainian Rada declares autonomy of Ukraine.
June 18	Opening of Kerenskii offensive; by early July, Russian army is retreating.
July 3–5	"July Crisis": uprising against Provisional Government in Petrograd subdued by force; Bolshevik leaders arrested, flee.
July 10	Women's Battalion of Death enters combat.
July 24	Second coalition Provisional Government formed, headed by Kerenskii.
August 25–30	Kornilov rebellion.
October 25/26	Provisional Government is overthrown; formation of new temporary Soviet government by Bolsheviks.
October 26	Decree on Peace, announcing intention to seek negotiated end to war.
October 27	Decree on Press authorizes closure of oppositional ("counterrevolutionary") press.
November 10	Demobilization of part of Russian army begins.
November 23	Finland declares independence from Russia.
December 10	Armistice signed between Soviet and German governments.
December	Formation of anti-Bolshevik Volunteer Army begins in southern Russia.

1918

January 5	Constituent Assembly opens, is disbanded by Soviet authorities after one day.

January 14	Ukrainian Rada declares independence of Ukraine.
January 15	Decree on "Formation of Worker–Peasant Red Army."
January 25/February 9	Representatives of Ukraine conclude separate peace with Central Powers.
January 28/February 11, February 21	Peace negotiations break down; Soviet government issues decree "The Socialist Fatherland Is in Danger."
March 3	Peace treaty concluded with Central Powers at Brest-Litovsk; Russia exits war.

Introduction
Mobilizing a Nation
Patriotism and Citizenship in Russia's Great War, 1914–1918

On the morning of July 20, 1914, Russians learned that Germany had declared war on their country. Mobilization had been announced several days before and hundreds of thousands of men were already en route to join their units. Railroad stations were mobbed with crowds who had come to see them off. People wept, people wondered what the war might bring, and many people joined their communities in large patriotic demonstrations and prayer services. A few have left records of what they felt. The 33-year-old Baron Nikolai N. Vrangel', a writer and son of a wealthy and prominent family, wrote in his diary, "It is impossible to describe the emotion and enthusiasm that have seized Petersburg since the declaration of war. I have never seen such excitement, delight, and acceptance of the will of Fate." Like a number of intellectuals in other European capitals that day, he was swept up in the sense of unity: "Only in such exalted moments, when people are joined together by their every thought and feeling, do you understand all the grandeur and necessity of war."[1] Longing to aid his country in some meaningful way, he threw himself into the work of war relief.

More than 3,000 miles away, in the Yakut village of Amga in Siberia, a semi-literate peasant woman was also stirred by the call-up for war: "There was something holy about the nation's response to it ... It was an elevating, glorious, unforgettable moment." Mariia Bochkareva was 24 years old; having fled a drunken, abusive husband, she then followed a common-law husband into unhappy political exile. Now, she was gripped by the idea of becoming a soldier and heading for the front – as

---

[1] Baron N. N. Vrangel', *Dni skorbi. Dnevnik 1914–1915 godov*, ed. A. A. Murashev (St. Petersburg: Zhurnal "Neva," 2001), 19. Vrangel''s reaction immediately calls to mind that of Stefan Zweig as he joined enthusiastic crowds in Vienna at the outbreak of war: "I should not have liked to miss the memory of those first days. As never before, thousands and hundreds of thousands felt what they should have felt in peace time, that they belonged together ... All differences of class, rank, and language were flooded over at that moment by the rushing feeling of fraternity": Zweig, *The World of Yesterday: An Autobiography* (Lincoln: University of Nebraska Press, 1964), 223.

she recalled it, an inner voice called to her, "Go to war to help save thy country!" Doggedly overcoming opposition and ridicule from almost every corner, she successfully petitioned the tsar to enter the active army as a combat soldier.[2]

Neither of these individuals – the literary baron and the barely literate woman soldier – can be considered, by any measure, "typical." They also differed from each other in almost every respect. Yet the two characterized their response to the outbreak of war in very similar terms. Both were moved by the patriotism and unity of those around them, and both acted decisively on their desire to assist their country. In this they were not so different from millions of their compatriots. When Russians learned they were at war with Germany, an enormous wave of patriotism swept across the landscape. As we shall see, these patriotic manifestations of national unity, and the corresponding outpouring of voluntarism and donations, impressed contemporaries profoundly.

Yet three and a half years later, Russia's war had ended disastrously. Trying to make sense of humiliating defeat, many Russians concluded that the patriotic outpouring of the early war was illusory, that in fact the people had *not* loved their country enough to sustain the fight to the end. Often, this deficiency was represented as a consequence of the common people's inability to think of themselves as constituting a nation. Such were the views of a number of prominent and oft-cited generals.[3] In the 1920s General Anton Denikin claimed that the "illiterate masses of the population" went to war without a perception of the necessity to sacrifice: they simply could not understand "abstract national principles." General Aleksei Brusilov blamed this state of affairs on an inept imperial government, which had failed to teach the people to know their own country: "How could they acquire that patriotism which would inspire them with love for their great Russia?"[4] Generals Nikolai Golovin and Iurii Danilov also argued along these lines, as did prominent ex-tsarist officials.[5]

---

[2] Maria Botchkareva, *Yashka: My Life as Peasant, Officer and Exile. As set down by Isaac Don Levine* (New York: Frederick A. Stokes Co., 1919), 21–25, 33–44, 64–65, 71–76.

[3] A rare example that predates Russia's defeat is General N. Ianushkevich's assertion that the masses could not grasp the idea of fighting for Russia: a person from Tambov "is ready to stand to the death for Tambov province, but the war in Poland seems strange and unnecessary to him" (in Michael Cherniavsky, ed., *Prologue to Revolution: Notes of A. N. Iakhontov on the Secret Meetings of the Council of Ministers, 1915* [Englewood Cliffs, NJ: Prentice-Hall, 1967], "The Meeting of 24 July 1915," 22–23).

[4] A. I. Denikin, *The Russian Turmoil: Memoirs: Military, Social, and Political.* (London: Hutchinson and Co., n.d.), 21–22; A. A. Brusilov, *A Soldier's Notebook, 1914–1918* (London: Macmillan and Co., 1930), 38–40.

[5] N. N. Golovine, *The Russian Army in the World War* (New Haven: Yale University Press, 1931), 244–45, and Iu. N. Danilov, *Rossiia v mirovoi voine, 1914–1915 gg.* (Berlin: Slovo, 1924), 112, 115–16.

Mobilizing a Nation

Many scholars have similarly contended – though not always on the same grounds – that the mass of the population did not think of itself as a nation. The government is said to have conceived of Russia in traditional, imperial terms, while the common people's imagined community, to use Benedict Anderson's phrase, was decidedly local. According to one scholar, for example, "In the three centuries preceding the 1917 Bolshevik revolution, a critical mass consciousness based on nation or nationality did not develop in Russia."[6] Noting the importance of heroic narratives of the past for consolidating modern national communities, some historians suggest that prior to the 1930s Russians lacked "a sense of a common heritage and an awareness of a glorious history."[7] Others believe that because print was still primarily an urban phenomenon in 1914, patriotic culture did not extend to the peasantry. Some discern a lack of positive content in wartime patriotic culture, alleging that Russians knew what they were fighting *against*, "but not for whom and for what."[8] Scholars who argue that Russians did come to think of themselves as belonging to a national community, thanks in part to the impact of the war, are in a minority.[9]

---

[6] Astrid Tuminez, *Russian Nationalism since 1856: Ideology and the Making of Foreign Policy* (Lanham, MD: Rowman & Littlefield, 2000), 38. See also Richard Pipes, *The Russian Revolution* (New York: Knopf, 1990), 203–04; and Robert J. Kaiser, *The Geography of Nationalism in Russia and the USSR* (Princeton: Princeton University Press, 1994), 33–89, who contends that limited geographic and social mobility, limited access to schooling, and the barriers imposed by a plethora of regional dialects all meant that, on the eve of the war, "a sense of homeland remained only weakly developed in the Russian countryside, while more localist sentiments continued to be dominant in the thinking of the Russian peasant." Similarly, Vera Tolz, *Russia* (New York: Oxford University Press, 2001), 6–7 and 180–81, believes that territorial nationalism did not greatly affect the lower classes prior to 1917. Ronald Grigor Suny, "The Empire Strikes Out: Imperial Russia, 'National' Identity, and Theories of Empire," esp. 43–44, points to "the failure of Russian elites to articulate a clear idea of the Russian nation, to elaborate an identity distinct from a religious (orthodox), imperial, state, or narrowly ethnic identity" (in Ronald Grigor Suny and Terry Martin, eds., *A State of Nations: Empire and Nation-Making in the Age of Lenin and Stalin* [New York: Oxford University Press, 2001], 23–66).

[7] David Brandenberger, *National Bolshevism: Stalinist Mass Culture and the Formation of Modern Russian National Identity, 1931–1956* (Cambridge, MA: Harvard University Press, 2002), 10–16.

[8] Hubertus F. Jahn, *Patriotic Culture in Russia during World War I* (Ithaca: Cornell University Press, 1995), 109, 172–74. Other scholars who contend that patriotic culture was largely an urban phenomenon include O. S. Porshneva, *Krest'iane, rabochie i soldaty* (Moscow: ROSSPEN, 2004), 86–91, 260–62; and Leonid Heretz, *Russia on the Eve of Modernity: Popular Religion and Traditional Culture under the Last Tsars* (Cambridge: Cambridge University Press, 2008).

[9] For example, Aaron B. Retish, *Russia's Peasants in Revolution and Civil War. Citizenship, Identity, and the Creation of the Soviet State, 1914–1922* (Cambridge: Cambridge University Press, 2008), esp. 4–7, 22–63; Joshua Sanborn, *Drafting the Russian Nation: Military Conscription, Total War, and Mass Politics, 1905–1925* (DeKalb: Northern Illinois University Press, 2003); and Melissa K. Stockdale, "United in Gratitude: Honoring Soldiers and Defining the Nation in World War I Russia," *Kritika* 7, 3 (Summer 2006), 459–85.

There were, admittedly, problems in promoting patriotism and national cohesion in Russia's Great War. For many citizens, uniting in support of the country's war effort was complicated by distrust of a repressive government, ideological divisions, deeply felt class antagonisms, or religious tensions and prejudices. The transitional nature of the period following the 1905 revolution further complicated questions of national identity: while Russia had ceased to be an absolutist regime, one in which the person of the tsar embodied the nation, it had not yet worked out its new basis of "nationhood." And, since some 50 percent of the population was not ethnically Great Russian (*russkii*), constructing a shared "all-Russian" (*rossiiskii*) national identity could be highly problematic.

Yet, until 1917, contemporaries were struck more by the perseverance of Russian patriotism than they were by its deficiencies. Preoccupied by Russia's defeat, we have not examined this love of country. It is thus simply asserted that the July 1914 wave of patriotism soon dissipated, when in fact we know very little about the nature, types, or evolution of patriotism in the war. We have more or less taken on trust the claim that the authorities were reluctant to mobilize the masses, and that relatively little was done to create and disseminate popular patriotic narratives. Similarly, in taking a weak sense of nationhood to be a critical weakness of the Russian war effort, most scholars have not considered how the crucible of the war might have *forged* a new or stronger sense of the broad Russian nation, as Mark von Hagen persuasively argues was the case for Ukrainian national consciousness.[10]

Certainly Russians themselves commonly regarded this gigantic conflict as "transformative," though they could differ as to what, precisely, was being transformed, and the changes they expected it to produce. For example, religious thinkers and philosophers spoke of spiritual rebirth and "moral renewal," political reformers talked about the transformation of subjects into citizens and anticipated postwar democratization, and the business community looked forward to the unleashing of Russian entrepreneurial talents. Peasants perhaps had the greatest expectations, including more equality of rights with other social estates, expanded access to education, and land. In fact, all these mobilized expectations would prove problematic in 1917.[11]

We have largely overlooked a related dimension of this question, which is how various sectors of the population expected to advance their collective interests through shaping and buying into the narrative of the

---

[10] Mark von Hagen, "The Great War and the Mobilization of Ethnicity in the Russian Empire," in Barnett Rubin and Jack Snyder, eds., *Post-Soviet Political Order: Conflict and State Building* (London: Routledge, 1998), 34–57.

[11] A good summary of educated society's expectations is the collection *Chego zhdet Rossiia ot voiny. Sbornik statei* (Petrograd: Kn-vo "Prometei," 1915).

national patriotic "sacred union": patriotism can have its rewards.[12] Such groups included political parties, social estates, national minorities, and also Russian women, who bore the greatest share of the burden on the home front and played a disproportionately large role in war relief. Finally, in Russia as in all the belligerent states, no entity had a monopoly on patriotic discourse. Governmental, civic, and private organizations engaged in efforts to define and appeal to the patriotic national community, as did individual citizens. The diversity of voices and values precluded the possibility of a single master narrative. But contestations over the meaning and content of patriotism, and efforts to rethink who was included in the national community, should not be mistaken for the absence of certain powerful, shared themes and myths. By exploring different efforts to define and mobilize patriotism, citizenship, and Russian national identity over the course of the Great War, I hope to contribute to our understanding of the ways the war influenced these critical concepts.

Origins and Structure

This study is in part an outgrowth of my first monograph, a biography of liberal leader Pavel N. Miliukov, who played a prominent part in Russia's war effort and was also a champion of Russia's national minorities.[13] When I began looking into the scholarly literature on the war years for that study, I was surprised to discover how little had been written on Russia, particularly in comparison to the vast literature on other Entente countries and on Germany. Delving deeper into the primary sources, and poring over the wartime press, I was still more surprised. They told stories of inclusive patriotism, civic activism, and voluntarism, on the one hand, and radical policies of persecution and exclusion, on the other, that were missing or undeveloped in the scholarly literature. This wartime Russia was unrecognizable and unknown, and I wanted to explore it.

Happily, the scholarly landscape has changed since I began this project. This book builds on an exciting new generation of work on wartime political culture, military mobilization, and the expanding powers of the

---

[12] Linda Colley, *Britons: Forging the Nation, 1707–1837* (New Haven: Yale University Press, 1992), 54–56, 93–94, makes this important point in talking about how a British nation was created, noting that different classes and interest groups came to see this new national amalgam as "a usable resource, as a focus of loyalty which would also cater to their own needs and ambitions" (55).

[13] Melissa Kirschke Stockdale, *Paul Miliukov and the Quest for a Liberal Russia, 1880–1918* (Ithaca: Cornell University Press, 1997).

state by Boris Kolonitskii, Peter Holquist, Josh Sanborn, Eric Lohr, and others.[14] I am also indebted to the superb work on refugees, the war in the village, and memory of the Great War by Peter Gatrell, Aaron Retish, Scott Seregny, and Karen Petrone, to name but a few.[15] These studies were made possible by two critical developments: the opening of Russian archives, and the post-Cold War rethinking of the relationship between Russia's Great War and the revolution that it precipitated. Now, instead of regarding February 1917 as a great divide, the point where scholarly studies end or begin, many scholars share a conceptualization of the war, revolution, and civil war as a period, a "continuum of crisis" or "seven years' war," as Holquist and Igor Narskii have influentially argued.[16]

I begin by exploring Russia's "sacred union," a grand patriotic narrative of unity, service, generosity, and sacrifice assembled at the start of Russia's Great War. I analyze representations of the patriotic demonstrations of the first weeks of war, the historic July 26 session of the State Duma, and the popular responses to the general mobilization. I then turn to efforts to connect this "Second Fatherland War" (a name we forget was initially applied to this conflict) with the heroic Russian efforts against invaders in the Fatherland War of 1812. The chapter ends with a brief look at several events that were *not* included in this master narrative, such as riots by reservists and by soldiers' wives, and the authorities' preemptive suppression of potentially dissenting views on the war.

[14] Boris Kolonitskii, *Tragicheskaia erotika. Obrazy imperatorskoi sem'i v Pervoi mirovoi voine* (St. Petersburg: Novoe literaturnoe obozrenie, 2010); Peter Holquist, *Making War, Forging Revolution: Russia's Continuum of Crisis, 1914–1922* (Cambridge, MA: Harvard University Press, 2002); Sanborn, *Drafting the Russian Nation*; Sanborn, *Imperial Apocalypse: The Great War and the Destruction of the Russian Empire* (New York: Oxford University Press, 2014); and Eric Lohr, *Nationalizing the Russian Empire: The Campaign against Enemy Aliens during World War I* (Cambridge, MA: Harvard University Press, 2003). An exhaustive and penetrating study of soldiers at the front, up to the revolution, is A. B. Astashov, *Russkii front v 1914–nachale 1917 goda: voennyi opyt i sovremennost'* (Moscow: Novyi khronograf, 2014).

[15] Peter Gatrell, *A Whole Empire Walking: Refugees in Russia during World War I* (Bloomington: Indiana University Press, 1999); Retish, *Russia's Peasants*; Scott J. Seregny, "Zemstvos, Peasants, and Citizenship: The Russian Adult Education Movement and World War I," *Slavic Review* 59, 2 (Summer 2000), 290–315; and Karen Petrone, *The Great War in Russian Memory* (Bloomington: Indiana University Press, 2011).

[16] Holquist, *Making War, Forging Revolution*, and Igor Narskii, *Zhizn' v katastrofe: budni naseleniia Urala v 1917–1922 gg.* (Moscow: ROSSPEN, 2001). Further testimony to this reperiodization is the international scholarly publishing project "Russia's Great War and Revolution, 1914–1922," the first two volumes of which are: Murray Frame, Boris Kolonitskii, Steven G. Marks, and Melissa K. Stockdale, eds., *Russian Culture in War and Revolution, 1914–1922*, 2 books (Bloomington: Slavica, 2014), and Eric Lohr, Vera Tolz, Alexander Semyonov, and Mark von Hagen, eds., *The Empire and Nationalism at War* (Bloomington: Slavica, 2014).

Chapter 2, "National Mobilization," explores governmental and public efforts to define and promote patriotism and an inclusive national identity after the outbreak of war. I examine efforts to promote unity by inciting hatred of the enemy, but my main focus is positive means, such as the content and nature of surprisingly large and sophisticated propaganda campaigns, publishing ventures, and massive war-loan drives.

Chapter 3, "'On the Altar of the Fatherland,'" examines the church's role in shaping and sustaining patriotism. We know how important the legitimizing function of the Orthodox Church was for the Soviet regime in 1941, when the church promptly declared the fight against the German invaders a "holy war," but we know very little about its far more extensive activities in the Great War. Here, I look at new prayers and public rituals to unify the people and memorialize the fallen; the new nationally distributed parish newspaper that apprised the population of war relief, war needs, and the holy nature of Russia's cause; and clerical writings and sermons on the meaning of the war and the necessity of sacrifice.

Chapter 4, "All for the War," explores how various groups involved themselves in war relief, and the meanings assigned to these efforts. This wartime outpouring of aid and labor, from all across the empire and from every social class, helped generate a positive image of a compassionate, generous, and inclusive "all-Russian" national community. Many people believed that this unprecedented national self-mobilization would transform passive, parochial subjects into conscious and active citizens. And many members of population groups subject to restricted rights hoped their patriotic service and sacrifice would earn them fuller access to citizenship at war's end.

Chapter 5, "'United in Gratitude,'" looks at efforts to sidestep vexing class, ethnic, and confessional differences by uniting a diverse population around the figure of the soldier. I do this by exploring three innovative wartime projects: the campaign to properly bury and memorialize every fallen soldier, to publicly celebrate and reward heroes, and to create a new national holiday honoring "Those Who Have Shed Their Blood for Russia." These efforts helped enmesh the duty of military service to the state with full membership in the national community, and the modern notion of rights owed citizens for that service.

The next chapter, "Fantasies of Treason," takes up the obverse side of unifying the national community: efforts to identify and exclude individuals or groups that did not belong within it. One long-suspect population group, the Poles, managed to win an honorable new place in the national community through their suffering and sacrifice. But for two other groups, Russia's Jews and Germans, patriotic service and sacrifice did not save them from identification as enemies within. As the war dragged on, speculators, profiteers, and an array of nebulously defined traitors and spies thought to have infiltrated the army and the court were added to the list of internal enemies. Widespread fantasies of treason eroded public confidence in the dynasty and government, as well as the very idea of a sacred union of the nation.

Chapter 7, "'For Freedom and the Fatherland,'" maps the altered political landscape of patriotic discourse and action after February 1917. The end of the monarchy, and proclamation of democracy and equal rights, greatly influenced conceptions of patriotism, citizenship, and the national community. So, too, did war-weariness, growing social tensions, and an imploding economy. I examine the voluminous public debate over patriotism and citizenship – issues that could now be freely contested thanks to the near absence of censorship – and efforts of the Provisional Government to remobilize public support for the war. I also analyze the mass phenomenon of volunteering for combat, especially by women, as a most concrete expression of love of country and the duty of the citizen.

Sources and Definitions

The source base for this study is vast. Nonmilitary archival materials include data on patriotic organizations and commemorative projects; the papers of political parties and wartime patriotic societies; materials from a wide variety of propaganda campaigns, including all kinds of photos and graphic images; and secret police reports based on intercepted private correspondence. The papers of prominent Russians – most particularly the 5,000 files contained in liberal leader Pavel N. Miliukov's collection in Moscow – are another important source for wartime views and activities.[17] The enormous synodal records for the war include material on church publishing and on clerical efforts to support the morale of the troops and the home front; monthly reports on parish war relief activities; and dossiers on several unique investigations into rural clergy accused of unpatriotic activities. Military archives provide

---

[17] Most of the material in Miliukov's vast personal collection (*lichnyi fond*) is not of a personal nature: as both a historian and one of the most prominent politicians of the era, Miliukov collected – or had given to him – thousands of politically relevant documents, newspaper clippings, communiqués, and secret reports; he also kept hundreds of letters and telegrams sent by constituents, colleagues, and political opponents. (There are an additional 1,500 files in the Miliukov collection – dating from 1919 on – acquired at the end of the Second World War and held in a different part of the archive.)

illuminating digests of soldiers' correspondence with the home front, made by military censors in 1916; material on projects for identifying and publicizing national popular heroes; information on operations to cleanse active military zones of Jews and other "suspect" groups in 1914 and 1915; and data on men and women volunteering for the regular army and the revolutionary battalions of death.

A particularly important source for a study of patriotic discourse and activities is the periodical press. Some 871 *new* periodicals came into being in 1914 and 1915, many of them war-related.[18] Newspapers and magazines allow us to follow patriotic narratives of the nation being disseminated to various audiences, citizens' efforts to organize war relief and philanthropy, and outcomes of mobilizing campaigns. For the period 1914–16, I make use of eighteen daily, weekly, and monthly periodicals, including high-brow "thick journals," the political press, mass-circulation dailies and tabloids, rural and church papers, and illustrated magazines. For 1917, I add new revolutionary and patriotic publications to the mix. Finally, I use other publications that were relatively short-lived or which have been only incompletely preserved (many periodicals directed at women and at rank-and-file soldiers fall into this category).

The stenographic reports of sessions of the State Duma are a valuable source for mapping the political discourse of sacred union, policy debates on who should be included in – or excluded from – the patriotic national community, and debates over how citizens' wartime service should be recognized and rewarded. (Equal rights for minorities? Land for peasants? The franchise for women?) Another fascinating source is wartime diaries and correspondence, many of them located in archives or only recently published. Particularly revealing is the marvelously detailed diary of the capital's wartime mayor, Count Ivan Tol'stoi. At the opposite end of the social spectrum is another rare and valuable source, the laconic diary of a middle-aged peasant, A. A. Zamaraev, from the northern province of Vologda.[19] Valuable insights also come from nurses, medics, or others working for major war-relief organizations, such as Vrangel' at the Red Cross and Jewish activist S. Ansky, for the Union of Cities; these were people who typically traveled along the various

---

[18] T. A. Belogurova, *Russkaia periodicheskaia pechat' i problemy vnutrennei zhizni strany v gody Pervoi mirovoi voiny (1914–fevral' 1917)* (Smolensk: Gody, 2005), 41–42; while a large number of these periodicals were published in the two capitals, periodicals were published in a total of 1,808 Russian cities and towns.

[19] I. I. Tol'stoi, *Dnevnik v dvukh tomakh*, vol. II, *1910–1916*, ed. V. B. Ananich (St. Petersburg: "Liki Rossii," 2010), and V. V. Morozov and N. I. Reshetnikov, eds., *Dnevnik totemskogo krest'ianina A. A. Zamaraeva, 1906–1922 gody* (Moscow: Rossiiskaia akademiia nauk, 1995).

fronts or between front and rear, and recorded their immediate impressions in letters or diaries.[20]

The rich scholarship on nationalism, citizenship, and patriotism, as well as on the European experience of the Great War, has informed this study in a variety of ways. Benedict Anderson's work on the nation as imagined political community has not only profoundly influenced my approach, but at times seems almost to have influenced the culture I study, so closely does wartime Russian national imagining follow his strictures on the importance of disseminating – via print culture, through "empty homogeneous time" – national maps, unifying rituals, and a sense of a glorious shared past.[21] Also important is the work of Eric Hobsbawm – particularly on appreciating the gap between national ideas that elites propagate and what ordinary people choose to make of those ideas – as well as that of Jay Winter, George Mosse, Linda Colley, Aviel Roshwald, John Horne, and other scholars.[22]

Because I pay particular attention in this study to words and their use – the languages of patriotism, citizenship, and exclusion – it is important to define some key terms. I understand the term "patriotism" fairly broadly. At its most basic, it connotes love of and loyalty to one's country or *patria* – that is, traditional, state-based patriotism. But alongside it there can be patriotism that is local, chauvinistic, pacifistic, or social, in the sense of making one's compatriots the fundamental object of concern and loyalty.[23] A strong current of aspirational patriotism emphasized

---

[20] Besides Vrangel''s long-unpublished diary, *Dni skorbi*, see S. Ansky, *The Enemy at His Pleasure: A Journey through the Jewish Pale of Settlement in World War I*, ed. and trans. Joachim Neugroschel (New York: Henry Holt and Co., 2002). An absorbing diary by a woman doctor and prominent socialist who worked on a medical evacuation train must be used with caution, since it was published during wartime and therefore subject to censorship constraints: Tatiana Alexinsky, *With the Russian Wounded*, trans. Gilbert Cannan (London: T. Fischer Unwin, Ltd., 1916).

[21] Benedict Anderson, *Imagined Communities: Reflections on the Origin and Spread of Nationalism*, revised edn. (London: Verso, 1991).

[22] E. J. Hobsbawm, *Nations and Nationalism since 1780: Programme, Myth, Reality* (Cambridge: Cambridge University Press, 1990), 11, and Hobsbawm, "Mass-Producing Traditions: Europe, 1870–1914," in Hobsbawm and Terence Ranger, eds., *The Invention of Tradition* (New York: Cambridge University Press, 1983), 263–307. Aviel Roshwald writes incisively on the function of "violation and volition" in national myths: Aviel Roshwald, *The Endurance of Nationalism: Ancient Roots and Modern Dilemmas* (Cambridge: Cambridge University Press, 2006).

[23] In addition to Colley, *Britons*, helpful discussions of patriotism include Rogers Brubaker, "In the Name of the Nation: Reflections on Nationalism and Patriotism," in Philip Abbott, ed., *The Many Faces of Patriotism* (Lanham, MD: Rowman & Littlefield, 2007), 37–51; Hobsbawm, *Nations and Nationalism since 1780*, 86–93; Eugen Weber, *Peasants into Frenchmen* (Stanford: Stanford University Press, 1976), 95–114; and Hugh Cunningham, "The Language of Patriotism, 1750–1914," *History Workshop Journal* 12 (1981), 8–33.

fighting for a fairer, more democratic future, rather than in defense of putative "age-old traditions."[24]

As Michael Billig has noted, "To have a national identity is to possess ways of *talking* about nationhood."[25] One aspect of the wartime Russian vocabulary of nation and country that can be particularly confusing is the nearly interchangeable use of the words fatherland (*otechestvo*) and motherland (*rodina* – also translated by some scholars as "homeland"). The word fatherland was more prevalent in official discourse, while the word motherland could have more intimate and "organic" connotations, and was also used to refer to one's own home region, along the lines of the French *petite patrie*. Nonetheless, in the Great War the words Motherland and Fatherland – especially when capitalized – were essentially synonyms, often showing up in the very same sentence. Frequently, they were used instead of, but as equivalents to, "country" *(strana)* and the loan-word "nation" *(natsiia)*.[26]

Citizenship is a hotly disputed concept and the subject of a voluminous literature, with various scholars stressing different attributes, and recognizing, as well, distinctive national citizenship traditions.[27] In the late imperial Russian context, the legally recognized inhabitants of the state were subjects *(podannye)*, sorted into specific categories enjoying distinct and by no means identical duties and privileges. Liberals and progressives aspired to replace subjecthood *(podannstvo)* with the modern category of citizenship *(grazhdanstvo)*, understood as

---

[24] Marxist Georgii Plekhanov, for example, argued that German victory would strengthen the old order, while Russian victory would aid the "liberation movement": G. V. Plekhanov, *O voine*, 2nd edn. (Petrograd, [1915]), esp. 25–32. On "aspirational patriotism," see David Monger, *Patriotism and Propaganda in First World War Britain* (Liverpool: Liverpool University Press, 2012), 95. A number of scholars distinguish between patriotism – a sentiment that is taken to be healthy, defensive, or benign – and nationalism, which is considered extreme and aggressive; for an overview and rebuttal of such distinctions, see Michael Billig, *Banal Nationalism* (London: Sage, 1996), 55–59, and Brubaker, "In the Name of the Nation."

[25] Billig, *Banal Nationalism*, 8 (emphasis added).

[26] For a study of the evolution of these two terms from the eighteenth century to the end of the Stalin era, see Melissa K. Stockdale, "What Is a Fatherland? Changing Notions of Duties, Rights, and Belonging in Russia," in Mark Bassin, Christopher Ely, and Melissa K. Stockdale, eds., *Space, Place and Power in Modern Russia: Essays in the New Spatial History* (DeKalb: Northern Illinois University Press, 2010), 23–48.

[27] I have drawn on Brubaker's influential discussion of two modern national citizenship traditions, *Citizenship and Nationhood in France and Germany* (Cambridge, MA: Harvard University Press, 1992), x, 39–49, and T. H. Marshall's classic formulation of citizenship understood as encompassing social rights no less than civil and political rights: Marshall, "Citizenship and Social Class," in Marshall, *Class, Citizenship, and Social Development* (Westport, CT: Praeger, 1973), 65–122.

entailing rights as well as obligations, equal for all and guaranteed by law.[28] These rights included certain material claims on the state, as well as the more usual civil and political rights. This concept of reciprocity forms the basis of my working definition, though in the context of wartime discourse I also emphasize the idea of citizenship rights as something one can earn through appropriate service and sacrifice for the nation's war.[29]

***

As we have now reached the centennial of the First World War, historians are again examining the war's huge significance in shaping our modern world. This study contributes to these appraisals by addressing gaps in our knowledge of what Russians thought about their country, their nation, and themselves in the crucible of the war. The only study of this subject is Hubertus Jahn's *Patriotic Culture in Russia during World War I* (1995), a pioneering work but one which limits its scope to popular culture in the first fifteen months of the war.[30] There are only partial studies on mobilization of the home front, and correspondingly little

---

[28] A wonderful exploration of imperial subjecthood is Jane Burbank, "An Imperial Rights Regime: Law and Citizenship in the Russian Empire," *Kritika* 7 (2006), 397–431. A study of the Russian citizenship tradition focusing on the concept of boundaries is Eric Lohr, *Russian Citizenship: From Empire to Soviet Union* (Cambridge, MA: Harvard University Press, 2012). See also Yanni Kotsonis, "'Face-to Face': The State, the Individual, and the Citizen in Russian Taxation, 1863-1917," *Slavic Review* 63 (2004), 221–46.

[29] Works that examine the connection between citizenship, soldiering, and war include Alan Forrest, "La Patrie en danger: The French Revolution and the First *Levee en masse*," in Daniel Moran and Arthur Waldron, eds., *The People in Arms: Military Myth and National Mobilization since the French Revolution* (Cambridge: Cambridge University Press, 2003), 8–32; Bertrand Taithe, *Citizenship and Wars: France in Turmoil, 1870–1871* (London: Routledge, 2001), 1–20; and Nicoletta F. Gullace, *"The Blood of Our Sons": Men, Women, and the Renegotiation of British Citizenship during the Great War* (New York: Palgrave Macmillan, 2002), 1–10. Conscription, citizenship, and the notion of "equality of sacrifice" are discussed in Margaret Levi, *Consent, Dissent, and Patriotism* (Cambridge: Cambridge University Press, 1997), esp. 80–130.

[30] Given the 1917 revolution, it is not surprising that politics and political parties have been the most studied aspect of Russia's wartime experience. Besides tendentious Soviet studies of the Bolsheviks and worker activism, there are more recent studies of other parties in wartime, including Iu. I. Kir'ianov, *Pravye partii v Rossii, 1906–1917 gg.* (Moscow: ROSSPEN, 2001); F. A. Gaida, *Liberal'naia oppozitsiia na putiakh k vlasti (1914–vesna 1917 g.)* (Moscow: ROSSPEN, 2003); and Michael Melancon, *The Socialist Revolutionaries and the Russian Anti-War Movement, 1914–1917* (Columbus: Ohio State University Press, 1990). Two older and broader political studies are V. S. Diakin, *Russkaia burzhuaziia i tsarizm v gody Pervoi mirovoi voine, 1914–1917* (Leningrad: Nauka, 1967), and Raymond Pearson, *The Russian Moderates and the Crisis of Tsarism, 1914–1917* (London: Barnes & Noble, 1977).

Mobilizing a Nation 13

work on the roles played by Russian women in the war.[31] We have no studies of Russian wartime patriotic or nationalist organizations, or on the role of the press in mobilizing society in the Great War, such as exist for most of the other combatant countries.[32] Surprisingly, no study exists of the Russian Orthodox Church's activities in support of the war effort, including its legitimization of the conflict and conflation of Christian and patriotic duties of sacrifice.[33] The war's impact on modern conceptions of citizenship, which has been so richly explored for France, Britain, and the United States, has been only partially examined for Russia.[34] Finally, the revolution's role in eroding public willingness to continue the war has caused us to overlook ways in which liberationist sentiments could inform and support, as well as undercut, patriotic and national feeling.

Despite Russian generals' postwar lament that the common people had failed to conceive of a nation or continue to sacrifice for it, one is struck by the endurance of soldiers and civilians, and the generosity of the entire population, through years of hardship and staggering losses. The nobleman Nikolai Vrangel' and peasant Mariia "Yashka" Bochkareva were in this sense not so unique, being two out of a multitude who volunteered, endured, and suffered terribly in the war. It is quite possible to conclude that the war experience helped consolidate in the

---

[31] The only book-length study of either of the two largest "public organizations" is more than eighty years old: T. I. Polner, V. Obolenskii, and S. Turn, eds., *Russian Local Government during the War and the Union of Zemstvos* (New Haven: Yale University Press, 1930); more recent articles on these organizations are cited in Chapter 4. See also Lewis H. Siegelbaum, *The Politics of Industrial Mobilization in Russia, 1914–1917: A Study of the War-Industry Committees* (London: Macmillan, 1983); Peter Gatrell, *Russia's First World War: A Social and Economic History* (Harlow, UK: Pearson Education, 2005); and Gatrell, *A Whole Empire Walking*. A thoughtful recent study of civic organizations and war work is A. S. Tumanova, *Obshchestvennye organizatsii Rossii v gody Pervoi mirovoi voiny (1914–fevral' 1917 g.* (Moscow: ROSSPEN, 2014). Laurie Stoff is completing a book on Russian nursing during the war which will help fill important gaps in our knowledge of women's wartime activities.

[32] Such works include Monger, *Patriotism and Propaganda in First World War Britain*; P. J. Flood, *France 1914–1918: Public Opinion and the War Effort* (New York: St. Martin's Press, 1990); Verhey, *The Spirit of 1914: Militarization, Myth, and Mobilization in Germany* (Cambridge: Cambridge University Press, 2000); and Mark Cornwall, *The Undermining of Austria-Hungary: The Battle for Hearts and Minds* (Cambridge: Cambridge University Press, 2000).

[33] The classic treatment is John S. Curtiss, *Church and State in Russia: The Last Years of the Empire, 1900–1917* (New York: Octagon Books, 1965), but his chapter on the war is devoted to church politics and the Rasputin scandal. There is little work on the church's efforts on the home front, with the exception of the fine article by Scott Kenworthy, "The Mobilization of Piety: Monasticism and the Great War in Russia, 1914–1916," *Jahrbucher fur Geschichte Osteuropas* 52 (2004), 388–401.

[34] See also Christopher Capozzola, *Uncle Sam Wants You: World War I and the Making of the Modern American Citizen* (New York: Oxford University Press, 2008), and Gullace, "*The Blood of Our Sons.*"

population a sense of membership in a great national community, rather than being a test of patriotism that they failed. By enriching our understanding of Russians' experience of the Great War, I hope to help shift discussion of the causes of Russia's defeat from a putative – and exceptional – cultural "backwardness" to such factors as relative economic underdevelopment, an unsustainable level of casualties, and political delegitimization. And, by locating the origins of modern Russian national identity in the pre-Soviet period, it allows us to evaluate Russian nationalism as more than a Stalinist project.

1 A Sacred Union
Patriotic Narratives and the Language of Inclusion

> Yesterday's discord is forgotten. Yesterday's enemies have extended hands to one another. Blessed be this great hour of all-Russian union.
> V. I. Nemirovich-Danchenko, *Russkoe slovo*[1]

In the opening days of the Great War, virtually every combatant nation followed the lead of the French parliament in declaring a sacred union – *union sacrée* – of the nation. Typically, this special wartime union had two components: a renunciation of political, class, and confessional differences in the face of the common threat, and declaration of a political truce until the enemy had been defeated. Typically, too, the populations of the combatant nations were depicted as enacting corroborative scenes of patriotic unity, spontaneously joining in enthusiastic demonstrations and parades, singing and waving flags, and emotionally sending off their soldiers.[2] Russians, too, constructed a version of a "united Russia" (*ob"edinennaia Rossiia* or *edinaia Rossiia*) or "sacred union" (*sviashchennoe edinenie*).[3]

The Russian narrative of sacred union was assembled in July–August 1914, embodying three central strands or components. One strand was the traditional union of tsar and people, symbolized by the public's reception of Nicholas II on Palace Square in St. Petersburg on the day

---

[1] "Vchera i segodnia," *Russkoe slovo*, reprinted in special edition of *Russkie vedomosti*, January 1, 1915, 95.
[2] On the creation and enactment of "l'union sacrée" in France, see P. J. Flood, *France 1914–1918: Public Opinion and the War Effort* (New York: St. Martin's Press, 1990), 16–24, and Leonard V. Smith, Stéphane Audoin-Rouzeau, and Annette Becker, *France and the Great War, 1914–1918*, French sections trans. Helen McPhail (Cambridge: Cambridge University Press, 2003), 27–29; an extended analysis of the German variant is Verhey, *The Spirit of 1914*.
[3] Liberal leader Pavel Miliukov titled the section of his memoirs describing the outbreak of war "Sviashchennoe edinenie": P. N. Miliukov, *Vospominaniia (1859–1917)* (Moscow: Politizdat, 1991), 394–403. An analysis of the "political truce" aspect of sacred union is Raymond Pearson, *The Russian Moderates and the Crisis of Tsarism, 1914–1917* (London: Barnes & Noble, 1977), 10–38, who contends that this union had virtually ceased to function by June 1915.

he announced that Russia was at war with Germany, and preceded by the end of a massive strike that had paralyzed the capital for days. A variation on this theme was the equally traditional, triadic union of "faith, tsar, and fatherland," a formula often repeated over the course of the war. It was best symbolized by the imperial family's ceremonial visit to "Holy Moscow" several weeks after the outbreak of hostilities. Both these aspects of the patriotic narrative drew heavily on the memory of Russia's victorious Fatherland War of 1812.

The second strand of the narrative of sacred union concerned the patriotism of *all* Russia's people, regardless of belief or ethnicity, and the burying of their differences in support of Russia's just war. It was symbolized above all by the historic one-day session of the legislature on July 26, and especially the session of the lower house, the State Duma. There, in a chamber recently characterized by bitter partisanship and nationalist rancor, representatives of the major parties and national minorities declared love of the fatherland and solidarity with one another and with the government as they faced the aggressor. This patriotic unity transcended religious, ethnic, and ideological differences. Big patriotic parades and prayer services in cities across the country in July 1914 fed into the trope of a far-flung nation united.

The third strand of the patriotic narrative celebrated the willingness of all Russians to serve and sacrifice in defense of their country. Here, the emphasis shifted from words to deeds. The most obvious embodiment of service and sacrifice was the bearing of arms, symbolized in the massive military mobilization of reservists and an unexpected rash of volunteering that accompanied it. But also important was the self-mobilization of the civilian population for war relief, in an outpouring of voluntarism and generosity. This apparent willingness to serve and sacrifice was read as proof of popular support for Russia's just war. Many contemporaries believed that the tsar's decision to impose prohibition contributed to the success of these mobilizations. Ending Russians' thrall to demon drink (the "green serpent") reinforced characterization of this war as righteous and transformative, as compared to the ignominious conflict with Japan in 1904–05.

These three strands enjoyed an almost unprecedented level of publicity in the first months of the Great War, helping to create the narrative of a vast nation united in a just cause. Many groups would invoke the patriotic narrative repeatedly over the next two years. Policies were represented as supporting, undermining, or restoring the sacred union; the government and various organizations were characterized as adhering to or rupturing it in spirit or in practice. Of course, different individuals and groups interpreted this sacralized unity in different ways.

For example, where conservatives saw in the successful military mobilization a demonstration of the people's devotion to their sovereign, liberals and leftists saw proof of the people's civic maturity and fitness for fuller rights of citizenship. Finally, as is the case with assemblage of any unifying national myth or narrative – particularly in wartime – some events were left out, some stories censored, and some voices silenced entirely.[4]

The Union of Tsar and People

Several weeks prior to the outbreak of war, the mood in St. Petersburg was anything but unified. Heavy-handed suppression of labor strikes in the city of Baku had provoked sympathy strikes in the capital, beginning July 4; these rapidly assumed alarming dimensions. Count Ivan I. Tol'stoi, Mayor of St. Petersburg – a position with limited powers that did not include preservation of public order – wrote in his diary on July 7 that the strikes were continuing to expand and were becoming political; clashes between strikers and police had produced casualties on both sides. On July 8, he noted that at least 150,000 workers were striking, crowds in the working-class district of Vyborg were derailing tram cars and smashing their windows, and the "police are powerless to do anything." The next day saw more armed clashes between strikers, police, and Cossacks, with more casualties; few trams were operating anywhere in the city.[5] By July 9, the secret police reported, more than 117,000 workers were striking at 259 enterprises.[6]

This backdrop of bloody labor conflict made all the more remarkable the patriotic tableau on Palace Square, on the day following Germany's declaration of war on Russia. On the afternoon of July 20, 1914, the imperial family and some 5,000 people – mainly officers, senior officials, and members of the court – assembled in the Nikolaevskii Hall at the Winter Palace. On an altar placed in the center of the room was the icon of the Virgin of Kazan, before which Field Marshal Mikhail I. Kutuzov had prayed in 1812. At the conclusion of the mass, the court chaplain read aloud the tsar's manifesto to his people, with its summons to unity:

---

[4] The literature on selective memory in the service of national myth-making has a long pedigree, stretching at least from Renan's 1882 essay "Qu'est-ce qu'une nation?" ("What Is a Nation?"); for an excellent discussion of the issue of memory, see Roshwald, *The Endurance of Nationalism*, esp. 104–11.

[5] Tol'stoi, *Dnevnik*, II, 570–74.

[6] "Doklad nachal'nika Peterburgskogo okhrannogo otdeleniia Ministru vnutrennikh del (9 July 1914)," in Iu. I. Korablev, ed., *Rabochee dvizhenie v Petrograde v 1912–1917 gg. Dokumenty i materialy* (Leningrad: Leninizdat, 1958), 226.

"At this hour of threatening danger, let domestic strife be forgotten. Let the union between the Tsar and His people be stronger than ever, and let Russia, rising like one man, repel the insolent assault of the enemy."[7] In the account of Maurice Paleologue, the ambassador of France and the only foreigner present, the tsar then went up to the altar, "grave and composed, as if about to receive the sacrament," and declared: "Officers of my guard, here present, I greet in you my whole army and give it my blessing. I solemnly swear that I will never make peace so long as one of the enemy is on the soil of the fatherland." A wild outburst of cheering answered this declaration, which was copied from the oath taken by Emperor Alexander I in 1812. Then, all those present knelt.[8] Afterwards, Nicholas and the empress moved to a balcony to acknowledge the enormous crowd gathered on Palace Square, one of the largest public spaces in Europe.

That morning, newspapers had trumpeted the news of Germany's declaration of war. Thousands of people in the capital's various districts began converging onto the streets: to learn more details, to talk, simply to be with others. V. A. Obolenskii, a leader of the liberal Constitutional Democratic Party, later recalled that no one knew where they were headed as they joined the throngs and began moving: "Everyone felt a need to unite with the largest possible number of his fellow citizens, and therefore we directed ourselves toward the center of the city and not toward its periphery. Only in crossing the Troitskii Bridge did the crowd, as it were, understand the goal of its movement. Voices rang out: 'To the Winter Palace!' and the entire human torrent rushed toward Palace Square." It was not shared political views that had necessarily drawn them to the square, he wrote; rather, everyone felt the need to "accomplish some sort of ritual that would sanctify the unity of our feelings, to testify to the fact that the country was in solidarity with he who had accepted for Russia the challenge thrown down by her enemies."[9]

---

[7] In the description printed in *Rech'*, the imperial family is described as coming to the Winter Palace from New Peterhof by water, on the imperial yacht *Aleksandria*: "V zimnem dvortse," *Rech'* (July 22, 1914), 4. This description also refers to huge throngs on the embankment hailing the family, dropping to their knees, and singing the anthem, a scene that did not make its way into the narrative of sacred union on Palace Square. A translation of the text of the imperial manifesto is in Frank Alfred Golder, ed., *Documents of Russian History, 1914-1917*, trans. Emanuel Aronsberg (New York: Century Co., 1927), 29–30.

[8] Maurice Paleologue, *An Ambassador's Memoirs*, trans. F. A. Holt, 3rd edn., vol. I (London: Hutchinson and Co., 1924), 50–52, and "V zimnem dvortse." (Note that the Russian text is slightly different than Paleologue's version: "I here solemnly declare that I will not conclude peace until the last enemy soldier has left our land.")

[9] V. A. Obolenskii, *Moia zhizn', moi sovremenniki* (Paris: YMCA Press, 1988), 458–59.

1.1 On July 20, 1914, a diverse crowd of approximately 250,000 people gathered on Palace Square to see Tsar Nicholas II, following Germany's declaration of war. Photo courtesy of Bettmann/Corbis.

The crowd had reached huge proportions by mid afternoon on that sunny, sparkling Sunday, perhaps as many as 250,000 people. A quiet, "human sea" filled the enormous public space to capacity; others stood on balconies and roofs, or leaned out of windows. People held banners, flags, icons, and portraits of the tsar. Surviving photos and film clips document the crowd's diverse composition: bourgeois ladies with large hats and slim waists, workers in cloth caps, young men in suits and straw boaters. Visually, it was as though all Russia's social classes were there, something newspaper accounts did not fail to note.[10] They also remarked the patience and good order of the enormous crowd. When Nicholas and Alexandra at last appeared on the balcony, at approximately 6:00 p.m., the square exploded with deafening cheers. And then the assembled people dropped to their knees and began to sing the national anthem, "God Save the Tsar." "At that moment," rhapsodized *Novoe vremia*

---

[10] "Shoulder to shoulder stood workers, *intelligenty*, women, and children. It seemed that the entire population of Petersburg had flowed here, to the square before the Winter Palace": "Ob"iavleniia manifesta i slova Gosudara," *Russkoe slovo* (July 21, 1914), 1–2.

1.2 Nicholas and Alexandra being greeted by throngs at the Kremlin in Moscow, August 1914. Photo reproduced from *Letopis' voiny*, courtesy of Harvard University.

(New Times), "it seemed as if the Tsar and his people had strongly embraced one another, and in that embrace stood before the great motherland. Everywhere people gazed at the sovereign through tears – and these were tears of emotion and love."[11]

This mass demonstration of patriotism could scarcely have been counted upon in a city that had been in the throes of violent strikes just ten days earlier. The scene made a profound impression on those there.[12] One correspondent wrote to his paper, "It is impossible to convey what happened in those instants on the square ... some sort of unearthly force connected the balcony with this voluminous mass – the people and the tsar standing before them formed an unbreakable chain which called

---

[11] "Tsar i narod," *Novoe vremia* (July 21, 1914), 3.

[12] Bernard Pares – who was not actually there – pictured July 20 on Palace Square as a "tremendous scene of national enthusiasm" and embodiment of Russian community: Bernard Pares, *The Fall of the Russian Monarchy* (New York: Alfred A. Knopf, 1939), 187–88. Obolenskii recalled it rather differently, contrasting the crowd's heartfelt outpouring of patriotic feeling with the restrained nods from the remote figure of the tsar on the balcony. What he remembered seeing was the gulf dividing monarch and people, not their union: *Moia zhizn'*, 459.

A Sacred Union

to Russia."[13] The patriotic scene on Palace Square was taken to be paradigmatic of something far greater. The *Kievlanin'* editorialized: "Just a few days ago we scarcely realized the existence of this mighty spirit, this suddenly blazing, deep love of the motherland, that is now revealing itself ... In the midst of terrible ordeals, the sacred union of the Tsar and his People gains in strength and scope."[14] The journalist Litovchenko wrote: "Here is that psychological moment which defines historic events, the fate of peoples and of states ... A sacred flame has been kindled, toward which every Russian will strive, gathering without distinction of tribe, faith, or condition in a united, mighty, and boundless force."[15]

Detailed accounts of this event immediately flew across the empire, thanks to the presence of many papers' correspondents and the services of the St. Petersburg Telegraph Agency.[16] Photo spreads appeared in Sunday supplements and magazines, impressing readers with the size of the crowd and its diverse makeup.[17] One of the new wartime illustrated weeklies, *Letopis' voiny*, enthused, "It was impossible to hold back tears at the sight of such closeness of the Tsar to his own true [*vernyi*] people. Whoever was at the Winter Palace on July 20 will remember those sacred moments until the end of his life."[18]

The size of the crowd, its diverse composition, and the apparent spontaneity of its patriotic reaction all set the stage for the narrative of sacred union. This was not a war supported by only a small segment of population: it was a united "people's war," a defensive and just one. The crowd on Palace Square was a grandiose spectacle, Paleologue wrote, adding that he could not help recalling the outcome of an earlier and fatal effort by Petersburgers bearing icons and portraits to see their tsar – Bloody Sunday, January 9, 1905, when they were shot down in

---

[13] "Peterburzhets," "Peterburgskie otkliki," *Kievlianin'* (The Kievan) (July 26, 1914), 1.
[14] Unsigned lead article, *Kievlianin'* (July 22, 1914), 1.
[15] Litovchenko, "Sobiraites', russkie liudi – v edinenii sila," *Kievlianin'* (July 3, 1914), 1.
[16] The Petersburg Telegraph Agency, established in 1904, constituted a national news network as well as being the government's official news agency; see Louise McReynolds, "Autocratic Journalism: The Case of the St. Petersburg Telegraph Agency," *Slavic Review* 49, 1 (Spring 1990), 50. A fascinating discussion of the telegraph's role in consolidating Russian space is Marsha Seifert, "'Chingis Khan with the Telegraph': Communications in the Russian and Ottoman Empires," in Jörn Leonhard and Ulrike von Hirschhausen, eds., *Comparing Empires: Encounters and Transfers in the Long Nineteenth Century* (Göttingen: Vandenhoeck & Ruprecht, 2011), 80–110.
[17] For example, numerous photos of the crowds on Palace Square appeared in *Niva* no. 31 (August 2, 1914), 617–20, and *Letopis' voiny* no. 1 (August 1914), 8–9. Pathé also filmed the scene; see Marc Ferro, *Nicholas II: Last of the Tsars*, trans. Brian Pearce (New York: Oxford University Press, 1990), 156.
[18] S. N-chin, "Na Rusi," *Letopis' voiny* (Chronicle of War) no. 1 (August 1914), 23.

their hundreds.[19] Paleologue's reflection was likely shared by many: the juxtaposition of these two very different gatherings contributed to the symbolic portent of the vast, patriotic, and orderly crowd on Palace Square in July 1914, an image which could be laid over and efface the memory of the earlier tragedy that began a revolution.

The imperial family's visit to "Holy Moscow" in the first week of August represented a variant of the union of tsar and people, the triadic union of faith, tsar, and fatherland; it also deliberately echoed Alexander I's trip to Moscow in late July 1812 to mobilize its population against Napoleon's invasion.[20] The centerpiece of this visit was celebration of a high mass in the Kremlin's Uspenskii Sobor (Cathedral of the Assumption), where Russian rulers were traditionally crowned. Upon the sovereign's arrival at the Kremlin, all the church bells in Moscow pealed a welcome. Dozens of prelates in rich vestments were gathered to celebrate the service, which British ambassador George Buchanan found "beautiful and impressive beyond description." The scene outside the cathedral was equally memorable: "Walking along a slightly raised narrow platform to the other wing of the place, with nothing but a low railing to separate him from the kneeling multitude of his subjects – some of whom even kissed the ground as he passed – the Emperor was acclaimed with one never-ending cheer."[21] *Letopis' voiny* called the imperial family's trip to the ancient capital a "pilgrimage," contrasting this act of piety with the boastful behavior of the German Kaiser. Nicholas was deeply moved by the patriotic fervor of his reception in Moscow, telling representatives of the city that, "All the tribes and peoples of our empire have merged without distinction into this mighty, universal upsurge. Russia and I will *never forget* these historic days."[22]

Peoples and Parties United

The second component of the narrative of sacred union was embodied in the historic one-day session of the legislative chambers. The legislature was on its summer break when war broke out; on that same day, an *ukaz* (decree) signed by Nicholas announced an extraordinary legislative

---

[19] Paleologue, *Ambassador's Memoirs*, 52.
[20] Dominic Lieven, *Russia against Napoleon* (New York: Penguin Books, 2009), 220–25.
[21] George Buchanan, *My Mission to Russia and Other Diplomatic Memories*, vol. I (Boston: Little Brown and Co., 1923), 214–15.
[22] "Pervyi mesiats voiny," *Letopis' voiny* no. 2 (August 30, 1914), 29–30 (emphasis added). See also Richard Wortman, *Scenarios of Power: Myth and Ceremony in Russian Monarchy*, vol. II, *From Alexander II to the Abdication of Nicholas II* (Princeton: Princeton University Press, 2000), 510–11.

session for July 26: "In view of the trials sent to Our Fatherland, and desiring to be in complete union with the people, We consider it right to call together the State Council and the State Duma." The legislature could approve the requested war credits, and in doing so demonstrate to the world the country's unity and resolve.[23] Immediately, elaborate plans were drawn up for the sovereign's reception of deputies prior to convocation of the session. Duma deputies, scattered across the empire for the summer recess, hastily booked train tickets for a return to the capital. The leaders of each of the Duma's political groups, who together constituted its Senior Council, began meeting daily to plan the special session.[24]

The tsar had met with the assembled legislative deputies only once before, in 1906 at the ceremonial opening of the short-lived First Duma, which invested the July 26 reception with special significance. Dignitaries and ladies of the court, clergy, military officers, and representatives of the press, as well as members of the State Council and the Duma, were present. Nicholas pronounced a solemn and gracious welcome, stressing again his unity with the people and determination to fight until victory. Deputies responded with thunderous cheers. I. Ia. Golubev, speaking for the conservative State Council, struck a statist note, declaring that the union of the sovereign and the population would increase the empire's might. He added, "We are prepared for every sacrifice for the preservation of the honor and dignity of the united, indivisible Russian state."[25] Long-time ideological opponents shook hands and embraced, as part of the ritual of political reconciliation.[26]

But pride of place in this strand of the narrative belonged to the session of the State Duma, whose members – unlike those of the upper chamber – were elected by the people. After an afternoon prayer service, Duma president Mikhail Rodzianko, a moderate conservative with a taste for

---

[23] The lead article in *Rech'* (July 22, 1914), 1, was one of many pieces which thus interpreted the symbolism of convening the people's representatives.

[24] *Rech'*, unofficial organ of the Constitutional Democratic Party, ran daily articles on planning for the Duma's extraordinary session: for example, "Vozobnovlenie zaniatii zakonodatel'nykh uchrezhdenii" (July 22, 1914), 3.

[25] *Gosudarstvennaia duma: stenograficheskii otchet* (hereafter, *GDSO*), IV, 4, special sess. (July 26, 1914), col. 5, and "Vysochaishii priem narodnykh predstavitelei v Zimnem dvortse," *Gazeta-kopeika* (July 27, 1914), 3.

[26] The most symbolic "reconciliation" was between right-wing Duma deputy Vladimir Purishkevich and liberal leader Pavel Miliukov; the flamboyant Purishkevich, who had called Miliukov a traitor and been censured by the Third Duma for throwing a glass of water in his face, approached his old foe and repeatedly shook his hand: "Priem chlenov Gosudarstvennego soveta i Gosudarstvennoi dumy v Zimnem dvortse," *Russkoe slovo* (July 27, 1914), 2.

rotund turns of phrase, called the session to order.[27] The visitors' gallery was full to overflowing. Rodzianko noted that peace-loving Russia had not sought or wanted this war, but would prove to be a formidable foe: "Take care, we can say: you thought we would be separated by dissension and strife, whereas in fact all the peoples inhabiting unbounded Rus' have merged into one brotherly family as misfortune threatens our common fatherland." His words evoked cheers and applause, as did his call for salutes to the representatives of "Russia's true friends," Britain and France.[28]

Next, Chairman of the Council of Ministers Ivan L. Goremykin and Foreign Minister Sergei D. Sazonov spoke to the chamber. Each repeated the theme that it was not Russia that had started this conflict: the government had sought a diplomatic solution to the crisis, in vain. In past appearances before the Duma, ministers could often anticipate a hostile reception, including boos and catcalls from at least some parts of the chamber. On this occasion, all was cheers and applause, with Sazonov receiving a standing ovation for his strong endorsement of the Duma: "With humble hope for God's help, with steadfast faith in Russia, the government turns with ardent confidence to you, the elected representatives of the people, certain that you reflect the image of our great motherland, at which our enemies dare not laugh."[29]

Then fourteen carefully selected deputies, each speaking in the name of a given political or national group, came to the podium to express their constituents' willingness to defend Russia and their unity with all Russians in the face of the common foe.

A crucial element in the Duma's performance of unity were these declarations from the representatives of significant national groups. Baron G. E. Fel'kerzam affirmed the devotion of Russia's German population to fatherland and throne, and their readiness to sacrifice. Representatives of Latvians, Estonians, and Lithuanians spoke of these groups' ardent desire to fight for the fatherland in its "just and holy war."[30] Ivan V. Godnev, deputy from Kazan – with its sizeable Muslim population – assured listeners that the non-Russian inhabitants (*inorodtsy*) of his province "wholeheartedly desire the complete victory of Russian arms and will lay down their lives, as Russians, for Russia."

---

[27] Newspapers also highlighted the pledge by Duma deputies to give a portion of their monthly salaries to fund a frontline medical unit, in which a number of deputies and their family members volunteered to serve; for example, *Novoe vremia* (July 27, 1914), 2, and "Organizatsiia pomoshchi. Etapnyi lazaret Gosudarstvennoi dumy," *Rech'* (July 29, 1914), 3.

[28] *GDSO*, IV, 4, special sess. (July 26, 1914), cols. 4–6.   [29] Ibid., cols. 7, 11–12.

[30] Ibid., cols. 20–21, 25–26, 22–23.

Deputy Viktor F. Iaronskii insisted that the Poles, despite being divided territorially between three warring states, constituted one whole in their feelings and sympathies toward their fellow Slavs: "God willing, Slavdom, under the supremacy of Russia, will give the Teutons the exact same rebuff they were dealt 500 years ago by the Poles and Lithuanians at Grunwald."[31]

Along with Iaronskii's declaration, Niftel Fridman's avowal for the Jews had particular symbolic value, since Russian nationalists widely regarded the Poles and Jews as among the least loyal of the empire's subjects. Despite the difficult circumstances under which Jews had to live in Russia, Fridman said, they had always been true sons of the fatherland. Russia's Jews would fight shoulder to shoulder with all its peoples, "stand as one man under the Russian banners, and put all our strength into repulsing the enemy." According to the stenographic account, Fridman's declaration, like that of the Poles, was greeted by shouts of "bravo" and "stormy applause" from the left, center, and right.[32]

Representatives of the major political parties also proclaimed adherence to the wartime sacred union. Petr N. Balashev, head of the Nationalist Party, spoke of Russia's "sacred cause," vowing they would fight to the end against aggressive Germanism. A. D. Protopopov, for the moderate Zemstvo-Octobrist group,[33] predicted that Russia would emerge from this just and historic struggle "united, indivisible, morally renewed, and strengthened." Pavel Miliukov, leader of the liberal Constitutional Democrats (Kadets) – the largest opposition party – declared that, while his party remained true to its goals, it was suspending parliamentary struggle during the fight to defend the motherland.

---

[31] Ibid., cols. 21, 23, and 28; see also "Zaiavlenie deputatov-musul'man," *Rech'* (July 28, 1914), 3, for the patriotic declaration issued by the three Muslim deputies unable to get to the capital in time for the one-day session. The term "*inorodets*" (pl. "*inorodtsy*"), often translated as "alien," has no exact counterpart in English. Legally, it encompassed mainly "eastern" and non-Christian peoples of the empire – native peoples of Siberia and Central Asia, mountaineers of the Caucasus, and Jews – but could informally be used to refer to all national minorities; see John W. Slocum, "Who, and When, Were the *Inorodtsy*? The Evolution of the Category of 'Aliens' in Imperial Russia," *Russian Review* 57 (April 1998), 173–90, and Robert P. Geraci, *Window on the East: National and Imperial Identities in Late Tsarist Russia* (Ithaca: Cornell University Press, 2001), 30–31, 259, 310.

[32] *GDSO*, IV, 4, special sess. (July 26, 1914), cols. 23–24.

[33] Zemstvos were the organs of rural self-government, established in the 1860s as part of the Great Reforms. They existed at the provincial and county level and almost exclusively in European Russia; the regime resisted calls for them to be extended down to the district level, thus involving more peasants, or introduced into Siberia or predominantly non-Russian borderlands. The Zemstvo-Octobrist fraction in the Duma often reflected the interests of large landowners.

"We are united in this struggle; we set no conditions and demand nothing; on the scales of the struggle we simply place our firm will to overcome the aggressor."[34]

In fact, the promise of unconditional support by opposition groups had required some arm-twisting to orchestrate. A number of Progressives and left Kadets agreed with Trudovik leader Aleksandr Kerenskii that their support should be conditional upon the government agreeing to concessions – he wanted an end to persecution of Finns, Poles, Jews, and socialist leaders. However, the majority opposed trying to bargain for the Duma's support at such a moment; Kerenskii was irate, but on July 26 not a single group made demands of the government and only the Social Democratic deputies condemned the war.[35]

Socialists did imbed warnings in their pledges of support for defense. While Kerenskii promised that Russian democracy would help vigorously defend "our native lands and culture," he also predicted that joint suffering on the field of battle would strengthen "the brotherhood of all the peoples of Russia, and give birth to a united resolve to liberate the country from terrible *domestic* fetters!" Valentin I. Khaustov, a Social Democrat from Ufa, insisted that the present war was the responsibility of the ruling circles of all the combatant countries, rooted in their policies of aggrandizement. But he also declared that the proletariat "will always defend the cultural welfare of the people from any infringement, no matter its source."[36]

Even the extreme right was on board. Nikolai Markov II, a leader of the monarchists and arguably the crudest defamer of ethnically non-Russian peoples, began, "We have just listened with rapture to the voices, the patriotic voices of the peoples populating Russia." As representative of Kursk province, he then shared his recent impressions of Kursk's reaction to the outbreak of war, which he took to be characteristic of all Russia: "I did not hear a single word, a single reproach on the subject 'Why war?' The entire people were as one – and among them

---

[34] Ibid., cols. 26–29. In July 1914, most of the Fourth State Duma's 442 deputies were distributed among 10 organized parliamentary groups (called "fractions"). The restrictive 1907 electoral law guaranteed disproportionately large representation to the Right (64 deputies) and Nationalists (60 deputies). The moderate-to-liberal section included the Zemstvo-Octobrists, left Octobrists, and Center group (totaling 117 deputies), the liberal Kadets (57), and the Progressists (47). The left was artificially small, composed of the Trudoviks (10), Mensheviks (7), and Bolsheviks (5); figures come from Pearson, *Russian Moderates*, 15. Additionally, there was a Polish group of deputies, a Muslim group, and those with no party affiliation.

[35] Richard Abraham, *Alexander Kerensky: The First Love of the Revolution* (New York: Columbia University Press, 1987), 77–79.

[36] GDSO, IV, 4, special sess. (July 26, 1914), cols. 17 and 19–20 (emphasis added).

I note were many factory workers and railroad men, all those who are called proletarians ... all thought of only one thing: Lord, let there be victory."[37]

Once the speeches had concluded, the Duma voted unanimously for the formula whereby the chamber would move on to business. This resolution affirmed the Duma's conviction that "all the peoples of Russia, united by a single feeling of love for the motherland, firmly believing in the righteousness of its cause, according to the appeal of its Sovereign are prepared to stand to the defense of the motherland, its honor, and dignity." The war credits also passed unanimously, since the Trudoviks abstained and the Social Democrats walked out prior to the vote. A few months earlier, the bitterly divided Fourth Duma had found it difficult to agree on anything at all, which made its July 26 show of solidarity all the more striking. Moderate socialist A. Peshekhonov noted approvingly in *Sovremmenik* that, despite the lower house's deep political differences, when the country was in danger "it expressed its thoughts and feelings with one accord, its thoughts and will in unanimous votes."[38]

The press gave voluminous coverage to the Duma's historic display of unity in support of Russia's just war. *Sel'skii vestnik* (Rural Herald) told its rural readers about the Duma's overcoming of divisions along party and national lines: "All have become fiery sons of our great, common Motherland. Poles, Jews, leftists, all have set aside old scores and in the face of the terrible danger to Russia have merged into a single soul [*slilis v dushu edinu*] with the Russian people."[39] In Russia's highest-circulation popular daily, *Russkoe slovo* (Russian Word), V. I. Nemirovich-Danchenko enthused about a patriotic upsurge such as he had never seen: "The Pole, Russian, Jew, Latvian, Georgian, and Tatar stand shoulder to shoulder. There is no Hellene and no Jew. All are children of a common motherland." However dreadful war might be, he concluded, "How good it is to be alive in such moments!"[40] The historic session of the people's representatives not only reflected but also helped create solidarity, the liberal paper *Rech'* (Speech) suggested: "One feels that moments such as yesterday forge genuine national unity ..."[41]

---

[37] Ibid., col. 27.
[38] Ibid., col. 29, and A. Peshekhonov, " Na ocherednye temy," *Sovremennik* (September 1914), 297. It seems likely that the behavior of the Trudoviks and Social Democrats was also orchestrated in advance, in order to secure unanimous passage of the war credits.
[39] *Sel'skii vestnik* (July 29, 1914), 2.
[40] Nemirovich-Danchenko, "Vchera i segodnia," 95.
[41] *Rech'* (July 27, 1914), 1 (ellipsis in original).

1.3 Some 20,000 people joined a patriotic demonstration in Moscow in front of the statue of Kuz'ma Minin and Prince Dmitrii Pozharskii, July 1914. Photo reproduced from *Letopis' voiny*, courtesy of Harvard University.

Prayers and religious services helped sacralize this newfound unity. On July 22 in all the Orthodox churches in the capital the official manifesto announcing Germany's declaration of war was read aloud, followed by a Te Deum asking God to grant victory to Russian arms. Places of worship were full to overflowing, and prayer services were by no means confined to Orthodox churches. Newspapers carried briefs about celebration of services for Russian victory in Petersburg's Lutheran church, the Catholic Cathedral of St. Catherine, in the choral synogogue on Lermontovskii prospekt, and in the new mosque on Kronverskii prospekt.[42] In Moscow, an outdoor Te Deum on Red Square drew an estimated crowd of 20,000, which was followed immediately by a patriotic demonstration (*manifestatsiia*) in front of the monument to Kuz'ma Minin and Prince

---

[42] *Niva* (August 2, 1914), 651, and "Molebstvie musulman," *Russkoe slovo* (July 28, 1914), 2.

1.4 A wartime session of the State Duma; in July 1914, the Duma symbolized the people's patriotic transcendence of political, national, and religious differences. Photograph courtesy of Bettmann/Corbis.

Dmitrii Pozharskii, the heroes of 1613.[43] All over the Russian empire, similar services were celebrated, often accompanied by processions of the cross that drew thousands of participants.[44]

Patriotic parades and demonstrations contributed to the perception that this war enjoyed widespread support. There had already been patriotic demonstrations in the capitals and a number of large towns in the days following Austria's declaration of war on Serbia, but from July 20 they became more widespread.[45] Newspapers printed dozens of briefs on parades and gatherings in cities across the country, while telegrams received by the St. Petersburg Telegraph Agency described departing troops being seen off by "endless demonstrations in which the population of the Empire, without distinction of faith or nationality, participates with identical delight."[46]

The ecumenical character of many demonstrations drew special note. In Petersburg, the prayer service at the choral synagogue turned into a

---

[43] "Molebstviia," *Rech'* (July 23, 1914), 4; for an interesting analysis of how illustrated weeklies patriotically depicted such gatherings, see Christopher Stolarski, "Press Photography in Russia's Great War and Revolution," in Frame, Kolonitskii, Marks, and Stockdale, *Russian Culture in War and Revolution*, Book 2, 154–56.

[44] "Nastroenie v Rossii," *Rech'* (July 24, 1914), 3.

[45] A list of twenty-five towns where patriotic demonstrations were held following the Austrian declaration of war was published in "Manifestatsii v provintsii," *Gazeta-kopeika* (July 19, 1914), 3. See also *Sel'skii vestnik* (July 18, 1914), 2.

[46] "Matushka-Rus'," *Gazeta-kopeika* (July 23, 1914), 4. In addition to the largest cities of the empire, towns mentioned include Eisk, Kostroma, Nizhnyi Novgorod, Novocherkass, Omsk, Simbirsk, Sevastopol, Tomsk, Pernov (Estonia), and Aleksandropol (Armenia): "Manifestatsii," *Russkoe slovo* (July 21, 1914), 2, and *Novoe vremia* (July 23 and July 24, 1914), 3 and 5.

large public demonstration as Jewish crowds carrying portraits of the tsar, placards, and tricolored national flags, singing the national anthem and Jewish hymns, marched from Nevskii to Palace Square. Along the way, they were joined by hundreds of Christians; outside the Anichkov Palace, the confessionally mixed throng knelt and sang the national anthem together. Similarly, in Moscow, a large patriotic demonstration by Armenians – featuring the ubiquitous flags, portraits of the tsar, and singing of the national anthem – was joined by thousands of other citizens, ending up at the Kremlin, at the statue of the "tsar-liberator" Alexander II. In Odessa, some 10,000 Jews, Ukrainians, and Orthodox Russians marched about the city together, waving flags and singing the national anthem; onlookers were astonished to observe members of the antisemitic and anti-Ukrainian Union of Russian People joining in.[47]

The nationalist press depicted all these events as a sort of referendum on Russians' attitude toward the war. "The entire people has already spoken its mind on the subject of the war," *Golos naroda* (Voice of the People) confidently declared. "It said it in front of the Winter Palace, falling to its knees. It has said it in unending, enthusiastic patriotic demonstrations in the capitals, in Kiev, and numerous cities of the empire."[48] In Petersburg, one paper wrote about "crowds thousands strong, in their overwhelming majority the lower class, the simple people, yesterday's strikers," who were "harmoniously and decorously expressing their opinion of the position Russia has taken."[49]

Some observers doubted the authenticity of all these patriotic displays, suspecting they had been orchestrated by nationalist groups or the police, or that they were composed of young hooligans enjoying the chance to make a ruckus.[50] They were not, in other words, a reflection of the authentic people's sentiments. Others, however, believed they constituted a genuine show of patriotism by all classes – even when such a conclusion was not necessarily welcome. For example, in one letter intercepted by the police, a man in Petersburg morosely wrote to a friend in Irkutsk about the wholesale transformation in recently striking workers: "after the declaration of war these self-same gentlemen began

---

[47] "Nastroenie v Rossii," *Rech'* (July 23, 1914), 4, and (July 24, 1914), 3; "Manifestatsiia moskovskikh armian," *Russkoe slovo* (July 21, 1914), 2; "Liudi-brat'ia," *Gazeta-kopeika* (July 24, 1914), 4.
[48] Article from *Golos naroda* (July 25, 1914), reproduced in *Kievlianin'* (July 26, 1914), 1.
[49] "Peterburzhets," "Peterburgskie otkliki," *Kievlianin'* (July 21, 1914), 1; the same article describes army officers "moved to tears by the popular enthusiasm."
[50] For example, Gosudarstvennyi arkhiv Rossiiskoi federatsii (hereafter, GARF), f. 102, op. 265, d. 977, ll. 2–3, 6, 28, letters of September 1, 1914, August 23, 1914, and August 26, 1914, and remarks of Richard Merry, quoted in Wortman, *Scenarios of Power*, II, 511, to the effect that the police orchestrated these demonstrations.

going around from early morning with national flags, singing 'God save the tsar' and smashing windows and breaking up everything that appears to them to be German ... how could one not be disillusioned with such a quick about-face?"[51]

Most people recording their thoughts, however, rejoiced in the displays of patriotism. One young man wrote his father, "The mood in Moscow is amazing! And I repeat – woe to the Germans, the outburst is colossal, a unity such as history will remember." In the provincial town of Nizhnii Rybinsk, a woman wrote "The unity and fervor of Russian society so gladdens me ... Say what you like, though Russia might be wretched and have wretched policies ... still there is no Russian soul who would not stand up for the fatherland."[52]

Mobilization and Mass Sentiment

Evidence for urban patriotism is powerful, but it is more difficult to gauge rural support for Russia's war. Just as historian Jeffrey Verhey identifies mass, rural sentiment as the most problematic aspect of the myth of widespread German enthusiasm at the outbreak of war, so too in Russia evidence about the mood in the countryside at the outbreak of war is mostly fragmentary and anecdotal.[53] The patchiness of the evidence – and the simple fact that not all rural people thought alike – did not prevent contemporaries from frequently ascribing views to the peasant mass of the population.

How did peasants respond to the outbreak of war? In the narrative of sacred union, part of the answer was provided by the success of the military mobilization. Mobilizing the enormous Russian army was a giant logistical task, entailing the calling-up in three stages of more than 3.1 million men from the reserves, an additional 800,000 men from the militia, and the requisitioning of hundreds of thousands of horses. Approximately 96 percent of reservists reported for duty, providing a

---

[51] GARF, f. 102, op. 265, d. 967, Department of Police: Perlustrated Letters, 1914; letter of V. V. Kolosovskii to V. V. Prussak, August 5, 1914, l. 111.
[52] GARF, f. 102, op. 265, d. 990, l. 974, "Letter from 'Kolia,' Moscow, 21 July," and d. 992, l.1104, "Letter from 'Tvoia Katia,' Nizh. Rybinsk, 30 July."
[53] Verhey, *The Spirit of 1914*, 68–69, 91–92. As he notes, gauging how small farmers and villagers actually responded to the war is incredibly difficult: they did not have the national sites that served urbanites as focal points for big parades and gatherings, nor could they easily assemble in large crowds to demonstrate their feelings. Moreover, such humble citizens did not typically record their views in diaries or letters. Nonetheless, contemporaries tended simply to fold rural dwellers into the narrative of the "Spirit of 1914," thereby making enthusiastic support for the war a truly national and mass phenomenon.

stark contrast to the evasions and disorders that had marred mobilization for the unpopular war with Japan. Contemporaries celebrated it as a great achievement, testified to by the tsar's decision to strike a medal commemorating the successful mobilization of 1914. As Lieutenant General Nikolai Golovin later recalled, workers and peasants displayed equal consciousness of duty; "those who had witnessed the mobilization for the Russo-Japanese war could not help being amazed at the immeasurable difference of feeling in all classes of the Russian nation."[54]

Historian Joshua Sanborn has analyzed the military mobilization and its dynamics, revealing that, its success notwithstanding, there were more disorders and protests than contemporaries realized. Draft rioting occurred in 16 provinces and the Region of the Don Host, resulting in the death or wounding of 60 state officials and 352 rioters, as well as untold property damage. The biggest disorders occurred in Barnaul, in Tomsk province, where fighting between reservists and police claimed more than 100 lives. Since rioters often attacked and looted the liquor stores closed down during the mobilization, officials were quick to blame draft disorders on alcohol. But, as Sanborn shows, this handy excuse papered over a more complex reality. Besides looking for the liquor denied them, reservists were protesting lack of provisions for their families and themselves and the requisitioning of their horses, or demonstrating their reluctance to go off to fight. In some riots, alcohol played no role at all.[55]

Unpublished sources not subject to censorship constraints attest to varying reactions in different regions. For example, in a July 20 letter intercepted by the police, a young woman in Perm province wrote to her father about serious disorders that followed the order for mobilization: workers began smashing up local shops and shooting, eight were killed and fifteen injured. A letter of July 18 sent from Orenburg province to one Isidor Fater, in Odessa, spoke of the moans and lamentations of the countryside: "The harvest will be in two or three days, the most important time for a peasant ... and suddenly you have to leave everything and go to fight. There are homes here from which they've taken two or three workers and only women remain. You can imagine the state of the entire

---

[54] With the addition of the reservists and first-tier militia to the peacetime army of 1,423,000 men, the mobilization plan accounted for 5.5 million men; see Nicholas N. Golovine, *The Russian Campaign of 1914: The Beginning of the War and Operations in East Prussia*, trans. A. G. S. Muntz (Fort Leavenworth, KS: Command and General Staff School Press, 1933), 25–26, 77.

[55] Josh Sanborn, "The Mobilization of 1914 and the Question of the Russian Nation: A Re-examination," *Slavic Review* 59, 2 (Summer 2000), 275–77.

rural population."⁵⁶ In a rare peasant diary, A. A. Zamaraev, in the northern province of Vologda, described the news of mobilization as a thunderclap shocking everyone in the very midst of haymaking, and cursed the "treacherous Austrians." On July 21 he went to town to see the masses of soldiers and horses being assembled, noting: "All day, lots of people in town, and much weeping."⁵⁷ A letter written in Odessa on July 18, to N. D. Ivanov in the Second Siberian Artillery Brigade, painted a more positive picture: the patriotic upsurge in Odessa was continuing and "Mobilization is going wonderfully and peacefully, not at all like it was [for us] in Omsk in 1904."⁵⁸ A number of letters testified to a mood that was subdued rather than enthusiastic, as in a letter of July 20 from Kreitsburg, Latvia, to L. A. Tikhomirov in Moscow. The writer praised the impressive orderliness of the reservists, who "neither cried nor complained," continuing, "True, the picture was in general a somber one, but it was evident that everyone understands the necessity of the sacrifices being borne."⁵⁹

Thanks to censorship, few accounts of disorders, riots, or protests evoked by the mobilization made it into the press. Instead, newspapers hymned reservists' measured resolve, tender farewells to loved ones, or patriotic high spirits – depending upon the publication – as they joined their units. In *Sel'skii vestnik*, for example, reservists called up for service were depicted as "expressing not just complete willingness but even joy, conscious that they have been summoned to the great cause of defense of the Motherland."⁶⁰

Contemporaries could therefore take the apparent smoothness of mobilization as revealing what the inarticulate mass of the population felt about the war. The mobilization was "miraculous," *Letopis' voiny* wrote in early September. All the true sons of Russia "appeared at their units in the twinkling of an eye, having put aside wives, children, and all their business."⁶¹ One "Nika" in Moscow wrote to Countess E. P. Lamsdorf-Galagan, in Poltava, about the patriotic demonstrations and success of the mobilization in Moscow, concluding, "given such demonstrations of popular feeling, war does not terrify us, for Russia can muster

---

[56] GARF, f. 102, op. 265, d. 990, "Perlustrated Letters, 1914," ll. 971 and 944; a letter of August 1, 1914 from "Vera" to B. P. Dudov in Moscow, testifies to serious disorders in Tsaritsyn over distribution of aid to soldiers' families, resulting in some eighty wounded and twenty killed: d. 992, l. 1121.
[57] Morozov and Reshetnikov, eds., *Dnevnik totemskogo krest'ianina*, 86–87.
[58] GARF, f. 102, op. 265, d. 990, "Perlustrated Letters, 1914," l. 946.
[59] GARF, f. 102, op. 265, d. 990, "Perlustrated Letters, 1914," ll. 956, 966; also a letter from G. Veselyi in Helsingfors, July 19, to M. G. Veselyi in St. Petersburg, l. 954.
[60] *Sel'skii vestnik* (July 22, 1914), 4. [61] *Letopis' voiny* no. 3 (September 6, 1914), 53.

a force of up to 10 million and one is somehow confident that all will fulfill their duty." Bernard Pares, a British historian who spent much of the war in Russia, later insisted that "the brilliant success of the mobilization [was] due to the sympathy of the population. The war seemed to be the moment for the long-awaited reconciliation between country and monarch."[62]

Reservists' seemingly superb compliance could be attributed in part to prohibition. The imperial government banned the sale of vodka during mobilization, excluding only first-class restaurants and clubs. This edict made sense, given the longstanding custom of reservists getting drunk before showing up at draft centers. During the Russo-Japanese war, alcohol was clearly a factor in the widespread rioting and violence that accompanied mobilization. Contemporaries were sure that the success of the 1914 mobilization was "in significant degree assisted by the general sobering up of Rus'."[63] Soon, the government extended the ban on vodka for the duration of the conflict. As virtually every historian of the war has noted, this highminded step was a fiscal disaster. The government's vodka monopoly had accounted for 26 percent of its prewar annual revenues; to cover growing shortfalls, the treasury increasingly resorted to printing money, fueling inflation. And since peasants soon realized the advantages of turning their grain into illicit moonshine – for which there was brisk demand – temperance proved hard to maintain.[64]

But in 1914 many welcomed general prohibition as a powerful force for good, one of the profound changes wrought by the war. "The war has given the people sobriety," noted the venerable journal *Vestnik Evropy* (Herald of Europe). "What was unattainable in peacetime has now been achieved."[65] Besides anticipating that it would decrease domestic violence and crime, enhance labor productivity, and leave more money in family budgets for food and other necessities, liberals and conservatives alike believed that prohibition would renew Russians and Russia.[66] Konstantin Arsen'ev described a great spiritual upsurge, particularly among the peasantry, thanks to the dry laws. The penny paper *Malenkaia gazeta* (Little Gazette) insisted, "If you had said three months ago that

---

[62] Quoted by prominent liberal Vasilii ("Basil") Maklakov in his review of Pares's book: "On the Fall of Tsardom," *Slavonic and East European Review* 18, 52 (July 1939), 74.
[63] "Na Rusi," *Letopis' voiny* no. 3 (September 6, 1914), 53–54.
[64] On wartime prohibition and its disappointing results, see Patricia Herlihy, *The Alcoholic Empire: Vodka and Politics in Late Imperial Russia* (Oxford: Oxford University Press, 2003), 138–42.
[65] Kuzmin-Karavaev, "Voprosy vnutrennei zhizni," *Vestnik Evropy* (January 1915), 384.
[66] Rural educators and zemstvo activists were particularly enthusiastic about prohibition, since "alcohol and education are mortal enemies;" see Seregny, "Zemstvos, Peasants, and Citizenship," 295.

they don't trade in vodka in Russia, no one would have believed it. *The holy war has accomplished this miracle!*"[67] The war's role in curing the government of its dependence on liquor sales added to the perception of it as not merely righteous, but transformative.

A Second Fatherland War

The tsar had deliberately evoked the memory of the victorious 1812 Fatherland War in his official manifesto, his speech in the Winter Palace, and his pilgrimage to Moscow in August 1914. The ordeals and ultimate triumph over the invader symbolized in the 1812 war were part of the national myth and popular consciousness, celebrated in folk songs and tales as well as in the symphonic music and literary works of high culture. But Nicholas's allusions to one of Russia's defining national moments could also build on more recent memories of the elaborate, nationwide celebration of the hundredth anniversary of the war.

Commemoration of the Fatherland War involved production of material objects meant to have an enduring presence in Russian public space and publication of war-related texts and graphics, as well as organizing more ephemeral observations and festivities. The special committee set up in 1910 to plan the centennial decided to strike a commemorative medal, featuring the images of Alexander I and Nicholas II on one side, and a cavalry battle on the other, to be given to every active-duty soldier, employees of the Holy Synod and government ministries, teachers, and workers in naval factories, among others. More than 1.6 million of these 1812 jubilee medals were ordered, creating an exceptionally widespread and durable visual reminder of the Fatherland War.[68] By 1912, more than 600 publications about the war had appeared, ranging from scholarly editions of significant primary sources to snappy pamphlets on battles and heroes of 1812 that were distributed in tens of thousands of copies to government employees, workers, schools, policemen, and zemstvos.

A number of cities erected monuments or refurbished existing ones, among them Smolensk, which built a commemorative ensemble featuring a bronze map of European Russia with the inscription "From a Grateful Russia to the Heroes of 1812." Across Russia, cities and towns

---

[67] K. Arsen'ev, "Blizhaishee budushchee," *Russkie vedomosti* (January 1, 1915); "Otrevlenie naroda," *Malenkaia gazeta* (September 23, 1914), 1; and S. P. Fridolin, "Probuzhdenie derevni," *Derevenskaia gazeta*, nos. 3–4 (March 1915), 8 (emphasis in original).

[68] Rossiiskii gosudarstvennyi voenno-istoricheskii arkhiv (hereafter, RGVIA), f. 2000, op. 2, d. 1043, "O prazdnovanii 100-letnego iubileia Otechestvennoi voiny," ll. 12, 38, 42, 46, 48.

planned religious services, parades, performances, banquets, and festivities to coincide with the anniversary of the Battle of Borodino, on August 26–27, 1912. The Ministry of Internal Affairs sent out a circular in May 1912 emphasizing the importance of attracting to these commemorations the "broadest possible layers of the population of the empire," and the Council of Ministers assigned 500,000 rubles to help fund them. Other monies came from regimental committees, zemstvos and municipal governments, and private donations.[69]

Schoolchildren and soldiers were the greatest objects of attention. In the Kazan educational district, teachers gave talks with slides on the Fatherland War for primary school pupils, while all secondary students studied the events and significance of the war for the entire fall semester. Educators prepared programs of recitations, songs, and dramatic performances (including scenes from *War and Peace*), while school orchestras diligently practiced Tchaikovsky's *1812 Overture* and the national anthem. Elsewhere in the Volga region, in the city of Saratov schoolchildren participated in sporting events put on at the hippodrome in honor of the centennial, while the city of Ufa sponsored a patriotic spectacular, "The Burning of Moscow," with free performances for schoolchildren and soldiers.[70]

Military authorities were quite alive to the centennial's value as a teaching moment, and various military districts produced detailed plans for commemorating the 1812 jubilee in the army. Leading up to the actual anniversary there would be lectures for the men on the history and significance of the war, and distribution of historical picture postcards and brochures; barracks were to be freshly painted and decorated with relevant maps and portraits. On August 26 and 27 there would be military parades, religious observances, and speech-making. And to make sure there was pleasure as well as edification, most districts planned two days of superior victuals in the mess hall, sporting competitions with prizes, banquets, and a trip for the soldiers to town for evening shows or festivities.[71] A number of planners wanted a handsome badge to be given to every member of historic units that had participated in the

---

[69] A. A. Smirnov, L. V. Mitroshenkvoa, and S. N. Seledkina, "Pamiatniki," in V. M. Bezotochnyi et al., *Otechestvennaia voina 1812 goda. Entsiklopediia* (Moscow: ROSSPEN, 2004), 543–45.

[70] T. A. Magsumov, "Prazdnovanie stoletnego iubileia Otechestvennoi voiny 1812 g.," *Voprosy istorii*, 9 (2012), 137–42; and I. A. Kuznetsov, *Liubov' k otechestvu. Istochniki sily narodnoi. (K iubileiu "Otechestvennoi voiny" 1812 goda)* (Ufa: Gubernaia elektricheskaia tipografiia, 1912), 4–9.

[71] RGVIA, f. 2000, op. 2, d. 1040, "O prazdnovanii iubileia Otechestvennoi voiny 1812 gody – perepiska," ll. 1–2, 17, 23–29, 33–38.

Fatherland War; when these men left active service and returned home wearing their badges, "they would be communicating about the war to their families and acquaintance and the memory of the Fatherland War will have been deepened among the people."[72]

The memory of the 1812 Fatherland War was therefore broadly diffused and ready for invocation in 1914. But what story was being invoked? At its most basic level, it was a narrative of unity, patriotism, and perseverance. France had invaded Russia, making Russia's war defensive and just. And since the fighting took place on Russian soil – unlike the Russo-Turkish War or the war with the Japanese – it was a true "fatherland war," a fight for the country's independent existence, dignity, and wellbeing. Particularly important to this story was the way all classes, indeed the entire people – from noble to merchant to peasant – responded to Tsar Alexander's call to repulse the invader. Despite devastating losses, Russians did not cave in. Instead, they chased the invader out of Russia and all the way to Paris, breaking Bonaparte's power, "saving Europe," and gaining a new appreciation of themselves as a whole, united people. Some accounts stressed the tsar's leadership, his staunch refusal to make peace with the invader; other more liberal or populist accounts might stress the initiative and sacrifice of the people, or the role of partisans in driving out the French. But whatever the emphasis, the reassuring message was the same: Russian unity, resolve, and willingness to sacrifice ultimately beat even the mightiest foe.[73]

This inspiring myth, and obvious parallels between the powerful German aggressor and Napoleon's Grande Armée, made the 1812 Fatherland War a particularly usable story for 1914. Columnist A. Savenko, in *Kievlianin'* (The Kievan), immediately predicted that "Russia will save Europe again, as she did 100 years ago." The official organ of the Ministry of War, *Russkii invalid* (The Russian Disabled Veteran), was convinced by the patriotic demonstration on Palace Square that, "We are present at the rebirth of the popular spirit

---

[72] RGVIA, f. 2000, op. 2, d. 1040, "O prazdnovanii iubileia Otechestvennoi voiny 1812 gody – perepiska," ll. 2, 15, 42, 62. Most of the proposals sent to the central planning committee hoped films would be made which they could show to their troops.

[73] For example, V. Efremov, "Otchego voina 1812 goda nazyvaetsia 'otechestvennoi'?" in Kuznetsov, *Liubov k otechestvu*, 10, 17, which states that the war "reflected the moral grandeur of the Russian people" and that "the entire people, every social estate in the country, sacrificed its life and property for the salvation of the fatherland." See also S. I. Dmitriev, *Stoletie Otechestvennoi voiny 1812–1912. Ocherk dlia rabochikh i ikh detei* (St. Petersburg, 1912), 21, who concludes that, if an enemy should again attack "Holy Rus'," "we will enjoy complete victory over him if only 'we join together as a single heart' and, imitating the patriots of 1812, shout in unison 'For faith, tsar, and fatherland!'"

of '1812.' We will inscribe in the history of Russia a *Second Fatherland War*."[74] Indeed, while no single, agreed-upon name was applied to the new conflict – it was variously referred to as the Great War, the European War, the Teutonic–Slavic War, and the War of 1914 – variations on the name "Second Fatherland War"(*Vtoraia otechestvennaia voina, Velikaia otechestvennaia voina*) were also widely applied.[75] On July 20, *Russkoe slovo* announced the war with the bold banner headline: "A Second Fatherland War."[76] Other periodicals referred to the Second Fatherland War in headlines and articles, and this name appeared in war-relief posters, postage stamps, speeches, and private correspondence as well. Ten months later, as Russia's terrible "Great Retreat" unfolded, the reminder that things had looked very black before Russia defeated Napoleon would be used to bolster public spirits.[77]

Controlling Information in Wartime

One reason the narrative of universal patriotic support for Russia's just war enjoyed the credence it did was the suppression of dissenting views. Not surprisingly, Russia, like all the continental powers engaged in the Great War, trusted more to official censorship than media self-restraint in managing both written and nonwritten communication.[78] The relative freedom enjoyed by the Russian press since 1906 came to an abrupt halt with the outbreak of hostilities; censorship, like surveillance, would thereafter expand as military authorities, conservative government ministers, and right-wing pressure groups agitated for

---

[74] "Nezabvennye istoricheskie minuty," *Russkii invalid* (July 22, 1914), 5 (emphasis in original). Other newspapers noted the way the tsar had chosen to quote from Alexander I's speech: for example, "1812–1914," *Kievlianin'* (July 23, 1914), 1.

[75] At least one author, noting that "many among us have experienced difficulties in giving a precise name to the present war," argued that it could *not* be considered a fatherland war, given that "it is not being conducted solely against us, and does not in the least threaten our national existence and national independence": "Inostrannoe obozrenie," *Vestnik Evropy* (September 1914), 367.

[76] *Russkoe slovo* (July 20, 1914), 2. See also "Otechestvennaia voina," *Gazeta-kopeika* (July 20, 1914), 2.

[77] "Vtoraia otechestvennaia voina," *Soldatskii vestnik* (August 31, 1914), 1; *Sel'skii vestnik* (May 30, 1915), 1, reminded readers that the Napoleonic war "started badly and ended in victory."

[78] For wartime censorship in other countries, see Adrian Gregory, "A Clash of Cultures: The British Press and the Opening of the Great War," in Troy R. E. Paddock, ed., *A Call to Arms: Propaganda, Public Opinion, and Newspapers in the Great War* (Westport, CT: Praeger, 2004), 15–50; David Welch, *Germany, Propaganda, and Total War, 1914–1918: The Sins of Omission* (New Brunswick, NJ: Rutgers University Press, 2002), 28–40; and Mark Cornwall, "News, Rumour, and the Control of Information in Austria-Hungary," *History* 77 (February 1992), 50–64.

greater control, and the military superseded civilian authorities in larger chunks of the empire.[79]

Two statutes established conditions of military censorship at the outset. On July 20, 1914, the imperial authorities issued the "Temporary Position on Military Censorship," intended to prevent the proclamation or dissemination of information which could "harm the military interests of the state" during mobilization or war. All printed matter – from books to periodical literature to graphics – all correspondence and telegrams, and all public lectures and speeches were subject to review. In "zones of military activity," full military censorship was established, which included preliminary censorship of publications.[80] Military zones included not just the active fronts but also regions contiguous to the fronts and extending well into the rear: significant swathes of European Russia, including the capital, in addition to Finland, Poland, and the Caucasus, came under military rule and censorship. Penalties for the elastically defined prohibition against disseminating "information harmful to military interests," contained in article 31 of the wartime censorship statute, were severe. For example, distribution in zones of military activity of a periodical publication not given prior approval by the censors drew fines ranging from 100 to 2,000 rubles. Calling for an end to fighting, whether in a public speech or in print, was subject to imprisonment for a period of two to eight months.[81]

The July 16 "Statute on Field Administration of Troops in Wartime" gave General Headquarters the right to close publications it deemed to be in violation of provisions of the censorship. On July 26, instructions appeared spelling out exactly what was prohibited, which turned out to include discussion of the contents of letters or telegrams from the front, discussion of Russian losses in materiel or personnel, or even writing about "alarms" among the civilian population.[82] Obstacles to printing

---

[79] On the expansion of wartime surveillance and its postwar afterlife, see Peter Holquist, "'Information Is the Alpha and Omega of Our Work': Bolshevik Surveillance in Its Pan-European Context," *Journal of Modern History* 69 (September 1997), esp. 417–23, 426–32.

[80] The main provisions of the statute, "Vremennoe polozhenie o voennoi tsenzure," are excerpted in *Vlast' i pressa. K istorii pravovogo regulirovaniia otnoshenii 1700–1917. Khrestomatiia* (Moscow: Izd. RAGS, 1999), 204–10.

[81] My overview of the 1914 censorship provisions is based on the excellent treatments by A. F. Berezhnoi, *Russkaia legal'naia pechat' v gody Pervoi mirovoi voiny* (Leningrad: Leningradskii gosudarstvennyi universitet, 1975), 19–21, and Eric Lohr, "The Russian Press and the 'Internal Peace' at the Beginning of World War I," in Paddock, ed., *A Call to Arms*, 91–114.

[82] "Perechen' svedenii i izobrazhenii, ne podlezhashchikh oglasheniiu i rasprostraneniiu," in *Vlast' i pressa*, 211–13. The stiffer penalties included fines as high as 10,000 rubles or a prison sentence of two months to one year.

military-related information were in fact so formidable that they profoundly exasperated a public hungry for solid news about the fighting. Moreover, the lack of reliable information from the front encouraged the spread of fantastic rumors, as Baron Nikolai Vrangel' noted in his diary on August 18: "At such moments people must nourish their imaginations with at least a few facts of some sort – not having information, they invent all sorts of rubbish which passes from mouth to mouth and so achieves a Herculean scale of stupidity."[83] In mid 1915, the military top brass came to this conclusion themselves and significantly relaxed limitations on reporting from the front.[84]

Besides keeping news from the front out of the press, the military authorities also closed approximately eighty periodicals in the first months of the war. Some of these were produced in the two capitals and aimed at a national audience, but many others were regional or provincial organs. The majority were either socialist in orientation – including the so-called workers' press – or periodicals published by and for the empire's national minorities. The press in Ukraine and the Caucasus was particularly hard hit; according to one Duma deputy, closure of two dozen Ukrainian publications had virtually destroyed the Ukrainian-language press.[85] These closures were mainly preemptive in nature: the authorities assumed – incorrectly, as it turned out – that the entire socialist camp would oppose the war, and obviously entertained doubts about the reliability of sectors of the national-minority press as well.

Military censorship constituted only one sphere of censorship in wartime Russia, overlapping with but never entirely superseding the regular civil censorship exercised by the Ministry of the Interior's Chief Administration for Affairs of the Press. This body's powers of control over the press were also enhanced in wartime. Within a week of the outbreak of war, the entire empire was placed in a state of extraordinary safeguard, a condition approaching that of martial law and allowing for greater control over the printed word. However, the Chief Administration for Affairs of the Press did not wield as much control over censorship in practice as in theory, for the simple reason that it was underfunded and understaffed. In 1914, fewer than 100 censors were supposed to review publication of some 32,000 books and pamphlets and 3,111 periodicals

---

[83] Vrangel', *Dni skorbi*, entry of August 18, 1914, 43; many *intelligenty* made similar complaints.
[84] Rossiiskii gosudarstvennyi istoricheskii arkhiv (hereafter RGIA), f. 2003, op. 1, d. 1484, letter and report on changing military censorship (October 14, 1915), ll. 1–5.
[85] Berezhnoi, *Russkaia legal'naia pechat'*, 26–27.

throughout the empire, and the number of civilian censors grew scarcely at all through the war. Civil censorship was therefore not so onerous as was the military's, and information that failed to pass the military censors in Petrograd and Kiev could often legally be published in Moscow – at least until Moscow was also placed under military censorship in March 1915, despite its not being located anywhere near a "zone of military activity."[86]

This censorship apparatus – often arbitrary and overreaching, but not consistently so – helped bury critiques or events that might challenge the narrative of a patriotic nation united behind the war. I have already noted how disorders among reservists during mobilization were not reported in the press, a silence that contributed to the belief that mobilization was not just successful, but "miraculously" so. Similarly, popular disorders connected with temporary food shortages or problems with stipends for soldiers' families in the first weeks of war were rarely reported. For example, in a letter of August 1 intercepted by the police, a resident of Tsaritsyn told one B. P. Dudov, in Moscow, that after a good start to mobilization riots had broken out over distribution of the stipend to soldiers' families; eventually orders were given to shoot, resulting in approximately twenty people dead and eighty wounded.[87] No mention of this tragedy surfaced in the national press. In Odessa, more than 1,000 frustrated soldiers' wives (*soldatki*) demonstrated on August 11, angered by the city's tardiness in distributing family stipends. They threw rocks at the police called in to disperse them, injuring several; not a word about this confrontation – or any other protests involving women in Odessa – appeared in print prior to March 1917.[88]

Isolated political protests and expressions of antiwar feeling were also kept under wraps. According to historian Iu. I. Kir'ianov, from the announcement of mobilization to the end of 1914 there were no antiwar strikes in Russia, though in Petersburg three small antiwar demonstrations were attempted. There was only one political strike, in November 1914, also quite small.[89] But no overtly political expressions of

---

[86] Benjamin Rigberg, "The Efficacy of Tsarist Censorship Operations, 1894–1917," *Jahrbucher für Geschichte Osteuropas* 14 (Fall 1966), 340–42, and Berezhnoi, *Russkaia legal'naia pechat'*, 64; censors included approximately forty censors employed in Petrograd by the Chief Administration for Press Affairs, and Russia's vice-governors, who were formally responsible for civil censorship in the provinces.
[87] GARF, f. 102, op. 265, d. 990 (excerpted letters, 1914), l. 1121, letter from Vera, Tsaritsyn, August 1, 1914.
[88] Ieugen Dzhumyga, "The Home Front in Odessa during the Great War (July 1914–February 1917): The Gender Aspect of the Problem," *Danubius* 31 (2013), 226–27.
[89] Iu. I. Kir'ianov, "Rabochie Rossii i voina. Novye podkhody i analizu problemy," in V. I. Malkov, ed., *Pervaia mirovaia voina. Prolog XX veka* (Moscow: Nauka, 1998), 437–38.

discontent with the outbreak of war or the authorities' response to it, however minor, were reported. In a letter intercepted by the police, a student wrote to a friend about the big patriotic demonstration at St. Petersburg University in early fall 1914. It was strongly supportive of the war, he said, but there were a few signs calling for a political amnesty, and some derisive shouts and whistles, about which "the newspapers were silent."[90]

In the narrative of sacred union, some events were not so much omitted as revised. The end of the massive labor strikes in St. Petersburg in July 1914 is a case in point. As we have seen, the strikes broke out on July 4, rapidly becoming larger, more politicized, and violent. Besides using local police and Cossacks to suppress the strikes, the authorities also called in a cavalry brigade from Tsarskoe Selo; Mayor Tol'stoi noted in his diary that the disorders were largely over, and trams running regularly, by July 11.[91] On July 14, news of Austria's bombardment of the Serbian capital prompted "patriotic manifestations" in St. Petersburg; these demonstrations increased in size as general mobilization was declared late in the evening on July 16.[92] But in the patriotic narrative, the strike was not put down by force several days before the order of mobilization; rather, Russian workers spontaneously ended their strike when they saw that the fatherland was under threat. The end of those massive protests was too potent a symbol of wartime transformation, of the "cessation of discord and strife," to be attributed to governmental force applied days before the population realized that war was imminent.

Another kind of "silencing" was enabled by the empire-wide state of "extraordinary safeguard," which simplified the arrest and internal exile of individuals deemed likely to oppose or disrupt the war. These were, overwhelmingly, revolutionary activists. Police had already arrested labor leaders and socialist agitators in St. Petersburg during the strike, also shutting down the Bolshevik paper *Pravda*. After July 20, they conducted more sweeping round-ups of suspected members of revolutionary parties in various cities. With the exception of the provocative arrest of the five Bolshevik Duma deputies in November 1914, and their subsequent trial

---

[90] GARF, f. 102 OO, 1914, op. 244, d. 343, otd. 2, Letter from Gennadii, Petrograd, to A. M. Vasil'ev, October 13, 1914, l. 143. The police vice-director's note at the bottom of this letter said simply "Ascertain and detain the author."

[91] Leopold H. Haimson, "General Introduction," in Haimson and Giuli Sapelli, eds., *Strikes, Social Conflict and the First World War: An International Perspective* (Milan: Feltrinelli Editore Milano, 1992), 19, and Tol'stoi, *Dnevnik*, II, entry of July 11, 1914, 574. Police reports offer a slightly different picture of timing, characterizing the political strike as waning on July 11, but not ending until July 14: reports of July 11 and July 14, 1914, to the Minister of the Interior, in Korablev, *Rabochee dvizhenie*, 237–38, 241–42.

[92] For example, *Novoe vremia* (July15, 1914), 2, and (July 17, 1914), 1–2.

and conviction, these operations were not discussed in the press; they were decidedly not enshrined in the patriotic narrative of sacred union.[93]

Conclusions

The wartime unity and political truce that constituted Russia's version of sacred union did not endure through the entire war, any more than it did in other combatant countries. A conflict that lasted for years instead of months, that claimed so many casualties and imposed so much hardship, inevitably stoked social tensions and exacerbated ideological differences. Given the unexpected scale and carnage of the Great War, perhaps we should be more surprised that it took so long for fissures to develop. Powerful censorship and policing operations by the continental powers meant critics of the war were rounded up and their criticisms silenced, while the public was long kept in the dark about the true scale of losses. Also important for the preservation of unity, however, were the patriotic narratives crafted at the start of the war.

In Russia, as elsewhere, narratives were created through rituals of solidarity and reconciliation, at sacred places and national monuments as well as in political spaces. They featured vows, oaths, and stirring appeals, often invoking the nation's past but also looking forward to a nation transformed. They attracted, and symbolically represented, the active participation of crowds of ordinary citizens. These rituals helped constitute patriotic narratives that drew on, mobilized, and, I would argue, helped to forge national sentiments.

The Russian narrative of sacred union depicted the entire population unified in a just cause. No one was left out or excluded from this narrative, which insisted upon the patriotism of national minorities, the humble and the mighty, the city and the village. The depiction of the war as purely defensive legitimized the service and sacrifice required of the population, while prohibition helped reinforce depiction of the conflict as both righteous and transformative. Invoking familiar narratives of past victories against aggressors, most especially the 1812 Fatherland War, suggested that Russia would win in this conflict, too.

The inclusiveness of the patriotic narrative of sacred union explains much of its power. The "union of tsar and people" is primarily a *vertical*

---

[93] Melancon, *The Socialist Revolutionaries and the Russian Anti-War Movement*, 60–68. A detailed – and entirely partisan – treatment of the government's crackdown on Bolsheviks is A. E. Badaev, *Bolsheviki v Gosudarstvennoi dume* (Moscow, 1929), 303–85; on the activities of the security police in the first year of the war, see Jonathan W. Daly, *The Watchful State: Security Police and Opposition in Russia, 1906–1917* (DeKalb: Northern Illinois University Press, 2004), 159–75.

union – it envisions "all layers" or social estates and classes united with their sovereign. In contrast, the ecumenical union of all nationalities and all political orientations, symbolized in the Duma's extraordinary session, is more *horizontal*. Finally, the last strand of the narrative, concerning the mobilization of troops and of public donations for the war effort, is fundamentally a *spatial* union: from city and from farm, from every corner of the empire, men march out to defend their country while donations of money, goods, and labor flow from the civilian population to the front.

It was also an accommodating narrative, in the sense that different emphases and orientations could find a place in it. The prominence of Nicholas in the patriotic unity of 1914 provides a good example. Conservatives believed that the renewed union of tsar and people would shore up the prestige of the absolute monarch, while reformers believed that same union would transform the postwar political landscape along more democratic lines. But, for this inclusive narrative to be truly effective, to inspire and mobilize the population, it had to be fleshed out and disseminated widely. We will explore attempts to do precisely that in the next chapter.

2 National Mobilization
Government, Propaganda, and the Press

> In our time ... priority belongs to the task of the mobilization of morale, not just of the army alone but of the entire country.
> Sergei Runin, "The Mobilization of Morale," July 1915[1]

General Anton Denikin, in his influential memoirs, devotes many pages to the imperial government's failure to promote Russia's war effort in public opinion. He contends that neither the civil nor the military authorities in Russia had any organ "which was even in some degree reminiscent of the mighty Western propaganda institutions." Thanks in part to the high command's fear of introducing politics into the army, no effort had even been made to foster "wholesome patriotism" in soldiers; the government's track record was little better in regard to the general population. In consequence, as the Great War dragged on it became increasingly hard to persuade an uncomprehending population that they must continue to serve and sacrifice until victory.[2]

Denikin's was not an isolated postwar critique. Other generals, including Nikolai Golovin and Aleksei Brusilov, contrasted the Russian government's failure to instruct and inspire the people with the highly successful efforts of the German authorities to maintain the spirit of sacrifice in their people. Conservative former official V. I. Gurko similarly asserted that "the government did nothing" to explain to Russians the real meaning of the struggle or inspire morale by publicizing heroes.[3] Taken altogether, these critiques constitute an indictment of a regime too hidebound in its approach to governance and too fearful of unleashing the energies of its own population to prosecute successfully a modern war

---

[1] Sergei Runin, "Sim pobedish' – mobilizatsiia dukha," *Otkliki. Politicheskii zhurnal-fel'etony* (January 1916 reprint edition of article of July 10, 1915), 3–4.
[2] Denikin, *The Russian Turmoil*, 28, 191–93.
[3] Golovine, *The Russian Army in the World War*, 244–45; V. I. Gurko, *Features and Figures of the Past: Government and Opinion in the Reign of Nicholas II* (Stanford: Stanford University Press, 1939), 543–46.

of nations in arms. Contemporary critiques of the Russian government's failure to foster and mobilize patriotic sentiment are also a substantive part of the explanation proffered for a more fundamental problem, the putative lack of patriotism in Russia among the predominantly rural population.

Today, scholars of the Great War typically characterize it as a total war, one in which national mobilization of the home front is a crucial component of victory. As John Horne puts it, national mobilization is "the engagement of the different belligerent nations in their war efforts both imaginatively, through collective representations and the belief and value systems giving rise to these, and organizationally, through the state and civil society." Its function is to "generate unity and a sense of inclusiveness."[4] Most scholars of Russia in the Great War would argue, as did contemporaries, that the Russian imperial government failed here, both imaginatively and organizationally.[5]

However, a closer look at the imperial government's efforts to define, inculcate, and mobilize state patriotism in the Great War presents a more complex picture. In truth, the authorities relied more on supervising public opinion than on generating it. The lack of unity in the organization and control of information and propaganda could undermine the coherence of the patriotic narratives being created. At the same time, governmental efforts and expenditures in producing patriotic materials for a national, mass audience were far greater and far more innovative than contemporaries appreciated. The content of these materials, along with those being produced by the commercial press and various individuals and groups, was not simply traditionally monarchic, or nationalistic – and thereby potentially exclusive – along religio-ethnic lines. New narratives of what it meant to be "Russian" and new grounds of inclusion within the national community were being created.

---

[4] John Horne, "Introduction: Mobilizing for 'Total War', 1914–1918," in Horne, ed., *State, Society and Mobilization in Europe during the First World War* (Cambridge: Cambridge University Press, 1997), 1, 7, 9. A good comparative context is provided by the exprience of the Austrian empire: see Cornwall, *The Undermining of Austria-Hungary*, 16–39.

[5] An important exception is Holquist, *Making War, Forging Revolution*, who argues that propaganda, surveillance, and other techniques of mass persuasion were being employed in 1914–17 in Russia and then drawn upon by both Reds and Whites in the civil war. A representative view is S. Ia. Makhonina, "Russkaia legal'naia zhurnalistika XX v (1905–fevral' 1917). (Opyt sistemnogo issledovaniia)," in B. I. Esin, ed., *Iz istorii russkoi zhurnalistiki nachala XX veka* (Moscow: Izd. Moskovskogo universiteta, 1984), 12, who writes that tsarism did not have its own print organs capable of advancing government policy, trying instead to influence the press through "censorship, administrative suspensions, and prohibitions."

Moving Images: The Skobelev Committee

Scholars surveying Russia's cultural landscape during the Great War have noted the extreme modesty of the semi-official Skobelev Committee's propaganda efforts. As Richard Stites puts it, the committee "produced some films, concerts, and unimaginative graphics but remained relatively inactive."[6] Had the Skobelev Committee been the imperial government's sole or even main venue for positively shaping public opinion in the war, the story of the state's role in promoting patriotism could be told very briefly.

The Skobelev Committee, founded during the Russo-Japanese war as a philanthropic organization for aiding disabled soldiers, was named for the hero of the Russo-Turkish war, General Mikhail D. Skobelev. The committee partially funded its charitable work through publishing and cinematography operations, and shortly after the outbreak of hostilities in 1914 it began to publish war-related pamphlets and posters and to organize patriotic benefit concerts. Its publications bore the statement that the committee enjoyed the patronage of the sovereign.[7] The committee also received the exclusive right to film moving pictures in areas of military activity.[8]

That monopoly helped limit the use of cinema as a propaganda tool in Russia's Great War. The Skobelev Committee's military-cinematographic division did manage to enlist the talents of well-known Russian filmmakers, such as P. Novitskii and N. Ermolov. But, as Hubertus Jahn notes in his discussion of wartime film in Russia, the committee lacked sufficient personnel and resources to cover the enormous Russian front. That shortfall meant it could not produce nearly enough newsreel or documentary footage to satisfy the public's hunger for authentic images from the war. Owners of movie theaters had to try and satisfy this demand by filling in with the much more plentiful newsreels of the western front.[9] Russian film audiences were therefore more likely to see moving pictures of devastated Belgium or the defense of Verdun than to be moved by images of their own troops or territory.

---

[6] Richard Stites, "Days and Nights in Wartime Russia: Cultural Life, 1914–1917," in Aviel Roshwald and Richard Stites, eds., *European Culture in the Great War: The Arts, Entertainment, and Propaganda, 1914–1918* (Cambridge: Cambridge University Press, 1999), 9.

[7] RGVIA, f. 1620 (Skobelevskii komitet), d. 1, ll. 1, 17; d. 92, ll. 21–22. How the Skobelev Committee assumed its wartime propaganda role is a matter of speculation, since many of its records are too poorly preserved to be available to researchers.

[8] RGVIA, f. 2003 (Staff of the Supreme Commander – Stavka), op. 2, d. 15, "O kinemagraficheskoi deiatel'nosti Skobelevskogo komiteta, 27 ianvaria–6 sentiabria 1915 g.," ll. 15, 16.

[9] On film, see Jahn, *Patriotic Culture*, 155–58, and RGVIA, f. 2003, op. 2, d. 15, ll. 15–16.

This failure to provide an eager public with war-related footage was also the fault of the high command. Conservative generals such as Nikolai N. Ianushkevich – the supreme commander's chief of staff until August 1915 – were not keen to permit filming in military theaters of activity. In March 1915 Ianushkevich took exception to scenes filmed by a Skobelev Committee crew, most particularly the burial of a fallen soldier. He fired off memos demanding that the film be suppressed and that all works produced by the committee in future be subject to prior military censorship, noting reports that images in the film had "actually upset the public."[10]

In their reluctance to embrace the propaganda possibilities of film, the Russian military behaved more like their opponents than their allies. In Germany, however, wariness eventually turned into appreciation of film's unique appeal across class lines, and potential for influencing public opinion. In January 1917, the German high command set up a Photographic and Film Office to coordinate the wartime activities of the German film industry; throughout 1917 General Erich Ludendorff stressed the importance of film for propaganda. In Russia, restrictions on filming near the theaters of war do not seem to have been significantly relaxed, and the Skobelev Committee retained its monopoly until December 1916.[11] Given that Russia had approximately 4,000 movie theaters attracting 2 million people daily, this was indeed a missed opportunity.[12]

Publicizing Enemy Atrocities

In the first two weeks of August 1914, German troops brutally sacked the small border city of Kalisz, in Russian Poland, killing many residents and destroying much of the town. The Russian press, smarting at German depictions of barbarous Cossacks, reported avidly on this horrifying incident; as one paper indignantly commented, "Germany has the audacity to accuse us Russians of barbarity. Now it has revealed its true self."[13]

---

[10] RGVIA, f. 2003, op. 2, d. 15, ll. 31, 36–37, 44–45, 50, 55–57, 65–66.
[11] Welch, *Germany, Propaganda, and Total War*, 45–48. The Skobelev Committee did produce several very popular feature-length films with war themes; see Jahn, *Patriotic Culture*, 159–69.
[12] Denise J. Youngblood, *Russian War Films: On the Cinema Front, 1914–2005* (Lawrence: University of Kansas Press, 2007), 12.
[13] D. Danilov, "Chetyre dnia germanskikh varvarov," *Birzhevye vedomosti* (July 31, 1914), 2, cited in Laura Engelstein, "'A Belgium of Our Own': The Sack of Russian Kalisz, August 1914," *Kritika* 10, 3 (Summer 2009), 449.

National Mobilization

In Russia, as among other belligerents, demonization of the enemy was an important means of mobilizing the citizenry behind the war effort. Stories of German and Austrian atrocities and violations of the rules of warfare filled the pages of the Russian press from the very start of hostilities. Commercial publishers such as Sytin produced big print runs of cheap, brightly colored woodcuts (*lubki*) featuring swaggering or barbaric Germans doing all manner of despicable things.[14] Circulated widely, at every level of society, these stories and images could have a powerful effect. Depictions of enemy atrocities and outrages created an object of hatred around which everyone could unite: internal differences paled in comparison before the terrible, external foe. Showing the enemy's contempt toward one's own people and the indignities he visited upon them – and most especially upon women – played to national pride and personal honor. It also fed fear of the horrors he would wreak should he win, which presumably hardened the population's resolve to continue the fight, no matter the costs.

But for these shocking acts to have maximum effect, their credibility had to be established. An effective way of verifying allegations about enemy misdeeds was to create an extraordinary investigatory body composed of individuals worthy of public respect. The British, by far the most sophisticated of the belligerents in the use of propaganda, led the way with establishment of the Bryce Commission, which published its influential report in 1915.[15] Russia, too, wasted little time in creating a commission. The idea for such a body was raised at the special January 1915 sessions of the legislative chambers, and on April 9, 1915, the Council of Ministers announced formal creation of an Extraordinary Investigative Commission. Chaired by Senator Aleksei N. Krivtsov, the committee had members from the

---

[14] For a discussion of portrayals of the enemy in *lubki*, see Stephen M. Norris, *A War of Images: Russian Popular Prints, Wartime Culture, and National Identity, 1812–1945* (DeKalb: Northern Illinois University Press, 2006), 136–39, 143–46; on the gendering of the enemy in wartime images, see Karen Petrone, "Family, Masculinity, and Heroism in Russian War Posters of the First World War," in Billie Melman, ed., *Borderlines: Genders and Identities in War and Peace, 1870–1930* (New York: Routledge, 1998), 95–119.

[15] See, for example, Gary Messinger, *British Propaganda and the State in the First World War* (Manchester: Manchester University Press, 1992); a classic study is James Read, *Atrocity Propaganda, 1914–1919* (New Haven: Yale University Press, 1941). However, as is pointed out by John Horne and Alan Kramer, *German Atrocities, 1914: A History of Denial* (New Haven: Yale University Press, 2001), exaggerations concerning atrocities in the Great War should not obscure the fact that atrocities were actually committed.

50   Mobilizing the Russian Nation

Звѣрство въ Калишѣ.

Насиліе дѣвушки, на глазахъ отца и 2-хъ братьевъ. Послѣ надѣвательства, дѣвушку убили, а братьевъ и отца разстрѣляли.

2.1 "German atrocities at Kalisz," 1914; depictions of a barbaric enemy were one means of promoting internal unity. Political Poster Collection, #RU/SU 374, courtesy of Hoover Institution Library & Archives, Stanford University.

legislative chambers, the Ministry of Justice, the Foreign Ministry, and the military. The Extraordinary Commission's original mandate was investigation of alleged violations of the rules of war by Germany and Austria-Hungary (the sack of Kalisz among them); those by

Turkey and Bulgaria were added subsequently. It was also tasked with disproving false accusations about atrocities committed by Russian troops.[16]

The Extraordinary Commission immediately issued public appeals for information about instances of atrocities or abuse (*zloupotreblenie*) by enemies. Military and civil authorities, individual eyewitnesses, and victims responded with some 8,000 allegations in its first year of existence. The commission tried to corroborate the allegations through testimony, medical examinations, documentary evidence, and photographs.[17] Its studied air of objectivity notwithstanding, the Extraordinary Commission found precisely what it expected to find: all manner of cruelty and abuses, some committed on the whim of individuals and others the result of deliberate policies. Violations of the rules of warfare included resort to inhumane weapons, such as poison gas, and mistreatment of prisoners of war. Other crimes were directed at civilians, including looting, physical injury, sexual assault, and murder. The commission also enumerated gratuitous destruction of animals and cultural monuments.

The sober findings of so distinguished a group of investigators gave credence to the sensational stories in the press and popular broadsheets. Steps were taken to make sure the Extraordinary Commission's findings were widely known. The first volume of its report was published in early 1916 in an edition of 10,000, but by then the commission had already released eight short pamphlets on its findings, all gruesomely illustrated. Copies of these were sent to members of the State Council and Duma, provincial governors, organs of the press, Orthodox bishops, and educational institutions. In 1916 five booklets specifically aimed at soldiers were printed in editions of 300,000 each; an additional 152,000 copies of two pamphlets on mistreatment of Russian POWs by Germany and Austria were given to Supreme Command and to reserve units. A million copies of the POW pamphlets were also distributed to rural officials and schools, clergy, and zemstvos. Finally, 50,000 inexpensive copies of "popular readings" about enemy atrocities were put on sale to the public.[18]

Significantly, General Mikhail Alekseev, by that time army chief of staff, was the impetus for the huge editions of atrocity literature tailored for soldiers. He wrote to Extraordinary Commission head Krivtsov in

---

[16] "Vvedenie," *Nashi vragi. Obzor deistvii chrezvychainoi sledstvennoi komissii* (Petrograd, 1916), i–ii, and RGIA, f. 1276, op. 20, d. 103, "Osobyi zhurnal soveta ministrov (1916)," l. 148.

[17] "Vvedenie," *Nashi vragi*, ii–iii. [18] Ibid., iv–v.

December 1915 asking about the possibility of such publications – the General Staff's representative on the commission had shown Alekseev some of their material, and he was enthusiastic that it could have "a wonderful influence on the lower ranks." The army would of course pay all production costs. Underlying this overture was the high command's profound concern about the rate at which rank-and-file soldiers had surrendered to the enemy in 1915: pamphlets graphically depicting the tortures and hardships awaiting soldiers who fell into German and Austrian hands would presumably act as a deterrent. Senator Krivtsov responded with alacrity to Alekseev's proposal; an initial outlay of 40,000 rubles was agreed upon, and pamphlets began reaching reserve units within the month.[19]

Reaching a Mass Audience

Governmental contributions to creation of wartime patriotic culture were by no means limited to negative tropes about what Russia was fighting against. The imperial authorities expended much money and effort in trying to shape popular opinion, particularly that of the peasantry, who furnished most of the army's soldiers. In early July 1914, the Chief Administration for Press Affairs, under the Ministry of the Interior, received permission to create a Committee for Popular Publications; its primary task was disseminating useful agricultural knowledge among the peasantry. Within weeks, this mission was radically reworked: now, the committee made its top priority informing rural people about the war and its significance for Russia.

In August 1914 the committee requested 150,000 rubles to fund improvements to the government-subsidized rural newspaper *Sel'skii vestnik* and its broader distribution; publication of a whole series of pamphlets on the war; and assemblage of small libraries of suitable readings that could be made available to wounded soldiers at hospitals and clinics.[20] Minister of the Interior Nikolai A. Maklakov and Minister of Agriculture Aleksandr V. Krivoshein – respectively among the most conservative and liberal of cabinet ministers – strongly supported this proposal, noting that "printing matters are in the highest degree useful,

---

[19] RGVIA, f. 2003, op. 2, d. 30, ll. 1–2, 3, 4, 10, letter of Alekseev of December 2, 1915, responses of Krivtsov of December 23, 1915, and January 11, 1916.

[20] On the history of the paper prior to the war, see James H. Krukones, *To the People: The Russian Government and the Newspaper Sel'skii Vestnik ("Village Herald")* (New York: Garland Publishing, 1987).

important, and demand further development."[21] Further requests for appropriations – 200,000 rubles in June 1915 and another 200,000 in December 1915 – were promptly filled.

The Committee for Popular Publications tackled its mission energetically. Within its first 18 months of existence it published 14 pamphlets in editions of 1–2 million each, distributing them free of charge to soldiers, field hospitals, zemstvos, some 22,000 primary schools, and various rural officials. (Committee members noted that demand for the brochures exceeded supply.) Similarly, the small libraries of 130 titles, distributed to the Red Cross and to hospitals run by the Union of Zemstvos and Union of Cities, were in great demand. The initial 1,000 libraries were snapped up so quickly that another 1,400 were assembled and distributed by the end of the year. Graphic images were also popular. A map of Europe that showed the various military theaters – including Russia's – was distributed free of charge as a supplement to subscribers of *Sel'skii vestnik*. Some 178 zemstvos also requested copies, inspiring a second printing priced for sale at a modest 5 kopeks each; in all, 130,000 copies of the European map were published, soon followed by others. More than 400,000 postcards with images of the tsar, the supreme commander, and other war leaders and heroes were distributed to soldiers and in hospitals and clinics. In addition, 200,000 color copies of a large portrait of Nicholas II – "The Sovereign Emperor – Powerful Leader" (*derzhavnyi vozhd'*) – were published and distributed.[22]

The first brochure produced by the Committee for Popular Publications, "The Great War" (August 1914), managed to instruct, vilify, and inspire in just four pages. Clearly written in easy-to-read language and a bold typeface, it explained that the war was entirely the fault of the greedy and perfidious Germans, who had long desired Russia's land for themselves. But the arrogant Germans were sadly mistaken in imagining they would beat their intended victim, for Russia was strong and had strong allies, her tsar was resolute, and her people united. While Germany was fighting for base goals, the Russian people were fighting for the honor and integrity of their country, for their native fields and their families. Above all, it was the justice of the cause which ensured that Russia would prevail, for hers was a "holy war." The text concluded stirringly, "Remember brothers, Russian people,

---

[21] RGIA, f. 1276, op. 10, d. 1090 (1914), l. 1.
[22] RGIA, f. 1276, op. 11, d. 1418 (1915), ll. 1–4, 74. The figure on state schools comes from Jeffrey Brooks, *When Russia Learned to Read: Literacy and Popular Literature, 1861–1917* (Princeton: Princeton University Press, 1985), 41.

behind us is the motherland; before us is victory; and everywhere, in labor and in battle, God is with us!"[23]

Many of the other pamphlets take up predictable themes. "War with Turkey" describes an enemy that is contemptible and beatable – historically an oppressor of Christians, and regularly bested by Russia in every past conflict. "Our Glory" celebrates the sturdy heroism of the simple soldier and the common people, from the days of General Aleksandr V. Suvorov's eighteenth-century triumphs over the Germans, to the Fatherland War of 1812, to the present. But in insisting, too, on the heroism of the noble officers, the pamphlet reminds readers that *all* social estates in Russia love their country and willingly sacrifice for her. "War in Galicia," illustrated with photographs of Nicholas II, the heir Aleksei, and various generals, builds pride and confidence by detailing past Russian victories over Austria. It also reinforces the theme of the just nature of Russia's war, for Russia is not conquering another people, the reader is assured, but rather liberating her "own": Galicia was once part of Russia and 500 years' separation "has not caused the Galicians to forget their Russian origins."[24]

Consistency is not always apparent from pamphlet to pamphlet. "What Victory Will Give Russia" justifies the need to keep fighting by demonstrating how the fruits of victory will far exceed the costs; some of the enumerated benefits – such as acquisition of the Dardanelles – scarcely correspond to the picture of Russia's disinterested motives. However, even here a defensive theme is proclaimed: with victory, Russia will finally be liberated from the economic dominance of Germans, "who in peacetime, making use of our Russian good nature, little by little have taken into their hands our land and our trade and our factories and plants."[25]

At least one of these pamphlets develops themes one might not expect from an official committee of the tsarist government. "War and the State Duma" (1915) looks at the historic July 1914 special session that demonstrated the sacred union of the tsar and the people's representatives, and how this union was reaffirmed in the special session of January 1915.[26] Quoting extensively from the speeches of Duma

---

[23] "Velikaia voina," in RGIA, f. 1276, op. 11, d. 1418, ll. 10–12.
[24] "Nasha slava," l. 21, "Voina s Turitsiei," l. 34, "Ottorzhennaia vozvratikh (voina v Galitsii)," ll. 25–26, all in RGIA, f. 1276, op. 11, d. 1418. Many Galicians did not consider themselves "Russian," and the heavyhanded military occupation of Galicia in 1914–15 managed to alienate almost everyone: see Mark von Hagen, *War in a European Borderland: Occupations and Occupation Plans in Galicia and Ukraine, 1914–1918* (Seattle: University of Washington Press, 2007), 19–42.
[25] RGIA, f. 1276, op. 11, d. 1418 "**Chto dast' Rossii** pobeda," ll. 36–38.
[26] The government had initially intended to keep the State Council and State Duma closed for the war's duration, following the special one-day session. But, as it became clear that

president Rodzianko, the pamphlet identifies three main duties of the "people's electors": preservation of the fraternal union of all the peoples of Russia, discovery and fulfillment of the people's aspirations, and care for the country's military might, a duty the Duma "has always fulfilled on the grounds of deep patriotic feeling." While this depiction of the Duma makes it the loyal prop of the monarch rather than stressing its role as tribune of the people's will, it is nonetheless a warm endorsement of the people's elected representatives. It is difficult to imagine any official representation of the Duma so positive since its opening in 1906.[27]

The success of the government-subsidized paper *Sel'skii vestnik* illustrates both the importance attached to reaching rural dwellers and peasant appetite for news of the war.[28] The Committee for Popular Publications invested great effort in improving this daily newspaper, since it considered it "the most important and reliable instrument for influencing the rural reader."[29] This realization apparently came from outside the government. At the end of July, Baron Nikolai Vrangel' and two friends – all with publishing experience – came up with the idea of putting out a newspaper for soldiers, and submitted a formal proposal to Minister of Agriculture Krivoshein. They pointed out the need for a paper written in accessible prose that would interpret the war for the troops and demonstrate the strong connection between the country's defenders and the people for whom they were fighting. Besides reporting on war news, the paper would keep soldiers abreast of agricultural news, tell them about everything that was being done for their families, and inform them about patriotic demonstrations all over the country. Krivoshein praised the idea, but said there was no money for such an undertaking. On September 16, Vrangel' saw an issue of the refurbished *Sel'skii vestnik* and wrote in his diary that Krivoshein had behaved rather treacherously: "Having grasped that this was a good and needed undertaking, he decided to apply *none other than our program* to the Ministry of Agriculture's organ *Sel'skii vestnik*, and managed to find for this the

---

the conflict would last for more than a few months, public pressure mounted to reconvene them, and the authorities reluctantly authorized a special three-day session for January 27–29, 1915. The chambers were then prorogued until July 19, 1915 – much to the Duma's dismay – though various committees continued to meet. See Pearson, *Russian Moderates*, 28–31, and Gaida, *Liberal'naia oppozitsiia*, 66–70.

[27] RGIA, f. 1276, op. 11, d. 1418, "Voina i Gosudarstvennaia duma," ll. 46–48.

[28] The war's impact on peasant interest in the world outside the village was a topic of tremendous interest to contemporaries; see, for example, Seregny, "Zemstvos, Peasants, and Citizenship."

[29] RGIA, f. 1276, op. 11, d. 1418 (1915), ll. 4–5.

needed 150,000 rubles!"[30] Vrangel' was of course glad to see these ideas put into practice, even if not specifically for soldiers.

The new incarnation of *Sel'skii vestnik* borrowed from the proven methods of the commercial press by switching to a bolder typeface, attracting more literary talent, and providing all sorts of free supplements to subscribers, such as war-related maps, pamphlets, and posters.[31] With an enlarged staff, it increasingly freed itself from the necessity of printing undigested governmental communiqués – all but incomprehensible to most peasant readers – and instead wrote its own copy.[32] These improvements, along with expanded reporting on the war, attentive coverage of the situation of rural soldiers' families, and a weekly supplement answering readers' questions, brought in a slew of new subscribers. In summer 1914, *Sel'skii vestnik*'s circulation stood at 34,053; by May 1915 it had grown to 86,731 paid subscriptions, and by early 1916 circulation was expected to exceed 150,000 (including free subscriptions delivered to the army and hospitals).[33]

Sel'skii vestnik was in most respects quite traditional in its representation of Russian patriotism. Early articles from July and August 1914 spoke of devotion to faith, tsar, and country in highly formulaic terms: "an immemorial, firm faith in God, deep loyalty to the Tsar, and the greatest love for the Motherland – these are the feelings that have seized everyone in Russia."[34] A slight but also traditional variant to this theme stated that "We are defending the Motherland, the Tsar, our wives

---

[30] Vrangel', *Dni skorbi*, 27–31, 60–61, entries of July 31, August 1, August 2, and September 16. The group approached Krivoshein because he was a friend of one of them, L. K. Stefanskii. They planned to call their paper *Voina za mir* (The War for Peace) and estimated it would take 100,000 rubles to launch.

[31] One cheap, mass-circulation paper, for example, just three months into the war, reminded subscribers that it had already sent them two large, colored maps of the theaters of war and at the end of the year would be sending "a lavishly produced War Album": "Ot izdatel'stva," *Gazeta-kopeika* (October 1, 1914), 3. On incentives used by the popular commercial press, see Louise McReynolds, *The News under Russia's Old Regime: The Development of a Mass Circulation Press* (Princeton: Princeton University Press, 1991), 228–44.

[32] A perceptive analysis of how peasants read newspapers is Corinne Gaudin, "Circulation and Production of News and Rumor in Rural Russia during World War I," in Frame, Kolonitskii, Marks, and Stockdale, *Russian Culture in War and Revolution*, Book 2, esp. 56–66.

[33] RGIA, f. 1276, op. 11, d. 1418 (1915), ll. 4–5. The most popular daily at this time, *Russkoe slovo*, saw its wartime circulation climb to over 1,000,000, but no other publication came close to these figures. On readership and the popular press in this period, see Brooks, *When Russia Learned to Read*, 115–18, 131.

[34] *Sel'skii vestnik* (July 22, 1914), 4; see also (July 17, 1914), 1, "with faith in God, with deep loyalty to the Tsar, with an ardent willingness to give all to the Motherland we will await the days to come"; and (July 23, 1914), 1, "we stand strongly, all as one, for Faith, Tsar, and Fatherland."

and daughters, we are defending our entire existence." Thus, in addition to the triadic formula of faith, tsar, and fatherland, defense of family, of the land of one's ancestors, and of a way of life were the inspiration offered to rural Russians.[35]

The paper also followed the lead of the commercial press in emphasizing the popularity of the war, due largely to the righteousness of the cause. The patriotic demonstrations that occurred prior to and following Germany's declaration of war showed that "the firm and calm policy of the government has found a sympathetic response in the broad circles of the population."[36] The success of the mobilization was also invoked, as when Duma deputy N. L'vov of Saratov remarked that it showed how, "In general, war with the Germans is extraordinarily popular." Almost every article reminded readers that Germany had attacked Russia, that Russia's war was a strictly defensive one.[37]

But the most important theme in *Sel'skii vestnik* during the first year of the war, as with virtually all periodicals in the empire, concerned the sacred union: the population's united resolve to defend the country transcended class, nationality, and political party. Drawing the common parallel between the Napoleonic war and the current conflict, the paper editorialized that, "Entering into the second Fatherland war, Russia meets it as she did the first. All classes of Russian society, the entire Russian people, have merged into a single spirit."[38] An article about the July 26 reception at the Winter Palace for the members of the legislature celebrated the union of Russians with their tsar: "Tsar and people have merged together and in the highest sense of selfless love for the Motherland given their mutual vow to conduct this war, which we did not begin, to a glorious conclusion." Covering the historic one-day session of the Duma, the paper stressed there were no exceptions to the patriotic display: Baltic Germans, Poles, Muslims, and Jews all made speeches declaring themselves "profoundly loyal to the Motherland, prepared for any sacrifice for her."[39]

The patriotic narrative presented in *Sel'skii vestnik* was a remarkably durable one, altering little until the dark days of late fall 1916. Patriots were full of love for faith, tsar and fatherland and for their families and

---

[35] *Sel'skii vestnik* (July 23, 1914), 1, and (August 13, 1914), 3.
[36] *Sel'skii vestnik* (July 15, 1914), 1; (July 17, 1914), 1; see also (July 18, 1914, 2), and (July 19, 1914), 3.
[37] *Sel'skii vestnik* (July 22, 1914), 4, and (July 24, 1914), 3.
[38] *Sel'skii vestnik* (July 23, 1914), 1; the parallels with the 1812 Fatherland War, when "every social estate responded with high patriotic feeling and gave their all for defense of the Motherland" were noted again on May 30, 1915, 1.
[39] *Sel'skii vestnik* (July 29, 1914), 2 and 3–4.

land: that which was familiar, dear, handed down from old times, was what inspired loyalty and sacrifice. Patriots' loyalties were founded on the past and present, rather than on hopes for a better future (in contrast to the aspirational trope stressed by progressive society and national minorities). Patriots were of course strong and brave, and gave unstintingly of their labor, goods, and even their lives. Thus, steadfast service and generous sacrifice were patriots' defining features. Equally important, patriots were to be found among all classes and every national group in Russia – all were, at least potentially, true sons and daughters of the motherland. This theme of unity of the peoples of Russia, which was by its nature an inclusive construction of the patriotic national community, one depending on loyalty to a common geographic territory and ruler rather than on race, social estate, or religion, persevered despite the obvious fractures in national unity from summer 1915 onward.

The one striking exception to this harmonious picture is the paper's increasingly hostile treatment of Russian subjects of German origin, and particularly the so-called German colonists. German colonists did not really consider themselves Russian, the paper informed its readers; they had proved to be traitors.[40] Otherwise, fissures in the national united front made themselves felt in *Sel'skii vestnik* only in late fall 1916, when the desperate public mood could no longer be kept out of its pages. On December 3, a lead article reminded readers of the need to be strong "not only in weapons but strong in spirit, strong in our boundless love for the Motherland." The motherland is "the home of the Russian people," it explained, and "If in a home all is right [*blagopoluchno*], if in a family there is harmony," then no external trial is frightening. But now "among us all is not right." Unity and agreement had to be reforged so that Russia would be strong and win.[41]

Besides publishing materials aimed at popular audiences, the imperial government also covertly funded a number of existing, mostly privately owned periodicals, which ranged from the conservative to the reactionary. Progressive Russians complained about secret subsidies to the right-wing press; though the government blandly denied the charges, when the subsidies were revealed after the February revolution, the only real surprise was their scale. An examination of the recipients and the sums given demonstrates both the degree to which the imperial government tried to influence public opinion, and the degree to which its message could be contradictory. The narrative disseminated by what censors routinely called the "monarchic" or "patriotic" press – which

---

[40] *Sel'skii vestnik* (September 4, 1916), 3.   [41] *Sel'skii vestnik* (December 3, 1916), 1–2.

progressive Russians labeled the "Black Hundred" or "reptile" press – was in many cases not the narrative sponsored by the government in its own publications.[42]

Subsidies to the press predated the war; Minister of the Interior Petr A. Stolypin had employed them during his tenure, 1906–11, and his successors continued the practice. According to one published source, subsidies to the right-wing press were approximately 600,000 rubles in 1912.[43] In 1915 the very substantial sum of 1,122,071 rubles was assigned from a discretionary fund to the Chief Administration for Press Affairs to use for publication subsidies; roughly 76 percent – approximately 853,500 rubles – went to right-wing undertakings. Of this, 62,000 rubles went to a small number of "monarchic" organizations in Moscow; the remainder, approximately 791,600 rubles, went to 53 monarchic newspapers and journals all over the empire. The subsidies increased in 1916.[44]

What the government received for its largesse can only be called problematic. Clearly, one consideration underlying the subsidies was to ensure the existence of a conservative, loyalist regional press, as is revealed by the titles of many of these organs: *Severo-zapadnaia zhizn'* (Northwestern Life), *Golos Samary* (Voice of Samara), *Tambovskii krai* (Tambov Territory). Several religiously oriented publications received money, among them *Pastyrskii sobesednik* (Pastoral Interlocutor) and *Mir Islama* (The World of Islam), directed at Muslim readers. But among the secular right-wing organs were a number of publications that directly contradicted or undermined the narrative of sacred union. These included *Russkoe znamia* (Russian Banner), the organ of the Union of Russian People, and *Korennik*, published in Moscow by the Russian Monarchic Union. Doubting that ethnically non-Russian subjects of the empire could be as patriotic as the "core population," narrowly construing Russianness on ethnic (*russkii*) and religious grounds,

---

[42] The Chief Administration of the Press's "Review of the Press" for 1914 identified twenty-two publications as monarchic, many of these also being characterized as "patriotic": RGIA, f. 776, op. 10, d. 1957, ll. 148, 162.

[43] On Stolypin's subsidies to the press, see Abraham Ascher, *P. A. Stolypin: The Search for Stability in Late Imperial Russia* (Stanford: Stanford University Press, 2001), 121–22; Ascher estimates an annual dispersal of about 3 million rubles from the discretionary fund, but this figure includes monies given to political parties as well as to some thirty newspapers; figures for 1912 and 1914 come from Berezhnoi, *Russkaia legal'naia pechat'*, 26.

[44] GARF, f. 601 (Personal Archive of Nicholas II), op. 1, d. 1067, "Otchety, spravki i perepiska Glav. Uprav. po delam pechati o sekretnykh raskhodakh na subsidirovan. Monarkhicheskikh i pravykh gazet i zhurnalov, 1915–1916," ll. 1–3, 11–12, 24. Half of the sum dispersed to monarchic organizations in 1915 went to one prominent right-wing monarchist, Vladimir M. Purishkevich.

and – after a hiatus of some months – preaching hatred of Jews, the far-right press threw into doubt the inclusive and familial tropes of national unity being officially propagated. Although right-wing periodicals had small circulation figures, educated society perceived them as enjoying an outsize influence.[45] At the very least, government tolerance of such publications sent a confusing message to the public and undermined the persuasive power of the official narrative of sacred union.

A second anomaly in government spending on the press involves workers. From the outbreak of war, the authorities had been concerned about working-class loyalty and support for the war effort; its concerns had obvious foundations. In 1914, workers' discontent was higher than it had been at any time since the massive strikes of 1906; workers' patriotism once war was declared was therefore almost as surprising as it was welcome. And, as scholars have noted, in the years immediately preceding the war the authorities were highly conscious of the nexus between war and revolution in Russia that had existed in 1904–05. They were correspondingly apprehensive that another war, or at least one that began to go badly, would spark a second wave of revolutionary unrest. By summer 1915, as military debacle unfolded on the front, there was renewed concern about attitudes in urban, working-class circles, particularly given worsening living conditions and the urgent need to step up industrial production.[46]

Yet positive measures to influence workers' views on the war, as opposed to surveillance, censorship, and arrests of factory agitators, were fairly nominal. It is true that a number of the pamphlets written and disseminated by the Committee for Popular Publications could be of interest to urban dwellers, such as the pamphlet on support for soldiers' families. But relatively little was done specifically to target workers. One isolated effort was the pamphlet "The Working People and the War," by one A. Panov. The pamphlet invokes the authority of Georgii Plekhanov, the founding father of social democracy in Russia and one of the only prominent Social Democrats to come out in support of Russia's war effort. It quotes copiously from Plekhanov's open letter of July 21, 1915, to Duma deputy and fellow socialist A. F. Burianov, in which he contends that, should Germany win, the workers would suffer most of all. Noting the "great truth" of these words, the author details how a victorious Germany would destroy Russia's factories and virtually

---

[45] On the Russian far right in the war, see the excellent book by Kir'ianov, *Pravye partii v Rossii*, 8–11, 217–31. A liberal perspective on the far-right press is A. S. Izgoev, "Pod flagom primireniia," *Russkaia mysl'* (December 1914), 166–75.

[46] Gatrell, *Russia's First World War*, 70–72, 113–17; on workers' attitudes, see Kir'ianov, "Rabochie Rossii i voina," 432–46.

enslave the population. Russian workers therefore had to make sure their soldiers had the supplies they needed to fight; to miss work was to help the Germans.[47]

Since this message was delivered in a single pamphlet, not a series or barrage of publications along the same lines, we might suspect its impact was limited. By autumn 1915, at any rate, a number of extreme-right groups had concluded that a patriotic message could not be gotten to workers on a regular basis given the absence of solid, monarchic working-class newspapers. In a memo to the Department of Police, the right-wing Union of Russian People proposed a solution: the government needed to create just such a daily paper, or subsidize and expand upon a suitable existing working-class paper. *Russkii rabochii* (Russian Worker) began appearing in Petrograd on December 2, 1915. Formally, a group of Duma deputies of working-class origin initiated the newspaper but, according to testimony given after the February revolution, the Ministry of the Interior and Department of Police were actually the driving force.[48]

The editorial in the first issue declared that social democratic ideas were alien to the Russian people, a "German toxic gas, poisoning the soul of the worker." Workers had therefore decided to publish "their own nonparty paper," which would steer clear of political intrigue and partisan stands. Blackening social democracy by reference to its close ties with Germany was a recurring device of this paper, along with editorials and columns urging workers not to strike and to work hard to ensure victory. According to a Soviet historian, though the paper lasted until February 1917 it attracted few readers, since no one was in doubt as to its real provenance.[49] Whether or not this assertion is accurate, the meager annual subsidy of 2,000 rubles given the paper is telling, especially when compared with the hefty sums pumped into other publications. Although the authorities worried mightily about worker attitudes toward the war, they did not dedicate correspondingly large sums to influencing their views.[50]

"Selling" the War

Governmental, civic, and commercial entities were all involved in a vigorous effort to support and publicize the war, the war-loan campaigns.

---

[47] A. Panov, "Rabochyi narod i voina," RGIA, f. 1276, op. 11, d. 1418 (1915), ll. 104–12.
[48] P. E. Shchegolev, ed., *Padenie tsarskogo rezhima. Chrezvychainaia sledstvennaia komissiia*, vol. IV (Moscow and Leningrad: Gosudarstevennoe izdatel'stvo, 1924–27), 127.
[49] "Ot izdatel'stvei," *Russkii rabochii* no. 1 (December 2, 1915), 1. For a discussion of the paper, see Berezhnoi, *Russkaia legal'naia pechat'*, 38, 57–58.
[50] The figures from Nicholas's archive are 2,000 rubles for 1916; no sum is mentioned for 1915: GARF, f. 601, op. 1, d. 1067, ll. 24 and 12.

There had been domestic, publicly subscribed loans in previous conflicts, but these were on a smaller scale and also aimed at larger investors, since the very smallest share denomination one could purchase was 100 rubles. But, in the Great War, the enormous costs of waging total war necessitated borrowing on a vast scale; over the course of the conflict the government floated 7 internal war loans worth a total nominal value of 12 billion rubles. To support this undertaking the imperial government began in 1915 a massive effort to mobilize the savings of even its humblest subjects behind the loan – offering a more accessible 50-ruble loan denomination, expanding the opening of savings banks in rural areas and at the front in order to sell loan subscriptions, and undertaking publicity campaigns to popularize the loans.[51]

An All-Russian Committee for Civic Aid to the War Loans was organized, and war loans were heavily publicized in the press, by lecture campaigns, and, from 1916, through the Orthodox Church and the medium of the poster. In 1916 the Skobelev Committee sponsored a series of thirty posters to support the loan drive, and other public organizations and governmental entities commissioned loan posters as well; a total of 1 million copies of posters and 10 million copies of pamphlets were issued in 1916, and the effort was still more concerted in 1917.[52] Featuring striking imagery by some of Russia's best graphic artists, pithy slogans, and exhortatory texts, the innovative war-loan posters are an excellent source for studying the depiction of the patriotic nation.

War-loan posters, like other wartime propaganda genres, drew on a variety of symbols and sources for their images and allusions. A good example is the simple, graphically effective poster from 1916 by an unknown artist featuring the silhouette of the monument to Minin and Pozharskii, the heroes of the Time of Troubles who mobilized a people's army in 1612–13 to drive the occupying Poles out of Russia. Each figure holds a shield, and one raises his arm in summons to the viewer; behind

---

[51] On wartime borrowing, see Gatrell, *Russia's First World War*, 139–44. The classic treatment of Russia's war loans is Paul N. Apostol, "Credit Operations," in Alexander M. Michelson et al., *Russian Public Finance during the War* (New Haven: Yale University Press, 1928), 247–52, 263–77; a more critical appraisal of the loans is V. V. Strakhov, "Vnutrennie zaimy v Rossii v Pervuiu mirovuiu voinu," *Voprosy istorii* no. 9 (2003), 8–43.

[52] Apostol, "Credit Operations," 247–48, 263, 268–71, and N. I. Baburina, catalog essay for *Russkii plakat Pervoi mirovoi voiny* (Moskva: Isskustvo i kul'tura, 1992), 9; this handsomely produced catalog contains twenty-one war loan posters from 1916. Many other war-loan posters are held in the World War I poster collection of the Hoover Institution.

National Mobilization

the silhouettes, against a dark yellow background, rises a mighty double-headed eagle, emblem of the Romanov dynasty. Beneath the words "WAR LOAN" the legend reads simply: "The fatherland needs your help. Subscribe to the loan."[53] With great economy – two colors, three figures, ten words – this poster unites Russian national heroes, the dynasty, a reminder of how the people have previously mobilized themselves to save their country, and subscription to the loan in a single, patriotic appeal.

War-loan posters often explicitly appeal to a common duty. One poster, showing a doubled-headed eagle attacking an eagle representing the enemy, bears the legend, "Participation in the loan according to one's means is everyone's patriotic duty." The same legend appears in a poster featuring a machine-gunner ensconced behind bushes in a snowy field and another depicting two sailors, one seasoned and one young, working together to load a shell into a giant gun. The artist Ianovskii's poster featuring St. George killing the dragon reads, "Our valiant troops, spilling their blood for the motherland, are sacredly fulfilling their duty. Fulfill yours, too – subscribe to the loan." Yet another poster depicts a handsome and resolute young worker making artillery shells, with the exhortation, "Patriotic and profitable! Buy into the 5 1/2% war loan." Here, the flattering depiction of a worker laboring for his country on the home front reminds the viewer that all classes are crucial in the war effort, and doing their part.

A central focus of many posters is the materiel the army needed for victory. They show giant munitions factories working at full speed even on the night shift, male and female workers producing weapons, trucks, and train cars loaded with ordnance headed for the front, and gunners loading shells into enormous, sleek guns. Many of the posters bear the legend "All for the war!" or "All for victory!" and many make explicit the connection between supplies and outcome: "The more money there is, then the more shells, the fewer the casualties, and the closer is victory over the enemy."[54] These are quintessentially mobilizing posters, calling on the people of the empire to help supply the army by representing not only mobilized, active soldiers – young and old, peasant and urban – but also civilians of both sexes working in munitions. They are also reassuring the viewer about eventual victory, by showing the mountains of supplies being produced and the cutting-edge technology now available

---

[53] *Russkii plakat*, 64.
[54] *Russkii plakat*, 71–77, and Library of Congress, Photography and Graphics Division, Lot 5452, "Russian War Loan Postcards, 1915–16."

2.2 A symbolic map of Russia and Europe, from 1915; mass editions of maps of Russia and the war theaters were distributed throughout the war. Political Poster Collection, #RU/SU 780A, Courtesy of Hoover Institution Library & Archives, Stanford University.

to the troops. This tactic was an astute one, given public outcry over the terrible shortfalls in supplies in 1915 and the connection between shortage and defeats in that crisis year.

Many loan posters were also produced in postcard size, with text on the back amplifying the messages relayed in the pictures. For example, one card spells out concretely what one got for one's money: "Each 100-ruble loan share buys three shrapnel shells. Let our army bombard the Germans sitting in the trenches with your shrapnel." Several remind of the need to sacrifice: "Selflessly, with his own breast, the soldier at the front deflects the enemy attack. You, too, take part in the common struggle – subscribe to the war loan!" Patriotism could also be personally beneficial: by putting one's money into the war loan "you'll fulfill your duty to the motherland and after the war, thanks to your savings, you'll arrange your life along new lines!" In more familial terms E. Cheptsov's image of four soldiers loading a heavy artillery gun, set in a devastated, shell-pocked landscape, insists on the bond between front and rear:

2.3 The slogan of this 1916 poster tells the viewer that buying into the war loan is "Patriotic and profitable!" Its depiction of a handsome young worker making munitions conveys the all-class nature of the sacred union. Political Poster Collection, #RU/SU 1226, Courtesy of Hoover Institution Library & Archives, Stanford University.

"Brothers and sisters, help us soldiers defend you from the enemy hordes. Buy into the war loan!"[55]

The financial success of the internal war loans is a matter of dispute. Those of 1916, in part thanks to the bigger publicity campaigns, were the most successful, being subscribed overall at better than 94 percent. Some scholars compare this level unfavorably to rates of subscription in Germany and Britain.[56] Contemporaries, however, regarded the level of 1916 subscriptions with pride. Moreover, in every combatant nation, war-loan campaigns were as much about involving civilians in their country's war effort as they were about raising revenue. Subscribing to the loan, just like collecting scrap metal or planting a victory garden, invested even humble citizens in the struggle, allowing them to act as patriots and demonstrate their membership in the national community.

Making Russians Heroes

Heroes and heroic martyrs are an important means of building modern national identity and solidarity. Aviel Roshwald notes the pairing of "violation and volition" in many nationalist ideologies: the idea of self-determination – the free exercise of collective volition – is often given meaning and focus by an image of violation. "Indeed, a common yardstick for the measurement of a nation's strength and tenacity is the degree to which its individual members are willing to risk all and even sacrifice themselves on its behalf."[57] Valerie Rosoux suggests that devotion to the heroic memory of martyrs is a significant means whereby communities – be they political or religious – maintain their internal cohesion.[58] In Russia's Great War, later critiques notwithstanding, the authorities did appreciate the value of publicizing the nation's heroes and incorporating them into the patriotic narrative.

The best-known popular hero of Russia's Great War was the Cossack Koz'ma Kriuchkov. Supposedly, in August 1914 Kriuchkov single-handedly killed eleven Germans in one day with his lance, despite suffering sixteen wounds himself. For this incredible feat he was awarded a St. George Cross, the highest decoration for valor. The commercial

---

[55] Library of Congress, Photography and Graphics Division, Lot 5452, "Russian War Loan Postcards."
[56] Apostol, "Credit Operations," 252, 273–77.
[57] On the role of heroes, see, for example, George L. Mosse, *Fallen Soldiers: Reshaping the Memory of the World Wars* (New York: Oxford University Press, 1990), and Roshwald, *The Endurance of Nationalism*, 88–97.
[58] Valerie Rosoux, "The Politics of Martyrdom," in Rona M. Fields, ed., *Martyrdom: The Psychology, Theology, and Politics of Self-Sacrifice* (Westport, CT: Praeger, 2004), 3.

National Mobilization

2.4 The legend of this 1916 war loan poster reads "Our cities, villages, and churches await liberation ..." Political Poster Collection, #RU/SU 1241, Courtesy of Hoover Institution Library & Archives, Stanford University.

press, filmmakers, and publishers immediately seized upon Kriuchkov, and his image was widely disseminated. His popular appeal is easy to understand. As Jahn notes, Cossacks had long been the standard heroes of Russian war imagery, smart and daring, "with peasant instincts and horseback acrobats."[59] The idea of the clever Cossack getting the better of arrogant enemies was also reassuring: Germans might have superior technology, but they were no match for brave and more resourceful Russians.

Besides the phenomenon of Kriuchkov, there were other heroes who enjoyed a national reputation. Kiev's big war hero was Captain P. N. Nesterov, an aviator shot down over Galicia in late August 1914. Local and national newspapers carried detailed stories on his dashing career,

---

[59] On the Cossack as military hero, see Jahn, *Patriotic Culture*, 23–24, 174, and Judith Deutsch Kornblatt, *The Cossack Hero in Russian Literature: A Study in Cultural Mythology* (Madison: University of Wisconsin Press, 1992), esp. 14–20.

68 Mobilizing the Russian Nation

> Храбрый нашъ казакъ Крючковъ,
> Ловитъ на полѣ враговъ,
> Много-ль, мало-ль—не считаетъ,
> Ихъ повсюду поддѣвляетъ,
> Какъ догонитъ—не милуетъ,
> Сзади, спереди шпигуетъ,
> По возможности елику,
> Сколько влѣзетъ ихъ на пику.

2.5 A *lubok*-style poster depicting the feat of heroic Cossack Koz'ma Kriuchkov, the first recipient of the St. George Cross for valor in the Great War. Political Poster Collection, #RU/SU 83, Courtesy of Hoover Institution Library & Archives, Stanford University.

and covered the giant funeral of this "exemplary son of Russia."[60] Yet another hero was Prince Oleg Konstantinovich, the only member of the Romanov house to die on active duty in the war. A 22-year-old cornet in a Hussar Guards regiment, Oleg died of wounds in September 1914; his handsome photograph was reproduced widely in postcards and illustrated Sunday supplements. His death in service to the Fatherland was immediately lauded as symbolic of the dynasty's love of Russia and willingness to make the supreme sacrifice on its behalf.[61] Sisters of Mercy could also become heroes. The most famous was Rimma M. Ivanova, who in summer 1915 assumed command of a small unit during battle when all its officers were killed; she led a successful charge before being

---

[60] Press coverage of Nesterov includes a long story on his funeral in the military newspaper *Russkii invalid* (September 5, 1914) and an illustrated story in the weekly magazine *Lukomor'e*: "P. N. Nestorov-Nekrolog," no. 18 (September 12, 1914), 12, which concludes "Happy the country that gives birth to such sons!" For hometown coverage of this hero, see *Kievlianin'* (August 28, 1914), 2; (August 29, 1914), 3; (August 31, 1914), 3; and (September 1, 1914), 2 and 3.

[61] For example, "Kniaz' Oleg Konstantinovich," *Letopis' voiny* no. 8 (October 1914), 125; *Derevenskaia gazeta* no. 39 (October 1914), 8; and Boris Nikol'skii, "Ego vysochestvo kniaz' Oleg Konstantinovich," *Istoricheskii vestnik* (November 1914), 12–15.

fatally wounded herself. Ivanova was posthumously awarded the Order of St. George, fourth degree, and hailed in the press as a true "daughter of the fatherland."[62]

Heroic acts cannot foster unity or resolve if no one knows about them. The importance of widely publicizing the heroes of the "Second Fatherland War" was appreciated early on, by a variety of individuals and groups. For example, in October 1914 Father Georgii Shavel'skii, head of Russia's Military Chaplaincy, came up with the idea of requesting that military chaplains record all the feats (*podvigi*) of Russian troops, medical personnel, and clergy at the front, both to preserve these deeds for posterity and to show the "entire world the great soul of the Russian person."[63] Here, we see a shrewd new use of chaplains as "chroniclers of war." Another proposal came from a newly coalescing "committee of patriots" in December 1914, which planned to publish inexpensive pamphlets describing the feats of present-day Russian heroes.[64] The pamphlets were intended to acquaint "millions of people" with the deeds of the motherland's defenders.[65] From a purely commercial perspective, publishers wasted no time in catering to public interest in heroes, producing hundreds of prints and dozens of cheap pamphlets in big press runs, and running regular photo spreads of decorated heroes in illustrated magazines.[66]

It was in this context that the heroic deeds and tragic death of Stefan Veremchuk were brought to the attention of higher military authorities.[67] On September 7, 1915, in Dubenskii district, Volynia province, units of the 76th Kuban Infantry regiment neared the right bank of the river Ikva.[68] They were fighting Austrian forces at the tail end of Russia's

---

[62] For example, "Pokhorony geroiny," *Gazeta-kopeika* (October 1, 1915), 3.

[63] "Voennye sviashchenniki – letopistsy voiny," *Prikhodskii listok* (October 29, 1914), 2, and Otets Georgii Shavel'skii, *Vospominaniia. Poslednego protopresvitera russkoi armii i flota*, 2 vols. (New York: Izd. imeni Chekhova, 1954), vol. II, 93–95. His published instructions asked for concrete details and information about witnesses who could testify to the deeds.

[64] RGVIA, f. 2005, op. 1, d. 71, "Dokladnaia zapiska," l. 16.

[65] RGVIA, f. 2005, op. 1, d. 71, "Vozzvanie," December 5, 1914, l. 17, and letter of January 7, 1915, ll. 17, 19.

[66] Besides frequent photo spreads on heroes in magazines such as *Niva* and *Solntse Rossii*, and illustrated weekly supplements to newspapers such as *Novoe vremia* and *Russkoe slovo*, heroes featured prominently in the new commercial periodicals devoted entirely to the war, such as *Letopis' voiny*, *Voina*, and *Nashi geroi*. On Russian heroes in wartime imagery, see Norris, *A War of Images*, 139–56, and Petrone, "Family, Masculinity, and Heroism."

[67] RGVIA, f. 2005, d. 45, report of General Alekseev of December 1, 1915, ll. 1–2.

[68] This area lies within an old Polish–Russian swathe of borderland, or *kresy*, tellingly characterized by Kate Brown as "the ruins of a remote place of no central historic importance on the periphery of an empire which no longer exists": Kate Brown,

terrible "Great Retreat."[69] Stefan Veremchuk, a 30-year-old peasant, rowed his small boat across the river from his village of Babaloki to tell the Russian command about the strength and placement of enemy forces near the village. His information allowed the Russians to direct their fire effectively, forcing the Austrians to retreat to a second line of trenches near the forest. The next day, Veremchuk rowed Russian scouts over to his village. The Austrians opened fire, but Stefan managed to ferry all the scouts back safely despite being wounded himself. He then returned to his village, where his family remained, despite the soldiers' efforts to convince him that the "Magyars" would kill him. He was indeed captured, and his screams could be heard for hours; purportedly, he shouted a willingness to undergo torture for his fellow Orthodox and the tsar. A day later, the Russians succeeded in driving the Austrians from the area. Stefan's wife, Iustiniia, accompanied by fellow villagers and soldiers, recovered his disfigured body and buried it.[70]

As a sizeable file of military, church, and governmental correspondence shows, a number of people in authority found this story deeply compelling. In late 1915, it was decided to publicize Stefan's inspiring deeds and martyr's death on an unprecedented, mass scale. The why and how of this huge project of valorization has much to tell us about official efforts to promote patriotism, as does analysis of the meanings his narrative was meant to convey.

Having been informed about Veremchuk, Major General Nechvolodov, Commander of the 19th Infantry Division, made sure that his surviving family was given shelter in a neighboring women's monastery. Inquiries were made about Veremchuk and his family. Villagers were interviewed and stated that Stefan was distinguished by great religiosity and deep love for his family. Despite his extreme poverty, he took to heart the misfortunes of others and shared the little he had. He also "passionately loved his motherland." The family he left behind included his blind mother, his wife, and three small sons. Nechvolodov drafted a petition to the emperor relating Veremchuk's inspiring heroism. He proposed that the mother and widow be assigned state pensions; that the three sons be awarded personal nobility, and upon reaching the proper age be sent at

---

A Biography of No Place: From Ethnic Borderland to Soviet Heartland (Cambridge, MA: Harvard University Press, 2004), 3.

[69] It is worth noting that Nicholas II arrived at Stavka at Mogilev to assume supreme command of the army on September 5, 1915 – three days before Veremchuk's death; for an overview of Russia's military fortunes at this point, see Bruce W. Lincoln, *Passage through Armageddon: The Russians in War and Revolution, 1914–1918* (Oxford: Oxford University Press, 1994), 136–83.

[70] RGVIA, f. 2005, d. 45, report of General M. V. Alekseev of 1 December 1915, ll. 1–2.

state expense to a military academy; that a detailed description (*opisanie*) of Veremchuk's life and deeds be published and widely distributed; and that there be an open subscription to build a memorial chapel at his grave.

This petition sped up the military chain of command. Chief of Staff General Mikhail Alekseev received the petition in early October and had the story verified: members of the 76th Kuban Infantry were prepared to testify to Vermechuk's patriotic assistance, and to his having been tortured and "disfigured." On December 1, 1915, Alekseev presented to the tsar a slightly modified version of the original petition – the request to grant nobility to the sons was dropped, and the educational proposal was changed to agricultural school. Besides asking that a pamphlet about Stefan's life be printed and distributed to all army units and among the civilian population, Alekseev also asked that clerics of every church explain to their congregations, through sermons and conversations, the "deep meaning and significance of the upright life and high deed of Stefan Veremchuk." Just one day after receiving Alekseev's petition, the emperor approved it in its entirety, including granting annual pensions to Veremchuk's mother and widow. The pensions were assigned on December 7 and the educational arrangements completed a week later.[71]

By late May 1916, the all-important story of Veremchuk's life and deeds was in print. The distribution for this free, 32-page pamphlet throws light on its intended audience: 200,000 copies were designated for the Ministry of Internal Affairs, presumably for distribution to government employees, zemstvos, municipal dumas, and the wartime public organizations; 100,000 copies went to the synod, explicitly for distribution in parish churches and parish schools; and 100,000 copies each went to the Chief Administration of the War Ministry and to the staffs of the military districts.[72] The synod's Printing Office also produced an additional 60,000 copies as a free supplement to its nationally distributed parish newspaper, *Prikhodskii listok* (Parish News), an important new link to Russia's Orthodox parishes.[73] In sum, a surprising 560,000 copies of the pamphlet were printed. To put this figure in context, consider that the combined total press run of *all* biographies in the 1930s of famous Soviet boy hero Pavlik Morozov was 175,000.[74]

---

[71] RGVIA, f. 2005, d. 45, report of General M. V. Alekseev of 1 December 1915, l. 3.
[72] RGVIA, f. 2005, d. 45, report of General M. V. Alekseev of 1 December 1915, ll. 21–22.
[73] RGIA, f. 800, op. 1, d. 590, l. 60.
[74] Catriona Kelly, *Comrade Pavlik: The Rise and Fall of a Soviet Boy Hero* (London: Granta Books, 2005), 180.

Why was it Veremchuk who was fashioned a national hero-martyr? After all, by late summer 1915 Russia had, tragically, hundreds of thousands of dead defenders to choose from. We can glean some clues from the timing and context, for different moments require different heroes. Given concern that the hero be authentic, and perceived as such, the large number of witnesses to Stefan's deeds and death was important. Also important were his good character and humble estate. But Veremchuk was not just from the peasantry, he was a civilian: it seems likely that in the context of mobilization of the home front in 1915, a civilian hero was particularly useful. It is also tempting to suppose that his torture at the hands of Austrians ("Magyars," as the soldiers put it) was doubly useful, since Russian authorities could depict these presumed Catholics as enemies of the Orthodox faith and as thoroughly barbaric as the German foe.[75]

Besides Veremchuk's bravery, piety, and love of family, the two virtues most exemplified in the description of his life are love of country and self-sacrifice. The official pamphlet opens with a four-page introduction in folksy language, which asserts that "From ancient times, the Russian people has been distinguished by love of its Motherland." Of course most human beings love their country, the text continues, but not all peoples cherish this feeling so deeply as to be willing to sacrifice even life itself: "In this respect, the Russian person, in general, stands very high." And while this supreme sacrifice is most often offered by military men, Veremchuk is cited as an example of the "not unusual" incidence of simple Russian civilians consciously sacrificing their lives for the good of the motherland.[76] Finally, it is intriguing that Stefan is not Great Russian. Although no explicit mention is made of this – Veremchuk is always described simply as representative of the *"russkii narod"* – the choice of a Ukrainian ("Little Russian") peasant as national hero-martyr bolsters the narrative of sacred union.

The message of the Veremchuk heroic narrative is that the Russian people (encompassing *all* the peoples of Russia) loves its country and will sacrifice itself for it. Veremchuk is explicitly said to represent a common national type, making him paradigmatic as well as exceptional. As a civilian, Veremchuk was not under orders. He understood and freely accepted danger and, ultimately, death for the sake of what he held most dear; in this sense, his actions exemplify nationalist myths' joining of

---

[75] Von Hagen, *War in a European Borderland*, 10–14, 54–71, demonstrates that the Austrians – and Russians – were as capable of harsh treatment of civilians in occupied areas as were the Germans.
[76] RGIA, f. 796, d. 329, ch. 1 (1916), ll. 116–17.

"violation and volition." Stefan's piety also underlies the broader narrative of the war as not only a "just war" against an aggressor but a Holy War, a crusade, to protect the true faith from defilement and to rid Russia of German "dominance" (*zasilie*). Last, but certainly not least, Stefan's martyrdom is not in vain. The Austrians are ultimately driven out, in part because of his aid to the Russian army: this small victory can be thought to prefigure the greater, national victory that is assuredly to come.

Despite all the effort invested in publicizing Veremchuk, his story does not seem to have caught on.[77] We can only speculate as to why this martyr from the common people did not become a well-known hero. Perhaps the extreme modesty of his life and situation was too colorless to capture the popular imagination. I suspect that his facelessness – the pamphlet has no portrait, fictive or otherwise – made it hard for people to connect with him. Nonetheless, this effort to fashion a national hero is instructive. The Veremchuk project demonstrates civil and military authorities' appreciation of the need for heroic narratives to inspire, mobilize, and unite the population, and a corresponding commitment to disseminating the story on a truly mass scale. It shows a shared belief in the desirability of having heroic exemplars who came from the common people (and not only the ethnically Great Russian people), as well as appreciation of the importance that society and the state be seen to honor them. That said, the apparent lack of success of this huge effort also reminds us that the popular reception of any given national narrative does not necessarily conform to expectations. This humble citizen's patriotic deeds and awful sacrifice did not "live on for posterity."

Conclusions

The Russian authorities spent tens of millions of rubles through 1916 on efforts to inform, influence, and mobilize the public in support of the war. In some cases, the initiative came from the government or the military; in others, private individuals, civic organizations, or the commercial press participated in these efforts, or made suggestions that the government implemented. But no distinction really need be drawn between the two types of activity, since this symbiosis of private,

---

[77] I have been unable to find any mention of Veremchuk in the commercial press, or any images published for a mass audience. A pamphlet published by a right-wing press does include a sketch of a heroic-looking Stefan about to be grabbed by Austrians as he returns to his village: Graf N. N. de-Roshefor, *Svetlo pamiati Stefana Veremchuka* (Petrograd: Tip. "Kolokol," 1916), 16; there is no information on how many copies were printed, but presumably the edition was small.

commercial, and governmental efforts was the hallmark of every society's mobilization in the first modern, total war.[78] The scale of these undertakings was enormous. For example, the imperial government paid for production and free distribution of 20 million copies of war leaflets and pamphlets for the 17-month period from the outbreak of war to the end of 1915. Increased attention to and investment in the rural newspaper *Sel'skii vestnik* demonstrate that the tsarist authorities were alive to the possibilities of shaping popular opinion through mass-circulation periodicals.

Although many publications offered traditional imagery and exhortations to fight for faith, tsar, and fatherland, there were also significant departures. A more modern and inclusive definition of the nation, based on common territory rather than ethnicity or religion, and an insistence that all peoples and classes were equally imbued with love for the motherland, coexisted with more traditional or ethnically exclusive constructions. The wide distribution of war-loan posters, inexpensive maps, and pictures of heroes helped the population visualize the nation and those defending it. In this way, in images as well as in words, the sacred union of the nation was shown to include everyone willing to serve and sacrifice for Russia.

There were also missed opportunities. The heightened appreciation for the power of the printed word and image extended only partially to film, a hugely popular medium that the Bolsheviks would effectively employ in the civil war. Despite concerns about the attitudes of workers toward the war, the government's effort to craft a newspaper that would engage the urban working classes was belated and poorly funded.

Overall, the efforts of the imperial authorities to disseminate mobilizing, patriotic themes were surprisingly ambitious, and amplified by enormous private and commercial efforts to publicize – and sell – the war effort. Another powerful means of mobilization was the Russian Orthodox Church, which not only had the ability to communicate with tens of millions of the faithful, but also to sacralize the nation's righteous cause. The church and its co-mingling of religious and civic duty are the subject of the next chapter.

---

[78] See Ian F. W. Beckett, *The Great War*, 2nd edn. (Harlow: Pearson Education, 2007), 392–408, and Leonard V. Smith, Audoin-Rouzeau, and Becker, *France and the Great War, 1914–1918*, 54–56.

3 "On the Altar of the Fatherland"
The Orthodox Church and the Language of Sacrifice

> Remember that shame and death will fall on the head of the lazy, self-seeking, and traitorous, while eternal glory is in store for those who place their property and their life on the altar of the Fatherland.
>
> Proclamation of the Holy Synod, July 1914

On July 20, 1914, the Holy Synod of the Russian Orthodox Church issued a proclamation calling on the faithful to defend faith, tsar, and fatherland from unprovoked German aggression. It exhorted all Orthodox people to put aside their differences, unite around the throne, and "go willingly and robustly to the defense of the Fatherland."[1] According to customary practice, this proclamation would be read aloud by every priest in every parish at Sunday services, along with the emperor's manifesto about the start of the war, thus speedily reaching tens of millions of Orthodox churchgoers.

The Russian Orthodox Church had always supported the modern state's military ventures, and the Great War was no exception. The zeal with which the church embraced this war effort, however, was striking. It was also of enormous importance to the state authorities, since the church was legitimizing and sanctifying the national cause. We know how valuable this legitimizing function of the Orthodox Church was for Soviet authorities in the Second World War, when the church immediately declared the fight against the German invaders a Holy War.[2] But there has been almost no exploration of the role and activities of the church in the First World War, significant though these were.[3]

---

[1] S. G. Runkevich, *Velikaia otechestvennaia voina i tserkovnaia zhizn'* (Petrograd, 1916), 19.

[2] On the day of the German invasion, Metropolitan Sergei – acting head of the Russian Orthodox Church – issued an appeal to the faithful promising that, "The Church of Christ will bless all Orthodox who defend the holy borders of our Motherland": quoted in Steven Merritt Miner, *Stalin's Holy War: Religion, Nationalism, and Alliance Politics, 1941–1945* (Chapel Hill: University of North Carolina Press, 2003), 69, 76–83, 93–114.

[3] The standard work is still Curtiss, *Church and State in Russia*, which was originally written in the 1940s without benefit of access to Soviet archives. Several histories of the synodal

75

In a preradio era, the church enjoyed unparalleled means for communicating with the majority of the rural population. According to the 1897 census, between 115 million and 125 million subjects of the Russian empire were Orthodox – that is, around 70 percent of the population. (In European Russia and Siberia, the figure was even higher, more than 81 and 85 percent, respectively.) While many rural subjects might not regularly come into contact with a newspaper, they attended church frequently and thus could bring home information about the war and its conduct provided by the priest.[4] Parish schools were a second avenue of influence, since one-third of all schoolchildren in the empire attended church-run primary and secondary schools. Third, with its enormous publishing operations, the Orthodox Church had the means to produce periodicals and all manner of instructional as well as devotional literature that could be distributed to clergy and laity. Finally, through its formal department of military chaplains, serving active units and military hospitals, the church had direct access to millions of mobilized men. For all these reasons, the Russian Orthodox Church was uniquely placed to shape the narrative of the war's meaning and conduct.

As the state church, the Russian Orthodox Church was profoundly aware of its unique responsibilities to the nation in this conflict.[5] The church also appreciated the huge benefits its activities might have beyond the war itself. In fact, for many clerics Russia's involvement in the war meant not only hardship, sacrifice, and loss but also opportunity: opportunity to contribute to national-patriotic renewal, after years of revolution and social discord; opportunity to revitalize rural parishes, and

---

era devote a few pages to the war years: for example, M. A. Babkin *Sviashchenstvo i tsarstvo (Rossiia, nachalo XX v.–1918 g.). Issledovaniia i materialy* (Moscow: Izdatel'stvo "INDRIK," 2011), and S. L. Firsov, *Russkaia tserkov' nakanune peremen (konets 1890-kh–1918 gg.)* (Moscow: Kruglyi stol po religioznomu obrazovaniiu i diakonii, 2002). One war-related topic which has attracted scholarly attention concerns clergy assigned to military units: see, for example, A. A. Kostiukhov, "O nekotorykh usloviakh sluzheniia voennogo dukhovenstva v gody Pervoi mirovoi voiny," *Vestnik Pravoslavnogo Sviato-Tihkonskogo Gumanitarnogo Universiteta. Istoriia. Istoriia Russkogo pravoslavnogo tserkvi* (Moscow, 2005), issue 1, 1, 24–44.

[4] M. A. Babkin, *Dukhoventsvo russkoi pravoslavnoi tserkvi i sverzhenie monarkhii. (Nachalo XX v.–konets 1917 g.)* (Moscow: Gosudarstvennaia publichnaia istoricheskaia biblioteka Rossii, 2007), 57. Russian Poland had the lowest proportion of Orthodox believers, at 6.47 percent, followed by Central Asia, at 8.28 percent. For a short overview of the rhythms of rural and urban church attendance, which could vary by age, gender, and region, and also according to season, see Page Herrlinger, *Working Souls: Russian Orthodoxy and Factory Labor in St. Petersburg, 1881–1917* (Bloomington: Slavica, 2007), 79–82.

[5] See, for example, *Deiatel'nost' otechestvennoi tserkvi vo vremia voiny Rossii s Germaniiu, Avstrieiu i Turtsieiu (v 1914 g.)* (Petrograd: Synodal'naia tipografiia, 1916).

improve the relations of the parish priest with his flock; opportunity to enhance the standing of "the Fatherland church" in a secularizing society by proving the supreme value of the church to the national community in time of trial. It was also an opportunity, in the eyes of some, to strengthen Orthodoxy in its contest with rival faiths.

The Church on the Eve of the War

A host of problems confronted the Russian Orthodox Church in the years immediately preceding the outbreak of the war. Since the late nineteenth century, growing numbers of clerics had desired church reforms, ranging from grant of greater autonomy to the church, down to reorganization at the most basic grass-roots level, the parish itself. Many parish clergy also felt stifled by the repressive atmosphere of the church hierarchy, with limited opportunity for debate of important issues or local autonomy of action.[6] While there was no consensus as to what reforms were needed, there was a widespread belief that reform must be undertaken. The revolution of 1905 had intensified hopes that a national church *sobor* (council) would finally be convened to do just that. But various proposals went nowhere, in good measure because Emperor Nicholas II, and the conservative chief procurators he appointed, had reservations about such change. Many clerics became frustrated and disillusioned, the more so as some prominent churchmen actively participated in right-wing political movements, behavior which seemed to associate the church in general with the forces of reaction.

Nor was the institutional reputation of the Holy Synod, as the ruling administrative body of the church, particularly lustrous in the post-1905 period. From 1912, as public indignation over the behavior of Grigorii Rasputin grew, the close association with Rasputin of several prominent church figures – among them Chief Procurator Vladimir K. Sabler and Metropolitan Pitirim of St. Petersburg – seriously damaged the authority of the synod and church hierarchy. The emperor's April 1905 Manifesto on Freedom of Conscience, by allowing greater religious choice than had previously been the case, exposed the church to more competition from

---

[6] As a group, hierarchs tended to be more conservative on questions of reform than parish clergy or academy professors, but even deeply conservative bishops favored some reform; see John D. Basil, *Church and State in Late Imperial Russia: Critics of the Synodal System of Church Government (1861–1917)* (Minneapolis: University of Minnesota, 2005), 20–33, and T. A. Bernshtam, *Prikhodskaia zhizn' russkoi derevni. Ocherki po tserkovnoi etnografii* (St. Petersburg: RAN, 2005), 48–51.

other denominations. Many clerics felt beleaguered, as the number of Baptists and other "Sectarians" increased.[7]

Small wonder, then, that the few studies touching on the church in the war tend to dwell on its problems. But these difficulties should not obscure important sources of vitality within the church, both as an institution and as a community of the faithful, or cause us to accept old perceptions of it as moribund. Despite contemporary concerns about society's secularization, popular piety was in fact making a comeback.[8] This piety in turn suggests that the regime's insistence on an important role for the church in its numerous mass public ceremonies celebrating the dynasty and state – what historian K. N. Tsimbaev terms its "jubilee mania" – had a practical basis beyond the religiosity of the imperial family itself.[9] Tapping into popular piety and sanctifying the state's secular events were two important means by which the church helped shape patriotism in Russia's Great War.

Mobilizing Altruism

The degree to which the Orthodox Church tried to mobilize itself and the faithful in support of the Great War was unprecedented, even as compared with the Russo-Japanese war ten years earlier. Then, it had conducted the customary services asking for victory, pledged 100,000 rubles for soldiers' medical care, established a hospital, and called upon the faithful to help with wounded troops. In contrast, within the first two months of the outbreak of the Great War the church broadened the scope of its prayers and religious interventions, massively expanded efforts to communicate with the faithful, and assumed substantial responsibilities for fundraising and provision of material assistance.

On July 20, 1914, the Holy Synod met in extraordinary session to determine how the church should respond to the war. Its first decisions were

---

[7] One study of the church in the late imperial period refers to the years 1907–17 as the "decade of despair": Jennifer Hedda, *His Kingdom Come: Orthodox Pastorship and Social Activism in Revolutionary Russia* (DeKalb: Northern Illinois University Press, 2008), 187–97. See also Curtiss, *Church and State in Russia*, 286–305, who paints an equally bleak picture.

[8] On the ebb and flow of popular piety see, for example, Gregory L. Freeze, "A Pious Folk? Religious Observance in Vladimir Diocese 1900–1914," *Jahrbucher für Geschichte Osteuropas* 52 (2004), 323–40, and Herrlinger, *Working Souls*, esp. 110–14, 216–23; both these studies make clear that popular piety could diverge from the formal teachings of Orthodoxy in many ways, also noting regional variations in beliefs and practices.

[9] K. N. Tsimbaev, "Pravoslavnaia tserkov' i gosudarstvennye iubilei imperatorskoi Rossii," *Otechestvennaia istoriia* no. 6 (2005), 42–51; Tsimbaev asserts, however, that this project of sacralization was not very successful.

fairly traditional, primarily involving the marshaling of church resources to help the Red Cross attend to the medical needs of the army. The synod announced it would organize and fund a large military hospital, and urged clergy and employees of religious departments to tithe 2 percent of their monthly salaries toward aid for wounded soldiers. It also pledged church monies for these goals and instituted a weekly collection for soldiers' needs after divine service. Monetary donations for war needs from the church and its personnel were significant: by June 1915, they had donated 3,736,069 rubles – directly or via the Red Cross – for aid to sick and wounded troops and 2,721,930 rubles for other war needs.[10] The weekly collection in all churches to benefit the wounded was soon followed by all sorts of one-time or annual collections for specific war-related causes – disabled veterans, soldiers' families, soldiers' orphans, the needs of "liberated Galicia," and so on. There were also huge collections of warm clothing, linens and bandages, foodstuffs, tobacco, and holiday gifts.

Monasteries and monastic clergy were understood as having special contributions to make to the war effort. In 1914, Russia had more than 1,000 male and female monasteries in operation, and some 94,000 monastics (more than 75 percent of whom were female), constituting significant human and material resources.[11] In the years immediately prior to the war the church had worked with the Red Cross to have monks and nuns trained to serve as reserve Brothers and Sisters of Mercy; now more monastics were exhorted to undergo this training. Monasteries and convents were urged by the synod to establish hospitals, clinics, or hospices on their premises and to provision as well as staff them. By the end of the first year of war, there were 670 infirmaries operating on monastic or church premises.[12] As the war entered its

---

[10] Runkevich, *Velikaia otechestvennaia voina*, 20–25, 30–31; *Deiatel'nost' otechestvennoi tserkvi*, 1–3, 12–21; and D. A. Pashentsev, "Blagotvoritel'naia deiatel'nost' russkoi pravoslavnoi tserkvi v nachalnyi period Pervoi mirovoi voiny," in *Rossiia v Pervoi mirovoi voine. Tezisy mezhvuzovskoi nauchnoi konferentsii, 4–5 oktiabria 1994 goda* (Riazan, 1994), 161–62.

[11] According to figures from I. K. Smolich, in 1914 there were 550 monasteries and 475 convents; numbers of women far outweighed numbers of men, and were also growing at a faster rate: 73,299 female monastic clergy, as compared to 21,330 male: cited in William G. Wagner, "Paradoxes of Piety: The Nizhegorod Convent of the Exaltation of the Cross, 1807–1935," in Valerie A. Kivelson and Robert H. Greene, eds., *Orthodox Russia: Belief and Practice under the Tsars* (University Park: Penn State University Press, 2003), tab. 1, 236.

[12] *Deiatel'nost' otechestvennoi tserkvi*, 5–7. In July 1915, this mission was slightly refined by the emperor's call upon male clerical institutions to make their premises as widely available as possible for medical facilities for soldiers, with state and public entities – such as the zemstvos and the Red Cross – assuming financial responsibility for provisioning them: RGIA, f. 796, op. 198, d. 329, ch. 1 (1915), l. 221.

second year, appeals to the monastic community to aid the war effort broadened. For example, a synodal directive (*opredelenie*) of July 28, 1915, explained that since the Lord had not yet seen fit to grant Russia and its allies victory, the Fatherland needed monastics to "deepen your sacrifices and labors for the fatherland" by establishing long-term convalescent facilities and retraining centers for disabled veterans and homes for the orphaned children of fallen soldiers.[13] Increasingly, these residential facilities would also be used to provide housing for tens of thousands of refugee women and children. However, some contemporaries believed well-endowed monasteries were not giving nearly enough, a charge the socialist newspaper *Den'* leveled at the wealthy Solovetskii monastery in fall 1915. The number of times that the synod exhorted monastics to do still more for the war effort suggests that there were in fact public doubts about their generosity and patriotism.[14]

No institution was so well placed as the church to address war-related needs in rural areas, which were underserved by public or private charitable agencies.[15] At its special session of July 20 the synod called for the creation of more parish guardianship councils in order to aid the families of mobilized soldiers; within a year 36,118 of Russia's 40,590 parishes reported having such councils. The guardianship councils were composed of elected members of the laity, with participation from the parish priest. In the war's first year they distributed some 6.3 million rubles in monetary aid – more than half of it raised within the parishes themselves – as well as disbursing food and organizing cafeterias for needy soldiers' families. Councils were also tasked with making sure that mobilized soldiers' families knew of their right to state aid, and helping them procure it. In 1915, assisting soldiers' families with field work and the harvest became a top priority, an effort that included finding and coordinating volunteers and setting up temporary daycare centers for children whose mothers were working in the fields.[16] The councils also took a lead

---

[13] Runkevich, *Velikaia otechestvennaia voina*, 335–36.
[14] In October 1915 the senior military censor banned circulation of these critical articles: RGIA, f. 796, op. 198, d. 329, ch. 1 (1915), l. 296. Examples of synodal exhortations for monasteries to do more include "Monastyri i voina," *Prikhodskii listok* (September 11, 1914), 2; "V zashchitu monastyrei i monashestvuiushchikh," *Prikhodskii listok* (August 11, 1915), 2; and F. V-b., "Monastyry i prikhody Moskovskoi eparkhii v dele sluzheniia ikh nuzhdam voiny," *Prikhodskii listok* (October 3, 1915), 3.
[15] On the basis of data for 1902 (the fullest statistics available), one scholar estimates that 7,998 of the country's 11,040 charitable institutions – 72.4 percent – were located in cities: G. N. Ul'ianova, *Blagotvoritel'nost' v Rossiiskoi imperii. XIX–nachalo XX veka* (Moscow: Nauka, 2005), 258–59.
[16] The directive on temporary daycares was issued April 8, 1915, and envisioned using the premises of church primary schools for the daycares, and the female teachers in those schools to staff them. On parish councils, see *Otechestvennaia tserkov i voina* (Petrograd,

role in organizing donations for the army, particularly of clothing and linens, and in late summer 1915 began helping with refugees.

This mobilization of rural charitable impulses was a tangible way of involving thousands of small, scattered communities, as communities, in the collective national war effort. The synod also anticipated that the parish guardianship councils, having proved so useful, would continue their social and philanthropic efforts in peacetime. It is hard to gauge the effectiveness of the councils, since data on their activities tend to be exclusively official in nature, and therefore reported in a wholly favorable light. (One might suspect that creation of thousands of councils within the space of a year would have resulted in a sizeable number of "Potemkin villages.") *Novoe vremia*, a frequent critic of "church stagnation," applauded the formation and activities of the councils, which showed the majority of the clergy "at the height of their position in the heavy time of war."[17] In any case, most councils continued functioning into 1917. By late summer of that year, however, the situation had deteriorated. The diocese of Nizhnyi Novgorod, for example, reported to the synod in August that the activity of its parish guardianship councils had "all but expired," since most had run out of money. By mid 1917 many dioceses were not capable even of gathering information to report.[18]

It seems likely that the church's stream of appeals for donations and volunteers, and collection of funds during and after divine services – a conjuncture of spiritual and material solicitation – had the effect of reinforcing the "sacred" nature of the war. Similarly, the church's willingness to publicize the two internal war loans of 1916 legitimized the connection between the church, the state, and the war. The synod directed priests to try and convince parishioners of the importance of buying shares in the war loan. Church publications ran articles explaining, "The people need to understand that participation in the loan is not only a matter of profit, but first and foremost a matter of conscience, a duty before the motherland and before the church, which are threatened today by such grave danger from the side of the enemy." Or, again, "Can a person with means who refuses to give money to the government loan

---

1916), 16–17; *Deiatel'nost' otechestvennoi tserkvi*, 4–5, 59–63; and "Opredelenie Sviateishago sinoda," *Voina* no. 9 (1915), 66–67.

[17] "1914 god," *Novoe vremia* (January 1, 1915), 12; the article goes on to complain that some hierarchs had been dilatory in organizing parish councils in their dioceses, just as not all monasteries had been unstinting in their aid to the war effort.

[18] By summer 1917, even councils that still had funds were reluctant to use them for soldiers' families, since "families of mobilized men are already handsomely provided for by the government" while clergy were themselves too impoverished to continue aid: RGIA, f. 796, op. 198, d. 329, otd. 1, st. 5 (1917), "Ob okazanii pomoshch' na voennye nuzhdy (o popechitel'nykh sovetakh)," ll. 5–6, 10.

for the needs of the troops, really call himself a son of the motherland, a citizen of the fatherland?"[19]

Sacred-Secular Rituals Uniting the Nation

Besides greatly expanding its efforts to assist with war relief, the Orthodox Church also significantly developed the conduct of prayers and rituals associated with the war. From the outset, the church mandated that after every celebration of the liturgy there be a prayer asking God to grant victory to Russia and its allies, adding to the prayers for the health of the emperor and heir the name of supreme commander Grand Duke Nikolai Nikolaevich. These traditional supplications were soon supplemented by new daily prayers for wounded soldiers and prayers for POWs. From September 2, 1914, the synod decreed that a requiem (*panikhida*) be held every Saturday in church for the fallen. The church also became involved in the memorialization of fallen soldiers in other ways, with construction of memorials inside churches, stand-alone monuments, and special fraternal cemeteries. It directed every parish school to erect a tablet inscribed with the names of its former pupils and teachers who had died serving their country in the war; women's patriotic sacrifice was not overlooked, since guidelines stipulated that Sisters of Mercy be listed as well as soldiers.[20]

Special national observances could unite all the faithful in thanksgiving, entreaty, or acts of sacrifice. From October 1914, "significant events of the war" were to be celebrated with all-Russian services of thanksgiving and the all-day ringing of church bells. Such occasions included Russia's occupation of eastern Galicia in September 1914 and the fall of the key Austrian fortress of Przemýsl in February 1915.[21] A different kind of all-Russian observance was on July 8, 1915, the day celebrating the Kazan Icon of the Mother of God, which the Orthodox Church designated as a national day of prayer for the troops. A description of one local observation of this day depicted a cathedral illuminated by hundreds of candles, as on a principal feast day, and overflowing with worshippers. The prayers were repeated four times, since this parish had sent four rounds of men to the army; with each cycle of prayers the men of each separate call-up were individually named. The priest evoked a

---

[19] L.T., "Novyi voennyi zaem i dukhovenstvo," (March 18, 1916), 3, and K.P., "Komu pomogat'?" *Prikhodskii listok* (November 1, 1916), 3; also, "Zaem pobedy" (March 23, 1916), which outlines how Russian clergy can follow the example of French priests and explain to their parishioners the necessity of buying shares in the loan.
[20] Runkevich, *Velikaia otechestvennaia voina*, 82–83, 124–25.
[21] Opredelenie No. 8480, reported in *Prikhodskii listok* (October 15, 1914), 2.

3.1 Crowds praying in front of Kazan Cathedral in Petrograd on the All-Russian Day of Prayer, July 8, 1915. Reproduced from *Letopis' voiny*. RP9.L6255, Houghton Library, Harvard University.

torrent of sobbing with his heartfelt, impromptu sermon: "Brothers and Sisters! Today we are carrying out the all-Russian day of prayer for our dear troops. All Russia is praying for them! ... Remember your wounded brothers and refrain from evil. They're dying on the field of battle and we should not forget this. We must help the sick, widows, and orphans ... Let us do everything like sincere Christians, loving each other."[22]

Besides the prayers and observances that were decreed from the center and were national in scope, churches, clerics, and believers initiated a wide range of war-related religious observances at the local level. A community might decide to build a memorial chapel (*chasovnia-pamiatnik*), as in the town of Pechenkino in Ufa in May 1915, where several thousand believers attended services at the local church and then processed to the site of the memorial to lay the foundation stone, carrying with them a temporary plaque bearing the names of the 300 men called up from their town thus far. The rector celebrated the divine service at

---

[22] G.P., "Kak narod molit'sia vo dni voiny," *Prikhodskii listok* (July 22, 1915), 3. For coverage of the Day of Prayer around the country, see "Vsenarodnye molebstviia o darovanii pobedy," *Russkie vedomosti* (July 9, 1915), 4. The popular preacher Ioann Vostorgov sermonized that this "day of national unity" was reminiscent of the days of Minin and Pozharskii; "Velikie edinenie," in Protoierei Ioann Vostorgov, *V dni voiny*, series 2 (Moscow: Russkaia pechatnia, 1915), 139–41.

3.2 "News from the War." Peasants listen attentively as a young man reads aloud from a newspaper; secular and religious authorities were particularly concerned to keep rural Russians connected to the war effort. Drawing by N. Bogdanov-Bel'skii, from the popular illustrated magazine *Niva*.

the site, gave a homily, then led prayers for victory, for the dynasty, and for the eternal memory of those who had laid down their lives for "faith, tsar, and fatherland."[23] We might also assume that local clergy offered many services simply for solace, without the valence of a patriotic message, like the one organized by a priest one Sunday afternoon in June 1915 in an unnamed village to comfort "the families crying for their dead." He observed, "we all cried together and these prayerful tears helped more than any words could, and then the eternal miracle of the liturgy worked upon us."[24]

Pilgrimages provide a particularly interesting manifestation of local initiative. As Chris Chulos has noted, pilgrimages to regional shrines, a popular expression of Orthodox piety in the late imperial period, might also be encouraged by the secular authorities as contributing to formation of popular national identity.[25] In wartime, these journeys to sacred places could assume explicitly patriotic meaning. One illustration is the procession of the cross (*krestnyi khod*) organized by Protoierarch Nikolai Florinskii in Vladimir province in June 1915, to pray for victory. He set off with six priests, three deacons, and a large group of pilgrims, traveling from the town of Aleksandrov to the Trinity–Sergius Monastery, and back. Over the course of four days, the procession stopped at 22 villages en route, with the number of pilgrims swelling to 4,000. At each stop the procession was greeted by a crowd of villagers with bread and salt, a prayer service for victory was held, and a sermon preached. Another example comes from Petrograd, where 20,000 people participated in a two-day pilgrimage to the miracle-working icon of St. Nikolai in Iam-Izhory, to honor fallen soldiers and pray for victory.[26]

Benedict Anderson has called attention to the role of the pilgrimage in creating identities and communities, both religious and secular-national ones. Describing medieval Europe's great religious pilgrimages, he notes the role of the small cohort of literate adepts who performed the unifying rites, "interpreting to their respective following the meaning of their collective motion." Whether the pilgrimage was sacred or secular in nature, Anderson argues, these common journeys promoted in individuals from different localities a "consciousness of connectedness."[27]

---

[23] "Dobroe delo," *Prikhodskii listok* (May 20, 1915), 3.
[24] I. Popov, "V derevne v dni voiny," *Prikhodskii listok* (June 7, 1915), 2.
[25] See Chris J. Chulos, "Orthodox Identity at Russian Holy Places," in Chulos and Timo Piirainen, eds., *The Fall of an Empire, the Birth of a Nation: National Identities in Russia* (Burlington, VT: Ashgate, 2000), 29–32, 35–40.
[26] Palomnik, "Narodnoe molenie," *Prikhodskii listok* (July 7 1915), 3, and "Krestnyi khod," *Gazeta-kopeika* (May 17 1915), 3.
[27] Anderson, *Imagined Communities*, 54–56.

In the case of the wartime pilgrimages, the unifying rites were simultaneously religious and secular, performed for a community of believers that was taken to represent the national community, as well. Moreover, detailed coverage of pilgrimages in the press ensured that the larger community would be informed of – and perhaps inspired by – this unifying rite.

Disseminating Patriotism

Next to the church itself, the most important institution in the parish was the church school. In 1913, on the eve of the war, the Orthodox Church employed some 40,000 teachers in its parish schools, which were attended by approximately 2 million children. Schoolchildren demonstrated a keen interest in the war, particularly as so many had fathers or brothers who had been called up to fight. Teachers in parish schools – no less than in secular ones – appreciated the myriad possibilities for responding to and building on this interest.[28] In giving schoolchildren the information they craved about the war and showing them on maps where the fronts were located, they could simultaneously animate a broader interest in history and geography. Many believed that children's interest in the war could also teach patriotism: teachers could explain to them Russia's historic mission and status as a great power, teach them to honor and wish to emulate soldiers' bravery and self-sacrifice, and involve them in the war effort in their own small way through organizing donations or holiday gifts for soldiers or refugees. In an article in October 1915, educator K. V. El'nitskii talked about making use of schoolchildren's rise in patriotic feeling: "We should rejoice in this upsurge and cultivate it. We should deepen in the consciousness of pupils the conviction that everyone is obliged to serve his fatherland, and help it flourish."[29]

Teachers looking for guidance on how to promote patriotism in their communities had a ready source of ideas and examples in *Narodnoe obrazovanie* (Popular education), the church's pedagogical magazine. Each month it featured recommendations on war-related readings, patriotic songs, and poems that children could learn, ways in which

---

[28] Runkevich, *Velikaia otechestvennaia voina*, 259; on zemstvo teachers' use of the war as a teaching moment, albeit for adults, see Seregny, "Zemstvos, Peasants, and Citizenship," 293–97.
[29] K. V. El'nitskii, "Voina i shkol'nye deti," reprinted from *Narodnoe obrazovanie* in *Prikhodskii listok* (October 18, 1915), 4.

teachers all over Russia were incorporating the war into lesson plans, or correspondents' descriptions of the brave service or splendid war-relief activities undertaken by their pupils and fellow teachers.[30]

Schoolchildren were particularly encouraged to correspond with soldiers at the front. Soldiers greatly appreciated these displays of attention and respect, teachers were told, and this correspondence would also help to instill patriotic feelings in children. The magazine published examples of letters from pupils and responses from soldiers; while most of the latter were clearly Orthodox in faith and ethnically Russian, there were a few non-Russian (*rossiiskie*) exemplars to demonstrate the sacred union of all Russia's peoples. A letter purporting to come from one Shamil Fridunov expressed thanks for a holiday gift and continued, "I thought everyone had forgotten us but it turns out not yet. I am a Tatar volunteer, an inhabitant of the Caucasus and wish to get acquainted with you by letter. I ask you to write me a letter often. And don't worry, so long as we live we will with pleasure shed our blood to defend you and our fatherland and the motherland and our precious Sovereign." Instances of pupils reading letters aloud to soldiers' illiterate families, and helping them write replies, also featured prominently, with much emphasis on the esteem accruing to the pupils who had such valuable skills.[31]

Creation of war-related rituals in parish schools was another means of inculcating patriotic sentiments. For example, in a long article of late summer 1915 – when Russia's military setbacks were evoking ugly rhetoric about enemies – one priest advised teaching patriotism in a positive way, by nourishing pupils' natural admiration for their soldier-heroes rather than teaching them to hate the enemy. He suggested that in the

---

[30] For example, I. P. Sokolov, "Sluchainyi urok," *Narodnoe obrazovanie* (November 1915), 396, on getting children to collect and write down *chastushki* (short, often humorous folk verses) about the war, an activity that would build on their love of these folk songs, and N. Kozmin, "Uchitelia-geroi," *Narodnoe obrazovanie*, 3 (November–December 1916), 267–68, on the inspiring activities of twenty-six teacher-soldiers from Arkhangelsk parish schools. A particularly interesting example is the admiring piece about schoolteacher Vera Nilovna Glushinskaia, whose desire to serve the motherland was so profound that she disguised herself as a man, volunteered for the army, and won a St. George Cross for valor: V.M., "Vol'noopredeliaiushchiisia Sergei Glushinskii," *Narodnoe obrazovanie* (November 1915), 397–99.

[31] A. Krasikov, "Iz perepiski shkolnikov s soldatami," *Narodnoe obrazovanie* 2 (July–August 1915), 17–20; Uch-tsa Nina M., "Otzyvchivyia serdtsa," *Narodnoe obrazovanie* 2, 9 (September 1915), 156–58; and S. Kirzhatskii, "Uchastie tserkovnykh shkol podol'skoi eparkhii v sovremennoi voine," *Narodnoe obrazovanie* 3 (January 1916), 96–97, who writes that in Podolsk "the majority of church schools have turned into a sort of writing bureau during the war, where on mail days soldiers' relations can come and the pupils help them read their letters from the front and immediately write replies. This epistolary connection between the army and the home front has enormous significance."

Holy Corner in each school, near the icon, there be placed a placard with the names of the village's soldiers written upon it. After morning prayers – where pupils were already beseeching God to protect the emperor and give Russia victory – they would read aloud every name on this list, a daily ritual that would "strengthen in their childish hearts a feeling of deep love and gratitude toward their defenders." This was the proper way for schools to develop a truly unconquerable popular spirit: "We desire to base both the unity of the state and the wholeness of spirit of each future citizen of the state on belief in a righteous and merciful God, on love toward our neighbor, no matter who he might be."[32]

The wartime influence of the parish school was not confined to its pupils. As one priest advised in summer 1916, the whole community could also be improved by the war's lessons: "The very spirit of the times prompts us – pastors, teachers, educators – more energetically to help implant in the public's consciousness healthy conceptions of the principles and foundations of state life and national self-respect, to inculcate patriotic ideas and feelings."[33] Clergy and parish teachers were encouraged to arrange informative meetings at times convenient for adults. At these gatherings they could read aloud stories and articles about the war, or organize discussions for the community on the war and "spiritual-patriotic topics," enlivened with magic lantern shows whenever possible. They could also orchestrate patriotic shows that would serve the joint function of generating war-relief funds while also keeping up the spirits of performers and audiences alike.

Church authorities, like the secular authorities, appreciated the power of the printed word during the war. The synodal presses published large, inexpensive editions of the gospels (some 1.2 million copies in 1914 alone) and other purely devotional literature for distribution to soldiers. They also produced mass editions of war-related leaflets and pamphlets such as "What We Are Fighting for" and "The Orthodox Russian Soldier: Conversations of a Pastor with Troops on the Duty of the Fighting Man and His Obligations." The synod's School Council assembled small, inexpensive libraries of secular and religious texts that donors could purchase and have sent to military hospitals and clinics.[34]

---

[32] Sv. Al-ov, "K nachalu novogo uchebnogo goda," *Narodnoe obrazovanie*, 2, 7–8 (July–August 1915), 159–64.

[33] Sv. P.S., "K chemu zovet nas dukh vremen," *Prikhodskii listok* (June 11, 1916), 3.

[34] "K voprosu o snabzhenii knigami lazaretov dlia ranenykh i bol'nykh voinov," *Prikhodskii listok* (October 30, 1914), 2–3. The committee offered collections of four different sizes – priced from 5 rubles to 20. The 5-ruble library featured forty-one titles, including the gospels, a psalter, saints' lives, some Russian history (mainly concerning past wars), and a few works of fiction by Pushkin, Gogol, and Turgenev.

More remarkably, the synod launched an ambitious national publication, its first-ever daily newspaper. Debuting in September 1914, *Prikhodskii listok* was cheaper and livelier than existing diocesan weeklies, and aimed at a much broader audience: the parish intelligentsia and, through it, ordinary parishioners. Its goal, editors M. Ostroumov and P. Mironositskii explained, was to provide the reader with timely and accurate information about current events, and discussion of them "on a church and state foundation."[35] The scale of the undertaking was enormous, requiring purchase of special, expensive presses, the hiring of additional press workers, and the creation of a transport and distribution system. The size of print runs was also ambitious, ranging from 45,000 to 47,500 copies a day, enough for each parish to receive at least one copy daily.[36]

The front page of each edition of *Prikhodskii listok* was devoted to news about the course of the war, both on Russia's fronts and those of its allies. Beyond military briefs, regular features included "The Clergy and the War," "The War and School," "The War and the Parish," and "Readings about the War." Here was the real heart of the paper: news from and about the wartime activities and needs of parishes all over the empire. The reader would learn details about what parish guardianship councils were doing to assist soldiers' families, the kinds of patriotic fundraisers undertaken by pupils in church schools, the outfitting of hospitals by monasteries great and small. Village priests and teachers sent in descriptions of the wonderful peasant response to the weekly readings on the war that they had arranged.[37] In this way, *Prikhodskii listok* provided clergy with vignettes for sermons, information that teachers and clerics could disseminate to pupils and congregants hungry for news about the war, and models for charitable and patriotic undertakings. This publication also reinforced readers' sense of belonging to a far-flung national-religious, patriotic community. They could see that the problems they confronted were faced by others, or be reminded that the same prayer services for the troops that they took part in were simultaneously being enacted everywhere in Russia.

---

[35] *Prikhodskii listok* (September 1, 1914), 2. According to Runkevich, church leaders had for some time discussed the desirability of publishing a popular daily to combat the influence of the commercial penny press, but it was the outbreak of war that finally brought the idea to fruition: Runkevich, *Velikaia otechestvennaia voina*, 270–72.

[36] RGIA, f. 800, op. 1, d. 590, "O pechatanii 'Prikhodskogo listka,'" ll. 12, 20, 50, 113; in September 1915 daily editions briefly dipped to 44,800 copies, but grew again thereafter. The price of 1 kopek per issue made it competitive with other mass-circulation dailies.

[37] "Ot redakstii," *Prikhodskii listok* (September 1, 1915), 4; this announcement reminded would-be contributors to provide the name of their village and names of all people mentioned in their articles.

3.3 "A Sign of the August Victory." The image of the Mother of God and Christ Child appearing to Russian troops in 1914, prior to their success in Galicia, reinforces portrayal of the conflict as a Holy War. Political Poster collection, #RU/SU 357, Courtesy of Hoover Institution Library & Archives, Stanford University.

As inflation worsened over the course of the war, the costs of producing the paper mounted. By mid 1916, V. A. Ternavtsev, administrator of the Synodal Printing Office in Petrograd, wrote to the chief procurator of the synod warning of deepening losses from *Prikhodskii listok*, an "abnormal situation" which the printing office could not sustain indefinitely.[38] That the synod chose to continue publishing the paper in the same large print runs, despite a predicted annual loss of more than 30,000 rubles, suggests the importance it attached to this vital new link with Russia's parishes.

The Church and the Army

Both the fighting spirit and the spiritual health of soldiers are of great importance in wartime; the Orthodox Church – which did not necessarily draw a distinction between these two concerns – became deeply involved with both. Perhaps its most important symbolic function was administering the oath to every soldier and sailor. The military oath was a solemn pledge of loyalty to the person of the sovereign himself, rather than to the state or the country.[39] Typically, a bishop or priest administered the oath to the individual, who swore on the cross in the presence of his fellow soldiers and officers, surrounded by the regimental flag and standard. The church also blessed these important symbols, as well as weaponry. The church's involvement in these rituals underlined their solemnity and legitimized the state's characterization of military service – enshrined in 1906 in article 70 of the Fundamental Laws – as a "sacred duty" of the citizen.[40]

The army's spiritual needs were attended to by a special Department of Military Clergy (*voennoe dukhovenstvo*), headed by Archpresbyter (*protopresviter*) Father Georgii Shavel'skii, an exceptionally able individual.[41] Just as the military itself had been extensively revamped by the reform laws of 1912, the chaplaincy underwent a similar reconceptualization on the eve of the war. The first All-Russian Congress of the Military Clergy

---

[38] RGIA, f. 800, op. 1, d. 590, ll. 62–63, 89–91 (*Dokladnye zapiski* of June 25, 1916).

[39] The new recruit swore to defend the sovereign and his interests, and to subordinate himself to his officers in "everything pertaining to the benefit and service of the state." For the text of the oath and its explication to soldiers, see D. Kashkarov, *Prisiaga pod znamenem. Osnovy soldatskikh znanii*, 4th edn. (St. Petersburg: Tip. N. V. Vasil'eva, 1900), 4–7, 13.

[40] On the Fundamental Laws' redefinition of this duty, see Stockdale, "What Is a Fatherland?" 23–48.

[41] The protopresviter came from the so-called White clergy, not the Black, celibate clergy from which most church administration was drawn: Shavel'skii, *Vospominaniia*, vol. II, 96–99.

convened in July 1914, drawing on the lessons of the Russo-Japanese war to work out new guidelines. Clerics attached to units were now expected to be at the front lines, even in the trenches. They were to help doctors evacuate the wounded to dressing stations, and initiate collection of the dead from the battlefield. They were responsible for collecting detailed information about fallen soldiers to send to relatives. Chaplains assigned to hospitals also had added duties, including visiting bedsides daily to converse with and comfort men, and writing letters home for the sick and wounded. Particular emphasis was laid on every chaplain's responsibility for keeping the men supplied with suitable reading material, by organizing small mobile libraries at the front and regular libraries in hospitals.[42]

Changing war conditions generated more new instructions. Chaplains were given guidelines on appropriate behavior toward soldiers who were not Orthodox (which included a responsibility to prohibit distribution of literature that could be "insulting to different faiths"). As we have seen, in fall 1914 Shavel'skii instructed chaplains to gather information about inspiring acts of heroism by soldiers, officers, medical personnel, and clergy and forward them to his office for broad public dissemination.[43] This was explicitly intended to help boost morale. Following the terrible retreat of summer 1915, a directive reminded chaplains that during battle their place was with the troops in the front lines, and that one of their most important roles was to talk with the men: as often as possible, at any time, in accessible language, and "like a father," not a superior.[44]

Although the army and navy had too few chaplains in the opening months of the war (the peacetime number in 1913 was 954), the number of clerics in or serving the army eventually grew to 5,000.[45] That would

---

[42] On chaplains' duties, see A. S. Senin, "Armeiskoe dukhovenstvo Rossii v Pervuiu mirovuiu voinu," *Voprosy istorii* no. 10 (1990), 161–62, and Shavel'skii, *Vospominaniia*, vol. II, 91–92.

[43] Shavel'skii, *Vospominaniia*, vol. II, 93–95, and "Voennye sviashchenniki–letopistsy voiny," *Prikhodskii listok* (October 29, 1914), 2.

[44] Directive no. 3287 (September 14, 1915) of Father Shavel'skii to military clergy, quoted in V. Vasilenko, *Ofitsery v riasakh* (Moscow and Leningrad: Gosudarstvennoe izdatel'stvo otdel voennoi literatury, 1930), 98. The fact that this injunction was repeated might suggest that chaplains were *not* in the front lines.

[45] The figure 954, which includes chaplains serving in 476 regimental churches, is the calculation of M. Ivashko, *Russkaia pravoslavnaia tserkov' i vooruzhennye sily (XVIII–nachalo XX vv.). Istoriograficheskoe issledovanie* (Moscow, 2004), 64; Shavel'skii gives the figure 750 for peacetime chaplains. In September 1914 and again in May 1915, the office of the protopresviter wrote to the Synod about the urgent need for more army chaplains: RGIA, f. 796, d. 329/9, tom 5, ll. 35, 95–96. Numbers for army chaplains for other faiths and denominations, including sects, are hard to come by. According to one Soviet publication, in 1916 there were sixteen Old Believer priests serving the army, a very small number given that so many Cossacks adhered to the Old Belief: B. Kandidov, *Sektanstvo i mirovaia voina* (Moscow: Ateist, 1930), 35.

have resulted in approximately 1 chaplain per 800 Orthodox soldiers – not an ideal ratio, but better than the French or even the Americans envisioned for their forces. The number of mullahs, rabbis, and Catholic and Protestant chaplains was apparently quite small.[46]

The church's work with troops was not confined to the important efforts of the Department of Military Clergy. In early 1915, military authorities asked that the church direct more attention to pastoral work with men called up for duty but not yet at the front, as well as with their families. The synod duly issued an *ukaz* January 8, 1915, instructing all dioceses to undertake such work and to report back on their activities. One of the most detailed responses came from the energetic and ultra-conservative Archbishop Antonii of Kharkov and Akhitskii. Antonii had not waited for directives to begin offering his own version of spiritual and patriotic support to soldiers in his diocese. From the end of July 1914, every battalion heading to the front through Kharkov first attended a religious service, after which each soldier was presented with a small cross and a printed sheet of prayers "useful in wartime." Beginning in November, pastors known for their "sermonizing talents and patriotic mood" were detailed to lead discussions on religious-patriotic themes in reserve battalions and with men in the reserve militia; nearly 120 such discussions with garrison soldiers were conducted from November 1914 through February 1915.[47]

We have some idea of the content of these discussions, thanks to surviving copies of the leaflets Antonii's diocese distributed. A fairly typical example is the "Exhortation to the Christ-Loving Host," featuring an excerpt from the 90th Psalm on its front page, followed by patriotic text. It explained that soldiers were fighting for their native land and for the liberation of Orthodox peoples oppressed by the Germans: "Russian warrior! Look at what a sacred, great cause your Tsar has summoned you to!" The pamphlet urged soldiers to be brave – "Russians have never

---

[46] Mullahs in the active army, and Muslim clerics' support of the war among the faithful, are discussed by Franziska Davies, "Pervaia mirovaia voina kak ispytanie dlia imperii. Musul'mane na sluzhbe v tsarskoi armii," in Katia Bruish and Nikolaus Katser, eds., *Bol'shaia voina Rossii. Sotsial'nyi poriadok, publichnaia kommunikatsiia i nasilie na rubezhe tsarskoi i sovestskoi epokh* (St. Petersburg: Novoe literaturnoe obozrenie, 2014), 41–57. The number of priests per soldier serving the Russian army far exceeded numbers for the French, who initially appointed 4 priests to each army corps – about 1 priest per 40,000 soldiers, in contrast to 1 per 1,000 anticipated by the USA. Later in 1914 the French authorities sanctioned adding 250 volunteer chaplains to supplement the 100 official military chaplains. See Michael Burleigh, *Earthly Powers: The Clash of Religion and Politics in Europe from the French Revolution to the Great War* (New York: Harper Collins, 2005), 455.

[47] RGIA, f. 796, op. 198, otd. 1, st. 5, d. 329, tom 1, ch. 2 (1915), ll. 1–2.

96   Mobilizing the Russian Nation

to inform the faithful of the outbreak of war, was repeated in subsequent synodal proclamations and also employed by civilians, as in Vladimir M. Purishkevich's August 1915 speech in the State Duma honoring "the sacrifices the Polish people have placed on the altar of our common fatherland."[53]

With such phrases, the Orthodox Church provided anyone writing or talking about the war, whether in religious or secular vein, a "language of sacrifice," a vocabulary and diction that was simultaneously elevated but familiar and comprehensible to members of the Orthodox Christian community. Adrian Gregory has made this point in regard to the role of religion in Britain during the Great War, suggesting that one reason the revivalist-inspired patriotic rhetoric of a Lloyd George resonated so effectively was that "the grammar and vocabulary of the language of sacrifice were deeply familiar to a Bible-reading and hymn-singing public."[54] Nationalist discourse in Russia, as in many other countries, did not simply draw on religion as a constitutive element: it was inflected by the familiar – and legitimating – language *of* that faith.

The Meaning of the War

One strand of the church's narrative of the war and its meaning was that it was sent by God in punishment for sin. In the opening weeks of the war Vladimir, Metropolitan of Moscow, composed a small conversation (*beseda*) explaining that war was a scourge God used to punish people, but also to teach them: people could learn from its terrible lessons and win forgiveness. If Russians repented of their sins and turned to God, if they learned to do good in the war and not evil, then goodness *would* triumph.[55] Similarly, in January 1916, A. Volynets, a regular contributor to *Prikhodskii listok*, reminded readers that St. Serafim of Sarov had foretold both the war and Russia's eventual victory, one that ultimately depended not on force of arms but spiritual purity. His message was reassuring: "The Lord will give Russia victory for its Orthodox faith, for

---

[53] For example, a synodal proclamation of December 30, 1914, talking about the needs of wounded soldiers asserts the obligation of "all those remaining at home to bring their energies and resources to the altar of the Fatherland": RGIA, f. 796, op. 198, otd. 1, st. 5, d. 329, t. VII/51, l. 6, and V. M. Purishkevich, *GDSO*, IV, 4, sess. 4 (August 1, 1915), col. 246.

[54] Adrian Gregory, *The Last Great War: British Society and the First World War* (Cambridge: Cambridge University Press, 2008), 152–85, who offers a fascinating dicussion of religion and the "languages of sacrifice."

[55] *O voine. Vnebogosluzhebnaia beseda Petrogradskogo mitropolita Vladimira 1914 g., avgusta 15 dnia* (Moskva: Tip. T. Dortman, 1914), 10–12, 16–18, 24–25.

fidelity to the Orthodox Church."⁵⁶ German atrocities and destruction of churches caused some writers to compare the Germans or their Kaiser to the anti-Christ.⁵⁷

The purely spiritual-moral interpretation often merged with more secular, broadly nationalist views that represented the conflict as a clash between the Teutonic and Slavic peoples and their respective civilizations. Prominent churchmen wrote and sermonized on this theme from the very start of the conflict. For example, in August 1914 *Prikhodskoe chtenie* (Parish reading) spoke of the war as the clash of the Teutonic world, headed by Germany, and the Slavic world, headed by Russia. An article by Archimandrite Lavrentii explained: "Clearly, in this great struggle Divine Providence has allotted to our dear Motherland a high mission and purpose: to become the liberator of all Slavic tribes in general from centuries-old German oppression and violence. What a great and glorious cause is in store for Holy Rus' to accomplish in the world war that has begun!"⁵⁸ Similarly, the diocesan newspaper of Poltava offered a distinctly Slavophile reading of the war as the clash of two cultures, an "external, material culture," growing in the soil of Catholicism and Protestantism, and a culture that is "interior, spiritual, arising in and fostered by the life-giving current of the universal spirit of Orthodoxy in the depths of the Slavic national character."⁵⁹

There were also more explicitly great power elaborations of the spiritual theme. In a 1914 pamphlet titled "For Faith, Tsar, and Fatherland," Father Shavel'skii, the army's head chaplain, stated that a people blessed by God had a sacred duty to strive for the "external greatness" of their country and the broadening of its domains. He also stressed the importance of making Constantinople Christian once more.⁶⁰ Another example comes from an article in early January 1916, explaining why there could not be peace until victory: at this most decisive moment in Russia's history, what was hanging in the balance was its right to "an independent life in the capacity and dignity of a great world power."⁶¹

Another major trope was the way the experience of war – as well as eventual victory – would contribute to the rebirth or regeneration

---

[56] A. Volynets, "Sila dukha," *Prikhodskii listok* (January 3, 1916), 2. He also asserted the primacy of the Great Russian people and their church: just as the Russian people (*russkii narod*) was "first and ruling in Russia," the Orthodox Church was also "first and ruling."
[57] A. Volynets, "Gordyni buistvo," *Prikhodskii listok* (July 2, 1915), 3, K.V., "Nevinnyi iagenok," *Prikhodskii listok* (September 1, 1915), 2–3.
[58] Arkhimandrit Lavrentii, "Pouchenie po sluchaiu voine," *Prikhodskoe chtenie* no. 6 (August 16, 1914), 190–91.
[59] Excerpted from *Prikhodskii listok* (September 12, 1914), 4.
[60] Quoted in Senin, "Armeiskoe dukhovenstvo Rossii," 162.
[61] S., "Bez pobedy ne mozhet byt' i ne budet mir," *Prikhodskii listok* (January 3, 1916), 2.

(*vozrozhdenie*) of Russia. It was not only that Russia, once freed from German domination, would be a freer and richer country. The experience of the ordeal of the war, of shared suffering and self-sacrifice, would make individual Russians better people and renew and fortify the entire nation. This regeneration was one of the "main rewards of the horrors we are living through," one priest wrote in late 1916: the war furnished rich material for the "awakening and planting in Russian society of sincerely patriotic feelings, the implantation of legitimate feelings of popular pride, and consciousness of national dignity."[62] For the many proponents of temperance, the tsar's wartime imposition of prohibition was both a cause and consequence of this transformation: no longer enslaved by demon drink, the Russian people were manifesting a better work ethic and stronger resolve.[63]

Of course, the tropes of renewal and regeneration through war were not unique to the church and clergy. Among the lay thinkers who developed this theme were Prince Evgenii Trubetskoi, who lectured on the way that the shared experience of sacrifice and confrontation with death was bringing out the "finest qualities of the Russian people," as well as deepening national unity, popular heroism, and old values that had been forgotten.[64] Regeneration was also a common trope in other countries' narratives of the meaning of the Great War: German intellectuals and British divines were not the only ones to wax metaphorical about steel being tempered in the heat of the struggle, impurities burned away by flame, or materialism repudiated thanks to experience of shared sacrifice for the common good.[65]

As the case of Galicia shows, reunification of a putatively dismembered religious community could also form part of the larger narrative of Holy War and "regeneration." For decades, Russian nationalists had harbored irredentist dreams of incorporating the eastern part of Austrian Galicia into the modern Russian state, thus restoring to "Holy Rus'" a core land separated from it in the sixteenth century. Part of the Orthodox clergy expressed such views, as well as the hope of restoring the primacy of the Orthodox Church to these "lost" lands where the Uniate Church was

---

[62] Sv. P.S., "K chemu zovet nas dukh vremen," 4.
[63] See, for example, "Uroki voiny," in Vostorgov, *V dni voiny*, 69–70.
[64] Kn. E. N. Trubetskoi, *Otechestvennaia voina i ee dukhovnaia smysl'* (Moscow: Tip. T-va I. D. Sytina, 1915), 14–21, 25; Trubetskoi acknowledged but did not choose to dwell upon the darker human qualities unleashed by war. Among other positive impacts he details are its deepening of love of the motherland, self-sacrifice, and a return to the "values of our forefathers."
[65] See Roland Stromberg, *Redemption by War: The Intellectuals and 1914* (Lawrence: University of Kansas Press, 1982), and Burleigh, *Earthly Powers*, 439–59.

"On the Altar of the Fatherland"

now predominant. After Russian forces occupied eastern Galicia in September 1914, Archbishop Evlogii of Volynia, a zealous proponent of bringing Galicia back into the fold, was named the region's new Orthodox prelate.[66] Into early spring 1915, the church press featured glowing accounts of the reunification of "Holy Rus'" and restoration of Orthodoxy to a supposedly grateful population. From this perspective, the liberation of Galicia was a constituent element in the narrative of Holy War, alongside the liberation of "Tsargrad" (Constantinople) from Muslim rule, and the protection of Orthodox Slavs from Germanic designs.[67]

An Ambiguous Sacred Union

The Orthodox Church's version of the narrative of sacred union was never quite so inclusive as that of the secular authorities, given the church's emphasis on Orthodox Christianity as a defining feature of the Russian nation. Nonetheless, during the first nine months of the war, most clerics, like most secular writers and thinkers in Russia, observed the sacred union's "internal truce." Unity and love of the motherland – transcending class, ideology, faith, and nationality – were celebrated, and open critiques of other members of the national community (apart from Germans) were at a minimum.

Once fissures in the union began to appear, in late spring 1915 with the disastrous turn in Russia's military fortunes, antisemitism reappeared. It was most pronounced and ugly on the far right, a political movement toward which some Orthodox clerics gravitated. Identifying Jews as bad citizens or even traitors was not an official position of the church administration, though it made little effort to discourage or rebuke antisemitic remarks and writings by various clerics and prelates. This circumstance makes the symbolic embrace of Jewish soldiers by one of the church's most prominent prelates – Metropolitan Pitirim of Petrograd – all the more striking. On several occasions in late 1915, he made public visits to

---

[66] Evlogii (Georgievsk), *Put' moei zhizni. Vospominaniia Mitropolita Evlogiia* (Paris: YMCA Press, 1947), 233–35, 239–44. Later, Evlogii insisted that he never supported the coercive measures attributed to him by his opponents, but the tsar was nonetheless prevailed upon to remove him in April 1915. See von Hagen, *War in a European Borderland*, 38–42.

[67] For example, S. Troitskii, "Nash dolg' pered Prikarpatskoi Rus'," *Prikhodskii listok* (September 5, 1914), 2; "Slovo episkopa Trifona," *Prikhodskii listok* (October 17, 1914), 2; and A. Belgorodskii, "Galitsiia – iskonnoe dostoianie Rossii," *Prikhodskoe chtenie* no. 8 (October 1914), 256–61.

infirmaries run by Jewish organizations, or stopped to chat with wounded Jewish soldiers and praise their patriotism in pastoral visits to hospitals.[68]

The war also provided a tempting opportunity to go after the church's most worrisome sectarian rivals, the Baptists and Evangelical Christians, given the "German" origins of their faith. The church's concern over the spread of evangelical Protestantism was decades old, fueled by Protestants' success in winning converts from Orthodoxy to their "heretical" teachings. The 1905 Manifesto on Freedom of Conscience, which gave these groups more possibility to proselytize, was a source of anxiety for the church and particularly its conservative members. For the Orthodox hierarchy, Protestant sects were doubly dangerous: as false faiths, they compromised individuals' salvation, and as foreign, fundamentally not *Russian* creeds, they potentially corrupted the nation. Great Russian adherents of Protestant sects were regarded as people who were forsaking their national faith, indeed, as people whose core identities as loyal Russians were now suspect.

As Heather Coleman notes in her study of Russia's Baptists, even before the outbreak of war some government officials had harbored suspicions about the Baptists' foreign ties, political loyalties, and putative pacifism. But war with Germany intensified these inchoate suspicions, particularly since some areas of particularly successful sectarian missionizing – such as Kherson, Bessarabia, and Taurida provinces – also happened to be regions adjacent to or near the active front. The Holy Synod alleged that Baptists were conducting propaganda among the troops and demanded the removal from the military theater of these people of German origin.[69]

Finally, doubts about membership in the true national community could run along political or educational lines. Some prominent clergy did not scruple to openly politicize their messages to the troops. Not surprisingly, a representative example comes from a 1915 sermon by Archbishop Antonii of Kharkov, where he stops just short of labeling liberals as traitors. According to Antonii, these unworthy sons of the motherland used the pretext of aiding the war effort to hold congresses

---

[68] "Mitropolit Pitirm sredi ranenykh," *Gazeta-kopeika* (December 6, 1915), 2, and "Mitropolit Pitirm v lazarete evreisko obshchiny," *Gazeta-kopeika* (December 23, 1915), 3.

[69] Letter of June 28, 1915, cited in von Hagen, *War in a European Borderland*, 29. Individual Orthodox clerics frequently pressed for, abetted, or welcomed actions ranging from petty harassment of individual congregations all the way to banning prayer services, arresting and exiling pastors, or outright closure of meeting houses: Heather Coleman, *Russian Baptists and Spiritual Revolution, 1905–1929* (Bloomington: Indiana University Press, 2005), 118–22.

at which they fomented revolutionary plans, demanding freedom and rights for Russia's internal enemies (i.e., the Jews), diminished the status of Russia's church, and diminished of the rights of its monarch. Antonii predicted that efforts to subvert popular patriotism would be in vain: "Brothers, we will patiently and uncomplainingly work against both external and internal enemies, we will stick to our faith and loyalty to the Tsar."[70] The diocesan press of Kharkov printed this divisive sermon and distributed it to soldiers en route to the front. In fall 1915, some anti-intellectual pieces – typically contrasting educated urbanites with a putatively more authentic Russian and patriotic rural *narod* – also began appearing in the church press: in Russia, one article in *Prikhodskii listok* lamented, "the patriotic professor is a rarity."[71]

Reception of the Narrative

The Orthodox Church poured enormous resources and energy into explaining the war's meaning and legitimizing the conflict. Clearly, the church's narratives did not always harmonize with the more inclusive narrative of the secular authorities, nor were they always internally consistent. Moreover, the clergy who were responsible for familiarizing their congregants with these narratives were not simply transmission belts. What did they make of the church's interpretation of the nation's war, and how did they modify it – intentionally or unintentionally – in sermons and discussions with their parishioners? And how, in turn, did congregants understand and process what clerics said? Although the sources rarely allow us to answer these questions, there is fascinating, if anecdotal, evidence on the reception and modification of wartime narratives. In particular, a close reading of several cases of alleged "political crimes" committed by members of the clergy can throw light on attitudes to the war and its conduct, and beliefs about how citizens of Russia ought to behave.

On August 5, 1915, at the very nadir of Russia's military fortunes prior to 1917, an official investigation began into one Il'ia Semin'skii, the 28-year-old deacon of Pokrovskaia church in the village of Sandat, Medvezhenskii district, in Stavropol province. Allegedly, on July 27 on the feast day of St. Panteleimon, in the presence of approximately 400 parishioners, Sem'inskii launched into an unauthorized sermon (*propoved*) on the subject of ongoing military reversals. Mentioning the recent fall of

---

[70] RGIA, f. 797, op. 86, otd. 3, st. 5, d. 17, ll. 8, 17, 18.
[71] "Professor-patriot u nas – redkost'": G.P., "Narodnoe chuvstvo i vozhdeleniia intelligentsiia," *Prikhodskii listok* (September 24, 1915), 3.

Warsaw and Ivangorod, he said that in the State Duma they explained that these reversals stemmed from the lack of popular rule in Russia:

in Russia we don't have shells or rifles, but we sacrifice our sons and our brothers for Russia and the fatherland. What will we fight with? With bare hands, apparently. The war minister Sukhomlinov who was recently fired is to blame for this, and he's turned out to be related to Colonel Miasoedev who was hanged for treason. We need to do something so there won't be any more ministers like Sukhomlinov and we'll have responsible ministers.

According to the informant, congregants listened "very attentively" and then asked the deacon, "What should we do about this?" At this alarming juncture, the priest, Father Ostretsov, managed to cut off his deacon by resuming the service.[72] According to subsequent testimony gathered by the investigating officers, on exiting the church some villagers were upset with Deacon Sem'inskii, but many others, "considering him a clever person, expressed dissatisfaction with Father Ostretsov for not giving the deacon the chance to finish his speech."

The investigation into these allegations by the civil authorities resulted in formal charges according to articles 128 and 129 of the criminal code. The church's Spiritual Consistory also began its own investigation. Unfortunately, the official file on this case is incomplete. The only remaining information on the affair relates to a brief certificate from Sem'inskii's personnel file, stating that he was the son of a priest, had completed the fourth class in the Stavropol seminary, and had a wife and three children. Prior to this outburst his conduct had always been rated as excellent.[73]

Although we do not know the outcome of this case, it still has much to tell us. Semin'skii had no history of trouble-making, but was so upset by Russian losses that he publicly condemned the authorities. He put his trust in the State Duma for the explanation of why these losses had occurred and their deeper source, which he understood to be the political system and traitors in the government. Presumably this information was gleaned from newspapers. Villagers were extremely interested in his thoughts and apparently few of them criticized what he said; rather, most wanted to hear more. Perhaps one of the most interesting things about the case of Il'ia Sem'inskii is just how *unique* it is. Files titled "On Political Crimes" exist in the Synodal Archives for the years 1914–16, but contain only a handful of cases. Of these, only three – Semin'skii's and two others – appear to have concerned genuinely actionable behavior

---

[72] RGIA, f. 797, op. 15, otd. 3, st. 5, d. 5, ll. 14–15, "Po politicheskim prestupleniiam" (1915). The Miasoedev scandal is discussed in Chapter 6.
[73] RGIA, f. 797, op. 15, otd. 3, st. 5, d. 5, ll. 17–20.

on the part of clergy. All the remaining cases were dropped, either for lack of evidence or because the allegations turned out to be maliciously motivated or simply based on a misunderstanding.[74]

An instructive example of the latter is the case of Father Aleksei Dobriakov, a pastor in the village of Proshkove, Vorovichskii district, in the province of Novgorod. On April 23, 1915, someone informed the Department of Police that during morning service Father Dobriakov had read war news to his parishioners, going on to say something to the effect that even if Russia won the war "there will be little benefit from it because even though Russia is big it doesn't have such smart people as the Germans so it would be better to give up." These remarks allegedly produced an uproar among parishioners, who "noisily left the church, continuing to openly censure the priest for so inappropriate and unpatriotic a pronouncement." The local gendarmes placed the priest under surveillance and informed Archbishop Arsenii of Novgorod, who began his own investigation.[75]

It took six weeks, and a mountain of interviews and paperwork, to sort out the misunderstanding. True, Archbishop Arsenii wrote to the Chief Procurator's Office, Father Dobriakov was in the habit of reading aloud war news to his parishioners and then discussing it. On April 23 he had read and discussed with them a government communiqué about German cruisers attacking a Russian coastal town, remarking that even if Germans did take the town it would not harm Russia that much. When parishioners responded with declarations about German dominance in Russia and how the Germans should have long since been tossed out, he said that "the dominance of the Germans was due to their cunning and wealth and that when we win the war everything will get better, only we'll need to take all industry into our own [Russian] hands." The majority of his listeners were apparently satisfied with this conversation. Although a few people maintained that Father Dobriakov had actually said something different and quite objectionable, this was because their "lack of development" caused them to misinterpret his words.[76]

---

[74] RGIA, f. 797, op. 15, otd. 3, st. 5, d. 5, ll. 17–20. An October 1914 incident involved a priest in Kursk province who condemned the tsar and his officials in church as nothing more than "sausage-eaters and Germans," for the un-Christian act of mobilizing soldiers on a Holy Day (l. 26). In December 1915 a parish priest in Enisei province was punished for cursing the emperor while in an intoxicated state, during a conversation with a peasant about the conduct of the war: (1916), ll. 1, 16–20. At least one charge proved to be completely fabricated, a form of payback over a financial grievance, ll. 1–7.

[75] RGIA, f. 797, op. 15, otd. 3, st. 5, d. 5, l. 8 (letter of May 29, 1915 to Over-Procurator from the Ministry of the Interior, Department of Police).

[76] RGIA, f. 797, op. 15, otd. 3, st. 5, d. 5, ll. 9–10 (Report of Archbishop Arsenii to Over-Procurator Sabler, June 2, 1915). Ironically, the newspapers Father Dobriakov read from

The archbishop emphasized the priest's exemplary record and his sincere patriotism, though he did express concern that Father Dobriakov was holding such discussions in church: "God's temple is not a reading room, but a house of prayer." The final element in the archbishop's defense of his priest was his hypothesis that the whole affair was an intentional slander started by "Germans," noting that there were several German brick-making factories in the neighborhood and thus quite a few Germans about. In sum, Father Dobriakov was not guilty of lack of patriotism, just lack of judgment for reading newspapers aloud in church, and to "semi-literates." For the latter mistake, Archbishop Arsenii urbanely remarked, he was dispatching the father to Makerevskii monastery for two weeks, where he would have the opportunity to live in quietude and thereby "come to appreciate the beauty of an opportune silence."[77]

The story of Father Dobriakov's accusation and exoneration is revealing on a number of levels. It shows us a priest discussing the war with his congregation, precisely what the secular and church authorities wanted the clergy to do, though perhaps not in exactly this way. We see that priest and parishioners shared a keen interest in the war, as well as concerns about German economic influence at home. The archbishop's suggestion that local Germans were the probable source of the slander of Father Dobriakov might have been a deliberate red herring, given that the denunciation to the police seems to have come from someone present at his discussion in church. But it clearly tapped into growing anti-German sentiment, and related worries about the loyalty of Russians who were of German origin. And whatever the source of the denunciation, the investigation revealed that at least some of Father Dobriakov's rural congregation *believed* he had advocated giving up in the war and were outraged by such a suggestion (a reaction common to virtually all the cases in the files). Also worth noting is the apparent problem some parishioners had in understanding the newspaper article. As Archbishop Arsenii understood, reading articles to ordinary citizens – even articles from the church paper *Prikhodskii listok* – could lead to surprising results.

Conclusions

The Rasputin scandal and the trials of the Orthodox Church in the first years of Soviet power have long overshadowed the church's vigorous

---

were the nationalistic, anti-German *Novoe vremia*, and *Tserkovnie vedomosti* and *Prikhodskii listok* – all publications staunchly in support of the war. This circumstance probably helped convince investigators that a misunderstanding had indeed occurred.

[77] RGIA, f. 797, op. 15, otd. 3, st. 5, d. 5, l. 11.

activities in Russia's Great War. The scale of the church's undertakings and its zeal in publicizing and supporting the war are striking. It had enormous human resources to draw upon and well-established networks of communications; it also expanded existing networks, such as the parish guardianship councils, and created new ones, like *Prikhodskii listok*. Tens of millions of Orthodox believers would have heard its messages – many on a regular basis. Whatever they made of the church's patriotic narrative, its underlying reinforcement of the sense of a vast national community, justly defending itself from a fearsome aggressor, appears very powerful.

The church marshaled material aid for soldiers, their families, and refugees, as well as using the pulpit and the press to sell the state's war loans. It created new prayers, rituals, and commemorative days that sacralized the struggle and helped unite the national community in collective acts of sacrifice, thanksgiving, and mourning. It offered narratives of the war as not only just but also "holy," reassuring the nation that God was on Russia's side. However unevenly, its patriotic message exhorted brotherly love and Christian charity within the broader community. Finally, in propounding the virtues of love of motherland, unity, and steadfast service, the church also provided a "language of sacrifice," elevated but familiar to believers, that was both legitimizing and mobilizational.

To our ears, the church's total embrace of the state's martial cause, along with insistence that all must serve and sacrifice in whatever capacity demanded, is, at the least, disquieting. In this, however, the Russian Orthodox Church acted identically to other national churches in the Great War – the Church of England, and the Lutheran Church in Germany, for example – and recent scholarship suggests that those populations were much more comfortable with such uncritical support of war than we would be today.[78] Given that the Russian empire was multiconfessional, the most serious problem with the church's narrative of sacred union and Holy War was its explicitly Orthodox coloration. While the church press occasionally showcased patriotic non-Russians fighting for the fatherland, its constant identification of church and state, Orthodoxy and Russianness, did not leave much space within the national community for the non-Orthodox citizen. Where that space was most deliberately carved out was in the secular sphere of war relief, the subject of the next chapter.

---

[78] See for example Gregory, *The Last Great War*, 183–85, and Burleigh, *Earthly Powers*, 439–59.

4 "All for the War!"
War Relief and the Language of Citizenship

> A world war, the clash of peoples, cannot be decided by armies alone. The entire people, the whole country must actively participate in the struggle ... Citizens of Russia, do not delay; the hour of trial has come.
>
> Nikolai Astrov, speech to the Fourth Congress of the Union of Cities[1]

On July 26, 1914, one week after Germany's declaration of war against Russia, daily newspapers in the major cities of the empire carried an announcement from the Society for Aid to Soldiers and Their Families, directed to "Russian Citizens." It asked for donations of money and goods, but above all donation of one's efforts: success depended upon "extensive participation in its activities by Russian citizens." Over the course of the next three years, the peoples of the Russian empire would be bombarded – and bombard each other – with such appeals: give, attend, volunteer, sacrifice! The patriotism and compassion of Russian subjects had been called upon for aid in previous wars, but the scale had never been so great, the need for mobilizing all of society's resources so huge. Nor had Russia's peoples been so insistently appealed to as *citizens*. They were, of course, appealed to in other ways as well: as Russians, as family to "brothers" at the front, and through urban or regional identities –"Muscovites!" or "Siberians!"[2] But the ubiquity of the appeal to the generalized citizen of Russia was something novel, yet another marker of the changes that had occurred since the 1905 revolution, and the way the experience of the war worked to deepen and consolidate those changes.

Organizing themselves for war relief in summer 1914, then remobilizing to deal with the catastrophes and military shortages of 1915, Russians

---

[1] "Organizatsiia tyla," *Izvestiia Vse-rossiiskogo soiuza gorodov* (March 1916), 9.
[2] "K Russkim grazhdanam," *Russkii invalid* (July 26, 1914), 6. See also, for example, the appeal on behalf of soldiers by the city of St. Petersburg, "Grazhdane!" *Russkii invalid* (August 12, 1914), 1; the appeal for donations, "Russkie Grazhdane!" from the Kiev Ladies' Committee, *Kievlianin'* (August 21, 1914), 1; the appeal to keep fighting, "Grazhdane!" from the Executive Committee of the Kiev Committee of Disabled Soldiers, *Kievlianin'* (September 5, 1917), 1.

drew on existing associational networks and created new ones. They worked together with the central government and military authorities to treat the wounded, succor orphans, and aid refugees. This joint work of the state and the people, which cut across class, faith, nationality, and politics, quickly became one of the constitutive strands of the narrative of sacred union. Most contemporaries read these public efforts for war relief as a profound demonstration of love of country, welcome proof that the Russian people was not so riven by class antagonisms, or lacking in "state consciousness," as was sometimes feared.

But it was also the case that different objects and understandings of patriotism existed, or came into being thanks to the experience of war. The love of country that inspired many Russians to apply themselves to war relief could be predicated on hopes for what a better, future Russia might be, rather than on semi-autocratic Russia as it was. Social patriotism – love for and loyalty to one's fellow countrymen – could reinforce, supersede, or outlive state patriotism. And as was demonstrated by the increasingly politicized and hostile relations of the imperial government, on the one hand, and the Duma and public organizations, on the other, the meaning of the patriotic sacred union was itself transformed by the war.

Service on the home front, like service at the military front, could also be constitutive of new loyalties, identities, and expectations. Many participants in war relief believed that the experience of freely uniting and working for the common good was transforming passive subjects into conscious citizens. Moreover, the language of citizenship, with its expectations of rights as well as obligations, was being joined to the more traditional wartime language of sacrifice. Those expectations would increasingly be voiced by the many subsets of the population with only limited access to citizenship rights.

Nationwide Networks of Relief

Despite the very real constraints imposed by state tutelage and oversight, Russians were creating and joining voluntary associations in ever greater numbers in the decades prior to the war. The reforms of the 1860s had ushered in a new era of associational activity, which also opened up new vistas for charitable and philanthropic activity. The scope widened further after the 1905 revolution: the provisions of the March 4, 1906, "Temporary Rules about Societies and Unions" allowed hundreds of new societies and associations to come into being. While overall figures for the eve of the war do not exist, scholars estimate that throughout the Russian empire there were at least 6,100 philanthropic or charitable societies as of 1910, as well as thousands of other voluntary associations in the form of professional and labor organizations, learned societies, cooperatives, clubs, sports and leisure groups, and so on. In Moscow alone, 365 new societies and unions were registered in the period 1906–09.[3] According to Joseph Bradley, these associations formed the institutional core of civil society and served, in effect, as workshops of citizenship: "[Associations] created and assiduously cultivated the spaces of initiative and autonomy where the capacity of citizenship could appear."[4] And by enabling members to forge local networks, learn skills, set and realize agendas, and raise funds, they furnished critical frameworks and cadres for the huge task of relief in Russia's Great War.

The scale and nature of the war itself essentially required the active involvement of the civilian population. Although the authorities did not truly understand the total nature of the war they were fighting until the military disasters of spring 1915, they did realize almost immediately that they would need the public's help in caring for the wounded. Moreover, by immediately invoking the heroic myth of the 1812 Fatherland War, with its narrative of an enemy repulsed by the united efforts of the entire people and their tsar, the government appeared to signal greater appreciation for – and acceptance of – public initiative in war relief. A space was opened up for creation of voluntary organizations with truly national networks; society made use of that space with alacrity.[5]

From the outset, the effort to supply the needs of soldiers and their families involved state, public, and private entities. A number of semi-official institutions for providing such aid already existed. Semi-official entities were philanthropic bodies receiving some state funding and

---

[3] A. S. Tumanova, *Obshchestvennye organizatsii i russkaia publika v nachale XX veka* (Moscow: Novyi khronograf, 2008), 245–46; Adele Lindenmeyr, *Poverty Is Not a Vice: Charity, Society, and the State in Imperial Russia* (Princeton: Princeton University Press, 1996). The impossibility of estimating the number of war-relief entities, or their revenues and outlays, is part of the larger problem of scanty statistics for most charitable entities in Russia, something contemporaries found deeply frustrating: see remarks from the 1916 assembly of the All-Russian Union of Institutions, Societies and Activists in Public and Private Charity, *Prizrenie i blagotvoritel'nost'* (May 1916), 437–40.

[4] Joseph Bradley, "Subjects into Citizens: Societies, Civil Society, and Autocracy in Tsarist Russia," *American Historical Review* 107, 4 (October 2002), 1120, 1122.

[5] This apparent welcome of public initiative posed a contrast to the experience of the Russo-Japanese war, when the government severely curtailed the scale of the zemstvos' medical organization, and in other ways alienated early support for the war effort. (Japan's surprise attack on Russia evoked an initial wave of support for the war among significant portions of the public, though not among most workers or national minorities.) See Tsuchiya Yoshifuru, "Unsuccessful National Unity: The Russian Home Front in 1904," in David Wolff, Steven G. Marks et al., *The Russo-Japanese War in Global Perspective: World War Zero*, vol. II (Leiden: Brill, 2007), 325–53.

enjoying royal patronage, but also dependent on private donations and including private citizens on their governing boards. Examples of these were the Aleksandrovskii Committee for the Wounded, dating back to the end of the Napoleonic wars, and the Russian Society of the Red Cross. Two organizations dating from the Russo-Japanese war were the Alekseevskii Committee, named for the heir to the throne, which concerned itself primarily with the needs of children of rank-and-file soldiers, and the Society for Aid to Soldiers and Their Families, which attended to things as diverse as finding work for soldiers' wives and affordable housing for their families. With some 880 local chapters across Russia by 1914, this society had a genuinely national reach.[6]

Two governmentally sponsored organizations created at the start of the war became highly effective avenues for coordinating local societies' efforts across the country. The Committee of Her Imperial Highness Grand Duchess Elizaveta Fedorovna for Extending Charitable Aid to Families of Individuals Called to the War (hereafter, the Committee of Elizaveta Fedorovna), was established on August 11, 1914 by Empress Aleksandra Fedorovna's sister, a widow in holy orders who had long devoted herself to charitable work.[7] The Committee of Elizaveta Fedorovna helped soldiers' families by constructing daycares for their children, providing affordable housing and shelters, free or reduced-price lunches, and other services. It also aided disabled soldiers by establishing invalid homes and providing training for new jobs and assistance in finding work.

The committee was explicitly intended to help unify war-related charitable activities, and rapidly became a nationwide organization, with nearly 600 branches. Almost every province established a branch, usually chaired by the provincial governor and with membership on their board of prominent clergy, representatives of municipal government or zemstvos, and other local notables. Provincial or regional committees then

---

[6] There was also the Romanovskii Committee, established to mark the tercentenary of the Romanov dynasty; its mandate expanded to address the needs of children of mobilized soldiers, and children left homeless by the war: Runkevich, *Velikaia otechestvennaia voina*, 126–29, and *Voina* no. 5 (December 1914), 70. An overview of some of the most important entities for aiding soldiers is N. Beliavskii, "Pomoshch' soldatam i ikh sem'iam," *Russkii invalid* (September 30, 1914), 3, (October 1, 1914), 3–4, and "Kratkii doklad Tsentral'nogo upravleniia o deiatel'nosti Obshchestva s vozniknoveniia voiny," *Vestnik Obshchestva povsemestnoi pomoshchi postradavshim na voine soldatam i ikh sem'iam* no. 9 (1914), 6.

[7] Grand Duchess Elizaveta Fedorovna was no mere figurehead, taking an active role in her committee's work throughout the war; see N. L. Matveeva, *Blagotvoritel'nost' i imperatorskaia sem'ia v gody Pervoi mirovoi voiny* (Moscow: Izdatel'stvo MGOU, 2004), 58–62.

organized district-level branches and established working relations with other charitable bodies in the area. Quite representative was the experience of Enisei province's branch of the Committee of Elizaveta Fedorovna, founded in September 1914, which pulled together a web of 107 new and already existing charitable bodies in the province that managed to raise more than 116,000 rubles in cash donations alone for soldiers' families in its first year of existence.[8]

The variety of societies brought together through the Committee of Elizaveta Fedorovna is illustrated by the annual report of its Sevastopol branch. Upon commencing its activities in September 1914, this committee found seven new war-relief societies already functioning, along with six other established charitable bodies prepared to work with it on war needs. These thirteen organizations included the Balaklava Municipal Guardianship, the Sevastopol branch of the Society for Aid to Soldiers' Families, the Sevastopol Jewish Circle, the Sevastopol Greek Ladies' Committee, the Society for Defense of Children, the Armenian Committee for Aid to Armenian Refugees from Turkey, and the Sevastopol Parish Guardianship Council.[9] Uniting and coordinating the work of diverse religious, civic, and private aid societies in local communities, the Committee of Elizaveta Fedorovna was helping to build a nationally inclusive network. It also served as a conduit for treasury funds to support this common effort on behalf of local needs.

In many ways, the Committee of Her Imperial Highness the Grand Duchess Tatiana Nikolaevna for the Temporary Relief of Victims of War (hereafter, the Tatiana Committee) worked in analogous fashion. Created by imperial decree on September 14, 1914, and named in honor of its patron, the emperor's second daughter, it became associated with aid to refugees early on. By late spring 1915, when the problem of displaced populations in the empire was reaching crisis proportions, the Tatiana Committee had made refugees its main mission. It had established 66 provincial and municipal branches and 220 district- and volost'-level branches by October 1915, creating yet another web of war-relief connections across the country.[10] Given that many refugees were not ethnically Russian, the central and local Tatiana Committees worked with national minority organizations and often numbered

---

[8] GARF, f. 6787, op. 1, d. 113, "Obzor deiatel'nosti blagotvoritel'nykh uchrezhdenii za 1914–1915 gg.," ll. 52–53.
[9] GARF, f. 6787, op. 1, d. 113, "Obzor deiatel'nosti," l. 54.
[10] "Sovremennoe polozhenie dela pomoshchi bezhentsam," *Prizrenie i blagotvoritel'nost'* (October–December 1915), 539.

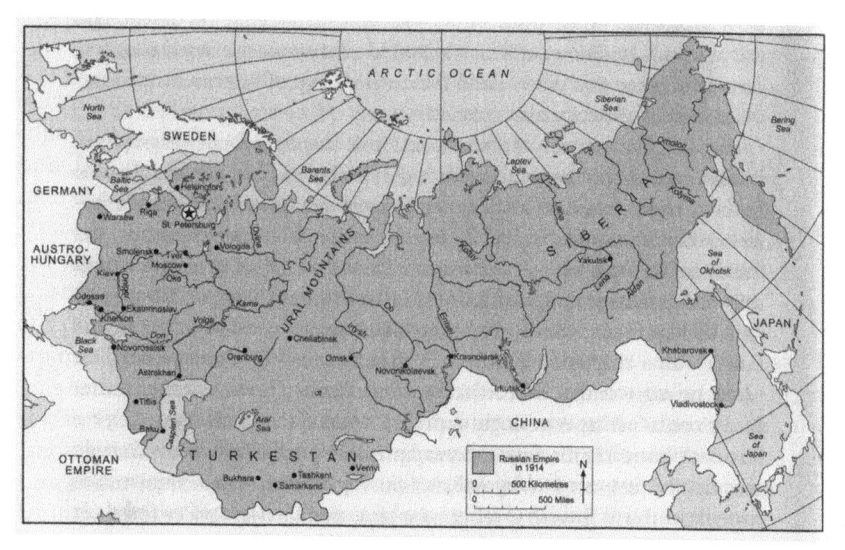

4.1 A map of the Russian empire in 1914; networks of war-relief organizations came into being across the country. Courtesy of the Drawing Office, School of Geography, Earth and Environmental Sciences, University of Birmingham.

representatives of those organizations among their members.[11] Tatiana Committees helped organize food, clothing, shelter, and desperately needed medical care for refugees, as well as employment, schooling, and daycare.[12]

In both its mission and rhetoric, the Tatiana Committee exemplified the "we are one family" dimension of sacred union. A good example comes from the appeal for its nationwide, three-day collection in late May 1915, "From Russia to the Ravaged Borderlands." The text of this appeal speaks movingly of the enemy's devastation of Russia's borderlands and the great need for assistance, but it begins with a proud declaration of multiethnic solidarity. Despite nearly a year of war,

the spirit of the Russian land is not weakening, its unity grows stronger, consciousness grows that all the peoples populating Russia are brothers in spirit, in culture, in love for the great Russia that unites us ... Russians, Poles,

---

[11] "Otchety komiteta," *Prizrenie i blagotvoritel'nost'* (May 1916), 447–55, features reports from provincial branches of the committee, detailing how they coordinated and helped fund the efforts of various public and national minority organizations aiding refugees.

[12] Gatrell, *A Whole Empire Walking*, 40–42, 60–61, 67, 77, 118.

Latvians, Lithuanians, Jews, Armenians, Tatars stand staunchly, a bulwark of the strength and greatness of Russia in the struggle for right and justice.[13]

Thanks to the vigorous publicity for the Tatiana Committee's nationwide collection, these inclusive words were "repeated a million times throughout the country," a columnist for *Gazeta-kopeika* approvingly noted, and "are meeting a fervent response." This collection alone raised more than 1 million rubles.[14]

When the war began, the Russian Society of the Red Cross was the country's largest organization dedicated to aiding sick and wounded troops. The Red Cross had provided admirable medical services in the Russo-Japanese war but, like the War Ministry's own medical department, had failed to anticipate the even greater number of casualties that would be produced by a general European war. With the outbreak of war the Red Cross could put into service only 118 field medical institutions, accommodating a grand total of 13,500 beds, plus 2 medical trains and 6 automobile detachments: this, for an army that mobilized almost 4 million men from the start of hostilities.[15]

Both the attractions and the problems of the Russian Red Cross are captured vividly in the diary of one of its many volunteers, Baron Nikolai N. Vrangel'. From the start of the war, the 32-year-old Vrangel' began to help out at the Red Cross in Petersburg, but longed to do more, writing in his diary that he felt superfluous, a fool, without a "right to exist," so long as he did nothing truly useful for the war effort.[16] Even as he pondered what that useful activity might be, and activated his manifold connections to try and line something up, he recorded difficulties at the Red Cross. On August 16 he wrote that "Everyone is indignant at the disorders in the military field infirmaries. The wounded are not being evacuated, lying for days on the ground, without food or drink. All the officers returning to Petersburg testify unanimously to this." On August

---

[13] "Rossiia – razorennym okrainam," *Gazeta-kopeika* (May 23, 1915), 1. The three-day all-Russian collection was timed to begin on the birthday of Grand Duchess Tatiana Nikolaevna.

[14] Tol'stoi, *Dnevnik*, II, 763.

[15] Red Cross figures come from "Zhurnal chrezvychainogo obshchego sobraniia R.O.O.K.," *Vestnik Krasnogo kresta* no. 8 (October 1914), 257. Newspapers openly wondered at the authorities' initial failure to provide evacuation for the wounded, since "they had to know there would be a huge need for this, given that there would be huge armies": "Sanitarnoe i evakuatsionnoe delo," *Kievlianin'* (October 29, 1914), 1. According to the Central Statistical Administration, the Russian army had mobilized 3.9 million men by August 1, 1914: "Tablitsa 1," in *Rossiia v mirovoi voine 1914–1918 goda (v tsifrakh)* (Moscow: Tsentral'noe statisticheskoe upravlenie, 1925), 17.

[16] Vrangel', *Dni skorbi*, 19, 26, 27. Nikolai Vrangel''s older brother, Baron Petr N. Vrangel', was a colonel at the outbreak of the war and later become famous as commander of the anti-Bolshevik Volunteer Army.

"All for the War!" 113

23 he noted that there simply were not enough hospitals to deal with the wounded. In early September he identified one important source of the disorder at the Red Cross: interference from the society's numerous imperial patrons. "The unity of authority necessary in wartime has been replaced by a royal muddle."[17]

These concerns notwithstanding, Vrangel' was overjoyed by his appointment in mid September to head one of the new medical evacuation trains. Over the course of the next nine months, first in charge of a medical train and then as a Red Cross inspector, he traversed Russia's northern and western fronts; unfortunately, his opinion of the Red Cross did not improve. He met capable and dedicated personnel, but was in general depressed by widespread waste, mismanagement, and internal squabbling.[18] Tragically for Vrangel', as for countless other medical workers, the hazards of wartime conditions proved fatal. He died of gastritis in Warsaw in June 1915.[19]

Shortcomings in the Red Cross help explain the meteoric growth of the largest and best-known "public organizations" of the war period, the All-Russian Union of Zemstvos and the All-Russian Union of Cities. Civic leaders founded these voluntary organizations during the first month of hostilities to assist in evacuating and treating the wounded; Russia's institutions of local self-government were naturally suited to assist in these tasks, since they were a critical part of the country's administration of health care.[20] In the opening days of the war the St. Petersburg Telegraph Agency issued the texts of dozens of patriotic telegrams sent from all over the empire by local zemstvos, announcing the amount of funds they were pledging for support of the war effort or plans to open and provision hospitals or infirmaries for the wounded.[21] Within a week of the war's outbreak, Moscow's provincial zemstvo met in extraordinary session to propose uniting and coordinating these disparate efforts by creating a nationwide union of zemstvos. A week later, representatives of dozens of provincial (*guberniia*) and district (*uezd*) zemstvos gathered in Moscow to hammer out preliminary guidelines for the new national

---

[17] Ibid., 49, 54, 57–59.
[18] Ibid., 61, 86–87, 91, 105–10; he was also becoming disheartened by the way Russia's heavy-handed "police tutelage" in the borderlands was stifling local relief efforts (123–24).
[19] Ibid., 143–44.
[20] The depth of zemstvo commitment to public health and to education is reflected in their allocations, which in 1913 constituted 25.1 percent and 31.4 percent, respectively, of their outlays; see Samuel C. Ramer, "The Zemstvo and Public Health," in Terrence Emmons and Wayne Vucinich, eds., *The Zemstvo in Russia: An Experiment in Local Self-Government* (Cambridge: Cambridge University Press, 1982), 307.
[21] *Novoe vremia* (July 25, 1914), 2; *Russkii invalid* (July 22, 1914), 3.

body; soon, all but one provincial zemstvo joined the new association (the ultra-conservative zemstvo of Kursk being the only holdout). The founding conference sent the customary telegram of loyal good wishes to the tsar, which read in part: "Today the representatives of zemstvo Russia have united to undertake the sacred duty of helping the sick and wounded, and they place their devotion and feelings of unlimited love at the feet of your Imperial Majesty."[22] Shortly thereafter, Russian municipalities decided to follow this example and organized a Union of Cities.[23]

The unions' role rapidly expanded. By September they were working at the front lines and not just in the rear, running medical trains that evacuated tens of thousands of men from the front to various treatments centers or redistribution spots, and operating canteens to feed them along the way, as well as presiding over nationwide networks of hospitals and convalescent centers. They also accepted orders from the military to begin supplying the army with warm clothing, footwear, and hospital linens (the Union of Zemstvos filled orders for more than 37 million such items by the end of 1915), and collected holiday gifts for the troops. They addressed acute shortfalls in medications and surgical instruments, most of which Russia had imported from Germany. In 1915, the unions took on the feeding and medical care of tens of thousands of civilian laborers constructing fortifications and trenches at the front. They helped create and run huge sanitation programs in the army and in urban areas to curb the spread of infectious diseases in cities whose health-care systems had been overwhelmed by refugees and the wounded. They sponsored educational programs on topics as diverse as the meaning of the war and the importance of clean drinking water in averting the spread of disease. And they established large departments in Moscow, Petrograd, and several provincial cities to organize aid for the hundreds of thousands of Russian POWs in Germany and Austria-Hungary.[24]

---

[22] Vserossiiskii Zemskii soiuz, *Obzor deiatel'nosti glavnogo komiteta, 1 avgusta 1914 g.–1 fevralia 1915 g.* (Moscow, 1915), 21–25; see also William Gleason, "The All-Russian Union of Towns and the All-Russian Union of Zemstvos in World War I," Ph.D. dissertation, Indiana University, 1972, 8–11.

[23] Tol'stoi attended the two organizing meetings of the Union of Cities, both held in Moscow, and describes them in his diary: Tol'stoi, *Dnevnik*, II, entries of August 8 and September 14, 1914, 592 and 614. On the Union of Cities, see William Gleason, "The All-Russian Union of Towns and the Politics of Urban Reform in Tsarist Russia," *Russian Review* 35, 3 (1976), 290–302.

[24] *Kratkii ocherk deiatel'nosti Vserossiiskogo zemskogo soiuza* (Moscow, 1916), 8–10, 13–19, 22, and N. Borodin, "Organizatsii pomoshchi voennoplennym. (Pis'mo v redaktsiiu)," *Vestnik Evropy* (August 1916), 394–404. It has sometimes been contended that the imperial state, disapproving of those who "surrendered," did not provide support to its POWs. While the state's aid was not generous, it did assign funds for Russian POWs and actively encouraged private aid.

Although the funding for these ambitious endeavors increasingly came from the state treasury, as well as resources assigned by the member zemstvos and cities, donations of money, products, and labor were crucial. The two unions' appeals for support were ubiquitous and, while invoking both patriotism and compassion, they tended to be cast most emphatically in terms of civic duty. For example, in its September 1915 appeal to aid refugees, the Union of Cities insisted that "Today, citizens of the Russian state who are not taking direct part in the great cause of defending the motherland have no duty more sacred than sheltering, feeding, and clothing refugees."[25]

Both the scale of operations and the nationwide network of the public organizations were unprecedented – at last, organs of local self-government were permitted to forge the broad horizontal linkages they had been desiring for decades. By February 1915, the Union of Zemstvos had helped its 582 provincial and district member zemstvos set up more than 174,000 hospital and infirmary beds for the sick and wounded, was operating 44 medical evacuation trains at the front and in the interior, and directly employed more than 9,000 medical personnel. It also employed tens of thousands of people – many of them refugees – in its workshops, warehouses, food-distribution centers, and other undertakings.[26] The Union of Cities had a still broader reach, since it extended to areas where zemstvos did not exist, such as Siberia and the Caucasus. In September 1917, the union had 630 member towns, stretching from Vladivostok to Tbilisi to Helsinki (Helsingfors), and more than 54,000 fulltime employees – 22,000 of them women – as well as legions of volunteers.[27] Each union published a monthly newsletter, which helped keep member towns and zemstvos informed about one another's activities as well as advertising those activities to the public. Twice-yearly all-Russian congresses of the unions brought together hundreds of

---

[25] "Vserossiiskii soiuz gorodov," *Gazeta-kopeika* (September 3, 1915), 3.
[26] On the eve of the war, zemstvo institutions existed in 43 of the 84 provinces and regions of the empire, comprising 441 districts: Kermit E. McKenzie, "Zemstvo Organization and Role within the Administrative Structure," in Emmons and Vucinich, *The Zemstvo*, 34; and *Vserossiiskii zemskii soiuz. Obzor deiatel'nosti*, 42–44. By the end of 1915, the Union of Zemstvos, Union of Cities, and city of Moscow provided a total of 318,000 hospital beds for sick and wounded soldiers, with the military and the Red Cross providing the remaining 208,000 beds: *Kratkii ocherk deiatel'nosti*, 11.
[27] The classic treatment of the voluntary organizations during the war is Paul P. Gronsky and Nicholas J. Astrov, *The War and the Russian Government* (New Haven: Yale University Press, 1929), 186–87, 193–96; an account of the Union of Zemstvos drawing on Russian archives is N. A. Sudavtsov, "Zemstvo v gody Pervoi mirovoi voiny," in A. P. Korelin, N. G. Koroleva, and L. F. Pisar'kova, eds., *Zemskoe samoupravlenie v Rossii, 1864–1918*, Book 2, *1905–1918* (Moscow: Nauka, 2005), 237–316. See also Gatrell, *Russia's First World War*, 40–43.

delegates from across the country, further consolidating members' sense of belonging to a national community.

With their enormous size, national scope, and vaunted energy and competence, the Union of Zemstvos and Union of Cities deeply impressed Russia's citizens. Importantly, military commanders were both generous and public in their praise, a good example coming from the July 1915 telegram of General Iu. Danilov, commander of the northwestern front, to Union of Cities chair Mikhail V. Chelnokov, which expressed "deep gratitude to all the members of the Union of Cities working within the boundaries of the northwestern front, and admiration of their inexhaustible energy and responsiveness."[28]

The unions did have critics. Ultra-conservatives increasingly accused them of wasting vast sums of treasury monies and also of playing politics, contending that they were trying to use their popularity to diministh the monarch's power.[29] More damagingly, a number of humble citizens, as well as conservatives, suspected that the public organizations were havens for bourgeois and upper-class men trying to avoid entering the military. This perception contributed to official efforts in 1916 and 1917 to comb out men with undeserved special exemptions and send them into the army. Overall, however, the perceived accomplishments of the public organizations became an important strand of the patriotic narrative of a competent, vigorous, and compassionate population.[30]

From the outbreak of hostilities, hundreds of charitable and civic organizations already in existence shifted the focus of their work to

---

[28] "Blagodarnost' Soiuzu gorodov," *Russkoe slovo* (July 31, 1915), 6. Leaders of both unions were quite adept in publicizing the accomplishments of the voluntary organizations

[29] Prince Georgii L'vov, head of the Union of Zemstvos, listed efforts to discredit the two voluntary organizations and rebutted the charges in a special meeting with reporters: *Den'* (July 2, 1916), 1–2. (Another accusation was that the unions had allowed themselves to be infiltrated by unreliable and even revolutionary elements.)

[30] It is impossible to determine how many men sought jobs in the public organizations in order to avoid active military service. Allan K. Wildman, *The End of the Russian Imperial Army: The Old Army and the Soldiers' Revolt (March–April 1917)* (Princeton: Princeton University Press, 1980), vol. I, 102–03, surmises that possibly as many as 200,000 shirkers with special exemptions ("white-ticketers" or *belobiletniki*) "nested in the swollen 'public organizations'"; however, Mark George, "Liberal Opposition in Wartime Russia: A Case Study of the Town and Zemstvo Unions, 1914–1917," *Slavic and East European Review* 65, 3 (July 1987), 383–84, contends that the Russian government greatly exaggerated this supposed draft-dodging in order to discredit the popular unions. On the question of the Union of Zemstvos' continuing effectiveness, William E. Gleason, "The All-Russian Union of Zemstvos and World War I," in Emmons and Vucinich, *The Zemstvo*, 365–82, suggests that worsening political tensions between the noble-dominated zemstvo administrations and their professional staffs meant "the reality of class in time overshadowed that of dedication to a patriotic cause" (378).

"All for the War!" 117

war-related needs, or created special committees to address them. For example, the Russian Women's Mutual Aid Society created a special committee "On Aid to Those Suffering from the War." The Society of Brotherly Love raised more than 70,000 rubles in 1914 to build two dormitories in Moscow for needy widows and dependants of soldiers killed in the war. The Municipal Guardianship for the Poor of Lefortovo District, in Moscow, spent 13,702 rubles through mid 1915 to operate cafeterias serving daily free lunches and run four shelters caring for

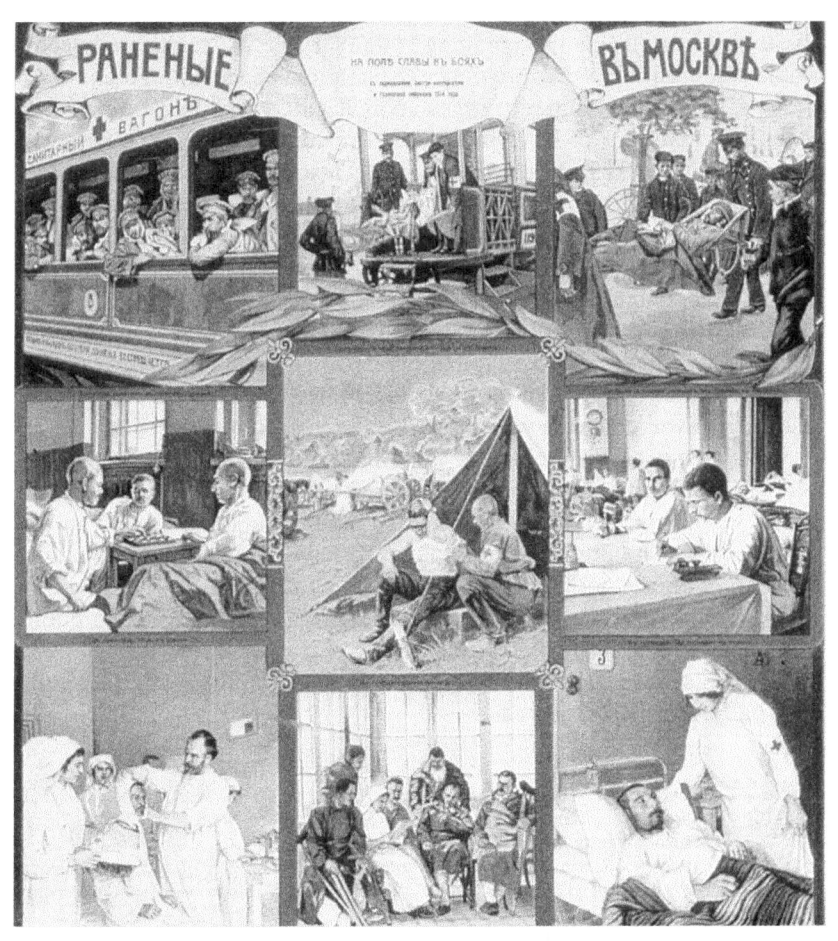

4.2 A 1914 poster, "Moscow Aids the Wounded," 1914, depicts how a caring and compassionate community looks after the country's defenders. Political Poster collection, #RU/SU 763, Courtesy of Hoover Institution Library & Archives, Stanford University.

children of mobilized reservists.[31] Rural cooperative societies in Riazan province "adopted" several hundred refugee families, helping them with food, housing, and finding work.[32]

A more traditional associative nexus that could be used to mobilize patriotic efforts was Russia's estate-based entities. Noble associations, existing since the reign of Catherine the Great, were the oldest of these, and still politically influential. Within days of the outbreak of war the association of the Moscow provincial nobility met in special session. Reminding its members – and all of Russia – of the heroic efforts of the Moscow nobility during the 1812 Fatherland War, it declared its intention to prove itself again by pledging 300,000 rubles to war-related needs. Noble assemblies in other provinces also made pledges, though not on so grand a scale.[33] Prominent nobles soon decided it would be advantageous to create an all-Russian nobles' organization for support of the war; by March 1915, 39 provincial noble associations had joined, with donations totaling 1.366 million rubles. The pooled resources of the member associations enabled the new organization to outfit and support twenty medical trains for the evacuation of the sick and wounded, an infirmary, a canteen, and other war-related causes.[34]

At the Eleventh Congress of United Noble Societies, held in Moscow March 10–11, 1915, these contributions were proudly enumerated, a testament to the patriotism of the Russian nobility. However, there were delegates to the congress who felt nobles' contributions were not nearly so well known to the public as they deserved to be. The reactionary Nikolai Markov II complained angrily about the lack of publicity for nobles' efforts on behalf of the fatherland, which he blamed on "an evil Jewish plan." The press was dominated by Jews, he insisted, and had no desire to publicize nobles' fine work or the fact that they footed the entire bill for their relief efforts rather than using treasury funds as the public organizations did. Markov's fulminations generated applause, suggesting that others shared his grievance that nobles were not getting the credit their patriotic work deserved.[35]

---

[31] *Novoe vremia* (July 27, 1914), 6, and (August 3, 1914), 3; *Russkoe slovo* (October 1, 1915), 1; *Otchet gorodskogo popechitel'stva o bednykh lefortovskoi chasti za 1915 god* (Moscow: Gorodskaia tipografiia, 1916), 1–2, 27.
[32] N. N. Chervakov, "Riazanskii gubernskii kooperativnyi komitet v gody Pervoi mirovoi voiny," in *Rossiia v Pervoi mirovoi voine. Tezisy mezhvuzovskoi nauchnoi konferentsii* (Riazan, 1994), 165.
[33] *Novoe vremia* (July 28, 1914), 3, and *Russkii invalid* (August 14, 1914), 3.
[34] "Dvorianskaia organizatsiia," *Novoe vremia* (August 17, 1914), 4, and *Stenograficheski otchety zasedanii XI S"ezda Upolnomochennykh ob"edinennykh dvorianskikh obshchestv* (Moscow, 1915), 32, 35, 37–38, 40.
[35] *Stenograficheskie otchety zasedanii XI S"ezda*, 41–42.

Professional and trade associations were another natural means of organizing for war relief. Not surprisingly, the business community raised the largest sums. For example, in the first month of war the Baku oil producers and Tbilisi Commercial Bank gave 115,000 rubles to the Caucasus Committee on Aid to Families of Reservists, while the Representatives of Trade, Industry and Credit institutions in Kiev pledged 155,000 rubles for local war needs.[36] Over the course of the first year of hostilities, the joint committee of the Moscow Merchants and the Moscow Exchange collected a whopping 7,326,496 rubles in subscriptions for war aid, with the Moscow Merchants' Society also donating eight buildings for use as hospitals and 300,000 rubles from its own means.[37] Lawyers' associations, the Society of Russian Teachers, rural cooperatives, and dozens of other groups drew on their associational ties to raise money, donate materials, or volunteer their time to support Russia's war effort. Frequently, they took out ads or published accounts in their monthly journals apprising their members, and the general public, of their patriotic contributions.[38]

Many Russians believed that, in mobilizing itself on this scale, society was demonstrating its own transformation. As one journalist remarked in fall 1914, through their scientific and professional associations the "laboring intelligentsia" had always responded to poverty in Russia, but what was now displayed was something new, "a capacity for brisk initiative and efficient organization." The deeply conservative *Kolokol* also noted the wartime transformation approvingly: Russian society's "latent store of energy and initiative has found its proper field of application. 'Bystanders' have turned into citizens. Everyone and everything have been gripped by the civic impulse to do whatever they can for the army."[39] The rural newspaper *Derevenskaia gazeta* (Village Gazette) put it more bluntly: the mighty work of war relief "shows how we have all

---

[36] *Russkii invalid* (July 22, 1914), 2.
[37] "Patriotizm moskovskogo kupechestva," *Kievlianin'* (July 24, 1914), 4, *Voina* no. 8 (1915), 56–58.
[38] For example, cooperative societies – whose numbers expanded substantially during the war – worked with other aid organizations to help soldiers' families, funded and supported their own infirmaries in seven provinces, and additionally donated an estimated 3.5 million rubles in money and goods to war relief by mid 1915; members and employees of cooperatives could read about these worthy endeavors in the magazine *Kooperativnaia zhizn'* (Cooperative life): cited in A. S. Orlov, *Kooperatsiia v Rossii nakanune i vovremia voiny*, 2nd edn. (Moscow: Izdanie "Pechat' T-va I. N. Kuchnerov i Ko.," 1917), 67–69.
[39] I.M., "Voina i obshchestvennaia samodeiatel'nost'," *Sovremennik* (October 1914), 192–93; the excerpt from *Kolokol* is quoted in "Obzor pechati," *Russkii invalid* (November 19, 1914), 3.

matured as *conscious citizens*, able not only to die for the common good but also to work for and *create* it."[40]

The Politics of Service and Giving

Linda Colley has called our attention to the way that patriotic activism, however sincere, can also be a useful way of accumulating political capital. In the case of creation of a new "British" nation in the eighteenth century, she argues, different classes and interest groups – many of them located well outside the corridors of power – came to see this national entity as "a usable resource, as a focus of loyalty which would also cater to their own needs and ambitions."[41] Similarly, one need not impugn the patriotism or compassion of various groups within Russian society to observe the potential utility for themselves of their engagement with war relief.

Over the course of the conflict, virtually every national minority group in Russia organized war relief or services. Many of these undertakings were concerned with assisting co-nationalists suffering from the war, as was the case with the Central Latvian Committee for Aiding Refugees. This body united the work of 77 independent associations around the empire aiding more than 252,000 Latvian refugees; they organized housing, ran elementary and middle schools, built clubs, and maintained clinics and sanitariums. Leaders of Muslim philanthropies received permission to organize a Provisional Muslim Committee of Assistance to Soldiers and Their Families, which speedily established sixty-six local chapters across the empire; it organized a medical unit that was sent to the front, but increasingly assisted fellow Muslims suffering hardship in the war.[42] As Peter Gatrell demonstrates, in a variety of ways the ordeals and experience of mass numbers of refugees, and collective action by national groups to aid their own, actually helped consolidate and deepen distinct national identities.[43]

---

[40] V. Anzimirov, "Sluzhba tyla," *Derevenskaia gazeta* no. 43 (November 1914), 2–3 (emphasis in original).

[41] Linda Colley, *Britons: Forging the Nation, 1707–1837* (New Haven: Yale University Press, 1992), esp. 54–56, 93–94.

[42] "Sredi latyshei," *Gazeta-kopeika* (November 22, 1915), 4, and Norihiro Naganawa, "A Civil Society in a Confessional State? Muslim Philanthropy in the Volga–Urals Region," in Adele Lindenmeyr, Christopher Read, and Peter Waldron, eds., *Russia's Home Front in War and Revolution, 1914–1922, Book 2, The Experience of War and Revolution* (Bloomington: Slavica, 2016), 59–78. Naganawa notes that the leaders who organized this new web of war relief were confident that it would help Muslim citizens gain fuller rights at war's end.

[43] Gatrell, *A Whole Empire Walking*, 168–70.

But minority communities and organizations also deliberately involved themselves in the broader, "all-Russian" war effort. They organized prayer services for victory, raised funds for the wounded, signed up as medics or Sisters of Mercy, and in other ways demonstrated their loyalty and membership in the Russian patriotic community. Most of the press appeared happy to write up these acts of giving and volunteering – briefs on them are ubiquitous – presumably because they so neatly corroborated the patriotic narrative of sacred union. Readers of various periodicals thus learned about generous Mennonite donations to the Red Cross, the gift of thirty-three yurts by the ethnically non-Russians (*inorodtsy*) of Akmola region for use by mobile medical units, and the Polish Committee of Irkutsk's fundraising campaign for wounded soldiers and refugees.[44] Jewish Committees in Riga, Kiev, and elsewhere raised large sums to outfit clinics, purchase gifts for frontline troops, and in other ways show their commitment to the national cause.[45] In May 1915, a medical-nutritional detachment (*otriad*) organized by and named for the "Buriat people" was sent to the front under the auspices of the Union of Cities. At the ceremony marking this unit's departure for the front, N. M. Kishkin, one of the leading figures in the Union of Cities, expressed deep thanks to the Buriat people and pointed to their detachment as demonstrating, yet again, that "the entire people is united in the struggle against the enemy, that the war being conducted is a people's war."[46]

During the Great War, in virtually every combatant country women engaged in work previously limited in scope or entirely prohibited for their sex, ranging from transportation and the civil service to making shells.[47] In Russia, too, the mobilization and self-mobilization of the civilian population opened new spheres of activity to women. Female street-car drivers, porters, and concierges became increasingly common urban sights. In the industrial sector, women moved into such male preserves as munitions, metalworking, and coal. By 1916, women made

---

[44] *Russkie vedomosti* (January 10, 1915), 6, and (May 15, 1915), 4; *Kievlianin'* (July 26, 1914), 3; "Irkutskii pol'skii komitet," *Voina* no. 3 (1914), 77–78.
[45] "Dlia armii" and "Rizhskaia evreiskaia obshchina," *Voina i evrei*, nos. 1, 2 (1915), 16 and 14. See also Tol'stoi's diary entry for November 30, 1914: Tol'stoi, *Dnevnik*, II, 654.
[46] *Russkie vedomosti* (May 16, 1915), 4.
[47] There is a rich literature on women's paid labor in the Great War; see, for example, Gail Braybon, *Women Workers in the First World War* (London: Croom Helm, 1981); Margaret H. Darrow, *French Women and the First World War: War Stories of the Home Front* (Oxford: Berg, 2000); Margaret Higonnet, Jane Jensen, et al., *Behind the Lines: Gender and the Two World Wars* (New Haven: Yale University Press, 1987); and Angela Woollacott, *On Her Their Lives Depend: Munitions Workers in the Great War* (Berkeley: University of California Press, 1994).

up 35 percent of all railroad employees. In addition to filling positions left open by men called to the war, Russian women engaged directly in war-related services and war relief. Whether as volunteers or paid employees, women could actively express social patriotism through the giant task of relief work for soldiers' families, disabled soldiers, and the millions of refugees.[48] We have no comprehensive numbers for how many women were involved in these critical efforts, since the history of Russian women in the war remains to be written. But taking into account the traditionally large role of women in volunteer work, and the shrinking numbers of able-bodied civilian men, the figures were not small: it seems certain that, in the mobilization of the home front for war relief, most of the "boots on the ground" were women's.[49]

During the Great War, in virtually every combatant country women's most ubiquitous contribution to war relief was sewing – the demand for bandages, linens, and clothing was seemingly insatiable. In Russia, too, women were called upon to patriotically ply their needles, as this front page appeal in the magazine *Zhenskoe novosti* (Women's News) illustrates: "Women, sew linens for the troops! Through your work you'll benefit the motherland and do your bit for our common cause."[50] Ladies' Committees (*damskie komitety*) in virtually every large city made supplying linens a primary concern, creating sewing departments to make these articles.[51] To coordinate the huge task of provisioning infirmaries and medical trains, large storehouses (*sklady*) were organized in various cities, the best-known being the Empress's Storehouse at the

---

[48] The fullest overview of Russian women in the war is Alfred G. Meyer, "The Impact of World War I on Russian Women's Lives," in Barbara Evans Clements, Barbara Alpern Engel, and Christine D. Worobec, *Russia's Women: Accommodation, Resistance, Transformation* (Berkeley: University of California Press, 1991), 208–24; see also Barbara A. Engel, "Not by Bread Alone: Subsistence Riots in Russia during World War I," *Journal of Modern History* 69, 4 (December 1997), 696–721, and Jane McDermid and Anna Hillyar, *Midwives of the Revolution: Female Bolsheviks and Women Workers in 1917* (Athens: Ohio University Press, 1999), ch. 5. On women in refugee work, see Gatrell, *A Whole Empire Walking*, 125–27.

[49] In addition to Lindenmeyr, *Poverty Is Not a Vice*, and Gatrell, *A Whole Empire Walking*, scholarship attentive to gender and identity creation through philanthropy includes Jean H. Quataert, *Staging Philanthropy: Patriotic Women and the National Imagination in Dynastic Germany, 1813–1916* (Ann Arbor: University of Michigan Press, 2001), esp. 2–5, 272–90. An approach linking war relief, patriotism, and women's citizenship claims is Capozzola, *Uncle Sam Wants You*, esp. 103–116.

[50] "Zhenshchiny mobilizaites' dlia nuzhdy voiny!" *Zhenskoe novosti* no. 1 (January 12, 1916), 1.

[51] "Damskie komitety," *Russkii invalid* (July 26, 1914), 4, and "Damskii komitet," *Kievlianin'* (October 30, 1914), 4; E. S. Trepova, head of the Ladies' Committee of the Red Cross in Kiev, estimated that as of October 15 volunteers and paid wives of soldiers had sewn 19,000 items.

Winter Palace. Storehouses actively solicited volunteer workers, most of whom were women, for sewing and other work. The paid work at these institutions – which included assembling gas masks as well as sewing – was reserved for family members of mobilized soldiers, and refugees (again, mainly women).[52] Masses of schoolgirls engaged in sewing for the troops, whether at school or through charitable societies; as one senior in a girl's gymnasium wrote to her mother, "We now have such a tremendous amount of work to do. Latin and mathematics are very interesting. Do you know how many sets of underclothing we made last week? 538!"[53]

Crucially, women provided medical care for the sick and wounded. Thanks to the inadequate supply of doctors for the front, the services of female doctors were welcomed. Tatiana Aleksinskaia was one such physician, and has left a fascinating account of her experiences. A socialist and critic of the tsarist regime, she was living in Paris with her husband, ex-Duma deputy Grigorii Aleksinskii, when the war began. As was true for a number of political exiles, love of country outweighed dislike of the regime: she returned as soon as possible to Russia and began working on a medical evacuation train run by the Union of Zemstvos. The train had thirty-two cars for wounded, accommodating twelve men each, and a medical staff of thirteen people, eleven of whom were women, including the chief surgeon. As Aleksinskaia described it, "Ours is a feminist train, and I am proud of it."[54]

But, in this conflict, nursing was the iconic patriotic service rendered by women. The need was terrific – the Russian Red Cross apparently had only 4,000 trained Sisters of Mercy in reserve at the outbreak of hostilities. Immediately, the Red Cross, larger zemstvo associations, and various polytechnics and medical institutes organized crash courses in nurses' training. In the opening months of the war, there were often

---

[52] Not surprisingly, the Empress's storehouse attracted exceptionally large donations, including 200,000 rubles from the St. Petersburg Municipal Credit Society: *Novoe vremia* (August 3, 1914), 2. By October 1914, the Chief Storehouse of the Red Cross, located in Petrograd, had organized dozens of voluntary sewing circles as well as a special committee to provide materials to sewing circles created by other organizations: *Vestnik Krasnogo kresta* no. 8 (October 1914), 263–64.

[53] Cited in Dimitrii M. Odinets, "Russian Primary and Secondary Schools during the War," in Dimitrii M. Odinets and P. I. Novgorodtsev, eds., *Russian Schools and Universities in the World War* (New Haven: Yale University Press, 1929), 77.

[54] Tatiana Alexinsky, *With the Russian Wounded*, trans. Gilbert Cannan (London: T. Fischer Unwin, Ltd., 1916), v–vii, 1–10. Other prominent socialist exiles who supported Russia's war effort included Georgii Plekhanov, Prince Petr Kropotkin, and Vladimir Burtsev, who became a *cause célèbre* when he returned to Russia to volunteer for the war effort and was immediately arrested: see "Delo V. L. Burtseva," *Gazeta-kopeika* (January 21, 1915), 3.

more women wishing to enroll than there were places on offer. Not unusual was the experience in Kiev, where 2,000 women showed up between July 20 and 24 to enroll for 500 openings in courses offered by the local Red Cross. The Red Cross also announced that in time of war it was suspending its usual prohibition against accepting non-Christians as Sisters of Mercy, and would enroll Jewish candidates for the courses.[55]

The empress and her two eldest daughters, Olga and Tatiana, enrolled almost immediately in nursing courses. After receiving their diplomas they nursed regularly at the Empress's Hospital in Tsarskoe Selo, attending to common soldiers as well as officers, and also visited other hospitals in the capital and the provinces. Photos of them, dressed in long white gowns and veils that fastened under the chin, were widely featured in illustrated magazines and Sunday supplements, as were nursing photos of other members of the imperial family.[56] This most exalted example of female patriotism may have inspired other women to become Sisters of Mercy, although it did not, in the case of the empress, convince the majority of the population of her love for her adopted country.[57] Many socially prominent women served as nurses, sometimes in infirmaries that they had organized themselves and financially supported.[58]

Initially, the great bulk of nurses came from the less exalted ranks of officers' wives and daughters, schoolteachers, and other "middle-class" women. But, as the war wore on, the requirement that candidates for nursing courses have at least two years' secondary-school education was relaxed, allowing women of humbler social backgrounds to enroll. This expanded pool helped ensure that, despite the low pay and often grueling nature of war nursing, no shortage of candidates developed.[59]

[55] *Kievlianin'* (July 26, 1914), 2; *Novoe vremia* (August 3, 1914), 3, 4; Red Cross statutes on requirements and training for Sisters of Mercy are contained in D. Mikhailov, *Krasnyi krest i sestry miloserdiia v Rossii i za-granitsei* (Petrograd and Kiev: Knigoizdatel'stvo "Sotrudnik," 1914), 65–67.
[56] For example, in Pskov, *Russkoe slovo* (October 15, 1915), 3–4. Grand Duchess Olga Aleksandrovna, the tsar's sister, was particularly active: "Samootverzhenie velikoi kniagini," *Soldatskii vestnik* (September 17, 1914), 3. A member of the imperial family who has left a detailed account of her years of wartime nursing is Marie, Grand Duchess of Russia, *Education of a Princess: A Memoir*, trans. from French and Russian under the editorial supervision of Russell Lord (New York: Viking Press, 1931), 165–247.
[57] The most detailed exploration of negative public perceptions of the Empress is Kolonitskii, *Tragicheskaia erotika*.
[58] For example, a spread in *Stolitsa i usad'ba* no. 36–37 (July 1, 1915), 18–24, was devoted to high-society women nursing in infirmaries organized in palaces and mansions; issue no. 40–41 (September 1, 1915), 13, pictured Countess Elizaveta Vladimirovna Shuvalov in nursing uniform in her 400-bed infirmary.
[59] One author, noting the enormous numbers of women volunteering for nursing courses, wrote that "the sisterly wave has not subsided in the least through ten months of war": V. S. Krivenko, "Zhenskaia voinskaia povinnost'," *Novoe vremia* (June 4, 1915), 5.

"All for the War!" 125

Total numbers of women nursing in the war are impossible to establish, but given that the Red Cross service alone accounted for some 18,000 sisters in mid 1917 – a figure which would not include women nursing in the hundreds of medical institutions run by the public organizations, or in monasteries – there were probably between 25,000 and 30,000 Sisters of Mercy in 1917.[60]

A variety of factors explain the sustained interest in nursing. Recalling the solemn ceremony in which she and fellow classmates received their nursing badges in October 1914, Mary Britnieva's memoirs stress pure love of country: "I am quite sure that not one of us young women had ever before experienced such profound feelings of reverence, patriotism and enthusiasm, all in perfect harmony, as were evoked in us by this memorable service."[61] Describing her first glimpse of the Red Cross flag flying over her first posting, Lydiia Zakhareva also pictures herself as part of a larger whole: "I recall the feeling of tender emotion and the desire to bow my head before the beautiful symbol of mercy under whose protection I planned to join battle, a little, unremarked foot soldier of a great army." Both these memoirists express deep affection and respect for the soldiers they cared for.[62]

Wartime nursing could also appear glamorous and exciting. Photos of Sisters of Mercy, often alongside their patients or doctors, appeared constantly in the press over the whole course of the war. Colorful drawings of Sisters – selflessly tending wounded soldiers on shell-torn battlefields, or ministering to them in hospital wards – were featured on wall calendars and commercially disseminated prints, as well as on posters for war relief. The feats of particularly heroic nurses were widely publicized. I have already mentioned Rimma Ivanova, who died in battle in 1915 after assuming command of a small unit whose officers had been killed.

---

[60] The figure for Red Cross nurses is given by V. S. Krivenko in *Russkii invalid* (May 25, 1917), 4. A total figure of 25,000 Sisters of Mercy for 1916 is given by one scholar, but without reference to sources: Iu. I. Ivanova, *Khrabreishie iz prekrasnykh. Zhenshchiny Rossii v voinakh* (Moscow: ROSSPEN, 2002), 106. Data on nursing staff from the Union of Zemstvos is hard to evaluate, given its unlikely ratios for nursing staff to hospital beds: the union was responsible for 171,519 hospital beds by February 1, 1915, but apparently employed only 2,170 Sisters and Brothers of Mercy, which would scarcely correspond to claims that numbers of nurses were adequate by 1915: *Vserossiiskii zemskii soiuz. Obzor deiatel'nosti*, 41, 43.

[61] Mary Britnieva, *One Woman's Story* (London: Arthur Barker, 1934), 9–10. Britnieva, the daughter of an English father and Russian mother, was 20 when she completed her nursing course.

[62] Lydiia Zakhareva, *Dnevnik sestry miloserdiia. Na peredovykh pozitsiakh* (Petrograd: Izd. Biblioteka "Velikoi voiny," 1915), 23; Zakhareva's memoir provides no data about her age, background, or training. See also Alexinsky, *With the Russian Wounded*, 31–35, 66–70, 75.

Ivanova was posthumously awarded the Order of St. George, fourth degree.[63] Several hundred Sisters of Mercy received other types of St. George decorations for valor over the course of the war and, at the grand banquet held annually in Petrograd to fete all St. George cavaliers, these female "Georgiis" were among the honorees.[64]

Of course, some people attributed baser motives to women who wished to nurse. There were peasant soldiers who put it down to female licentiousness, while a number of educated observers suspected husband-hunting was on at least a few women's minds. Occasionally, prostitutes or thieves masqueraded as Sisters of Mercy; press concern with such incidents betrays anxieties about female behavior.[65] But media reporting on authentic Sisters of Mercy, in virtually all periodicals and no matter the audience, was ample and glowing. *Sel'skii vestnik* told its peasant readers about these "angels in the person of women," with articles approving both their bravery and their caring hearts. A columnist in *Russkoe slovo*, Russia's highest-circulation daily, characterized all Sisters of Mercy as "selfless," ready to risk their health and even their lives for those in their care.[66] For most Russians, it would seem, nursing was a gender-appropriate way for women to aid their country.

Russian feminists lauded this kind of patriotic service, along with the whole spectrum of paid wartime work undertaken by women. These challenging jobs provided a unique opportunity for women to demonstrate their competence and civic-mindedness, and thus their fitness for full citizenship rights: "Women! Give the world proof of energy, courage, persistence and a broad, state understanding of the tasks that have been

---

[63] "Pokhorony geroiny," *Gazeta-kopeika* (October 1, 1915), 3. Also worth quoting is Skitalets, "Doch' otchizny," *Gazeta-kopeika* (September 20, 1915), 4, who asserts that "a people that creates such a great and shining soul cannot be defeated."

[64] A. A. Osviannikov, "Georgievskie nagrady Pervoi mirovoi voiny," in *Rossiia v Pervoi mirovoi voiny*, 108, and, for example, *Novoe vremia* (April 23, 1916, Saturday supplement), 139, and (July 2, 1916, Saturday supplement), 9; "Georgievskii prazdnik," *Russkoe slovo* (November 27, 1915), 4.

[65] On more salacious images of Sisters of Mercy that circulated during the war – including those of the empress and her daughters – see Boris I. Kolonitskii, "Obraz sestry miloserdii," in Katia Bruish and Nikolau Katser, eds., *Bol'shaia voina Rossii. Sotsial'nyi poriadok, publichnaia kommunikatsiia i nasilie na rubezhe tsarskoi i sovestskoi epokh* (St. Petersburg: Novoe literaturnoe obozrenie, 2014), 100–26.

[66] L. Poryvaev, "Angely v litse zhenshchiny," *Sel'skii vestnik* (July 22, 1915), 3; and A. Pankratov, "Sestry," *Russkoe slovo* (July 9, 1915), 1. A. I. Ksiunin, "Russkie zhenshchiny na pole bitvy," *Vechernoe vremia*, reprinted in *Vestnik Krasnogo kresta* no. 9 (November 9, 1914), 721–23, praises the bravery of Sisters at the front and predicts that "their names will be inscribed on the same plaques as the names of our [soldier] heroes."

4.3 This poster, "War and the Press," advertises a fundraising exhibit organized in 1914 by the Union of Cities; with 630 member towns, it constituted one of the largest war-relief networks. Political Poster Collection, #RU/SU 862, Courtesy of Hoover Institution Library & Archives, Stanford University.

put before you."[67] In 1915, Poliksena Shishkina-Iavein, head of the Petrograd branch of the League of Equal Rights for Women, wrote that the Russian woman, having proved again her "social consciousness and political maturity," expected to be recognized as "a citizen of her fatherland." She also made sure that women's patriotic work did not go unnoticed, shrewdly calling upon Mayor Tol'stoi to invite him in person to the dedication of the infirmary being opened by the League of Equal Rights.[68] In a July 1916 article in *Zhenskoe delo* (Women's Cause), feminist Mariia Blandova similarly contended that women's war work had proved them the equals of men, so that, "thanks to this monstrous war, the last argument against equal rights for women put forth by the enemies of women's freedom has fallen." Such opinions were not confined to women activists. Duma deputy Prince S. P. Mansyrev, best

[67] A. K. Iakovlev, "Voina i zhenshchiny" and "Prizyv k zhenshchinam," *Zhenshchina i voina* no. 1 (March 5, 1915), 4–5 and 15–16.
[68] P. N. Shishkina-Iavein, "Voina i zhenshchina," in *Chego zhdet Rossiia ot voiny*, 155, and Tol'stoi, *Dnevnik*, II, entries of January 23 and 25, 1915, 687, 689.

known for his anti-German campaigns, told the Russian Women's Mutual Aid Society in 1916 that women's energetic wartime work was winning "recognition that they should have all civic rights." He expressed confidence that Russian women would soon acquire political rights as well.[69]

Thus, for the many sectors of the population who had only "second-, third-, or even fourth-class rights" – to use Duma deputy A. I. Chkhenkeli's phrase – engaging in war relief could serve more than one purpose: in coming to the aid of their country, they also bolstered claims to fuller membership within the national community and greater access to the rights of citizenship.[70] Women and national minorities therefore had ample reason to shape and buy into the patriotic narrative of sacred union. Some conservatives in fact worried about precisely such expectations. An August 1914 letter from an unknown sender to one A. A. Savel'ov in Nizhnyi Novgorod, intercepted by the police, predicted that "the Georgians and Little Russians and Finns, and so on, all of them, will be presenting their promissary notes for 'loyalty' after the war. And then very likely the Great Russians, too, will request a parliamentary system as a tip for themselves."[71]

In fact, it would be hard to find a group involved in war relief that was oblivious to the advantages they might derive from such patriotic endeavors. I have already noted nobles' ire at not having their association's aid to the wounded receive sufficient attention. It seems fair to infer political considerations in the large donations made to the Empress's Storehouse and the medical units of both the State Council and the State Duma by the Committee of the Moscow merchantry and exchange, a group long desirous of acquiring political influence more commensurate with members' economic power. Possible advantage to educated society was discussed explicitly at the October 1, 1914, conference of the liberal Kadet Party. Liberals played an outsize role in both the Union of Zemstvos and Union of Cities, and party leaders anticipated that this patriotic, nonpartisan activity across the country would rebuild

---

[69] On Russian feminists in the war, see Rochelle Goldberg Ruthchild, *Equality and Revolution: Women's Rights in the Russian Empire, 1905–1917* (Pittsburgh: University of Pittsburgh Press, 2010), 213–17. Mansyrev's remarks are in "Russkaia zhenshchina-russkaia budushchnost'," *Zhenskie novosti* (February 29, 1916), 7.

[70] For example, M. Slavinskii, "Voina i natsional'nyi vopros," in *Chego zhdet Rossiia ot voiny*, esp. 103–08, 116–20, and A. I. Chkhenkeli, *GDSO*, IV, 4, sess. 53 (June 9, 1916), cols. 5054–55. British and French women nurtured similar expectations about winning citizenship rights through their patriotic war work; see Susan R. Grayzel, *Women's Identities at War: Gender, Motherhood and Politics in Britain and France during the First World War* (Chapel Hill: University of North Carolina Press, 1999), esp. 220–25.

[71] GARF, f. 102, op. 265, d. 967, "Perlustrated letters, 1914," l. 1142.

their party and other progressive organizations decimated by governmental repression. As party leader Miliukov put it, their resurrection would be effected "under the banner and on the grounds of philanthropy and aid to war victims."[72]

Mobilizing Resources

Self-mobilization for war relief meant, among other things, mobilizing resources: cash, clothing, foodstuffs, labor, even jewelry and real estate could be offered for the cause. In the first months of war, Russians surprised even themselves with a tidal wave of generosity. Of course, in every belligerent nation in the Great War, intense social pressure to conform and do one's bit could compel individuals to buy bonds, roll bandages, and pledge to observe "voluntary" meatless days. As Christopher Capozzola observes of the American home front, lending a hand in the war effort became for citizens "not just a good deed but a duty, and serious consequences ensued for those who failed to join in."[73] Similarly, it is not hard to imagine that, when a Russian workplace voted on whether all employees should pledge 3 percent of their monthly salaries to war relief, or a parish ladies' committee invited parishioners to sew for the troops, most people would have been reluctant to refuse.

But, while the role of informal coercion complicates our assessments of what all this giving and volunteering meant, there is still much we can learn from Russian war relief. The variety of fundraising strategies provides yet another perspective on the nature of public initiative and participation in war relief. Besides raising material support for their various causes, these collections, exhibits, and benefit shows could also raise consciousness of the nation at war, conveying solid information or satisfying stories about the war's goals and conduct, disseminating recognizable images, and bolstering morale.

One of the most common means of fundraising was to hold a city-wide street collection (*kruzhechnyi sbor*). Advance publicity alerted the public to the cause and the date. Hundreds or even thousands of volunteers – primarily women and young people – took collection boxes around public spaces, railway stations, and amusement spots. A small souvenir or device would be given to everyone who put money

---

[72] Melissa Stockdale, "Russian Liberals and the Contours of Patriotism in the Great War," in V. V. Shelokhaev et al., *Russkii liberalizm. Istoricheskie sud'by i perspektivy* (Moscow: ROSSPEN, 1999), 283–92; the quote comes from N. G. Dumova, *Kadetskaia partiia v period Pervoi mirovoi voiny i Fevral'skoi revoliutsii* (Moscow: "Nauka," 1988), 32.
[73] Capozzola, *Uncle Sam Wants You*, 8.

in a collection box, such as a badge or rosette; these functioned as an incentive but also provided participants with a means of displaying their patriotism. Particularly popular were tiny national flags of Russia and its allies, and many locales held a "national flags day" in the first year of the war.[74]

Organizers could draw on the rich panoply of money-raising strategies developed by Russian charitable groups over the years, including bazaars, auctions, lectures, movie screenings, and masquerade balls (an upmarket example being the pre-Lenten ball hosted by the Kiev Noble Association, in 1915). Throughout the war, different war-relief entities petitioned the authorities for permission to raise money by selling small items such as patriotic postage stamps, calendars, medallions, or postcards featuring the likenesses of military heroes, Allied rulers and generals, or the emperor and heir.[75] In 1915, many cities held a "Day of the Press," with the local press uniting to produce a special edition paper devoted to war-related news and information; Moscow's Day of the Press raised 85,000 rubles.[76] Patriotic giving did not have to be strictly self-denying. Besides the seven internal war loans, paying 5 to 5.5 percent interest, there was the 1914–15 charitable lottery for war relief, with a big array of cash prizes, which realized some 16 million rubles in ticket sales.[77]

The patriotic show (*spektakl*) was extremely popular during the first year of war. Hubertus Jahn has explored in detail the colorful and typically traditional patriotic content of these entertainments in his pioneering study of early wartime culture. Enthusiastic crowds turned out for shows featuring fantastically staged air and land battles, clowns mocking the enemy, heart-stirring anthems, and grand finales with

[74] On "Flag Day" in Viatka, see *Russkii invalid* (August 8, 1914), 2; in Kiev, *Kievlianin'* (September 5, 6, 13, 1914), 2, 4, and 3; and in Moscow, *Novoe vremia* (July 30, 1914), 4. On other collections see *Russkii invalid* (August 12 and 17, 1914), 1 and 3, (August 27, 1914), 3, and (October 22, 1914), 3; *Russkoe vedomosti* (May 15, 1915), 4. On Slavic Day, see *Voina* no. 8 (1915), 51–52.
[75] Organizations receiving permission to issue fundraising postage stamps were as diverse as the Imperial Women's Patriotic Society, the Russian Society of Railroads, and the Tashkent branch of the Society for Aid to Soldiers and Their Families: see *Russkii invalid* (September 7, 1914), 3, and Library of Congress (Lot 6540), Red Cross Stamps.
[76] "Den' pechati," *Russkie vedomosti* (June 7, 1915), 4, and "Na temu dnia," *Den' pechati* (Buzuluk) (February 20, 1915), which rather poignantly echoes the common theme of wartime transformation: "even in moribund Buzuluk district" (Samara province), as in all of Russia, "a change for the better has occurred ... for the people of Buzuluk, the war has been a mighty school for public engagement."
[77] On the lottery, see O. I. Averbakh, *Zakonodatel'nye akty, vyzvannye voinoiu 1914 goda* (Vilnius, 1915), 548, 631. Ticket sales for the lottery began in December and continued into mid June 1915. The figure of 16,035,000 rubles in lottery ticket sales as of May 15, 1915, is given in *Kievlianin'* (May 27, 1915), 2.

flags and symbolic figures of Russia and its allies.[78] The patriotic concerts of soprano Mariia Ivanovna Dolina, usually performed at the Circus Ciniselli in Petrograd, were the longest-lived example of this genre. Over the course of 2 years, Dolina put on 163 patriotic concerts. With ticket prices ranging from 32 kopeks to 12 rubles, they attracted a broad and diverse audience; proceeds from each show went to support her infirmary for wounded soldiers or to a different designated cause. Rousing entertainments were not confined to major cities: small towns and even rural communities organized benefit shows for war relief, usually making use of local talent, especially that of schoolchildren.[79] Besides raising money for war relief, such diversions were believed to promote the patriotic consciousness of performers and audience alike.

Exhibitions based on war themes raised money while also stimulating awareness of Russian heroes, Russia's allies, or the geographic sites of the conflict. In late 1914, the Union of Cities organized a three-month long traveling exhibit called "The War and the Press" which featured printed literature, recruiting posters, maps and photos, and other material drawn from all the Entente allies. The entrance fee was 30 kopeks, with proceeds benefiting services for sick and wounded soldiers undertaken by each host city.[80] Periodic displays of captured enemy trophies catered to popular fascination with weaponry while also conveying the satisfying subtext that Russia's enemies could indeed be beaten.

Creative artists donated their talents by designing the posters that advertised collections, bazaars, and other undertakings; contributing their work to exhibits and auctions; or performing for the wounded or in benefit shows. The Petrograd Society of Writers for the Benefit of War Victims hosted an evening of readings called "Poetry and the War" in late 1914, also publishing war verse by Fedor Sologub and other luminaries, with proceeds going to war relief.[81] In March 1916, the Union "Artists of Moscow to the Russian Army and Victims of War," raised almost 52,000 rubles by staging forty-six "flying concerts" in cafes and restaurants

---

[78] Jahn, *Patriotic Culture*, 39, 86–90, 100–02, 158.

[79] *Kievlianin'* (September 1, 1914), 3. On the Dolina concerts, see Jahn, *Patriotic Culture*, 116–18, who notes that she was the daughter of an army officer and had become an active promoter of national music long before the war.

[80] *Russkii invalid* (November 20, 1914), 5, and *Kievlianin'* (February 21, 1915), 5. A number of villages in Viatka province staged performances, with proceeds going to the war effort; see Aaron B. Retish, *Russia's Peasants in Revolution and Civil War: Citizenship, Identity, and the Creation of the Soviet State, 1914–1922* (Cambridge: Cambridge University Press, 2008), 25.

[81] *Russkie vedomosti* (January 1, 1915), 9.

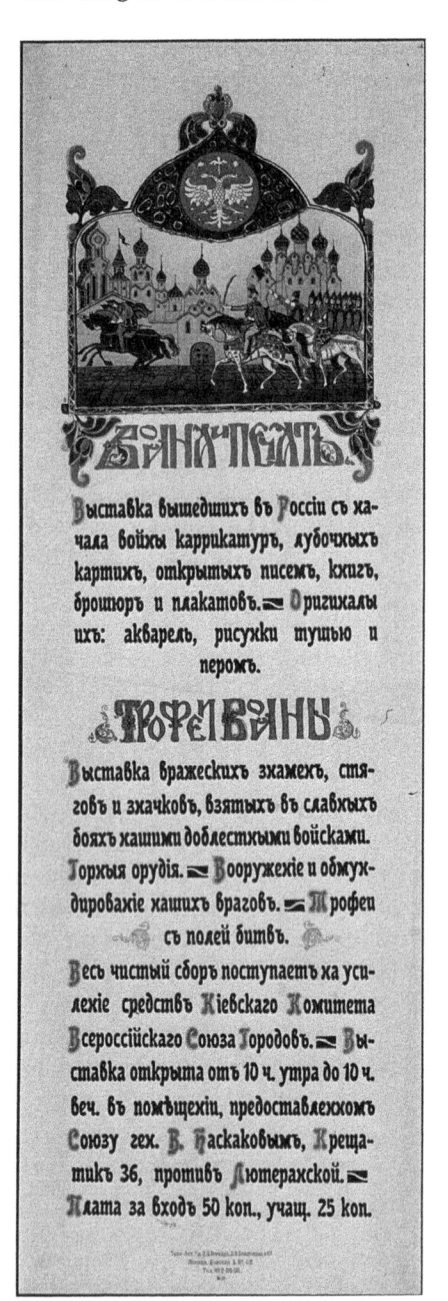

4.4 A poster depicting the heroic feat of Sister of Mercy Rimma Ivanovna during battle, in 1915; inspiring images of Sisters of Mercy were ubiquitous in wartime Russia. Political Poster Collection, #RU/SU 353, Courtesy of Hoover Institution Library & Archives, Stanford University.

"All for the War!" 133

around the city over the course of two days.[82] The number of benefit evenings could in fact become exhausting, given that there continued to be benefits for worthy causes *not* related to the war. In a three-month period in 1915, Petrograd mayor Tol'stoi noted in his diary his attendance at thirteen concerts, literary-musical evenings, and public lectures to benefit soldiers, Muslims of the Caucasus, Poles, Armenians, Jews, and Belgians, among others. Small wonder that after making his donation he sometimes slipped out during the intermission.[83]

The media was also attentive to humble donations, since an important trope of the patriotic narrative concerned the all-class nature of wartime giving. Invoking the 1812 Fatherland War, this conflict, too, was characterized as a "people's war," one which the whole people – not just the wealthy – helped support. We see this claim advanced in articles, editorials, and the literature of semi-official and voluntary organizations. The 1915 report of the Union of Zemstvos, for example, praised the ready sympathy of the entire national community in aiding the troops and victims of war: "100,000-ruble donations alongside those in kopeks express the great upsurge of *all* the Russian people, who thirst to lighten the suffering of their brother-soldiers." A newspaper brief on gifts to the Latvian Committee for refugee relief concluded that "judging by the dimensions of donations, the impulse has seized everyone. The highest figure is 3,000 rubles, the donation of O. I. Zubalova, and alongside it are modest sums in kopeks, brought by the compassionate common people of Moscow."[84] Periodicals reported on the generosity of the urban working class, such as the impressive sums collected by workers at the Petrograd Metallurgical Factory and the workers and employees of the Okhtenskii Factory in Petrograd in 1915 to buy Christmas presents for the troops.[85]

---

[82] *Russkie vedomosti* (April 8, 1916), 4 (April 13, 1916), 4, and L. Iu Rakhmanova and A. V. Rumanov, *V god voiny. Sbornik artist soldatu* (Petrograd: V tip. Akts. obshch. tipografskogo dela, 1915).
[83] Tol'stoi, *Dnevnik*, II, esp. 680, 684, 692, 713, 722, 727, 731.
[84] *Vserossiiskii zemskii soiuz. Obzor deiatel'nosti*, 296 (emphasis added), and "Chastnaia lepta," *Russkoe slovo* (July 30, 1915), 5.
[85] "Rozhdestvennye podarki voinam" and "Podarki rabochikh Okhtenskogo zavoda," *Gazeta-kopeika* (December 15, 1915), 3, and (January 7, 1916), 3. Collecting Easter presents for soldiers was also popular: "Rabochie v okopakh. (S podarkami v Svetlyi prazdnik)," *Russkii rabochii* (April 10, 1916), 3. An unpublished example comes from Mayor Tol'stoi: waiting with other dignitaries to greet a train of disabled Russian POWs returning from Germany, he was approached by a delegation of workers from a Petrograd cartridge factory, asking him to distribute the money they had brought for these disabled soldiers. "I shook hands with each one of them and in my greeting to the arriving men, drew attention to this [donation]": Tol'stoi, *Dnevnik*, II, entry of September 2, 1915, 803–04.

Peasant giving often took the form of food or material items, or taking in refugees or soldiers' orphans. A rare record of such giving comes from the diary of A. A. Zamaraev, a peasant farmer of Tot'ma, in the northern province of Vologda. On November 23, 1914. he noted: "Today I bought a water-proofed shirt for sending along with other things to the army. In the first half of November we took 50,000 prisoners and 600 officers." His entry for February 6, 1915, reads, "There was a collection in town for wounded soldiers, they went around on horses, it's said that they collected a lot." On December 15 of that year he wrote, "Again cold and clear. I went to the forest, then in the evening went to town and bought tobacco, paper, pencils, and envelopes as Christmas presents for soldiers in the active army."[86] The press praised peasant generosity, which could be interpreted as proof that the people did indeed "care about state interests."[87]

Although comprehensive figures for wartime giving do not exist, considerable anecdotal evidence documents a national outpouring of aid. Newspaper editorial offices often acted as collection points for war causes; since many papers published accounts of donations received, we can glean from them some sense of the nature of giving. In March 1915, for instance, the nationalist organ *Kievlianin'* published a list of 14,973 rubles in donations sent to its offices for fifteen wartime causes over a seven-month period. Donations made by individuals were mostly in the range of 1 to 5 rubles, with the rare individual donation of a sum as big as 25 rubles. Many donations were made collectively, by the employees of a business or office, or a group of artisans or workers.[88] Much the same picture of giving comes from the mass-circulation daily *Russkoe slovo* and the penny press, though donations to the latter were often measured in kopeks rather than rubles.[89] Occasionally, lists provide the geographic origins of the contributions, an example coming from *Russkoe slovo* in July 1915 for a campaign to buy gas masks for the troops.

---

[86] Morozov and Reshetnikov, eds., *Dnevnik totemskogo krest'ianina*, 95, 101, 121.

[87] For example, A. Borisov, "Vnutrennye dela i voprosy," *Russkie zapiski* no. 2 (December 1914), 336–75, and "Krest'ianskaia pomoshch'," *Malenkaia gazeta* (October 1, 1914), 2. A writer in the Far Eastern city of Khabarovsk insisted that all the fundraisers organized and donations made by humble citizens showed that the Russian public was "passing the exam" in civic maturity: N. S. Aref'ev, "Ekzamen na obshchestvennuiu zrelost'. Obshchestvennaia samodeiatel'nost' i voina," *Den' pechati* (Khabarovsk) (June 30, 1915), 4.

[88] *Kievlianin'* (March 5, 1915), 4; I have omitted kopeks from these figures.

[89] *Russkoe slovo* ran a monthly summary of donations sent to the paper, and their intended causes; see, for example, the issues of (October 20, 1915), 6, and (November 26, 1915), 6. *Gazeta-kopeika* sometimes published the notes readers sent in with their modest donations; for example, "Podarok voinam ot chitatelei 'Gazety-Kopeiki'" (December 22, 1914), 2.

"All for the War!" 135

4.5 This 1916 Calendar, passed out by a rural credit co-operative, features drawings of rural people aiding the war effort in a variety of ways, including making boots for the army and sending gifts to soldiers. Political Poster Collection, #RU/SU 1091, Courtesy of Hoover Institution Library & Archives, Stanford University.

Over the course of two days, readers sent in a total of 1,733 rubles from dozens of locales across the country, including Ufa, Kurgan, Riazan, Tashkent, Kokand, Petropavlovsk, and Mariupol.[90]

Despite seasonal ups and downs, levels of giving appear to have been high well into spring 1916. Donations to the Union of Zemstvos and the Union of Cities, for example, increased fairly steadily through the first six months of the war.[91] Many war-related causes saw a worrisome drop in early 1915, but the military setbacks of late spring and summer regalvanized public giving, particularly for the tidal wave of refugees created by the German–Austrian offensive and Russia's Great Retreat.[92] In fact, the Union of Cities reported its largest numbers of donations for the entire war period in August and September 1915. Swelling numbers of Russian POWs also prompted increased donations.[93] Another indication of sustained support is the ongoing success of Mariia Dolina's patriotic concerts. Dolina raised a total of 304,178 rubles through 162 concerts. We do not have exact figures for every concert, but that of December 23, 1914, for the Black Sea Fleet, realized 2,228 rubles and that of January 3, 1916, benefiting the charitable society "National Ring," realized 1,868 rubles, suggesting a fairly consistent level of attendance.[94]

But as remarkable as was the durability of wartime giving in Russia, donor fatigue inevitably set in. Again, our evidence is fragmentary. One set of statistics comes from the province of Kaluga. In the thirteen-month period from December 1, 1914, to December 31, 1915, Kaluzhans donated 4,718 rubles to local infirmaries treating wounded soldiers,

---

[90] "Na protivogazy," *Russkoe slovo* (July 5, 1915), 6. This list reflected donations reaching the paper on June 23 and 24, which brought the grand total for gas-mask donations to 13,786 rubles.

[91] *Vserossiiskii zemskii soiuz. Obzor deiatel'nosti*, 396. August 1914 was actually the largest month for donations, at 253,079 rubles, but 200,000 rubles of that sum came from the extraordinary one-time donation of millionaire industrialist S. Morozov. If that single donation is excluded, the monthly upward trend of donations is clear: *Izvestiia Vserossiiskogo soiuza gorodov* (March 1916), 196–98.

[92] For example, the Petrograd correspondent of one paper noted in early June that people still gave to all sorts of wartime causes, "but one doesn't see the enthusiasm of the first few months": "Petrogradskie otkliki," *Kievlianin'* (June 4, 1915), 3. See also V. Kuzmin-Karavaev, "Khronika," *Vestnik Evropy* (June 1915), 357–58, who was confident that the big drop in yields for war-related collections in Petrograd reflected an exhaustion of resources rather than a decline in patriotism. For the Union of Zemstvos, the overall total of monetary donations for February through December 1915 was 640,000 rubles, which is comparable to roughly 460,000 rubles (excluding the Morozov donation) for the first six months of the war.

[93] "Sbor 'Petrograd-bezhentsam,'" *Gazeta-kopeika* (October 1, 1915), 3; Borodin, "Organizatsii pomoshchi," 395–96.

[94] "Material'noi itog 38-mi patrioticheskikh kontsertov," *Gazeta-kopeika* (December 31, 1914), 4, and "Patrioticheskii kontsert," *Novoe vremia* (February 2, 1916), 2.

"All for the War!" 137

but gave only 965 rubles to those institutions in all of 1916.[95] In late 1916, the Holy Synod began turning down requests for permission to hold various war-relief collections after Sunday services, explaining that the multitude of collections was exhausting parishioners' capacities. Russians still managed to dig deeper into their pockets to give money for war orphans or for Christmas presents for the troops in 1916, but the worsening inflation that undercut the buying power of the sums donated also made it increasingly difficult for many sectors of the population to give.[96]

Whatever the sums or labor donated, wartime giving and the publicity it received made three significant contributions to patriotic culture. The massive reporting on war relief in the periodical press helped tie the national community together spatially, providing a positive image of generosity and service occurring everywhere in Russia. Besides its encompassing geographic dimension, this generosity was shown to be organized from below as well as from above, and to come from different classes and national groups.[97] It therefore contributed powerfully to the narrative of a patriotic citizenry that was not only united but conscious and active. The portrayal of unstinting generosity also presented a positive national image that had deep cultural roots. As Adele Lindenmeyr notes in her study of charity in imperial Russia, the Russian Orthodox Church fostered "a self-conscious ideology of Russians' exceptional benevolence, which it linked to a vision of national identity." Russians practiced true compassion for the unfortunate; theirs was a culture of giving.[98] During the Great War, that benevolence was shown to be characteristic of all patriotic Russians, in the broad (*rossiiskii*) rather than ethnic (*russkii*) sense of the word.

Gifts, supplies, and letters sent to the troops also helped consolidate the bond between the motherland and those sent to fight for it. That "motherland" (*rodina*), in Russian parlance, might be a regional or "small" one – cities or provinces took particular care of "their" regiments – but could also signify the nation writ large. In turn, men at

---

[95] I. S. Pisarneko, N. S. Voshchenkova et al., *Blagotvoritel'nye organizatsii kaluzhskoi gubernii v gody Pervoi mirovoi voiny* (Kaluga, 2001), 22–23, 46; this decline in giving did not reflect declining numbers of patients: nearly 37,000 wounded soldiers had passed through Kaluga by the end of 1915, but that figure had jumped to 97,703 by late June 1917.

[96] RGIA, f. 796, op. 198, otd. 1, st. 5, d. 329, "O proizvodstve v tserkvakh sborov na nuzhdy voennogo vremeni" (November 9, 1916), l. 191.

[97] Contemporaries often saw the generosity of peasant giving as proof that the mass of the population *did* "care about the interests of the state": A. Borisov, "Vnutrennye dela i voprosy," *Russkie zapiski* no. 2 (December 1914), 336–75.

[98] Lindenmeyr, *Poverty Is Not a Vice*, 7–8.

the front sent back letters of thanks; frequently, these were directed to newspaper or journal offices and published, allowing givers to see that their contributions had reached the troops and were valued by them. We also have a few private descriptions of the impact made by gifts and letters from the home front. One particularly eloquent example comes from a letter signed "Evgenii," sent from the army to one Colonel S. I. Sipiagin in Moscow, and intercepted by the police, in early 1915:

> The broad river of willing donations that flows unceasingly from Russia supplies us in abundance not only with everything necessary, but also with articles of luxury. Let them know in Russia that an army which finds in society and the people such tremendous moral support can't help but be strong in spirit, can't help but be victorious. All the difficulties and deprivations and even torment from wounds and illness disappear in the sea of love and sympathy expressed to us in the millions of letters from Russia.[99]

Conclusions

Surveying the effects of six months of war, in January 1915 *Derevenskaia gazeta* hailed a new era in Russian history: "The Petersburg period of Russian history has concluded and the Petrograd period has begun. At its basis lie these long- desired and henceforth acknowledged foundations: national consciousness, cultural self-determination, the independent activity of society."[100] As this statement suggests, many people regarded the vast effort of war relief, which joined grass-roots activism with state and religious efforts, as something profoundly new in Russia, part of the transformative effect of the Great War. Working and sacrificing for the nation's cause was proof positive of the patriotism of the entire population.

On one level, at least, people were right to interpret the sustained effort of war relief as a gauge of patriotism pure and simple. Social pressure to give certainly played a part, but ultimately loyalties to and a sense of belonging within the national community helped nourish the ongoing effort and sacrifice of war relief, which in turn helped consolidate that sense of far-flung community. Generous support of a whole slew of war-related causes contributed to the self-conception of a uniquely generous and compassionate Russian nation. Participation in war relief, the creation of networks for administering it, and the media's extensive reporting on it all helped unite the nation spatially – aid for the

---

[99] GARF, f. 102, op. 265, d. 1042, letter of 2 January 1915 from "Evgenii" to Polkovnik S. I. Sipiagin in Moscow, l. 129.
[100] "Vnutrenniaia politika Rossii v 1914 g." *Derevenskaia gazeta* no. 1 (January 1915), 12.

common cause was seen to come from everywhere in Russia, and from every category of the population.

Service and sacrifice for the war effort also mobilized expectations. People from the educated and property-owning classes anticipated that the public's patriotic labors, and that of their representatives in the Duma, would result in broader scope for public initiative with the winning of the peace. Certain social estates and professional groups believed, consciously or otherwise, that they would accrue political capital through their work for the war effort, and with it the opportunity to protect or advance their interests. And subsets of the population with access to only limited rights of citizenship, such as women and many national minorities, hoped that by demonstrating their loyalty, competence, and civic "maturity" through war work they would win full inclusion in the national community as well as greater rights at war's end.

In this way, the language of citizenship joined the language of sacrifice and giving as a constitutive element of the war's patriotic discourse. With the constant references to duty and obligation, the concept of wartime relief was also transitioning from notions of charity to those of rights, at least in the person of the defender of the motherland: those who were asked to make the supreme sacrifice for the nation had unique reciprocal claims upon it. Soldiers, and the honor and rights due to them, are the subject of the next chapter.

5 United in Gratitude
Honoring Soldiers and Defining the Nation

> In the Japanese war, soldiers were sent off to fight. In this war, citizens have gone to defend their fatherland.
>
> "Dve Rossii," *Russkoe slovo* (October 17, 1915), 1

The huge social dislocations and enormous casualties that accompanied the outbreak of the first total war required powerful public and state responses. Millions of conscripted men needed reassurance that the sacrifices they and their families had made did not go unnoticed, and that such sacrifices had meaning. Tens of thousands of grieving families sought consolation for their losses. As the war dragged on, local and national communities needed to reaffirm their unity and will to continue the fight. For these reasons, public recognition of citizen soldiers' service and sacrifice became practical and moral imperatives. Moreover, identifying such service and sacrifice, investing it with a particular meaning, and involving the public in commemorating and honoring it were all potentially powerful means of promoting patriotism and a common sense of the nation. As Jay Winter has argued of the war in general, after August 1914 the very act of commemoration was an act of citizenship: "To remember was to affirm community, to assert its moral character, and to exclude from it those values, groups, or individuals that placed it under threat."[1]

Virtually every belligerent nation of the war created ways to recognize and honor the citizen in arms; Russia was no exception, though these efforts have been largely forgotten. In addition to the great outpouring of war relief and charity on the part of individual Russians and their organizations, private and state initiatives produced three innovative projects to honor, memorialize, and reward the defenders of the motherland. These projects represent another embodiment, however imperfect, of the wartime narrative of sacred union. Examining them, and the diverse

---

[1] Jay Winter, *Sites of Memory, Sites of Mourning: The Great War In European Cultural Memory* (Cambridge: Cambridge University Press, 1995), 80.

motives underlying them, also allows us to explore the intertwining in Russia of notions of patriotism, citizenship, and membership in the national community. As will become evident, formal and informal appraisals of the soldier's wartime performance of duty were closely tied to discussion of what was therefore owed *him* by the state and his fellow citizens. In this way, a key component of the modern understanding of citizenship, as entailing rights as well as obligations, equal for all and guaranteed by law, was disseminated and enmeshed with ideas of the patriotic national community.

Obligations Owed Every (Worthy) Soldier

In the decade following the abolition of serfdom, Russia moved closer to European practices on universal male military service by introducing much broader conscription. But it was only after the debacle against Japan that military reformers gained greater support for their efforts to more thoroughly modernize the Russian army, and make it a truly national one. A national army was not only *of* the nation, and imbued with loyalty to it; it should also be embraced and supported by the nation. Major military reforms passed in 1912 abolished all sorts of previous exemptions to the 1874 law on military service, so that bearing arms for Russia became a much more nearly universal, national obligation.[2] In their provisions on material support the 1912 reforms also reflected the new thinking on the need to support Russia's defenders: the treasury would fully fund pensions for disabled soldiers, and during wartime every soldier's family would be entitled to receive state aid.

A key innovation of the law on family aid was its inclusive nature, since eligibility was not dependent on a family's economic circumstances. This provision for universal assistance replaced a more traditional and selective conception of state assistance to soldiers' wives (*soldatki*), one that looked on aid as charity for the impoverished. As Emily E. Pyle has demonstrated in her study of this important legislation, the Duma's bill on aid to families was informed by the conviction that wartime assistance must be extended as a legal right due all soldiers in return for sacrifices on behalf of the state. By making state aid to families an entitlement that soldiers earned by virtue of serving, rather than assistance benevolently

---

[2] On military elites' deliberately nationalizing project in making military service more universal, see William Fuller, *Civil–Military Conflict in Imperial Russia, 1881–1914* (Princeton: Princeton University Press, 1985), 197, 243–44, and Sanborn, *Drafting the Russian Nation*, 6–14, 20–38. Pockets of exemption from service remained, and during the war were greatly resented, the Mennonites and the Central Asian Muslim nomads being two such cases.

extended, and by making aid universal rather than something offered selectively, this legislation created an obligation of the state to its defenders that had not previously existed in imperial Russia.[3] And, though legislators did not frequently employ the term "citizen" (*grazhdanin*) in their debates over this provision, what was being created was clearly a right of citizenship: the universality of the military obligation required from the state a similarly universal and equal provision of aid to the family of the mobilized soldier.

Among the elite and educated classes, acceptance of aid as a right owed citizens subject to universal military conscription was broad-based, cutting across political orientations. As one letter to the nationalist *Kievlianin'* said of wartime assistance, "there could be no second opinion" on helping soldiers' families – this was part of the "common civic obligation" (*obshchegrazhdanskaia povinnost'*).[4] Or, as another writer put it in 1916, "Each fighting man going into battle with the enemy should have only one duty – his duty in relation to the Motherland. His duty in relation to his family the Motherland has taken upon herself."[5]

Popular awareness of the new right to state aid was probably not widespread until the outbreak of war and the start of mass mobilization, when more than 8.3 million close relatives of soldiers began receiving aid in the *first month* of hostilities.[6] Additionally, the authorities expended great effort in acquainting soldiers' families with their claims upon state support. One of the first and largest efforts of the new Committee for Popular Publications was the pamphlet "Aid to Soldiers' Families," which had an astonishingly large print run of some 3 million copies.[7] Intended for distribution at the front and among reservists, it explains in detail the unprecedented government support and services offered to soldiers' families during wartime, including the monthly stipends (*paiki*) due the members of soldiers' households, reduced rates for railroad travel, home fuel assistance, education opportunities for soldiers' children, and survivors' pensions. The pamphlet also enumerates additional

---

[3] Emily E. Pyle, "Village Social Relations and the Reception of Soldiers' Family Aid Policies in Russia, 1912–1921"(Ph.D. Diss., University of Chicago, 1997).

[4] *Kievlianin'* (August 22, 1914), 4.   [5] Runkevich, *Velikaia otechestvennaia voina*, 16, 21.

[6] According to figures used by the Council of Ministers, 8,387,000 soldiers' relatives had a right to the monthly state stipend as of late August 1914, with another 1,050,000 becoming eligible by September 17 as mobilization continued: RGIA, f. 1276, op. 10, d. 747 (1914), "Ob otpuske kredita na prizrenie semeistv...," ll. 1, 3.

[7] "Pomoshch' soldatskim sem'iam" (1914) and the revised version by M. Pletnev, "Popechenie o soldatskikh sem'iakh," (1915), RGIA, f. 1276, op. 11, d. 1418, ll. 23–24 and 39–42; 800,000 copies of the first printing were sent directly to soldiers in the regular army.

support and services provided by charitable committees and by members of society, from the exalted to the humble.[8]

One goal of the pamphlet was to assuage soldiers' concerns about their loved ones by showing the enormous scope of the aid undertaking, as well as to reinforce the image of the benevolence of tsar and state.[9] Its detailing of the broad, supra-class support for soldiers' families also implicitly played to the narrative of sacred union, reminding men in arms that a united, national community stood behind them and was doing its part, too. Perhaps the most striking feature of this pamphlet, however, was its message that all this support was not simply a manifestation of paternalistic goodwill, but what soldiers had a *right* to expect from their government and fellow citizens, based upon the provisions of the 1912 law.[10] Commercially published newspapers and periodicals, along with government-subsidized papers, reinforced this message, widely disseminating information about the legal rights to state aid and also informing readers about the panoply of public and private services available to defenders of the fatherland and to their families.[11]

The degree to which rank-and-file soldiers and their families internalized the idea of aid as a legally guaranteed right is difficult to gauge. A batch of twenty-one petitions for state aid from soldiers' families in Riazan province shows that most of the petitioners looked upon aid traditionally, as a form of charity extended to the needy, rather than laying claim to aid as a legal right owed them by the state.[12] In contrast, two studies of the behavior of soldiers' wives in wartime subsistence riots suggest an internalized sense of entitlement vis-à-vis the state on the part of *soldatki*, who called for larger stipends or better access to consumer goods as the war dragged on. These women in part justified their demands on the traditional basis of material need, but they also

---

[8] RGIA, f. 1276, op. 11, d. 1418, "Pomoshch'," l. 23.
[9] RGIA, f. 1276, op. 11, d. 1418, "Popechenie," l. 41.
[10] RGIA, f. 1276, op. 11, d. 1418, "Pomoshch'," l. 23.
[11] See *Novoe vremia* (July 25, 1914), 1, (July 27, 1914), 5, *Russkii invalid* (July 22, 1914), 2, and the two-part article by N. Beliavskii, "Pomoshch' voiskam i ikh sem'iam" (September 30 and October 1, 1914), 3 and 3. Shortly after the outbreak of war, *Sel'skii vestnik* began a regular column called "Aid to Troops and Their Families": see, for example, issues of September 16, 1914, 3, and May 2, 1915, 3.
[12] On these petitions, see Pyle, "Village Social Relations," 242, 270, 277. Petitions, however, constitute a rather unique body of literature, one whose traditional rhetorical strategies might continue to be employed even as the petitioner's own self-conception changed or was changing. See, for example, Golfo Alexopoulos's fascinating analysis of petitions for reinstatement of rights made by outcast Soviet citizens: Alexopoulos, *Stalin's Outcasts: Aliens, Citizens, and the Soviet State, 1926–1936* (Ithaca: Cornell University Press, 2003), 99–102, 115–25.

understood material considerations as something owed them because of their husbands' service and sacrifice for the fatherland.[13]

Even as the civilian authorities worked to disseminate the connection between bearing arms for the motherland and earning a right to state assistance for one's family, military authorities began to press for the negative realization of this reciprocal relationship: families of soldiers who served dishonorably should not receive state aid. The military was not considering soldiers' claims upon the state in the abstract – in the spring of 1915, as cases of Russian soldiers voluntarily surrendering to the enemy assumed alarming proportions, the General Staff urgently sought ways to discourage this dangerous phenomenon. If a soldier's meritorious service earned a right to state assistance, the authorities reasoned, failure to perform one's duty should terminate that assistance; while the 1912 law did not explicitly state this to be the case, they believed the intention was to care only for families of "worthy defenders of the state."[14] The Council of Ministers agreed with the recommendations of the General Staff, on March 27, 1915, determining that the families of lower-rank soldiers who voluntarily surrendered to the enemy or deserted would be deprived of their stipends. Further, the new rules stipulated that accounts of the disgraceful behavior of such soldiers were to be broadly disseminated in their villages or home towns, for such conduct "lays a stigma on their families as well."[15]

Deprivation of rights to state aid, along with public shaming, was meant to deter dereliction of duty, in part by legally and symbolically excluding the unworthy soldiers' families from the true national community. This extreme measure – which not surprisingly lent itself to overzealous application and abuses – came on the heels of a decree which physically excluded from the community those soldiers who had failed their country and fellow citizens. In early March Nicholas II decreed that soldiers who voluntarily surrendered to the enemy would

---

[13] Barbara Alpern Engel, "Not by Bread Alone: Subsistence Riots in Russia during World War I," *Journal of Modern History* 69, 4 (December 1997), 721, and Mark Baker, "Rampaging *Soldatki*, Cowering Police, Bazaar Riots and Moral Economy: The Social Impact of the Great War in Kharkiv Province," *Canadian–American Slavic Studies* 35 (2001), 137–55.

[14] RGVIA, f. 2003, op. 2, d. 784, Memo of 19 March 1915 from the Bureau of Pensions to the Staff of the Supreme Command, ll. 13–14.

[15] RGVIA, f. 2003, op. 2, d. 784, Memo of 29 April 1915 from the Ministry of the Interior to Chief of Staff N. N. Ianushkevich, ll. 17, 20, and letter of General M. V. Alekseev to the Minister of War of 22 December 1915, l. 50. It had already been decreed on March 9, 1915, that lower-rank soldiers who voluntarily surrendered would be sent to Siberia upon their return to Russia, but such a fate could obviously appear too distant and uncertain to deter desertion.

be sent to Siberia upon their return from captivity. As a *prikaz* (order) of June 14, 1915, to the troops explained, voluntary surrender was a shameful act of treason and "Traitors [*izmenniki*] will be given no mercy. Only those who are prepared to fight for her to the end should be allowed to live in the Russian land."[16]

Memorializing Fallen Soldiers

In the nineteenth century, as George Mosse, Jay Winter, and other scholars have noted, war memorials became an important means by which the state and society promoted national identity, national unity, and the idea of the worthiness of sacrificing oneself to save one's country. It was not the case until the Great War, however, that the idea of memorializing every single fallen soldier, no matter how humble his rank, came into currency. France passed a law creating military cemeteries as early as 1914; in mid 1915 Britain established a special commission on burials, and in fall 1915 Germany established regulations on caring for war graves in perpetuity.[17]

Planning to commemorate the fallen was one area in which Russia did not lag behind the other European powers. Exactly two months after the start of the war Nicholas II approved a proposal of the Aleksandrovskii Committee – a semi-official body traditionally concerned with the welfare of wounded and disabled soldiers – to perpetuate the memory of victims of the current war by setting aside lands for fraternal cemeteries (*bratskie kladbishchi*), erecting tablets in parish churches inscribed with the names of the fallen soldiers, and building memorials in their home towns. City governments and zemstvos in Arkhangelsk, Novgorod, Poltava, and Kharkov provinces, as well as the two capitals, responded generously to the committee's appeal, setting aside land and funds for war cemeteries and memorials.[18] As we have seen, in September 1914 the Holy Synod had instituted a new form of memorialization by instructing all churches in the empire to celebrate a weekly requiem for

---

[16] RGVIA, f. 2003, op. 2, d. 784, ll. 52, 116, and 126, "No. 559, Prikaz voiskam armii, 14 June 1915"; by September 1915, internal memos were already complaining of overzealous extension of this measure to families of soldiers who had been taken prisoner against their will.

[17] On Britain, see Catherine Moriarty, "Private Grief and Public Remembrance: British First World War Memorials," in Martin Evans and Ken Lunn, *War and Memory in the Twentieth Century* (Oxford: Berg, 1997), 125–42; for Germany, see Mosse, *Fallen Soldiers*, 80, who holds that "the war cemetery was central to the cult of the fallen soldier."

[18] RGVIA, f. 2003 (Stavka), op. 2, d. 36, "Aleksandrovskii komitet," l. 2.

fallen soldiers, for the duration of the war. Religious authorities and parish clergy also took an active part in the Aleksandrovski Committee's commemorative efforts, working with it to raise funds and organize placement of inscribed tablets in parish churches.[19]

Private citizens came forward with their own proposals. In September, several Petrograd families who had already lost loved ones in the war approached the municipal authorities with a request that they set aside a parcel of land to establish a "Field of Honor" cemetery for fallen heroes. Remains of Petrograd's fallen soldiers could be repatriated home for burial there, and the new space would also accommodate soldiers who died in the city's many war hospitals. The military newspaper *Russkii invalid* printed in full a reader's elaborate plan for a memorial "Temple of Russian Glory" that combined commemorative, educational, and practical features. N. M. Shugurov's envisioned complex would include a war museum and library, a cathedral named for St. George the Victorious, a home for disabled soldiers, and a military school for the orphaned sons of the fallen. This ensemble would perpetuate for future generations the memory of the heroes of the "Great Patriotic War," he believed, and in doing so would also be a monument to the unification of all Russians that the war had effected, to the "burying of old hatreds and national divisions."[20]

In April 1915, the project of commemorating Russia's fallen soldiers became more genuinely national and better organized with the creation of the "Russian Society for Remembrance of Soldiers of the Russian Army Who Fell in the War [of 1914–16] against Germany, Austria, and Turkey." The Society for Remembrance enjoyed extremely influential backing. General N. V. Ruzskii was its president and the tsar agreed to be its official patron; the governing board was composed of high-ranking officers and government officials, prominent clergy, representatives of the two legislative chambers, and other notables. The primary goals of the society can be divided into two areas, the first of which concerned burial. It would attempt to identify the remains of every fallen soldier insofar as possible, make sure that they were appropriately

---

[19] *Russkii invalid* (September 5, 1914), 2.
[20] *Russkii invalid* (September 12, 1914), 3, (November 19, 1914), 3. In Shugurov's scheme, memorializing soldiers was only one element of a larger memorialization of the war itself; moreover, as his plan suggests, burial grounds and memorials to soldiers were not the only means of preserving the memory of the war. The impulse to collect materials about the war "for posterity" in special museums, libraries, or archives was fairly widespread. Even villages could assemble their own archives of the war, as is outlined by P. N. Luppov, *Chto mogla by sdelat' derevnia dlia sokhraneniia pamiati o Vtoroi otechestvennoi voine* (Petrograd, 1916).

buried – which could include helping create special graveyards – and see to upkeep of cemeteries and communal graves. It would also provide assistance to family members desiring to take a loved one's remains back home for burial. The second goal of the society was to make sure that the memory of the fallen was indeed honored. It proposed that memorials be built – both sacred-symbolic ones at appropriate sites, such as battlefields or cemeteries, and practical ones, such as orphans' homes and hospitals. Annual, commemorative church services should be arranged. Finally, details about the heroic deeds of individuals and units were to be gathered and preserved for posterity.[21]

These efforts could serve several functions. They sacralized the loss of life, making the dead soldier a hero-martyr, and endowed the loss with larger, enduring, national meaning. Families and local communities could in this way take pride in their contribution and be comforted in their loss, while war memorials themselves would provide people places to grieve, both individually and collectively. Efforts to memorialize the patriotic sacrifice of the fallen reassured fighting men that they would be remembered and their effort honored should they not return from the war. For this reason, the Society for Remembrance was particularly concerned that the military authorities publicize its activities among troops at the front, and in June 1916 sent them thousands of copies of its pamphlet on memorialization for distribution to soldiers.[22] Anecdotal evidence from soldiers' letters suggests that such efforts did make an impression. A soldier in the 15th Siberian Rifle Regiment wrote of a future when "a heroic and mighty Russia would be renowned in the whole universe and would remember our heroes who laid down their lives for faith, Tsar, and Fatherland." Similarly, in fall 1916, a soldier wrote to his brother, "To stand up for our tsar and motherland, we may have to lose our young heads for this holy cause, but for centuries they'll remember us with a good word."[23]

The various memorials and acts of collective remembering also had an important "didactic-patriotic significance" (*vospitatel'no-patrioticheskoe znachenie*), as organizers explicitly noted, explaining that they taught

---

[21] RGVIA, f. 2003, op. 2, d. 752, "O strukture i deiatel'nosti Vserossiiskogo obshchestva pamiati voinov Russkoi armii," ll. 42, 63.

[22] RGVIA, f. 2003, op. 2, d. 752, ll. 42–43, letter of 31 July 1916 from society president General N. Ruzskii to General M. V. Alekseev.

[23] Letters read by the military-censorship department for the armies of the southwestern front, quoted in Petrone, *The Great War in Russian Memory*, 168–69. Of course, even soldiers who believed that their sacrifice was both meaningful and appreciated were not eager to make the "supreme sacrifice," and we have no way of determining how many soldiers doubted the value of such a sacrifice.

lessons about love of country and sacrifice to future generations: "We must honor their memory and hold it sacred. We must raise future generations with stories of their feats; by their blood we must consolidate for all time that national unanimity [*edinodushie*] that proclaimed itself from the very first day of the Second Fatherland War."[24]

War memorials, in spelling out who was to be remembered, and how, helped the nation to define its membership. This is how the Society for Remembrance of Fallen Soldiers' public pamphlet put it in an "Appeal to Citizens": "Perpetuating the bright memories of heroes should be a national cause [*delo obshchenarodnoe*]; it should be a united cause accomplished without distinction of religion, estate, or nationality, by the united, miraculously heroic Russian people [*Chudo-Bogatyr' russkii narod*], with the exact same unanimity with which [the people] has repulsed its enemies." In its founding statute, the society stated that it would attempt to seek out, make known, and keep in good order the burial place of *every* fallen soldier, ascertaining insofar as possible the individual's full name, faith, nationality, the name of his unit, and the date of his death. Clearly, the community thus defined was an all-inclusive and in some ways egalitarian one, formed not on an ethnic or religious foundation but on the basis of performed civic duty and sacrifice. Appropriately, membership in the society was similarly inclusive: it was open to all individuals of both sexes regardless of faith, nationality, education, or occupation, as well as to military units and public and private societies and clubs.[25] The Society for Remembrance, in effect, would permanently memorialize the wartime sacred union.

To what degree did the Aleksandrovskii Committee and the Society for Remembrance of Fallen Soldiers achieve their goals? Since most memorialization was envisioned as occurring after the war – as was the case in all the other combatant countries – it is difficult to judge success. In 1919 and 1920, when France, Britain, Germany, and other states began erecting or unveiling memorials by the hundreds, Russia was embroiled in civil war.[26] Subsequently, monuments in Russia would be

---

[24] RGVIA, f. 2003, op. 2, d. 752, "Vozzvanie Vserossiiskogo obshchestva pamiati," l. 45.
[25] RGVIA, f. 2003, op. 2, d. 752, "O strukture i deiatel'nosti Vserossiiskogo obshchestva pamiati voinov Russkoi armii," ll. 43, 45; only citizens of Germany, Austria-Hungary, and Turkey were excluded from membership.
[26] Most memorials were planned and built in the decade after the war: Winter, *Sites of Memory*, 79–85. There were 102 war memorials built in London alone in 1919–21: Mark Connelly, *The Great War, Memory and Ritual: Commemoration in the City and East London, 1916–1939* (London: Royal Historical Society, 2002), 143. For the French experience, see Antoine Prost, "Monuments to the Dead," in Pierre Nora, dir., *Realms*

built to commemorate the Bolshevik victory in that conflict, not to the memory of those who fought in what was now termed the "Imperialist War."[27] However, in 1916 the Society for Remembrance did manage to hold a national competition for memorial designs, in conjunction with the Imperial Society of Architects and Artists, awarding 3,000 rubles in prize money. The Aleksandrovskii Committee in 1914 helped establish a communal plot able to accommodate up to 10,000 soldiers in the Preobrazhenskoe cemetery in Petrograd. In Moscow, it worked with the municipal duma and the Grand Duchess Elizaveta Fedorovna, sister of the empress, to acquire a wooded estate on the city outskirts, the Usadba Golubitskaia, as the site for a fraternal cemetery that opened in February 1915. A small church was built there by private subscription, and in Easter week 1916 – a traditional time in the Russian Orthodox Church for visiting graves – city authorities ran special trains to the cemetery. They also approved plans to erect at the cemetery a large memorial church and war museum, designed by the prominent architect A. V. Shchusev (later selected to design Lenin's tomb); the church was completed, though the museum was not. Outside the capitals, the Aleksandrovskii Committee also helped build a number of soldiers' cemeteries on battlefields and in the provinces, though there is no precise data about these latter sites.[28]

Shortages of money and personnel also hampered efforts to memorialize soldiers. Severe manpower problems in the army's field division of the Military-Scholarly Archive prevented the Society for Remembrance from working with the field division in order to gather information about fallen soldiers. The field division was itself attempting to assemble

---

of Memory: The Construction of the French Past, vol. II, ed. Lawrence D. Kritzman, trans. Arthur Goldhammer (New York, 1998), 307–30. On Belgian memorials, see Laurence van Ypersele, "Making the Great War Great: 1914–1918 War Memorials in Wallonia," in William Kidd and Brian Murdoch, eds., *Memory and Memorials: The Commemorative Century* (Aldershot, UK: Ashgate, 2004), 26–40.

[27] The most detailed treatment of Soviet Russia's uneven effacement of public memory of the war is Petrone, *The Great War in Russian Memory*, esp. 1–30; see also Catherine Merridale, *Night of Stone: Death and Memory in Twentieth-Century Russia* (New York: Penguin, 2001), 96–100, and Aaron J. Cohen, "Oh, That! Myth, Memory, and World War I in the Russian Emigration and the Soviet Union," *Slavic Review* 62, 1 (Spring 2003), 69–86.

[28] RGVIA, f. 2003, op. 2, d. 36, l. 2. Additionally, see "Bratskie kladbishche pamiatnik," *Russkii invalid* (October 22, 1914), 3, and (October 24, 1914), 3; *Russkie vedomosti* (April 7, 1916), 6; and a work written in 1916 but only later published, A. T. Saladin, *Ocherki istorii moskovskikh kladbishch* (Moscow: Izd. "Knizhnyi sad," 1997), 4, 257–58. Karen Petrone discusses further plans for the site, which was to include sculptor I. D. Shadr's "monument to world suffering," thus significantly broadening the memorial scope: Petrone, *The Great War in Russian Memory*, 36–40.

"albums of graves of Russian troops" from the mountains of data it received – also an act of remembrance – but with a staff of exactly three people said it was unable to help the Society for Remembrance by sharing its data.[29]

Recognizing and Rewarding Soldiers

Just as honoring the memory of fallen soldiers could help unite the national community and teach valuable lessons about patriotism and service, so too could recognizing the country's heroes. Publicizing one's heroes occurred everywhere during the war, but the idea of awarding privileges and benefits (*l'goty*) to exceptional sailors and soldiers was a Russian conception that does not appear to have had contemporary parallels among the other European powers. The question of special benefits was taken up several times in Russia during the war, twice by the Council of Ministers in 1915 and at great length by the Committee for St. George Cavaliers (Georgievskii komitet) in early 1916.

The Order of St. George had constituted Russia's highest recognition of personal valor in the armed forces in time of war since 1807. In 1913, in keeping with the spirit of the 1912 military reforms, eligibility for such recognition was significantly widened with creation of the St. George Cross, which could be awarded even to rank-and-file troops. The St. George Cross had a hierarchy of classes, from fourth to first, but all St. George recipients were referred to by the prestigious title of "cavalier" (comparable to the title "chevalier" for members of the French Legion of Honor).[30] In January 1916, thanks to the efforts of Grand Prince Mikhail Aleksandrovich, the Committee for St. George Cavaliers was formally created to attend exclusively to the interest of these heroes. The committee's projects included organizing exhibitions, concerts, and other public fundraisers to support its mission and to raise public consciousness of the cavaliers' deeds, as well as undertaking specific forms of aid, such as sanitariums for sick or wounded cavaliers. The task was a huge one: according to the committee's own estimates, at the start of 1916 there were already 800,000 cavaliers and it was anticipated that by war's end

---

[29] RGVIA, f. 2003, op. 2, d. 752, ll. 33–34, undated response of the field division of the Voenno-uchenyi arkhiv, Western Front, to a letter of May 20, 1916, from the President of the Society for Remembrance.

[30] In 1769, Catherine II created an order named for St. George, which was exclusively for officers; a Mark of Distinction (*znak*) for lower ranks was added in 1807. On the history of the St. George awards, see A. V. Korotkov, "Georgievskie kavalery," *Voenno-istoricheskii zhurnal* no. 11 (1989), 20–22.

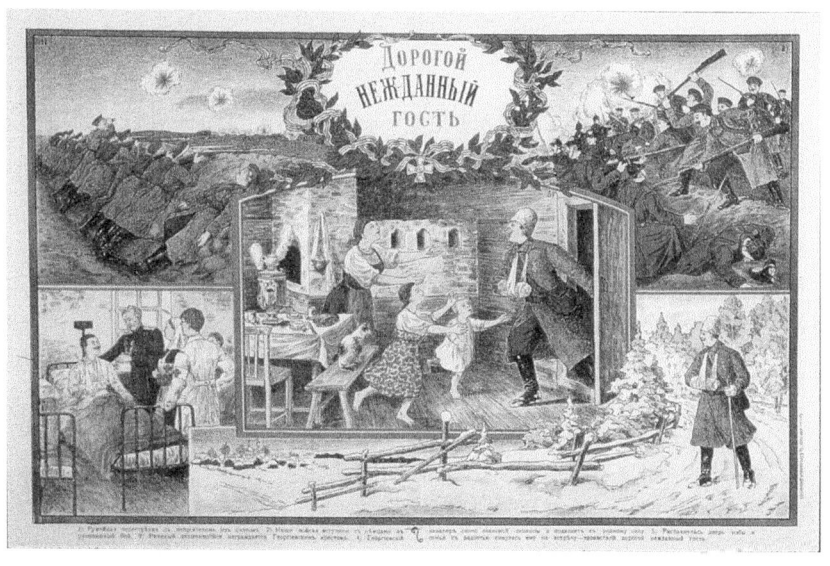

5.1 "Dear Unexpected Guest." This poster conveys the esteem given the country's defenders, depicting a soldier being wounded, cared for in a hospital, awarded a St. George Cross for valor, and returning home to the surprise and delight of his peasant family. Political Poster collection, #RU/SU 684, Courtesy of Hoover Institution Library & Archives, Stanford University.

the number of individuals awarded a St. George distinction of some sort (a medal, a cross, or weapons) would be at least 2.5 million.[31]

The committee's most successful effort in publicizing cavaliers' deeds was an exhibition of trophies of the war. Publicly displaying military trophies in wartime was by no means a new practice in Russia, but the 26-person exhibition committee decided to go beyond the usual static displays in the capitals and also organize a smaller, traveling version. The purpose of the traveling exhibit was to "strengthen in the broad layers of the population consciousness of the importance of concern for the most glorious defenders of the Fatherland." In July 1916, the traveling exhibit went on an extended trip down the Volga, leaving from Petrograd and ending in Astrakhan, stopping at forty-four cities and towns along the

---

[31] RGVIA, f. 29 (Chancellery of the War Minister), op. 3, d. 2549, "Kratkii otchet Georgievskogo komiteta," ll. 9–10. Russia was not nearly as lavish in distributing medals as Germany, which awarded 5.2 million Iron Crosses during the Great War: Holger H. Herwig, *The First World War: Germany and Austria-Hungary, 1914–1918* (London: Arnold, 1997), 192.

5.2 Crowds gather in Petrograd for the formal launch of the St. George Cavaliers traveling exhibition, July 1916, one of the more innovative wartime efforts to celebrate the country's heroes. From *Letopis' voiny*, courtesy of Harvard University.

way. In each town, the exhibit of military trophies was accompanied by popular lectures on the feats of individual cavaliers and units, and the screening of films about the war. The exhibit drew enormous crowds and raised more than 200,000 rubles through the modest entry fees and collections taken in many towns; as organizers proudly noted, realization of such a huge sum from such tiny fees was "proof of how willingly the *narod* visited the exhibition." Every place the exhibit went it evoked local organization of public prayer services, parades, and a plethora of patriotic telegrams. Nicholas was extremely pleased, praising the way the traveling exhibit had "created a new connection between the population and our glorious armies." With the onset of winter, the exhibit was transferred from boats to railroad cars; it was to head out to Siberia and then Turkestan in February 1917.[32]

Another important goal of the committee was to improve the quality of life of St. George Cavaliers. The subcommittee charged with this task

[32] RGVIA, f. 29, op. 3, d. 2549, ll. 8–9, 77; an article publicizing the planned exhibit is in *Sel'skii vestnik* (April 16, 1916), 3.

included members from the Duma, and in 1916 it drafted a bill for submission to the legislature, which would codify in law a series of privileges (*preimushchestva*) and benefits for cavaliers. An explanatory memo accompanying this draft bill provides a fascinating glimpse into what the committee's members believed ought to be done for this group of heroes, and why.

The opening declaration stressed the particularly deserving nature of all the St. George Cavaliers, both officers and lower ranks. Their labor and blood had secured for Russia the possibility of "material development and moral growth," so that they had "a full right to the substantive reward [*nagrada*] of a grateful motherland, quite independent of whether they had lost capacity for productive work." The St. George Cross "gives the fighting man [*voin*] the *right* to a large reward for faithful and distinguished service to the Motherland."[33] This reward could most practically be realized as aid in making a living and, since an estimated 90 percent of soldiers came from the ranks of agriculturalists, that meant above all helping them obtain sufficient land for farming. Such an approach conformed nicely to custom, committee members felt, since "Russian thought instinctively connects participation in a great war with land rewards to its participants." Additionally, the land reward would have a strategic payoff for the state, improving defense of the frontiers by settling ethnic Russians in the borderlands. The St. George Committee noted that, "The present war has graphically demonstrated what harm is done to the state by the absence of the core element of the population in the theaters of war, which nearly always turn out to be the frontiers of the state."[34]

The anticipated basis of the land fund for the St. George Cavaliers would be the properties that enemy aliens were forced to sell by the decrees of February 2, 1915, including the lucrative lands of certain Russian subjects of German origin, the so-called German colonists. (The Council of Ministers, in its 1915 project for land to soldiers, similarly intended to use German colonists' lands.) Monetary supplements were also envisioned, so that the new farmers could be properly set up on their land.[35] Members agreed that nonagriculturalists would receive different sorts of aid and rewards.

---

[33] RGVIA, f. 29, op. 3, d. 2549, "Ob"iasnitel'naia zapiska," l. 105.
[34] RGVIA, f. 29, op. 3, d. 2549, "Ob"iasnitel'naia zapiska," l. 105.
[35] "Ob"iasnitel'naia zapiska," ll. 105–06 (emphasis added); the project of the Council of Ministers is in RGIA, f. 1405, op. 539, d. 779, "Osobyi zhurnal soveta ministrov," 3 March and 17 April 1915, ll. 11–18; on the question of using German colonists' lands to settle ethnic Russians on the borderlands, the council roundly approved "settlement of the western border zone with trustworthy Russian people." For discussion of the expropriation of lands of enemy and Russian subjects, see Chapter 6.

However, the committee's proposals ran up against the limitations of the Russian economy and the large number of heroes to be rewarded. The Resettlement Administration of the Ministry of Agriculture warned that it could settle no more than 200,000–300,000 people per year, at an annual cost of up to 30 million rubles. Thus, taking the committee's own estimate for the number of cavaliers by war's end would mean resettling about 2.5 million men, which would require 8–9 years to realize and some 250 million rubles, a quite fantastic sum considering the other, enormous postwar outlays the state would be confronting. The Council of Ministers had apparently been similarly constrained a year earlier in trying to work out its own land program to reward soldiers. As one minister pointed out in those discussions, at the end of the Russo-Japanese war the council had considered a similar project for giving land to deserving soldiers, mostly in the Far East, but financial issues had prevented most of it from being put into practice.[36] Thus, after much discussion, the committee drafted a very modest bill on recognizing Russia's most heroic soldiers: St. George Cavaliers would be entitled to the status of "honored citizen" (*pochetnyi grazhdanin*); officers would get a good pension; lower ranks would get various forms of assistance and the right to buy land from the Peasant Land Bank at 90 percent of the asking price, with first crack at the choicest lots and with the help of government loans. Several generals who were members of the committee grumbled that offering better terms for purchase of land was in no way an adequate or worthy reward to the "flower and soul of the army," but such were the economic realities: rewarding patriotism was expensive.[37]

Prior to the deliberations of the St. George Committee, Chief of Staff General Nikolai N. Ianushkevich had made a more peremptory demand that soldiers be promised land, one issued in July 1915 as Russia's military reversals assumed catastrophic proportions. His thinking in calling for land for soldiers, and the storm of indignation it evoked in the Council of Ministers, offers another perspective on elite attitudes toward Russian soldiers' understanding of their membership in, and duty to, the nation.

On July 24, 1915, Minister of Agriculture Krivoshein appeared at the meeting of the Council of Ministers in a passionate rage. He informed the council that Stavka (General Headquarters) was demanding immediate

---

[36] RGIA, f. 1405, op. 539, d. 779, l. 18. Lohr, *Nationalizing the Russian Empire*, 108, 120, offers a conservative estimate of 6 million *desiatin* of enemy-alien land explicitly marked for expropriation by early 1917; the Peasant Land Bank had actually acquired only 920,000 *desiatin* by March 1, 1917. Clearly, these lands were insufficient to take care of all eligible heroes. A *desiatina* was equivalent to 2.7 acres.

[37] RGVIA, f. 29, op. 3, d. 2549, "Ob"iasnitel'naia zapiska," ll. 112, 134–35.

promulgation of a decree announcing a generous gift of land – 6–9 *desiatiny* per person– to soldiers who had greatly suffered or greatly distinguished themselves in the war. Since Krivoshein himself had put a very similar proposal to the council just three months earlier, it was not the principle of rewarding deserving soldiers that angered him, but rather the thinking underlying the demand.[38] According to Krivoshein, General Ianushkevich had written him a letter asserting that "fairytale heroes, idealistic soldiers, altruists are encountered very rarely" in the army and that they constituted no more than 1 percent; all the others were thinking of payday. Ianushkevich also maintained that the masses did not understand the idea of fighting for Russia, that a person from Tambov "is ready to stand to the death for Tambov province, but the war in Poland seems strange and unnecessary to him," and that this was why Russian soldiers were surrendering in huge numbers. He concluded from these two circumstances that the Russian soldier required a material interest in resisting the enemy, and that the principal lure should be land allotments. In Krivoshein's angry summation, the opinion of the supreme commander's right-hand man was that "Heroes must be bought."[39]

The minister represented this derogation of Russia's soldiers as basely self-serving: Ianushkevich was trying to shift responsibility for the ongoing military debacle from the high command onto the alleged deficiencies of the rank and file. For Krivoshein, such views called into question the chief of staff's fitness to lead. "How can General

---

[38] In his own 1915 proposal for giving land to soldiers, Krivoshein rejected any conception of benefits for soldiers as some sort of fee for their services, "the very thought of which would be inappropriate" given the enormity of their sacrifice and the depth of their feeling of duty. Rather, benefits should be understood as the state's natural and just concern for the economic needs of its defenders: RGIA, f. 1405, op. 539, d. 779, "Osobyi zhurnal soveta ministrov," l. 13.

[39] Unofficial notes on the council's meetings of summer 1915, taken by Arkadii N. Iakhontov, were later expanded into the piece "Tiazhelye dni," published in *Arkhiv Russkoi revoliutsii*, vol. 18 (Berlin, 1926). I have quoted from the translation by Cherniavsky, *Prologue to Revolution*, "The Meeting of 24 July 1915," 22–23. Iakhontov's original, terser notes for this meeting, and the text of Ianushkevich's letter to Krivoshein, can be found in R. Sh. Ganelin et al., *Sovet ministrov Rossiiskoi imperii v gody Pervoi mirovoi voiny. Bumagi A. N. Iakhontova* (St. Petersburg: "Dmitrii Bulanin," 1999), 203–04, and nn. 285, 401. In the letter itself, Ianushkevich put it this way: "To fight *for Russia* is very idealistic, high-sounding talk, but ... this is theory. People from Tambov will fight when we fall back behind the Dnepr, people from Ufa when we're behind the Volga, and so on. If one promises, on the one hand, the land of the German colonists to the St. George Cavaliers and the wounded; [if one promises] confiscation of land from all those who voluntarily surrender, and transfer of their allotments to those same St. George Cavaliers (and then the St. George Cavaliers will not permit them back and will *demand* their exile to Siberia) – then all will go differently. One must hurry with this. There is still time" (emphasis in the original).

Ianushkevich have the courage to continue to direct military operations when he no longer believes in the army, in the love for the fatherland, in the Russian people? What utter horror!"[40]

Krivoshein's revelations produced general outrage among the ministers. All those who spoke out concurred with his two implicit assumptions: Russian soldiers understood full well that they were fighting for their own country, not some alien entity; and they did not perform their duty to the motherland in expectation of material rewards. The profoundly conservative P. A. Kharitonov declared that, "if Ianushkevich thinks to buy heroes, and only by this method to guarantee the defense of the motherland, there is no place in headquarters for him." Newly appointed Interior Minister N. B. Shcherbatov said scathingly, "one must explain to him (apparently, such aspects of the human soul are not understandable to him) that no one has ever been able to buy heroes, that self-sacrifice and love for the motherland are not commodities. How could such a thought even enter his head?" The moderate and pro-Western foreign minister, Sazonov, similarly rejected Ianushkevich's view that "our soldiers cannot resist, that one must start to form a new army by bribing and luring future heroes."[41]

A second motive probably underlay some of this righteous indignation. Ianushkevich, a xenophobic Russian nationalist, was a driving force behind military policies on mass deportations from the western borderlands of Jews and other "suspect," non-Russian peoples. These brutal measures had seriously swollen the tide of refugees pouring into the heartland, as well as complicating the Russian army's retreat. But despite the fact that Ianushkevich was widely blamed for many of Stavka's poor decisions in 1915, he enjoyed the firm backing of Supreme Commander Grand Duke Nikolai Nikolaevich. According to one well-informed insider, Krivoshein saw in Ianushkevich's politically thoughtless remarks a perfect pretext for trying to remove him and thereby force changes in how Stavka conducted the war; all the other ministers, save Prime Minister Goremykin, supported Krivoshein's view.[42]

But even given such calculations, the minutes of this meeting convey quite genuine outrage at Ianushkevich for scapegoating Russia's soldiers with his claim that they did not feel themselves part of a national community for which they were willing to fight to the end. As we have seen, the council agreed in 1915 to approve draconian measures against

---

[40] Cherniavsky, "The Meeting of 24 July 1915," 23–24.   [41] Ibid., 24–26.
[42] Baron B. E. Nol'de, *Dalekoe i blizkoe. Istoricheskie ocherki* (Paris: Sovremennye zapiski, 1930), 127–30. On the unsavory figure of Ianushkevich, see Lohr, *Nationalizing the Russian Empire*, 130–34, 137–44.

"unworthy" soldiers, in an effort to stop the high rates of surrender that had prompted Ianushkevich's proposal on land, but privately the council shifted blame for the surrenders from the soldiers themselves to the incompetence of the high command. To the ministers, at least, it seemed clear that ordinary soldiers were not deficient in bravery or national commitment, but rather that their superiors' blunders had put them in an unbearable position. A "person from Tambov" indeed knew himself to be a Russian, and understood he was defending his motherland.

These various perspectives on recognizing and rewarding soldiers for outstanding service illustrate a number of important points. Two similar proposals to earmark land for especially deserving soldiers were endorsed in principle by two separate bodies, the St. George Committee in 1916 and the Council of Ministers in 1915 (though neither was eventually implemented). Both groups were informed by the belief that outstanding service to and sacrifice for the motherland give a *right* to tangible reward, but also by the belief that soldiers do not fight in expectation of such reward but rather act upon love of country.

Two other, less positive assumptions expressed by the St. George Committee, and shared by the Council of Ministers, reveal the more problematic aspects of envisioning a united national community in a multinational polity. First, their enthusiasm for settling the "core population" in the borderlands shows doubts as to whether the ethnically non-Russian population really was as patriotic as the Russians, and thus as prepared to defend the frontiers. Second, both groups assumed that the main source of land to be awarded to outstanding soldiers would be the properties enemy aliens *and* Russia's German colonists were being forced to relinquish: that is, they were quite comfortable with the principle of using land virtually expropriated from those excluded from membership in the patriotic and loyal nation to reward exemplary defenders of the nation.

There was also an exception to the broader efforts to recognize and publicize heroes: the differential treatment of Jewish heroism undercut the national inclusiveness of such efforts. From the early days of the war, progressive and liberal newspapers discovered that military censors often prevented mention of Jewish soldiers' bravery in print. In some cases, the portraits of Jewish recipients of the St. George Cross could not be published, or censors allowed a decorated Jewish soldier to be identified only by his initials, not by his more revealing, full name or by the adjective "Jewish." This policy was not a uniform and centralized one, and strong protests occasionally succeeded in wringing from the military censors publication of the feats of some Jewish soldiers. Papers not subject to military censorship could regularly report on

Jewish heroism.[43] The overall effect, however, was to mask from at least part of the public the patriotism and service of one particular group within the larger nation. This tendency, coupled with meretricious stories permitted in print about draft evasion and treachery on the part of Jews in the war zones, helped feed a popular perception that Jews were not loyal and did not serve. By extension, how could they be considered members of a national community founded on common patriotic service and sacrifice?[44]

Creating a Patriotic National Holiday

In the years immediately following the conclusion of the Great War, Russia was the only major belligerent that did not officially commemorate the war's fallen soldiers. But during the war Russians had formalized detailed plans for an annual holiday to honor those who had shed their blood in any of the country's wars, thereby anticipating in some measure the commemorative holidays other countries would establish. With its weaving together of solemn, patriotic, charitable, and purely festive elements, the "Holiday in Honor of Those Who Have Shed Their Blood for Russia" provides a unique example of an officially sanctioned, prerevolutionary attempt to create a genuinely "popular," secular national holiday.

The holiday was the brainchild of the Aleksandrovskii Committee on the Wounded, which had worked out the proposal for a "popular military holiday" (*voenno-narodnyi prazdnik*) prior to the Great War, in order to

---

[43] Numerous examples of military censors' prohibiting mention of Jewish feats of valor are contained in an unsigned memo, probably of 1915, "Voennaia tsenzura i evreiskii vopros," sent to Duma deputy and liberal leader Pavel N. Miliukov and contained in his personal archive: GARF, f. 579, op. 1, d. 2027, ll. 6–8, 13–15. See also "Iz 'Chernoi knigi' rossiiskogo evreistva. Materialy dlia istorii voiny 1914–1915 g.," in *Evreiskaia starina. Sbornik statei za 1917–1918 gody*, vol. X (Petrograd, 1918), 219–21. A good example of a paper that regularly reported on Jewish patriotism is the popular Moscow-based *Gazeta-kopeika*.

[44] Heinz-Dietrich Lowe, *The Tsars and the Jews: Reform, Reaction and Anti-Semitism in Imperial Russia, 1772–1917* (Chur, Switzerland: Harwood Academic Publishers, 1993), 323–24, notes that in fact some 500,000 Jews – approximately one-tenth of the empire's Jewish population – served in the Russian army. An example of unhindered derogation of Jewish soldiers comes from *Kievskaia kopeika* (May 24, 1915), 4, which reported on a Jewish soldier who received his St. George fraudulently and concluded, "That's how Yids become St. George Cavaliers." Unequal recognition of the valor of Jewish soldiers occurred again in the Second World War, when skewed reporting by the Soviet press created the perception that "there are no Jews at the front"; see Amir Weiner, *Making Sense of War: The Second World War and the Fate of the Bolshevik Revolution* (Princeton: Princeton University Press, 2001), 216–21.

commemorate its hundredth anniversary in 1914. In this format, the holiday would resemble other, one-time "jubilee" celebrations, such as the centennial of the 1812 Fatherland War and the tricentennial of the Romanov dynasty, lavishly celebrated in 1913.[45] The outbreak of the war prompted the Aleksandrovskii Committee temporarily to shelve its plans, but by early 1915 the committee resumed planning: the holiday would be a splendid means of raising money to aid the families of the wounded, while also providing Russians an opportunity to express esteem for those who were even then shedding their blood for the motherland. Nicholas II endorsed the proposal, and the holiday was given a sort of test run in Tula and Kursk provinces, with the intention of observing it in 1916 on a truly national scale.[46] In this way, what had originally been planned as the one-time commemoration of the Aleksandrovskii Committee's founding was now envisioned as an annual, patriotic event. Organizers believed the holiday honoring wounded and fallen soldiers would both reflect and help perpetuate the national unity the war had wrought: "All, all have come together in a single feeling of love for the motherland and her defenders."[47]

Great care was given to selecting the date for the new holiday, which was to be the first Sunday after Easter, "Fomino Voskresenie." Organizers noted that this feast day was always considered "particularly a people's holiday" in Russia. A spring date meant children would still be in school and troops (during peace time) still in winter quarters, making possible the especially desirable participation of these two groups in holiday events; spring weather also lent itself to parades and outdoor fetes. Anxious that the day be observed properly, the Aleksandrovskii Committee produced remarkably detailed sets of guidelines for community observances, which it distributed widely in pamphlet form. The ideal community commemoration would begin with the solemn celebration of the liturgy, followed by a parade of troops and schoolchildren of both sexes, a lunch for wounded veterans with distribution of gifts, and a second parade of troops and schoolchildren with flags, banners, and orchestral music. At some point, donations for the wounded would be collected. In the afternoon there would be a carnival with games and diversions and, in the evening, concerts, performances, films, and firework displays. While not every community

---

[45] A rich analysis of the dynastic patriotism embodied in the 1913 jubilee celebrations is Wortman, *Scenarios of Power*, II, 439–80; deliberate exclusion of local governments' elected representatives from official celebrations generated much ill-feeling.
[46] RGVIA, f. 2003, op. 2, d. 36 (1916), "Aleksandrovskii Komitet o ranenykh," ll. 1, 5–7.
[47] RGVIA, f. 2003, op. 2, d. 36 (1916), "Aleksandrovskii Komitet o ranenykh," l. 6.

could undertake so ambitious a program, county committees could work together to produce big local celebrations.[48]

Because most of the population did not live in towns, the guidelines paid particular care to explaining how rural people could mark the new holiday. In villages, schools should be the central site of the celebration, with student recitations and songs, and ceremonies honoring the villages' own veterans. The guidelines even advised on how to decorate the school hall – besides using portraits of the tsar, the new national flag, and banners, it was particularly desirable to display "portraits of war heroes." The place of honor in the hall should of course be accorded to wounded veterans and their families. Finally, there were suggestions for songs and poems to perform on the holiday. Songs could include the anthems of Russia and its allies, military songs, and "patriotic and folk songs in general." As a rule, the program guidelines advised, readings should not be too somber in mood: "It is best of all to select verse depicting those moments in the fatherland's history when our people manifested a special unity of spirit and a special upsurge of patriotic feeling, and Russian troops, defending the Motherland, covered themselves and Russia with everlasting glory."[49]

Organizers were clear that they wanted this holiday to be a permanent annual affair as well as genuinely popular and national (*vsenarodnyi*), both in terms of participation and appeal and by virtue of being held on "a grand scale." They also stressed its moral and educational significance. Besides gaining material aid, the wounded would derive tremendous consolation from these exertions by the whole people, for "in the esteem, attention and care for them and their families they will see a well-deserved gratitude." The younger generation, it was hoped, would be inspired to emulate these soldiers: "Let youth, seeing how Russia honors her best sons, themselves set out on their glorious road!"[50]

The similarities between these plans for the new national holiday in Russia and the postwar commemorative practices worked out by other combatant nations are striking. Ceremonies were highly participatory, involving much of the community and particularly the young. The celebrations emphasized the sacrifice and service of humble subjects or

---

[48] RGVIA, f. 2003, op. 2, d. 36 (1916), pamphlet by P. Borzakovskii, "O prazdnike v chest' prolivshchikh krov za Rossiiu (dlia shkol i naroda)," ll. 3, 5, 11.

[49] RGVIA, f. 2003, op. 2, d. 36 (1916), "O prazdnike v chest' prolivshchikh krov za Rossiiu," l. 12. Among the recommended poems, all of which could be found in schoolbooks, were Pushkin's "To the Slanderers of Russia" and "The Battle of Poltava"; Lermontov's "Borodino"; Viazemskii's "Holy Rus'" and "Song of the Russian Warrior"; Ostrovskii's "Koz'ma Minin"; Nekrasov's "Rus'"; Miakov's "Cossack"; and Koltsov's "Hurrah!"

[50] RGVIA, f. 2003, op. 2, d. 36, l. 6.

citizens, not those of civil or military leaders. They were particularistic, in that each community honored its own, but were also part of a larger, collective national celebration going on simultaneously all over the country. And by publicly honoring citizens who had done their duty, and expressing gratitude for their sacrifices, they offered both consolation and instruction. As Antoine Prost writes of the French postwar commemoration, "Armistice Day was a time for citizens to celebrate themselves. It strengthened their civic spirit and passed it on to the younger generation."[51] The "Holiday in Honor of Those Who Have Shed their Blood for Russia," as envisioned by its architects, also conformed to Russian practices. According to James von Geldern, tsarist celebrations were traditionally composed of two elements, a dynastic observance and popular entertainment: "solemnity and merriment stood side by side." Bolshevik festivals evolved into a similar pattern by late 1918. Holiday mornings were marked by long demonstrations, eulogies, and speeches. The afternoon and evening provided the merriment: carnival games, entertainments, and fireworks.[52]

Ultimately, the Aleksandrovskii Committee decided to delay introduction of the new holiday until the war was over, so we have no means of gauging how the population might have responded to it.[53] What is important for this discussion is that the idea of creating a secular, popular holiday, one so quintessentially national as the honoring of those who have spilled their blood for their country, debuted at precisely this time. It suggests, again, the influence of the Great War in helping to create in Russia a sense of national community, membership and identities within it, and loyalties to it.

"The Era of the Peasant Citizen"

The sketchiness of the sources makes it impossible to know the degree to which ordinary Russians internalized a connection between military service to the nation and citizenship rights.

---

[51] Prost, "Monuments to the Dead," 317–25, 329. Armistice Day in London was more somber and less secular than in France, but celebration of civic duty and the common soldier, community participation, and instruction of children were similarly important elements: Connelly, *The Great War*, 160–65.
[52] James von Geldern, *Bolshevik Festivals, 1917–1920* (Berkeley: University of California Press, 1993), 18, 40–41. See also the appraisal of early revolutionary ritual by Richard Stites, *Revolutionary Dreams: Utopian Vision and Experimental Life in the Russian Revolution* (New York: Oxford University Press, 1989), 79–100.
[53] Weber, *Peasants into Frenchmen*, 389–90, notes that it took nearly a decade for Bastille Day to be popularly embraced as the national festival of France after its introduction in 1880, so one might assume that the Russian holiday honoring dead and wounded soldiers would also have required time.

But we do know that peasant deputies to the State Duma insisted upon this connection, strongly and forthrightly, in the debates over the 1916 bill to make the peasant estate's rights closer to those of other social estates.[54] In the Russian empire, subjects had different privileges and obligations assigned them on the basis of their legal social estate; despite improvements effected between 1903–06, peasants remained in many respects a second-class category of citizens. They were located largely outside the formal, written system of law, had their votes weighed disproportionately in the curial system of voting for the zemstvos and State Duma, and faced obstacles to obtaining an internal passport or entering the civil service.[55] The bill would rectify some – though by no means all – peasant legal disabilities. On May 31, Vasilii Maklakov, a liberal Kadet and prominent lawyer, reported to the Duma on the bill on behalf of the judicial reform committee. Carefully explaining what it did and did not do – and why it did not try to address the legal disabilities of *all* categories of the population – he endorsed the bill as a realistic first step in extending greater rights to peasants. Its passage, he said, would begin a new era in Russia, "the era of the peasant-citizen."[56]

In the debates that followed, a series of peasant deputies rose to urge passage of the bill; all but one invoked peasant service and sacrifice in the war as a primary justification. P. M. Shmiakov, a peasant of Vitebsk province, noted that there was not a peasant family that had not given its fathers, brothers, or sons to the cause of defending the country. He urged, "Let our legislative chambers and our government see to it that there be no more stepchildren in Holy Rus', that all sons of great Russia merge together, bearing the name Russian citizen." A. I. Mukhin II, also from Vitebsk, put it more emphatically: "We, peasant sons of the great Russian people, creators of the great Russian state, are demanding for ourselves what should belong to us by right. Secure to us, peasants, the fullness of civil and political rights in our fatherland, built on the bones and blood of our ancestors."[57] A deputy from Petrograd province spoke of peasant martyrs defending their motherland, even when they had no weapons: peasants needed and deserved "genuine equality and the title

---

[54] Technically, the bill applied to "rural dwellers" rather than the peasant estate per se, but it would primarily affect the latter and was referred to in debates and reporting as the peasant bill (*krest'ianskii proekt*).

[55] Improvements to peasants' civil rights promulgated in the period 1903–06 were consolidated in the law of October 5, 1906; see Jane Burbank, *Russian Peasants Go to Court: Legal Culture in the Countryside, 1905–1917* (Bloomington: Indiana University Press, 2004), 29–30.

[56] *GDSO*, IV, 5, sess. 50 (May 31, 1916), cols. 4700–27.

[57] *GDSO*, IV, 5, sess. 52 (June 7, 1916), cols. 4876–77 and 4882–83.

of Russian citizen." A. I. Chistov, spokesman for a group of peasants, reminded the chamber of the burdens borne by peasants in the war and the blood they had spilled for defense of their native land, continuing that the Russian peasant had "an inalienable right" to be an "equal-rights citizen of the great Russian empire."[58]

After days of heated debate, and despite disappointment that the bill did not go far enough – or alarm that it went too far – support was sufficient to see that every "bill-killing" amendment was rejected; on June 18, the entire bill passed its third and final reading.[59] This landmark bill had made its way onto the agenda at the insistence of the peasant deputies, who dismissed conservatives' objections that war was "not the time" to take up the peasant question. As I. P. Demidov of Tambov province sarcastically remarked, "Really, last fall the army didn't say this was not the time for it to defend the motherland, although it had practically nothing [to fight with]."[60] Peasants and their supporters made a powerful case for extending equal rights to those who fought for their country. They also effectively conveyed how disillusioned the largely peasant army would be if news reached the front that "the Duma didn't manage to do this." At least one peasant deputy, M. P. Tyvonchuk, made explicit the connection between the war and support for the bill: "No one has thought about or passed laws for peasants in ten years, it's only when the war starts that they start to say here that something must be done for peasants ... I think that if there were no war, we wouldn't be looking at this law now. It would lie around for another ten years."[61]

---

[58] Ibid., cols. 4931 and 4890.

[59] Ibid., sess. 56 (June 14, 1916), col. 5340, and sess. 59 (June 18, 1916), col. 5668. The bill's tight focus on equalizing the rights of rural dwellers did nothing to aid most national minorities. This was a strategy adopted to try and ease its passage, since equal rights for Jews stood no chance of success, but it was the feature of the bill most objected to by nonpeasant deputies. Interestingly, the group of Muslim deputies announced they were not proposing any amendments to the bill in spite of this disappointing feature, since they did not want to be reproached with using the peasant question to gain something for *inorodtsy*: sess. 52, cols. 4921–26.

[60] Ibid., sess. 50, col. 4875; Demidov agreed that peasants needed rights, but felt that the top priority was getting land.

[61] Ibid., col. 4890, and sess. 53 (June 9, 1916), cols. 4992–93. Speeches highlighting the gulf between peasants' interests and those of the gentry became so heated that Boris Shtiurmer, who had replaced Goremykin as chair of the Council of Ministers, wrote to the emperor on June 7 warning that the Duma debate could incite the peasantry against the nobility: E. D. Chermenskii, *IV Gosudarstvennaia duma i sverzhenie tsarizma v Rossii* (Moscow: "Mysl'," 1976), 170–72. Peasant deputies also strongly supported introduction of a progressive income tax, which finally passed both legislative chambers in 1916; on the connection between the tax on individual incomes and understandings of citizenship, see the excellent discussion by Yanni Kotsonis, *States of Obligation: Taxes and Citizenship in the Russian Empire and Early Soviet Republic* (Toronto: University of Toronto Press, 2014), esp. 179–98.

While we cannot simply assume that ordinary peasants shared the views of peasant Duma deputies on this issue, extensive newspaper coverage of the debate means they would have been familiar with them.[62] Peasants' representatives in the legislature insisted on the connection between staunch service and enjoyment of equal rights of citizenship, and the Duma agreed. It seems likely that millions of peasant soldiers, at the very least, would have found such arguments appealing.

Conclusions

In Russia, as in other belligerent states during the Great War, we see extensive state and public efforts to foster and mobilize mass national sentiment through attentiveness to soldiers. For example, creation of a St. George Committee to identify, publicize, and reward heroes was a means of promoting love of and sacrifice for the nation through exemplars, as well as discharging a modern understanding of the duty of the state to its defenders.

A number of the means used to celebrate and honor those who took up arms in service of their country either expanded upon techniques employed in the immediate prewar period, or for the first time in Russia used techniques which would then be extensively employed in revolution and civil war. An obvious example is the effort to bring *to* the countryside examples of heroic valor on behalf of the motherland, in the form of the traveling St. George exhibitions. Another is the dissemination of mass editions of pamphlets to frontline soldiers to acquaint them with their right to state aid for their families. These undertakings reinforce important points made by Peter Holquist and other scholars concerning the First World War origins of many techniques of national instruction and mobilization we have habitually regarded as innovations of the revolution or Soviet regime.[63]

As befitted the narrative of sacred union, the sense of the nation that was being articulated for and around soldiers was an inclusive one. Given that there were various and competing visions of what constituted the Russian nation, and what precisely Russia was fighting for, the image of the soldier served as a handy focus of unity. Few extended families had not contributed a soldier; seemingly all people could agree that soldiers

---

[62] *Sel'skii vestnik* (June 2, 1916), 1–2, (June 8, 1916), 2–3, (June 11, 1916), 3–4, (June 15, 1916), 2, (June 19, 1916), 2, and *Russkoe slovo* (June 1, 1916), 3, (June 4, 1916), 3–4, and (June 19, 1916), 4.

[63] Holquist, *Making War, Forging Revolution*, has influentially argued that propaganda, "surveillance," and other techniques of mass persuasion and mobilization employed in the Great War were subsequently used by both Reds and Whites in the civil war.

were particularly worthy citizens and sons of the motherland, those called upon to leave their families and perhaps to make the ultimate sacrifice. Therefore, honoring, rewarding, and commemorating the nation's defenders constituted a way to sidestep vexing differences in the multinational state and bring all together on common ground.

We can also see how these efforts helped diffuse on a mass scale notions of equality of sacrifice, as entailed by universal military service, as well as of entitlements owed the citizen soldier by virtue of that service and sacrifice. The war experience laid the ground for the appearance of the vociferous citizens of 1917, who displayed a strong sense that they had earned consideration for their service to the country, and of the reciprocal relationship between the universality of sacrifice and equality of rights.

But the inclusive notion of the nation originally proclaimed in the sacred union, and embodied in many of the efforts to honor soldiers, was also subject to revision: over the course of the war various groups – such as Jews, Russian Germans, or other "traitorous" or unworthy citizens – were physically, legally, or symbolically excluded from the patriotic national community. Construction of those groups and how they tried to defend themselves are the subject of the next chapter.

6   Fantasies of Treason
Sorting Out Membership in the Russian National Community

> Whoever is branded with this scorching mark – "treason" – will rarely be saved.
>
> O. O. Gruzenberg, *Yesterday: Memoirs of a Russian-Jewish Lawyer*[1]

In 1917, a mass-edition pamphlet entitled "The Traitors and Betrayers of Russia" gave two reasons for Russia's many wartime defeats. It explained to readers that the tsarist authorities had done a bad job of preparing for the coming conflict. But making things still worse, "in the army and the rear there appeared spies and traitors who sold Russia out to our enemy." Internal enemies supposedly instigated the 1915 anti-German riots in Moscow, artificially created shortages and inflation, and generally sabotaged the war effort in any way possible. There were big traitors and little ones, "but both kinds worked for the death of Russia. They robbed it and drank its blood."[2]

Concern about internal security existed from the outset in all the belligerent states, providing an important rationale for censorship restrictions and surveillance of the population. But in Russia, worries about potential treachery went further. According to historian William Fuller, during the Great War Russia became obsessed with unmasking and destroying the internal foe: "the belief that 'treason is everywhere' became one of the most distinctive characteristics of wartime patriotism in Russia."[3]

---

[1] O. O. Gruzenberg, *Yesterday: Memoirs of a Russian-Jewish Lawyer*, trans. by Don C. Rawson and Tatiana Tipton (Berkeley: University of California Press, 1981), 141.

[2] Evgenii Gorets, *Izmenniki i predateli Rossii* (Moscow: Izd. Sytina, 1917), 5–6, 21, 25. The absence of reference to post-February discord and optimistic tenor of the pamphlet's conclusion suggest that it was written in spring 1917.

[3] William C. Fuller, Jr., *The Foe Within: Fantasies of Treason and the End of Imperial Russia* (Ithaca: Cornell University Press, 2006), 259–60. Alexander Prusin has demonstrated that in 1914–15 Austrian thinking about Galicia was characterized by the same obsessive fear of spies; he suggests this similarity might be explained by a structural commonality, "unpreparedness for war that entailed military setbacks." See Alexander V. Prusin, *The Lands Between: Conflict in the East European Borderlands, 1870–1992* (Oxford: Oxford University Press, 2010), 42–43.

The search for internal traitors intensified in 1915, a development related to fears about the unfolding national catastrophe, widespread demands for an explanation of its causes, and the need to deflect anger away from the authorities and onto other targets. Pecuniary motives also played no small role. But the hunt for enemies within was not solely a function of red herrings, scapegoats, and loot. Military debacles and their accompanying ordeals invited a national sorting and closing of ranks, a reckoning of who were the "true" patriotic sons and daughters of the nation, willing to serve and sacrifice even at the nadir, and who were not. Not only individuals but whole groups could be found wanting, often – though not exclusively – along ethnic or religious-ethnic lines. Once identified, those who did not deserve a place in the sacred union had to be distanced, stigmatized, even physically excluded from the national community. Or, to use phrases that circulated in this war and would subsequently gain much wider currency under Soviet power, the country had to be "cleansed" of alien elements, traitors, and "enemies of the people." It then turned out to be a short step in logic to move from punitive removal and relocation of disloyal groups to preemptive exclusion of groups deemed *likely* to engage in treacherous behavior.

Spymania

In the first weeks of the war, Germany, Austria, and France all suffered spasms of "spy fever," with anxieties about internal treachery and espionage sometimes assuming ludicrous proportions.[4] In this respect, Russia's experience was not exceptional. For example, in late summer 1914, the respected liberal "thick" journal *Vestnik Evropy* reported a popular furor in a region of Siberia where German zeppelins were rumored to be flying with bombs – thousands of miles out of possible range. In 1916, special police jumped into action at railroad stations when it was reported in a secret circular that Germans had set up a school for "underaged spies" in occupied Poland, and were infiltrating them into Russia by train.[5] One can only imagine the kind of scenarios produced by the instructions to monitor train stations for suspicious-looking children in school uniforms, who were to be arrested and questioned. One commercially published handbook, *Advice to the Young Officer*, featured a whole section on spies, warning that they were "everywhere" and could be of either sex – female spies supposedly posed as

---

[4] On spy fever in Germany, see Verhey, *The Spirit of 1914*, 75–76; for Britain, see David French, "Spy Fever in Britain, 1900–1915," *Historical Journal* 21, 2 (June 1978), 355–70.
[5] GARF, f. 63, op. 36 (1916) d. 385, "O maloletnykh shpionakh," l. 3.

Sisters of Mercy or refugees. At the front, spies were disguised in uniform; on the home front they could be found in "theaters, gardens, railroad stations, candy stores, and so on."[6]

However, for a number of reasons, spymania in Russia did not just fade away. One factor was a sensational case of treason that helped fuel panic about enemies within. On March 18, 1915, a special field court martial convicted Lieutenant Colonel Sergei N. Miasoedov of espionage on behalf of Germany and condemned him to death by hanging; the sentence was carried out within hours. Readers devoured press reports on the execution and ensuing investigations, which resulted in dozens of additional arrests in the following months. Most scholars who have looked into this case have concluded that Miasoedov – a shady character with still shadier companions – was probably innocent of espionage and quite possibly framed.[7] At the time, however, few doubted he had sold out to Germany. People were shocked by the idea that a Great Russian and officer of the Russian army would betray his country. If a Miasoedov could engage in treachery, how many other seemingly loyal people might not also be traitors? And could the people who advanced such a man really not have known anything about his evil doings? In February 1916, when ex-minister of war V. A. Sukhomlinov was arrested on charges of malfeasance and treason, his close association with Miasoedov figured heavily in assumptions of his guilt.[8] The Miasoedev case was a major factor underlying widespread beliefs that people were not necessarily what they seemed, and that the authorities were too incompetent – or too compromised – to protect the country from their plots.

Certain prominent individuals signally contributed to the climate of suspicion. One of these was General M. D. Bonch-Bruevich, who played a role in the Miasoedov case. Bonch-Bruevich was convinced that Germany and Austria-Hungary had been building vast espionage networks in Russia in the years leading up to the war, a threat Russia needed to root out. In April 1915, Supreme Commander Nikolai Nikolaevich tasked him with making recommendations for an overhaul of military counterintelligence; shortly thereafter, Bonch-Bruevich was appointed

---

[6] Rotmistr Kul'chitskii, *Sovety molodomu ofitseru*, 6th edn. (Kharkov, 1917), contained in RGVIA, f. 2005, op. 2, d. 766, ll. 28, 40.

[7] Fuller, *The Foe Within*, esp. 119–49 and 164–83; Fuller suspects that army officers keen to absolve themselves of blame for military failures conspired to set Miasoedov up as the fall guy.

[8] The survey of the public mood for 1915, created by the Ministry of the Interior's Department of Police on the basis of perlustrated letters, notes the large number of letters discussing "the traitor Miasoedev" and his association with Minister of War Sukhomlinov: GARF, f. 102, op. 265, d. 1042, "Obzor perliust-kh pisem za 1914–1915 gg., sostavlennyi v sekretnom chasti Osobogo otdela," ll. 133–35.

quartermaster-general of Sixth Army, whose area of authority included Petrograd and much of the Baltic area.[9] He immediately instigated far-reaching hunts and cleansing operations. Decades later, he insisted in his memoirs that the capital was heavily infiltrated by spies, that "the overwhelming majority" of Russia's German Baltic barons were spying for Germany, and that the hundreds of salesmen who traveled the empire for the Singer sewing machine company were part of an elaborate and impudent German intelligence adventure. He also unmasked alleged espionage groups in the army and within the Russian Red Cross. Bonch-Bruevich was finally removed from his position in February 1916, but the spymania he helped foster in the military, along with the departments he established for spy-hunting, outlived his tenure.[10]

The Poles and the Sacred Union of Peoples

On July 19, 1914, Petrograd mayor Count Ivan Tol'stoi wrote with great misgivings in his diary about the German ultimatum to Russia. His fears that a war could go badly stemmed in part from what he termed the "ill-fated and criminal nationality policy of the past twenty-five years, turning the Jews, Poles, and Finns against the Russian government ... Alas, we will have to reckon with all this now."[11]

A major strand of the narrative of sacred union forged in the following days, as we have seen, was the union of all the peoples of the multinational empire. In particular, the historic July 26 session of the Duma symbolized a new unity of Russia's political parties, faiths, and nationalities. And just as representatives of Muslims, Jews, and other sizeable national groups stepped up to the Duma rostrum to swear their people's passionate love of the motherland, all over the empire societies and associations organized along national or religious lines made similar pledges – usually accompanied by significant financial donations to war relief – in the opening weeks of the war.

Several national groups genuinely benefited from the wartime rethinking of the Russian national community. Latvians were one such group;

---

[9] Bonch-Bruevich denied contemporary charges of suffering from "spymania" but his memoirs, published decades after the events described, depict a man obsessed: M. D. Bonch-Bruevich, *Vsia vlast' sovetam. Voennye memuary* (Moscow: Voennoe izdatel'stvo ministerstva oborony SSSR, 1964), 54–58, 63–66; on his spy-catching zeal, see also Fuller, *The Foe Within*, 165–68.
[10] Bonch-Bruevich, *Vsia vlast' sovetam*, 70–83, 98. More generally, a 1915 Army General Staff appeal to the population, asking that it refrain from discussion of military events, implied that German spies were everywhere: "Boites' shpionov," *Sel'skii vestnik* (March 10, 1915), 2.
[11] Tol'stoi, *Dnevnik*, II, 578.

the Poles – rather surprisingly – were another. At the time of the 1897 census, there were more than 7.9 million Poles in the Russian empire, mainly in Russia's nine "western provinces" and the ten districts that made up the Kingdom of Poland (Tsarstvo Pol'ske).[12] Their position had deteriorated following the brutal suppression of the Polish uprising of 1863. Poles were limited in their right to buy land and excluded from holding higher governmental administrative positions in these provinces. Polish municipalities lacked rights of self-governance. Even many of the concessions extended to Russian subjects by the 1905 revolution, such as greater freedom of the press and religious tolerance, were less fully realized in Polish areas than elsewhere in the empire.[13] The emergent Russian nationalist movement in this area regarded Polish elites as separatists and oppressors of the non-Polish peasantry – especially the putatively Russian (i.e., Belorussian and Ukrainian) peasants. Many people were offended by what they perceived as Polish blackening of Russian national character all over Europe, believing that Poles assiduously propagated an image of Russia as the backward oppressor of the more civilized Polish people.[14]

Although not all Russian officials subscribed to the stereotyped image of the "arrogant and disloyal Pole" – some indeed appreciating that reforms and accommodation were practical necessities – on the eve of the war, Russian Poles had scant reason to feel satisfied with the government. Add to this the circumstance that Germany and Austria-Hungary would deal Russia heavy defeats *on* Polish lands, and the Poles would appear to have been prime candidates for the role of traitors. Yet Russia's Poles were not only not publicly accused of sympathizing with the enemy or excluded from the sacred union, but quite the opposite: they were rehabilitated, honored, and embraced.

The rewriting of the place of the Poles in the patriotic narrative began with the unexpected August 1, 1914, proclamation of Supreme

[12] Figures come from Andreas Kappeler, *The Russian Empire: A Multiethnic History*, trans. by Alfred Clayton (Harlow, UK: Pearson Education Ltd, 2001), 398. The official designation of this area was "Vistula country" (Privislinskii krai), but most people still referred to it as the Kingdom of Poland. My thanks to Ted Weeks for helping me sort out the intricacies of terminology.

[13] Poles living in the western provinces suffered even more disabilities than Poles in the Kingdom of Poland, in part due to fears of Polish economic influence over the non-Polish population. It should be noted that educated Poles could make careers in the civil service *outside* Polish areas; see Theodore R. Weeks, *Nation and State in Late Imperial Russia: Nationalism and Russification on the Western Frontier, 1863–1914* (DeKalb: Northern Illinois University Press, 1996), and particularly his discussion of Russian nationalist discourse on Poles and Poland, 32–34, 54–59, 96–109, 115–16.

[14] Even liberal leader Pavel Miliukov, one of the most determined champions of quality for all the empire's national minorities, kept separatist Poles at arm's length.

Commander Grand Duke Nikolai Nikolaevich, which promised reunification of the lands of partitioned Poland in union with Russia: "May the Polish nation be joined in one under the scepter of the Russian Emperor. Under that scepter Poland will be reborn, free in its own faith, language, and self-rule."[15] This proclamation was the brainchild of Foreign Minister Sergei D. Sazonov, and had a strictly instrumental purpose. It was a bid for Polish loyalty against the presumed blandishments of the Germans and Austrians, as well as an effort to stake Russian territorial claims prior to negotiation of the peace. For many progressive Russians, however, it seemed to augur a new era in nationality policy. One of these was Mayor Tol'stoi, who wrote in his diary, "This document has made me ecstatic. Can it really be that we've reached the long-desired collapse of militant Russian nationalism? It seems there are grounds for hope."[16] Polish reception of this promised rebirth was mixed, with some people jubilant and others quite skeptical.[17]

For some eleven months after its issue, Russian authorities did little to act on the manifesto, undermining faith in the state's intentions. But when the Duma reconvened July 19, 1915, as Russian troops prepared to abandon Warsaw, Prime Minister Goremykin's opening speech praised the Polish people and singled out Poland as a state priority.[18] While the Poles awaited liberation of their land from the enemy, he stated, it was important that they know and believe that the manifesto would be fulfilled. "The chivalrously noble, fraternally loyal Polish people, staunchly

---

[15] For the translated text of the manifesto, see Norman Davies, *God's Playground: A History of Poland*, vol. II (New York: Columbia University Press, 1982), 378–80. A thoughtful exploration of the manifesto and its impact on Russia's wartime policies on Poland is A. Iu. Bakhturina, *Okhrainy Rossiiskoi imperii. Gosudarstvennoe upravlenie i natsional'naia politika v gody Pervoi mirovoi voiny (1914–1917 gg.)* (Moscow: ROSSPEN, 2004), 23–29; for the back story on the manifesto, see Ronald Bobroff, "Devolution in Wartime: Sergei D. Sazonov and the Future of Poland, 1910–1916," *International History Review* 22, 3 (2000), 505–28.

[16] Tol'stoi also relates conversations the following day with Duma deputy N. N. L'vov, who felt similarly, and with the manifesto's author Sazonov, who was confident that it would be fulfilled: Tol'stoi, *Dnevnik*, II, entries of August 2 and August 3, 1914, 588, 590. In contrast, Nikolai Vrangel' considered the manifesto ill timed and illogical, and speculated as to what fears or intrigues had produced it: Vrangel', *Dni skorbi*, 31–32, entry of August 2, 1914.

[17] Initial reactions of Poles in the Kingdom of Poland to the manifesto included an exuberant street demonstration of 20,000 people in Lodz and a proclamation by the Polish National Committee describing it as "prefiguring the realization of our dreams: the reunification of the sundered body of Poland": Bakhturina, *Okrainy*, 29–31; a more negative picture of Polish views is offered in Davies, *God's Playground*, 380–83.

[18] According to Bobroff, "Devolution in Wartime," 514–17, conservatives on the Council of Ministers stonewalled Sazonov's efforts to work out concrete reforms for Poland. He managed to compel Goremykin's July 1915 speech only by persuading the emperor that Germany was preparing to declare Poland independent.

enduring innumerable hardships in this war, evokes in our hearts the deepest sympathy and wholehearted tribute of respect." At the emperor's behest, the Council of Ministers was working on a bill to grant Poland, at war's end, "the rights of freely constructing its national, cultural and economic life on the basis of autonomy under the scepter of the Russian Sovereign and with preservation of a unitary state." In a year of war and shared ordeals, he asserted, the Poles had "proved their loyalty to Russia."[19]

Public reaction to this renewed pledge was strongly positive. The Duma greeted Goremykin's speech with stormy and continued applause and shouts of "bravo." Columnists editorialized favorably in a broad spectrum of newspapers, and public organizations expressed heartfelt solidarity.[20] In September 1915, the government rescinded many of the legal disabilities of Poles and Catholics; when the Duma reconvened on February 9, 1916, deputies introduced a bill to abolish the remaining legal restrictions on the rights of Poles.[21]

How exactly had the Poles, so long considered disloyal, come to be regarded as patriotic? At the start of war, spokesmen for Polish communities, like other national groups, hastened to proclaim their patriotic bona fides, as well as to express hope for a better future for Russian Poland after the war. Duma deputy V. F. Iaronskii, for example, asserting Poles' eagerness to join the united forces of Slavdom in repulsing the Teutons, concluded: "Let the spilling of our blood and the horrors of what is, for us, a fratricidal war, lead to the unification of the sundered Polish people."[22] The Council of Ministers was confident that,

---

[19] For Goremykin's speech, see *GDSO*, IV, 4, sess. 1 (July 19, 1915), cols. 9–10.
[20] Ibid., col. 10. Examples of public reaction include a column by prominent nationalist Anatolii I. Savenko expressing his pleasure concerning Polish autonomy, "Mysli i vpechatleniia," *Kievlianin'* (July 26, 1915), 3, and, less surprisingly, an editorial in the same vein in the liberal *Russkie vedomosti* (July 22, 1915), 2. *Sel'skii vestnik* (August 2, 1915), 2, reported that on July 27 the congress of the War Industries Committees had sent a telegram to Polish members of the Duma and State Council expressing "greetings to the fraternal Polish people and its wish that they realize their national and state ideals, in union with great Russia." Compilers of the weekly survey of the press that was prepared for government officials noted that the press gave wide and favorable coverage to the Duma deputies' bill on equalizing Poles' rights: RGIA, f. 1470, op. 2, d. 103, "Obzor pechati, 1914–1917 gg.," l. 481.
[21] "Ob otmene soderzhashchikhsia v zakonakh ogranichenii poliakov ...," in "Spravka o dvizhenii zakonodatel'nykh predlozhenii, vnesennykh v poriadke st. 55 uchr. Gosudarstvennoi Dumy, chlenami Gos. Dumy," No. 60 (k No. 2, IV/3), 3., *Prilozhenie k GDSO*, IV, 4 (Petrograd, 1916), 3.
[22] Quoted in *Kievlianin'* (July 29, 1914), 1. Poles also participated in the common cause of war relief; at the solemn opening ceremony for a Polish-run infirmary in Petrograd, speeches "underlined the brotherhood of the Russian and Polish people and confidence in the happy future awaiting united Poland": Tol'stoi, *Dnevnik*, II, entry of September 7, 1914, 611.

thanks to the August 1914 manifesto, Russia's Poles were now animated exclusively "by feelings of loyalty."[23] Several prominent Russian Poles also wasted no time in proposing creation of volunteer Polish military units, to offset the Polish Legions being organized for the Austrian army by Jozef Pilsudski. Although Russia's Polish Legions (called *druzhiny*) numbered only several thousand men and played no significant military role, their very existence made a favorable impression, in the same way that the volunteer Latvian rifle units did.[24] The absence of reported cases of collaboration with the enemy on the part of Russia's Poles, along with numerous testimonies regarding their hostility toward the Germans, also invited a reappraisal of their loyalty.

The sheer calamity overtaking Polish lands animated Russian sympathies for Poles, one measure of which was a truly enormous public outpouring of aid.[25] Publicist Sergei Runin, in his pamphlet *Two Sisters: Russia and Poland*, emphasized the role of shared wartime suffering, which had engendered "all-forgiving, mutual love" between the long-estranged Slav "sisters." Suffering was transformative as well as redemptive; in an imagined dialog, Runin has Poland assure elder sister Russia, "Believe that I am not who I was formerly, that the suffering I have endured has not passed without trace."[26] In a war in which patriotism was demonstrated by service and sacrifice, the terrible suffering of the Poles, their apparently strong support for the Russian army, and the spilling of Polish blood in the fight against the invader were all powerful testaments to their right of inclusion.

The new representation of the Polish people as true sons and daughters of Russia was not just official rhetoric, although such rhetoric was significant in setting a tone for others to emulate. A host of unlikely people – from army officers to rabid nationalists to liberals – came to see Poles in a "new light." By far the most famous public embrace of the Poles came from far-right Duma deputy Vladimir M. Purishkevich, whose work with medics at the front had transformed his previously

---

[23] RGIA, f. 1276, op. 20, "Osobyi zhurnal Soveta ministrov," meeting of August 24, 1914, ll. 202–03.

[24] RGVIA, f. 2003, op. 2, d. 323, ll. 46, 52–54, 112. An initial Polish "legion" was formed in September 1914. In January 1915, more Polish units were authorized, though these were expressly to be called *druzhiny*, not legions; within weeks, the latter two had approximately 750 men each.

[25] For example, what appears to be Petrograd's biggest collection of the entire war was for Poland, yielding donations of 290,000 rubles and more than 900,000 items: Tol'stoi, *Dnevnik*, II, diary entry of October 23, 1914, 636. The Kiev branch of the Tatiana Committee raised 147,168 rubles for the Poles in fall 1914: *Kievlianin'* (January 15, 1916), 2.

[26] Sergei Runin, *Dve sestry – Rossiia i Pol'sha*, "*Otkliki*," issue 3 (Petrograd, 1915), 5, 9–10.

6.1 A symbolic rendering of the rapprochement of the two Slavic "sisters," Russia and Poland. Political Poster Collection, #RU/SU 854, Courtesy of Hoover Institution Library & Archives, Stanford University.

scathing opinion of Polish loyalty to Russia. Purishkevich championed rights for the Poles in articles, public lectures, and Duma speeches, as on August 1, 1915, when he paid tribute to Polish support of the Russian army even as Warsaw fell, referring to "the long list of material and spiritual sacrifices which the Polish people have placed on the altar of our common fatherland." On February 12, 1916, he told the Duma, "You know my attitude in the past toward the Poles. I was their hater. Now, a year of war at the front has made of me their greatest friend, for the Poles have conducted themselves valiantly ... And have the Poles not earned by their valor those rights which they ought to receive for fighting and dying side by side with Russian soldiers on the fields of battle?"[27]

Of course, we have no statistics for assessing the universality of the wartime reorientation; police evidence about attitudes toward Russia's Poles, gleaned from intercepted private correspondence, shows that many Russians still harbored doubts about long-term Polish aspirations.[28] For our discussion, the important point is that an ethnically non-Russian people professing a faith other than Russian Orthodoxy – moreover, a people that had long been stigmatized as disloyal – could be writ into the national narrative as a true member of the patriotic national community. With inclusion came greater rights, something that would not have been lost on other marginalized or second-class population groups who nurtured hopes that their wartime service and sacrifice would improve their position. In fact, the conclusion of Goremykin's speech on creating an autonomous, united Poland gave reason to hope:

[I]n the multinational great Empire it is not just the Poles who have demonstrated their loyalty to Russia in this year of war and common ordeals. And in response to this, our domestic policy must be imbued with impartial and benevolent care for the interests of all citizens loyal to Russia, without distinction of nationality, language, and faith. (Applause and shouts of bravo.)[29]

Further corroboration that loyal service prompted rethinking of discriminatory policies toward minorities comes from an unexpected source, the

---

[27] GDSO, IV, 4, sess. 4 (August 1, 1915), col. 246, and *Tribuna. Rechi V. M. Purishkevicha (stenogrammy) v Gosudarstvennoi Dume vo vremia voine* (Petrograd, n.d.), 16; Purishkevich also spoke to the Duma on behalf of the Poles on January 26 and August 16, 1915. Sizeable excerpts from his speech on Polish valor and loyalty were featured in *Sel'skii vestnik*, which commented that "the State Duma warmly welcomed this speech": (August 4, 1915), 2.

[28] GARF, f. 102, op. 265, d. 1042, "Obzor... 1915," ll. 79–82. While letters from the army quoted in police reports testify to a genuine sea-change in attitudes, the police concluded that most correspondents still believed the Poles wanted full independence. Above all, letters written by Ukrainians revealed deep skepticism about Polish intentions: GARF, f. 102, op. 265, d. 1056, l. 608.

[29] GDSO, IV, 4, sess. 1 (July 19, 1915), col. 10.

minister of war. After thirty deputies of the State Duma introduced a bill in February 1916 calling for immediate abolition of all restrictions on citizens due to religion or nationality, the president of the Council of Ministers sent the bill to the ministers for comment. While all agreed that the midst of war was *not* the time to introduce such fundamental changes, Minister of War A. A. Polivanov was among those who endorsed many of the proposed changes in principle. In his opinion, the wartime experience had greatly diminished doubts about national minorities' political reliability:

> Numerous nationalities populating the state are fighting valiantly in the ranks of the Russian army, and for the common Motherland endure the hardships of war equally with core Russians. Moreover, in the course of the war the experience of forming purely Polish, Latvian, Armenian, and Czech military units has proved their complete reliability and fitness in the military respect. These circumstances make it reasonable to conclude that many of the currently existing limitations on non-Russians need revision.[30]

"Traitors and Betrayers": The Jews

Great suffering was not in itself redemptive, for the Jews who lived in Polish areas – and also suffered grievously – found themselves more often branded as traitors than treated with compassion.

There were more than 5.2 million Jewish subjects of the Russian empire at the time of the 1897 census. Tens of thousands had assimilated to some degree into broader Russian society and carved out successful careers, despite numerous legal disabilities and prevalent antisemitism. The great majority of Jews, however, were still legally confined to residence within the Pale of Settlement, composed of fifteen western Russian provinces and tsarist Poland– that is, along several major Russian fronts in the war.[31] When things went badly for the Russian army, the Jews were on hand to blame. But even before major military setbacks along the southwestern front, part of the high command was inclined toward preemptive removal of the "disloyal" Jewish population, before they could have opportunity to betray the army.

Bonch-Bruevich later claimed in his memoirs that the army systematically inculcated antisemitism in soldiers. The truth of this charge is

---

[30] RGIA, f. 1276, op. 12, d. 3 (1916), ll. 36, 37. Polivanov went on to point out that many restrictions on Poles and Catholics had already been lifted by imperial decree of September 6, 1915.
[31] On Jewish assimilation, and its dilemmas, see Benjamin Nathans, *Beyond the Pale: The Russian-Jewish Encounter with Modernity* (Berkeley: University of California Press, 2002), esp. chaps. 3–5.

impossible to establish, particularly since the pervasiveness of antisemitism in the War Ministry and the high command was not necessarily replicated among field-grade officers.[32] We do see instances of profoundly antisemitic screeds appearing in some army newspapers for distribution to soldiers. *Poslednaia armeiskaia izvestiia* (Latest Army News), for example, published by the Staff of Third Army, featured a nasty little piece on December 26, 1915. "Germans are beasts," the article begins, and it is well known that "every big predator has a retinue of small, cowardly, and spiteful jackals"; the Jews were the Germans' jackals. "Before the war all the Jews constantly demanded that they be called Russians and considered Russians. Now these Jews are showing what kind of Russians they are."[33]

Sources suggest that the image of the Jews as alien and treacherous was widespread in the army in late 1914 and 1915. The secret-police overview of intercepted correspondence for 1915 observed that the majority of letters from the army touching on the Jewish population "note the negative side of [their] character and actions," that numerous letters spoke of treachery and betrayal on the part of the Jews, "who systematically shoot our troops in the back" and "treat Russian wounded badly" in their field hospitals. Many letters characterized the army as "full of indignation toward the Jews," and predicted massive pogroms at war's end.[34]

On the highly mobile eastern front (Russia's "western front"), control of areas changed hands repeatedly. The volatility of the front meant troops were extremely concerned about the loyalties of the local populations and keen to distinguish between "us" and "them." Drawing such distinctions was not always easy to do, for the otherness of the Orthodox Jews of Galicia and Poland was pronounced. They wore distinctive clothing, lived in separate areas, and rarely mingled socially with the rest of the population. Most spoke Yiddish rather than Russian, a language that soldiers commonly mistook for German. Longstanding friction between the Polish and Jewish populations in the region had worsened in recent decades and at least one Jewish observer – writer and activist Semen Ansky – contended that Poles energetically spread lies about Jewish treachery.[35]

---

[32] On antisemitism in the army in this period, see Yohanan Petrovsky-Shtern, *Jews in the Russian Army, 1827–1917: Drafted into Modernity* (Cambridge: Cambridge University Press, 2009), 240–64.

[33] GARF, f. 579, op. 1, d. 2016, "Iudy-predateli. Statiia Poslednykh armeiskikh izvestii," ll. 1, 2.

[34] GARF, f. 102, op. 265, d. 1042, ll. 91–93.

[35] S. Ansky, *The Enemy at His Pleasure: A Journey through the Jewish Pale of Settlement in World War I*, ed. and trans. Joachim Neugroschel (New York: Henry Holt and Co., 2002), 5, 7, 14–16, 18–21, recounts numerous examples of libels spread by Poles; he suspected that they did so not only to rid themselves of their longtime enemies, but also

The lure of loot certainly played a role. Property left behind by expelled Jews provided easy pickings for Cossacks, regular soldiers, and locals. When pogroms erupted, as they frequently did, physical violence against Jews was accompanied by the pillaging of their homes and shops. Often, the rationale for such eruptions was alleged signals to the enemy detected from windows, or shots at Russian soldiers from buildings. A number of observers caustically noted that these signals and shots – sparking searches for the culprits, accompanied by "retaliatory" looting – typically were identified as having come from tempting shops and warehouses, not miserable hovels. Pogroms and looting were decidedly not a policy of the Russian high command, rather being initiated on the ground, and most usually by Cossacks.[36] But efforts to avert mob violence, or halt it once it began, were not always successful. And though the high command was not happy about pogroms and their disruptive consequences, the directives it issued about wholesale Jewish espionage and treachery helped create the anxiety and anger that made such violence likely to erupt.

Thus, there was all too fertile ground for credulous or self-serving acceptance of fantastic allegations of Jewish treason. In the words of a 1915 report on the wartime plight of the Jews, prepared for a conference of the liberal Kadet Party, "It is scarcely surprising that in such an atmosphere there began to arise tall tales about gold taken abroad by Jews in coffins, about a Jew on a white stallion going ahead of troops and giving signals ... about long-distance telephones set up with the help of thick wires and ropes, and other fairytales which began to pass from mouth to mouth, morbidly affecting the fate of the Jews and creating within the army an infectious panic and abnormal spymania."[37]

The Jews' troubles began in areas controlled by military rather than civilian authorities. During the first six months of the war, there were

---

to hide their own pro-Austrian treachery. See also G. Kurnatovskii and I. Ia. Kleinman, "Pol'sko-evreiskaia otnosheniia. (1. Golos poliaka. 2. Golos evreia)," *Russkaia mysl'* (December 1914), 27–41, and, on factors underlying deepening Polish antisemitism, Theodore R. Weeks, *From Assimilation to Anti-Semitism: The "Jewish Question" in Poland, 1850–1914* (DeKalb: Northern Illinois University Press, 2006), 149–69.

[36] In a sample of fifty-four pogroms in four provinces during Russia's Great Retreat, Lohr concludes that all but three of the pogroms began with soldiers present and that the army – and more specifically Cossacks – initiated the violence in almost every case; see Eric Lohr, "1915 and the War Pogrom Paradigm in the Russian Empire," in Jonathan Dekel-Chen, David Gaunt, Natan M. Meir, and Israel Bartal, eds., *Anti-Jewish Violence: Rethinking the Pogrom in East European History* (Bloomington: Indiana University Press, 2011), 41–51. He also sees the 1915 pogroms as more nationalist than any previous wave of pogroms.

[37] "Iz 'Chernoi knigi' rossiiskogo evreistva," 209–11.

numerous instances of expulsion from localities of individuals deemed "unreliable," or even of the entire civilian population of a given village or town, on the grounds of military security. Jews were not the only ones subjected to these measures, but they predominated. The "Black Book of Russian Jewry" gives locations and figures for at least eight such group expulsions of Jews from August 1914 to January 1915, ranging in scale from several dozen people to more than four thousand. These ad hoc expulsions were usually followed by the looting or sequestration of the expelled persons' property. In November 1914, Polish Jews sent liberal Duma deputy Miliukov sworn declarations concerning twenty-five separate instances of pogroms and looting of Jewish property around Warsaw alone, carried out by Russian soldiers or by locals with tacit support from soldiers.[38]

More organized exclusion of Jews from the southwestern front began *prior* to the reversal of Russian military fortunes there, another circumstance pointing to the preemptive nature of the operation. In fact, Ianushkevich and several other officials had been writing memos since late fall urging wholesale deportation of the Jews before they had the chance to harm the Russian army.[39] In January 1915, all Jewish doctors and medics were banned from working on medical trains on the southwestern front, on the grounds that Jews in these positions were engaging in criminal antigovernmental propaganda among the troops. In early January 1915, the Supreme Command issued a proclamation that was posted on the streets of Russian-occupied L'vov, in Galicia, alleging that Jews were practicing espionage along the entire front. In order to protect the troops, Supreme Commander Grand Duke Nikolai Nikoaevich was forbidding the presence of (civilian) Jews in the area of the army and also ordering hostage-taking from the Jewish community. Hostages would be subject to "execution by hanging in the event of further espionage."[40] Hostage-taking had a practical underpinning – it was much simpler to guarantee the good behavior of a population through hostages than to deport tens of thousands of people from a given locale. But it also afforded expansive opportunities for extortion and bribe-taking.[41]

---

[38] GARF, f. 579, op. 1, d. 1994, "Zaiavleniia" (1914), ll. 1–13.

[39] See also Peter Holquist, "The Role of Personality in the First (1914–1915) Russian Occupation of Galicia and Bukovina," in Dekel-Chen et al., *Anti-Jewish Violence*, 62–65, who notes the role of influential memos urging such policies by a nonmilitary figure, V. Murav'ev, the Foreign Ministry's attaché to the southwestern front.

[40] "'Iz 'Chernoi knigi,'" 212–13, 15.

[41] Ibid., 217–19, and Lohr, *Nationalizing the Russian Empire*, 143–44, who says hostage-taking becoming more systemic in May 1915: First and Tenth Armies alone reported taking 4,749 hostages (nearly all of them Jews) by the end of May.

In March 1915 there began a more systematic program of expulsion of Jews from all the districts of tsarist Poland, as well as from the provinces of Kovno and Kurland, border areas containing approximately 30 percent of the Jewish population of the Russian empire. Expulsions were carried out rapidly and brutally, sometimes within hours of being announced, with little time given for the expellees to wrap up their affairs or pack belongings. In some cases they were able to leave in their own carts or wagons; in others, they were driven out on foot, or packed into freight cars. No exceptions were made for age, infirmity, or gender, so that the hordes of forcibly displaced people included tens of thousands of small children, their mothers, and the elderly.[42]

A detailed official account on how this cleansing process played out in Kovno province reveals the utterly fantastic character of the undertaking, as well as unsuccessful efforts to rein it in. On April 28, 1915 the governor of Kovno received a telegram from the chief of staff of Tenth Army, General Popov, demanding removal of all Jews from a broad region:

> In view of the information daily affirmed by the troops about the exceptional development of espionage among the Jews in a region of the province from the north to the Neiman, and likewise of the complete sympathy of the Jews for the Germans, the commander [*komanduiushchii*] has ordered taking the most decisive and urgent measures for the eviction of all Jews from the area of the armies ... The commander allots one week for carrying this out, after which the presence of Jews in the area of the armies will be punished according to the law of wartime, while officials of the administration who do not take eviction measures will be removed from their positions and prosecuted.[43]

The governor of Kovno was not keen to undertake this massive operation. Noting that some 250,000–300,000 Jews lived in the region described by the commander, the majority of them poor people for whom eviction would be economically disastrous, he immediately telegrammed the head of the Dvinsk military district, Prince Nikolai E. Tumanov, requesting amelioration of these orders. Tumanov responded on May 1, saying that in light of the difficulties entailed in wholesale eviction of the Jews from Kovno, the region would be divided into three categories: "1. Points from which all Jews will be evicted; 2. Points where only hostages will be taken; and 3. Points not subject to repression [*repressii*]." However, General Popov stuck to his original order: all Jews were to be

---

[42] *The Jews in the Eastern War Zone* (New York: American Jewish Committee, 1916), 61–63.

[43] GARF, f. 102, II, 1915, op. 73, d. 72 ("Po povodu nezakonomernykh deistvii vlasti po otnoshen. k evreiskomu naseleniiu"), Report of 26 August 1915 from Governor of Kovno to Department of Police, l. 11.

removed, and within a week. The governor of Kovno thereby sent out instructions for the expulsion of some 300,000 people from their homes and communities by a deadline of May 6. Because portions of four districts within this area were currently held by the enemy, it was determined that eviction of the Jews from these districts would be delayed until they had been "cleansed of enemy troops."[44]

The Jewish community of Petrograd presented a declaration to the Supreme Command protesting what was essentially a smear on the loyalty of the entire Jewish population. It spoke powerfully about the unjust and insulting accusations of Jewish betrayal of the army, and the horrible practice of hostage-taking, at the very time when Jewish sons were in the army, fighting for Russia. It concluded:

> Your Imperial Highness. In this grave hour of trials ... we would wish to preserve that bond of devotion to a common motherland, necessary for the good of all the peoples of Russia, which revealed itself with such force when the insolent foe threw down its challenge to Russia. We do not want to allow disorder, discord, and bitterness where unity and bright hopes should hold sway. And we boldly turn to your Imperial Highness in the hope that these measures which degrade us will no longer be put into effect, that the brand of outcasts will be lifted from us, that it be given to us, as the right of true sons of Russia, not to be suspected of failing to strain every nerve in the struggle with the common foe.

Military authorities did not respond to this appeal; the civilian authorities explained that they were powerless to control the conduct of the military administration of the war zones.[45]

It is impossible to establish exact totals for the numbers of Russian Jews affected by these policies. Scholars' estimates range from 500,000–600,000 to 1,000,000 Jews deported and expelled; total hostages probably numbered in the tens of thousands.[46] The Great Retreat swelled the numbers of displaced people; desperate civilians of various ethnicities quit their homes and fled into the interior, or were compelled to do so by the military. In order to deny the enemy of anything useful,

---

[44] GARF, f. 102, II, 1915, op. 73, d. 72 ("Po povodu nezakonomernykh deistvii vlasti po otnoshen. k evreiskomu naseleniiu"), Report of 26 August 1915 from Governor of Kovno to Department of Police, ll. 11–12. Some of the deportees were resettled in other parts of Kovno province; those that had to be moved further went by train.

[45] "Iz 'Chernoi knigi,'" 220–21.

[46] Lohr, *Nationalizing the Russian Empire*, 144, 146, and Oleg Budnitskii, *Russian Jews between the Reds and the Whites, 1917–1920*, trans. Timothy J. Portice (Philadelphia: University of Pennsylvania Press, 2012), 73. We have no statistics for the numbers of Jews killed by soldiers or mobs, or executed after being found guilty by military courts; a prominent attorney who attempted to defend many Jews paints a depressing picture of a judicial system also in the throes of wartime "delirium": Gruzenberg, *Yesterday: Memoirs of a Russian Jewish Lawyer*, 135–68.

the retreating troops torched fields, homes, and entire towns, a strategy which also compounded the immiseration of the populace. Complete abandon reigned in the final hours before evacuation of any given locale, one eyewitness recalled, with repeated scenes of robbery, violence, even murder: "No earthly power, no matter how good its intentions, could control the marauders. This was especially true when Jews were involved."[47]

One important result of the Great Retreat and uprooting of masses of the Jewish population was the de facto abolition of the Jewish Pale of Settlement. This momentous decision was debated in two meetings in early August 1915 of the Council of Ministers. New minister of the interior Prince N. B. Shcherbatov blamed the army's treatment of the Jews on "the all-powerful Ianushkevich," over whose policies the civil authorities had no control. He then painted a picture of crisis. The mass of Jewish refugees simply could not be accommodated within the small portion of the Pale of Settlement that was not under enemy occupation. Economic and sanitary conditions were deteriorating, social tension was escalating, and pogroms were likely. Moreover, Jewish leaders had met with Shcherbatov and urged that measures be taken, telling him that the Jewish population was being radicalized by despair, and that major unrest was possible. Finally, he noted pressure from outside Russia, as well: "It was pointed out to me that abroad, too, patience is wearing thin and the day may come when Russia will not be able to borrow a penny."[48] Although Shcherbatov did not allude to it, pressure was coming from non-Jewish quarters in Russia as well. Various city councils, appalled by the mass scale and suffering of Jewish refugees, were passing resolutions asking for permanent or at least wartime abolition of the Pale of Settlement.[49]

The ministers reluctantly agreed that Jews would have to be allowed to settle outside the Pale. In doing so, they acted more on pragmatic or humanitarian grounds than on the belief that Jews were part of the Russian national community and should be allowed to move about

---

[47] Hirsz Abramowicz, *Profiles of a Lost World: Memoirs of East European Jewish Life before World War II*, trans. Eva Zeitlin Dobkin, eds. Dina Abramowicz and Jeffrey Shandler (Detroit: Wayne State University Press, 1999), 182–85.

[48] Council of Ministers meeting of August 4, 1915, in Cherniavsky, *Prologue to Revolution*, 57–59. The Russian text is: *Sovet ministrov Rossiiskoi imperii v gody Pervoi mirovoi voiny. Bumagi A. N. Iakhontova. (Zapisi zasedanii i perepiska)* (St. Petersburg: "Dmitrii Bulanin," 1999), 211–12.

[49] GARF, f. 579, op. 1, d. 1999, ll. 2–3. In 1914, the city dumas of Vilnius and Smolensk voted by large majorities to petition for abolition of the Pale of Settlement. In 1915, as the Jewish refugee problem worsened, the volume of such petitions rose.

in their own country.[50] Minister of Transport S. V. Rukhlov found it impossible to countenance revocation of a policy meant to protect the Russian population from "the putrefying influence" of Jewish neighbors: "Russians are dying in the trenches, and the Jews who settle down in the heart of Russia will benefit from the public disaster and general ruination." But as Finance Minister Petr Bark told him, "we must not be guided by feelings but by the demands of an extraordinarily critical moment." Krivoshein expressed more bluntly the need to do something fast: "Let us hurry. One cannot conduct a war with Germany *and* with the Jews. Even though General Ianushkevich differs, I allow myself to insist that these wars must be separated." All the ministers, save Rukhlov, approved the issue of a circular authorizing Jewish settlement in cities lying beyond the Pale, excluding the war zones and capitals.[51]

Though other restrictions on residency were still intact, and it would remain for the Provisional Government to permanently abolish the Pale, opening the gates in summer 1915 remapped Russia's national landscape. A population that was largely segregated from the larger national community now gained far greater opportunity for geographic mobility and integration; approximately 40 percent of the Jewish refugees settled in regions that had previously been closed to them.

Countering the Narrative of Treason

Jews acted in a variety of ways to defend their communities. Like other Russian minority groups, they mobilized themselves not only to aid the common war effort but also to provide relief for co-nationals harmed by the conflict. In the first months of the war, wealthy public figures in Petrograd created a central Jewish Committee for the Relief of Victims of War (EKOPO), an umbrella organization that worked with local Jewish committees all over Russia. It helped establish shelters, soup kitchens, medical facilities, schools, and labor bureaus, distributing

---

[50] Jonathan Frankel offers an interesting appraisal of the 1915 decision on the Pale, seeing it as evidence of Jewish ability to influence wartime decision-making but also as resting on a myth of Jewish power (mainly financial) that would have devastating consequences after 1917: Jonathan Frankel, *Crisis, Revolution, and Russian Jews* (Cambridge: Cambridge University Press, 2009), 147–48, 153–54.

[51] Cherniavsky, *Prologue to Revolution*, "The Meeting of 6 August 1915," 65–71 (emphasis added). Other restrictions included a ban against settling in Cossack territories or in rural villages, and on purchase of immovable property by resettled Jews. For a detailed contemporary appraisal of the decree, see *Jews in the Eastern War Zone*, 20–31; see also Eugene M. Avrutin, *Jews and the Imperial State: Identification Politics in Tsarist Russia* (Ithaca: Cornell University Press, 2010), 183–84.

almost 31 million rubles in aid during the course of the war.[52] Besides the desperately needed assistance these undertakings provided to displaced persons, they were also important sources of agency, pride, and a sense of common community. As Peter Gatrell observes more generally of nationally based refugee relief, "Refugeedom *(bezhenstvo)* inspired among an emerging patriotic elite a sense of national calamity that in turn gave rise to a vision of national solidarity."[53]

Besides material aid, there were various efforts to stop the mass expulsions, hostage-taking, pogroms, and violence directed against Jewish populations, and to combat the incendiary stories of treachery and greed that served to justify these measures. Jewish leaders organized a political committee in Petrograd, consisting of the three Jewish deputies to the State Duma – Niftel M. Fridman, M. Bomash, and E. Gurevich – and representatives of the capital's Jewish organizations, which wrote petitions and open letters to civil and military authorities. Russian Jewish intellectuals also joined forces with their Russian counterparts. In late 1914, Maksim Gorkii took the lead in gathering a group of Jewish and Gentile writers and activists – Solomon Pozner, Z. I. Grzhebin, Leonid Andreev, and Fedor Sologub were among the other organizers – to form a league to combat antisemitism. In order to get the new entity legally approved, they chose the deliberately innocuous name the "Society for the Study of Jewish Life" and asked Mayor Tol'stoi to be its president.[54] The society organized a lecture series on the "Jewish question" and published a literary anthology, *The Shield* (Shchit'). It also published an "Appeal to Russian Society," signed by dozens of celebrated scholars, writers, artists, and politicians, which deplored the unfounded persecution of the Jews as traitors, reminding the public that "the welfare and might of Russia, the happiness and freedom of the Russian people, are inseparably linked with the happiness and freedom of *all* the peoples that make up the great Russian state."[55]

---

[52] Sources of funding for EKOPO's relief activities included an annual 5 percent tithe paid by all its members, donations from the Jewish diaspora, monies from other Russian voluntary organizations, and large sums from the Russian treasury; see Steven Zipperstein, "The Politics of Relief: The Transformation of Russian Jewish Communal Life during the First World War," in Jonathan Frankel, ed., *Studies in Contemporary Jewry: Jews and the European Crisis, 1914–1921* (New York: Oxford University Press, 1988), 22–40.

[53] Gatrell, *Russia's First World War*, 186.

[54] GARF, f. 579, op. 1, d. 2019, "Zapiska Sologuba," l. 1, and Tol'stoi, *Dnevnik*, II, entry of April 22, 1915, 737.

[55] Salo W. Baron, *The Russian Jew under Tsars and Soviets*, 2nd edn. (New York: Macmillan, 1964), 166. For a translation of the text of the appeal and discussion of the tumultuous "Society to Study Jewish Life," see Viktor Kel'ner, "The Jewish Question and Russian Social Life during World War I," *Russian Studies in History* 43,

In 1915, a handsome weekly, *Voina i evrei* (The War and Jews), was launched in Moscow. Again, contributors included prominent Russian Gentiles, among them Andreev, Prince P. D. Dolgorukov, and Prince Evgenii Trubetskoi. Featuring numerous articles about decorated or slain Jewish soldiers, field hospitals staffed and funded by Jews, and other patriotic Jewish undertakings, all lavishly illustrated with photos, the paper clearly aimed to counteract impressions that Russian Jews were not serving and sacrificing. Its inaugural issue declared that for the Russian intelligentsia the paper would provide "graphic evidence of the utter lack of foundation for antisemitic agitation," while for the Jewish intelligentsia it would commemorate

the great Fatherland war, where much Jewish blood was shed on the field of battle, where Jews with selfless courage defended the honor of their dear Russia.[56]

The State Duma provided another venue for speaking on behalf of persecuted groups, including the Jews. The day after the Duma's reopening, on July 20, 1915, deputies filed an interpellation (*zapros*) about mistreatment of the Jewish population, offering strong speeches in its support. Pavel Miliukov, for example, accused the government of violating the sacred union through its treatment of various national minorities. Worst of all was the treatment of the Jews, who despite their patriotism had been subjected to savage measures that "lower us in the opinion of the entire educated world." All citizens' interests were equally deserving of attention, something Premier Goremykin's recent speech belatedly acknowledged. When the far-right deputy Markov II interjected that the authorities had in mind only the interests of "loyal sons," Miliukov wrathfully responded: "Russian citizens *are* loyal sons of Russia, and no one has the right to doubt that any Russian citizen is a loyal son of Russia."[57]

The interpellation on the Jews – like others concerning suppression of workers, or suppression of the minority-language press – stood no chance of being passed, as its sponsors knew full well. But the Duma was an important national forum, thanks to its enormous popularity over the course of 1915 and 1916. Moreover, the authors of these interpellations and the orators who spoke in their support did not fail to make use of the language of unity, equality, and citizenship. Since newspapers could not be prosecuted for reporting what was said in the Duma, these speeches

---

1 (Summer 2004), 11–40. Signatories of the appeal included Konstantin Arsen'ev, Nikolai Berdiaev, Ivan Bunin, Zinaida Gippius, Anton Kartashev, and Dmitrii Merezhkovsii.

[56] The lead article also stressed that the paper was independent and unsubsidized: *Voina i evrei* no. 1 (1915), 2.

[57] *GDSO*, IV, 4, sess. 1 (July 19, 1915), 95–96.

helped disseminate and legitimize the inclusive rhetoric and characterizations of the patriotic Russian community.

Just as it is important to know how some groups were represented as belonging outside the true national community, it is also useful to know *to whom* these representations were made. Negative representations of treacherous Russian "Germans" appeared in most of the press, including state- and church-sponsored publications widely distributed in rural Russia: namely, *Sel'skii vestnik* and *Prikhodskii listok*. Interestingly, these latter two organs do not display analogous representations of Jews, about whom they are largely silent. A good comparison of the treatment of Jews and Germans comes from *Sel'ski vestnik*'s coverage of the much-anticipated reopening of the Duma on July 19, 1915, the first anniversary of the war. The paper reported, without comment, deputy Fridman's portrayal of Jewish service and sacrifice for the war, and his rebuttal of charges of Jewish treachery. In contrast, it noted of a similar defense of Russia's Germans by Baron G. E. Fel'kerzam that "In the State Duma, they didn't greatly believe this Baron."[58] Thus, the representations of unpatriotic or treacherous Jews that figured in the conservative and right-wing press were not being disseminated in the press organs most regularly reaching the countryside.

The Jews' position significantly improved in 1916, Ansky observed. The Great Retreat was over, and the two most powerful antisemites at General Headquarters – General Ianushkevich and Grand Duke Nikolai Nikolaevich – had been transferred to the Caucasus. Stories of widespread Jewish espionage ended, as did mass expulsions; some of the expelled people were able to return to areas not under German occupation. But just as important as the change in official policy, in Ansky's opinion, was the change on the ground. Antipathies still existed, but Russians and Polish Jews had "grown accustomed to one another. The Jews had shown that there was no reason to suspect them of collaboration with the enemy."[59]

Unite or Exclude? The Fatherland Patriotic Union and the Right

Ramping up the language of exclusion and reproach was not the only possible response to the worsening military situation in spring 1915.

---

[58] *Sel'skii vestnik* (July 21, 1915), 3. The legislature had been in recess since the special session of January 1915, despite increasing public demand that the State Duma be convened to help deal with the country's military crisis.

[59] Ansky, *The Enemy at His Pleasure*, 226–28; see also Holquist, "The Role of Personality," 58–61, 67–68.

Another was to seek ways to strengthen the sacred union proclaimed at the war's start. For the prominent monarchist Grigorii Orlov, head of the Moscow division of the Union of Archangel Michael, the latter approach entailed a fundamental rethinking of his worldview. He concluded that greater national unity was critical to the hopes of victory and that this unity required a broader understanding of who properly belonged in the Russian national community, including even Jews.

Prior to the war there was nothing unusual about Orlov's monarchist views. But, by spring 1915, he had begun to believe that Jews were *not* the enemy, and that monarchists should publicly recognize that Jews, along with Poles and other non-Orthodox, were indeed Russian citizens. His initial efforts to persuade other monarchists to embrace these views produced an uproar and resulted in his being kicked out of the Union of Archangel Michael.[60] Orlov and his followers therefore decided an entirely new monarchic organization was needed, one that could expand its membership and potential appeal by admitting minorities and the non-Orthodox.

The Fatherland Patriotic Union held its founding congress in Moscow on July 30, 1915, as Russia's Great Retreat assumed ever more calamitous proportions. Dozens of delegates from branches of the Union of Russian People and Union of Archangel Michael attended, along with representatives of smaller monarchic organizations.[61] The union's statutes stressed its commitment to "immemorial Russian foundations: Orthodoxy, unlimited tsarist autocracy, and Russian nationality [*narodnost'*]." But it deviated from standard right views in defining eligible members as "all true Russian citizens, all patriots loving above all else their Fatherland and serving their Sovereign," a statement it qualified in two ways. Germans were excluded, meaning, in essence, that no one of German descent could be regarded as a "true Russian citizen." But ethnically non-Russian and non-Orthodox persons *could* be accepted as members, when unanimously approved by the council of branch members.[62]

Orlov explained why he had taken this step in an August 10 letter to the main governing body of the Union of Archangel Michael. Members of the Moscow branch and local affiliates, he said, were amazed and

---

[60] GARF, f. 102, op. 265, d. 1006, letter of S. Obleukhova to V. M. Purishkevich, May 17, 1915, l. 17.

[61] Kir'ianov gives the dates of the founding congress as June 15–16 but, in an August 10 letter, Orlov himself gives the date as July 30, the birthday of the heir to the throne: Kir'ianov, *Pravye partii v Rossii*, 219, and letter from Orlov, "Perepiska s glavnoi palatoi russkogo narodnago Soiuza im. M. arkhangela ...," GARF, f. 117, op. 3, d. 4, ll. 2–4.

[62] Kir'ianov, *Pravye partii v Rossii*, 223–40.

angry at the leadership's continuing intransigence on the question of minority policies and at "the harshness in attitudes toward the Poles and Jews, the most suffering element of the Russian citizenry in the theaters of war." In the opinion of "a huge portion of the monarchists" whom he had united, Orlov claimed, such attitudes did not correspond to present needs or to the policy of social unity that the tsar himself approved.[63]

The Fatherland Patriotic Union quickly acquired an important print forum, the church newspaper *Kolokol* (The Bell). *Kolokol*'s November 1915 description of its positions provides the fullest expression of what patriotism and Russian nationality meant for the Patriotic Union. It offered an inclusive approach to national belonging, one that privileged ethnic Russians but ultimately assigned citizens rights on the basis of loyalty and sacrifice. While "sacredly preserving the sovereign primacy of the Russian people," it also declared that, "All who lay down their life for the happiness of Russia, all the peoples loyal to Russia, are worthy of enjoying the vital blessings of citizens with equal rights." It also ran counter to a major theme of the right, regarding the treasonous behavior of the lower chamber of the legislature in 1915, by praising the "patriotic work of the State Duma throughout the entire period of the war," which demonstrated Russian society's maturity and loyalty. In effect, *Kolokol* insisted on the transformative effect of the war: it was not tenable to remain "blind and deaf to the change in political mood and worldview that is taking place in every corner of our country." New realities dictated a new "progressive state path."[64]

Initial prospects for unifying the fractious right on the basis of a more inclusive vision of the nation looked somewhat hopeful. Some fifty-eight branches of existing monarchic organizations transferred their affiliation to the Fatherland Patriotic Union, which eventually numbered eighty-two branches; it claimed to have as many as a thousand railroad workers as members[65] However, the broader unity Orlov and his supporters sought eluded them. Most monarchist leaders were appalled by the thought of abolishing the Pale of Settlement, extending equal rights to Jews, or allowing Jews to join a monarchist organization. Even Vladimir Purishkevich, newly minted friend of the Poles, could not reconcile

---

[63] Orlov, "Perepiska," GARF, f. 117, op. 3, d. 4, l. 3.
[64] "Ob"iavlenie o podpiske na gazetu 'Kolokol,'" in Iu. I. Kir'ianov, ed., *Pravye partii. Dokumenty i materialy*, vol. II, *1911–1917 gg.* (Moscow: ROSSPEN, 1998), 478–79.
[65] Kir'ianov, *Pravye partii v Rossii*, 226, and the Department of Police report to the Ministry of the Interior on the Moscow conference, in Kir'ianov, ed., *Pravye partii. Dokumenty i materialy*, vol. II, 467–68.

Fantasies of Treason 189

himself to Jewish membership in a right organization.[66] In fact, the military and political crises of 1915 caused a significant portion of monarchists to begin defining the Russian nation even more narrowly than before, and to expand the list of internal enemies threatening the very existence of "Holy Russia."

This latter reaction was characteristic of the two best-known ultra-right leaders, A. I. Dubrovin and Markov II, as well as a significant swathe of provincial monarchists hailing from some of the most intransigently Right areas of the empire – the western borderlands and a portion of the Volga heartland. During the war, the most energetic of these unreformed rights was Nestor Nikolaevich Tikhanovich-Savitskii, a successful Astrakhan merchant and founder in 1906 of the Astrakhan Popular Monarchic Party. Party membership had long been dwindling, but the declaration of war regalvanized Tikhanovich-Savitskii.[67] According to police reports, from July 1914 he began recruiting new members and directing their activities toward uncovering German espionage and efforts to undermine the troops. In 1915, he started holding large meetings where he and his followers delivered fiery speeches urging the Russian people to fight German and Jewish influence. In the opinion of the police, Tikhanovich-Savitskii had become "a raging patriot-fanatic."[68] By mid June 1915, he was working to join his reanimated provincial forces to a larger, national union of monarchists that could hammer out a plan of action for dealing with the threats besetting Russia.

Tikhanovich-Savitskii helped organize the All-Russian Congress of Monarchists held in Nizhnyi Novgorod on November 26–29, 1915. This was the fifth gathering of monarchists in as many months, but the only one laying claim to nationwide significance. It was also the most incendiary in its language and the most radical in its proposals.[69] Nizhnyi Novgorod held special symbolic value as the place where Kuz'ma Minin

---

[66] Purishkevich gave a report summarizing the first year of war in which he assured his audience that he remained "firmly convinced of the perniciousness of the 'chosen people' [i.e., Jews]": RGVIA, f. 2003, op. 1, d. 151, "Vypiski iz pechati," l. 70.
[67] On dwindling numbers in extreme right parties, in general, see Kir'ianov, *Pravye partii v Rossii*, 17–18, and I. V. Narskii, *Revoliutsionery "sprava." Chernosotentsy na Urale v. 1905–1916 gg. (Materialy k issledovaniiu "russkosti")* (Ekaterinburg: "Cricket," 1994), 28–34, 113–16.
[68] GARF, f. 102 00, op. 245, d. 244, t. 1, l. 108, report of October 6, 1915, by the head of the Astrakhan provincial gendarme administration.
[69] Nationally prominent ultra-Rightists such as Dubrovin and Markov II were among the 100 people present; Orlov, Purishkevich, and men with pretensions to a more "statesmanlike" posture, such as Count A. A. Bobrinskii, did not attend. Tikhanovich-Savitskii missed the congress due to illness: "Soveshchanie upolnomochennykh pravykh organizatsii i pravykh deiatelei v Nizhnem Novgorode," in Kir'ianov, ed., *Pravye partii. Dokumenty i materialy*, vol. II, 496.

had helped raise a militia to drive the Poles out of Russia in 1612–13, during the Time of Troubles. The monarchists were presenting themselves as the true heirs to that patriotic act, having "gathered at Minin's tomb for defense of Russia's historic foundations" from the dark forces of destruction.[70]

The congress began with an affirmation of autocracy as monarchists' most fundamental value, absolute fidelity to which marked them off from all other political groups. But the congress spent less time affirming its positive values than it did identifying problems and assigning blame: in its view, Russia was rife with traitors and their dupes. Social Democrats were enemies, ruled by German Social Democrats and in thrall to the teachings of the "Jew-German Karl Marx." The Duma's recently organized Progressive Bloc was ruinous to Russia and the war effort, the tool of an international plot. Germans living in Russia, even if they were Russian subjects, in secret gave their allegiance to the Kaiser. Germans should forfeit their privileges and be subject to the section of martial law dealing with traitors and betrayers, since in threatening times "it is impossible to trifle with obvious enemies in the rear." The so-called Ukrainians were separatists who hated the Russian people and were working to dissolve the Russian state, which made impermissible the existence of Ukrainian literature, Ukrainian bookstores, or any organization whatsoever that aided the Ukrainian movement.[71]

But the most dangerous enemy was the Jews. They were practitioners of a bigoted religion that was ruinous to a Christian kingdom. Russia's Jews were traitors and betrayers, while worldwide Jewry was in cahoots with Germany, using its millions to manipulate national economies: wartime inflation and shortages in Russia were the work of the Jews. So insidious a threat called for extraordinary measures. In the short run, Jews needed to be excluded from the education system, barred from holding any position of authority over Orthodox Russians, and legally proscribed from owning land or engaging in trade. To better protect the Russian people, courses of instruction that revealed the real nature of "Yid-Talmudism" and the Jews' secret plots should be mandatory in all schools and universities. Jewish war refugees should be barred from receiving any aid and sent to special places of confinement. In the long run, however, Jews needed to be regarded as "foreign subjects" and expelled from Russia in their entirety; the congress resolved to petition for such a measure.[72]

---

[70] Ibid., 496, 500. [71] Ibid., 511–12, 514.
[72] Ibid., 508–10, 517, 519. The congress also proposed that vigilantes who used violence against "Yid-Talmudists" not be subject to prosecution.

Of course, the extreme right in Russia was not only a small minority, but also a beleaguered one. Contemporaries, however, believed right influence to be substantial, which is not surprising given that individuals holding high official positions – such as General Ianushkevich and Minister of Justice I. G. Shcheglovitov – were members of monarchic organizations. But a particularly significant way in which the intransigent right was out of step was its insistence on an essentialist discourse of membership in the Russian nation, at a time when the majority of educated Russians subscribed to a transformative understanding of the Great War and the national community. The monarchists who joined the Fatherland Patriotic Union believed, along with moderates, liberals, and the left, that the terrible ordeal of the war had either revealed the true, patriotic nature of Russia's minorities, or had transformed previously dubious groups – like the Poles and the Jews – into loyal members of the national community. For the far right, the war was not transformative and unworthy population groups were not redeemable: they could only be repressed or expunged.

Fears of German Dominance

For many Russians, hostility toward Germany and German nationals predated the war. This was partly a function of Germans' influential role in the industrializing Russian economy. In 1914, German capital accounted for 20 percent of foreign investment in Russia and hundreds of companies there were wholly owned by German subjects. Firms in Russia, whatever their ownership, typically employed many foreigners in managerial and technical positions, with Germans constituting the largest group. Although many educated Russians appreciated that foreign capital and expertise were aiding the rapid development of native-born skills as well as the national economy, others feared or resented foreign "dominance" (*zasil'e*) in the economy, desiring a more independent economy that afforded greater scope to Russian businessmen and specialists. This economic nationalism was gaining in importance in the years immediately before the war.[73] With the start of hostilities, anti-German feelings broadened and intensified. There was immediate, general outrage against the German aggressor who had started the war, most tangibly expressed when a large mob in the capital sacked and

---

[73] Lohr, *Nationalizing the Russian Empire*, 55–61, and John P. McKay, *Pioneers for Profit: Foreign Entrepreneurship and Russian Industrialization, 1885–1913* (Chicago: University of Chicago Press, 1970), 368–69.

burned the German embassy on July 21, 1914.[74] Press stories on German atrocities against civilians and whole peoples' cultural treasures helped stoke such feelings.[75]

Escalating animosity could easily blur the distinction between German nationals and Russian citizens of German descent, to the point where "Germanness" itself became suspect. In 1915, various governors began to limit or ban use of the German language.[76] In July 1916, the Council of Ministers more generally prohibited teaching in the German language in all educational institutions in the empire.[77] Even before such bans were formally promulgated, individuals speaking German in public – or, more often, mistakenly *believed* to be speaking German by ordinary citizens – might be chased off trolleycars, mobbed by angry crowds, or denounced to the police. In the workplace, individuals chafed at working under German "bosses" and sometimes voiced suspicions about their loyalty. In summer 1915, for example, workers at two large Petrograd factories with defense contracts, the Obukhovskii Steel Works and Erikson Co., sent Duma deputies anonymous denunciations of "German" personnel there, alleging efforts to slow production, destroy shells, or sell military technology. Exhaustive inquiries established that the individuals with foreign-sounding names were not actually Germans, and that nothing untoward was occurring at either plant.[78] While no quantitative data exist for the numbers of such denunciations, they can be seen as both a product of and contributor to the climate of suspicion.

Anti-German societies began to appear after the declaration of war and proliferate in 1915; they tended to be particularly interested in the economic threat posed by Germany and "German domination."

---

[74] *Novoe vremia* (July 21, 1914), 3; "Razgrom germanskogo posol'stva," *Gazeta-kopeika* (July 23, 1914), 3.

[75] For example, "Zvertsva nemtsev" and "V strane dikarei," *Novoe vremia* (August 1, 1914), 3 and 4; "Gunny XX veka," *Gazeta-kopeika* (July 31, 1914), 3; "Sataninskaia izobretatel'nost' nemtsev," *Kievlianin'* (August 31, 1914), 4.

[76] GARF, f. 102, op. 302, d. 30, "Perechen obiazatel'nykh postanovlenii izdannykh v sviazi s voennymi polozheniami," ll. 48–53. Prohibitions varied widely – in Voronezh, German could not be used on the telephone, spoken in public places, or used in writing for official business; in Omsk the ban was only on spoken German; in Moscow, use of German was apparently permitted in private phone conversations.

[77] Report of Trepov, chair of the Special Committee on Fighting German Dominance, to Interior Minister B. V. Shtiurmer, 16 October 1916, RGIA, f. 1483, op. 1, d. 1, 9.

[78] RGVIA, f. 369, op. 1, d. 113, "Zaiavleniia," ll. 27–31, 34–37. The Erikson Company, which supplied telephones to the military, had recently experienced a six-day strike by more than 2,700 workers, which probably helps explain the scope of the investigation. In each case, investigators concluded that Germanic last names, or German-sounding names (at least one of the accused supervisors was Swedish), had aroused workers' suspicions.

"Independent Russia," chartered in February 1915, was one such society. It identified the struggle against German influence in Russian economic and cultural life as the "unconditional obligation of each Russian citizen, his patriotic duty before the Motherland, his moral responsibility to future Russia."[79] Most of the anti-German societies did not aspire to a mass membership; their members came largely from educated society and the manufacturing classes, and they sought to shape public discourse by publishing pamphlets and broadsides, sponsoring lectures, writing Duma deputies to advocate tougher measures against Germans within Russia, and orchestrating consumer boycotts of German retailers and merchandise. They also kept the army in mind; the "Society of 1914", for instance, sent soldiers 40,000 free copies of its publications over the course of a year.[80] These groups' constant attention to the threat posed by German dominance helped heighten public concern about that danger, while their general disinclination to distinguish between German nationals and Russian subjects of German descent helped to blur the boundaries between the two.

At least one of these groups apparently crossed the line between inflaming passions and inciting violence. On the night of October 10, 1914, in Moscow, pogroms against stores allegedly owned by German or Austrian subjects also destroyed a number of Russian-owned establishments. The Ministry of the Interior investigated, determining that the society "For Russia" (Za Rossiiu) was largely responsible for the crowds' actions. It had tried to introduce into the population "the greatest possible animosity against German citizens" and on the day of the disorders had run newspaper ads calling on Muscovites to boycott firms it identified as German-owned. Such disorders did Russia no good at all, Interior Minister Maklakov angrily wrote to Moscow City Governor (*gradonachal'nik*) A. A. Adrianov, demanding that he rein in "For Russia."[81] Responding, Adrianov attributed the disorders to German

---

[79] *Obzor deiatel'nosti Obshchestva "Samodeiatel'naia Rossiia" za 1915 god* (Petrograd, 1916), esp. 1–2, 44–45, and 55–58; the society had 627 dues-paying members in 1915, including Duma deputies Purishkevich and Prince S. P. Manysrev. One of its more innovative proposals, made to the Duma, was for the authorities to award government distinctions to Russian factory workers who displayed a high civic-mindedness and work ethic.

[80] *Otchet Soveta o deiatel'nosti "Obshchestva 1914 goda" za 1915 god* (Moscow, 1916), 5–6, 13. This society's lack of concrete initiatives – beyond attacking those who were allegedly "pro-German" – eventually prompted public criticism in some quarters; for example, "Obshchestvo 1914 goda," *Kievlianin'* (August 26, 1916), 2; RGVIA, f. 2003, op. 1, d. 1491, "Izdaniia" (Letter from Council of Society of 1914, February 1, 1917,), l. 2.

[81] GARF, f. 63, op. 35 (1915), d. 453, "O pogromakh v mae 1915 g.," letter of October 21, 1914, to Moscow Gradonachal'nik A. A. Adrianov from Interior Minister Maklakov, ll. 28–29.

behavior and popular patriotism. The crowd knew about German atrocities and "German insolence" toward Russians. It was important to understand "how much people's sense of national pride and national self-esteem has been outraged. Many people feel so deeply insulted that they're in no state to understand the situation."[82]

On May 27, 1915, at a time when reports of serious Russian reversals on the southwestern front were fueling widespread anxiety, Moscow erupted in far more serious rioting. The disorders were initially directed against factories believed to be owned by Germans, where crowds severely beat a number of individuals, killing several.[83] According to the subsequent special investigation, on the afternoon of May 28 crowds smashing German shops on Red Square fanned out until almost all of Moscow "was engulfed by pogroms and looting." Fires were still burning when the disorders were finally brought under control the next day. The investigation estimated that 732 separate businesses and buildings were destroyed, worth 50,604,764 rubles.[84] Moreover, hundreds of the premises affected turned out to belong not to enemy subjects, but rather to Russians or citizens of Allied or neutral countries. The authorities' efforts to preserve order were initially complicated by the ostensibly patriotic disposition of the demonstrators, who were carrying portraits of the tsar and singing the national anthem: Adrianov and the chief of police worried that resort to force might turn the "deeply patriotic mood of the crowd" into a "sharply revolutionary one," and potentially outrage the troops as well.[85] Adrianov was nonetheless blamed for the inadequate police response and sacked.

The effects of these riots extended beyond the loss of life and enormous economic damage they wreaked. People across the country were horrified by the news, which gave rise to all manner of speculation about the *real* instigators of the violence; few of these theories redounded to the credit of the authorities. The unfortunate confluence of patriotic demonstration and street violence caused the new governor general of Moscow, Adjutant-General Prince Iusupov, to conclude that Russian popular patriotism was, in effect, too dangerous to let onto the street:

---

[82] GARF, f. 63, op. 35, d. 453, ll. 36–39, Report of A. A. Adrianov to Maklakov, November 6, 1914.

[83] Two detailed treatments of the Moscow riots are Iu. I. Kir'ianov, "'Maiskie besporiadki' 1915 g. v Moskve," *Voprosy istorii* no. 12 (1994), 137–50, and Eric Lohr, "Patriotic Violence and the State: The Moscow Riots of 1915," *Kritika* 4, 3 (Summer 2003), 607–26.

[84] RGIA, f. 1405, op. 533, no. 2536 (1915), "Doklad Senatora Krasheninnikova" (September 10, 1915), ll. 4, 6, 10.

[85] RGIA, f. 1276, op. 11, d. 169, "Chrezvych. Zasedaniia Soveta Ministrov, v stavke, 14 iiunia 1915 g.," Report of Prince Iusupov, l. 22.

he forbade *any* future demonstrations in the country's second-largest city.[86] A further conclusion drawn by Iusupov – that the presence of Germans and German-owned business was the red flag inciting popular outbursts – was shared by others in power. In his own report, Iusupov recommended that the authorities publish a decree exiling all German and Austrian subjects, without exception, and all Germans and Austrians who had acquired Russian citizenship within the past ten years. He was deeply convinced that "if, additionally, concentration camps were built for these individuals, then there would be no kind of disorders or disturbances at the present time."[87]

An important source of fears about German dominance and internal enemies was the press. One of the most influential papers in this regard was A. S. Suvorin's *Novoe vremia*, a Petersburg-based conservative daily that was almost rabidly anti-German. In the tense days leading up to the declaration of war, *Novoe vremia* sounded a steady drumbeat of approval for the coming conflict. When war was declared, besides carrying stories on German atrocities it stressed the need to cleanse Russia of German influence, both symbolic and real. In November, the regular installment of M. Menshchikov's wartime column, "We Must Be Victorious," advised Russian Germans to change their names, since it was important not only to be Russian but to *sound* Russian. An article in the same issue complained that, even though three months had passed since the declaration of war, "we still have not cleansed the capital of Teutonic physiognomies."[88]

Not even six months into the war, articles on the so-called German colonists and their allegedly divided loyalties became staples. There were more than 2 million of these farmers in Russia on the eve of the war, owning more than 12 million *desiatin* of land; many had lived in Russia for generations, while others were more recent immigrants.[89] *Novoe vremia*'s "Overview of 1914," after painting a glowing picture of the population's united, patriotic support for the war, pointed out two glaring exceptions: German colonists and Baltic Germans. "Only these

---

[86] GARF, f. 63, op. 35 (1915), d. 642, "Sekretnyi doklad," l. 19.

[87] RGIA, f. 1276, Report of Prince Iusupov, l. 24.

[88] *Novoe vremia* (July 31, 1914), 2 (August 18, 1914), 3, and (November 1, 1914), 13, 14. Wartime anti-Germanism in the United States offers some interesting parallels; see Capozzola, *Uncle Sam Wants You*, 179–82.

[89] These figures date from 1908; continued German in-migration until 1914 means the numbers had certainly grown: Kn. S. Mansyrev, *Nemetskoe zasil'e i pravila 2 fevralia 1915 g.* (Moscow: Tip. A. I. Mamontova, 1915), 7. A major source of concern were changes to German citizenship laws, which counted as dual citizens Germans who had emigrated and taken citizenship in their adopted country; though these immigrants to Russia did not regard themselves as German citizens, according to German law they were.

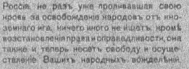

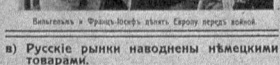

6.2 "Down with the German Yoke!" Headlines on this 1914 poster trumpet "The Secrets of German Intrigues" and "German Provocations in Poland". Political Poster Collection, #RU/SU 1123, Courtesy of Hoover Institution Library & Archives, Stanford University.

Fantasies of Treason

people, after nearly one and a half centuries' residence side by side with the Russian people, enjoying the special protection and favors of great Russia, have turned out to be alien to her and to the Russian people." Indeed, the Germans were so privileged that no one had even thought to doubt their loyalties. It finally fell to the Russian nationalist press to "reluctantly" assume the role of unmasker.[90] Actually, *Novoe vremia* unmasked with gusto, also going after officials or departments deemed insufficiently tough on Germans.[91] *Novoe vremia*'s inflammatory rhetoric spread far beyond its own readership, since its stories were often picked up and carried by other newspapers, including the Orthodox Church's *Prikhodskii listok*.

From late spring 1915, suspicions about the country's own Germans became common in most media outlets. In May 1915, the right-wing penny paper *Kievskaia kopeika* (Kiev Kopek) editorialized that every Russian needed to realize what any illiterate Russian peasant already knew: Russia's enemy was not just the German ruler and German army, but "all Germans in general."[92] The same paper occasionally paused in its vilification of Jews to point a finger of suspicion at Russia's German colonists. The soldiers' newspaper *Il'ia Muromets* explained to readers in late 1915 that with incredible foresight Germany had transplanted hundreds of thousands of German colonists to Russia decades ago, in order to have its spies and scouts in place when war eventually began.[93] From early 1915, columns condemning German dominance and the suspect loyalties of Russian Germans began appearing in the government-subsidized rural newspaper *Sel'skii vestnik*. In January 1916, that same paper promised all subscribers would be sent a free copy of the pamphlet "How We'll Be Saved from the German Colonists"; articles and letters supporting the authorities' efforts to liquidate these "nests of spies" continued to appear until the revolution.[94]

---

[90] "Obzor 1914 god," *Novoe vremia* (January 1, 1915), 12. Allegations in this article, as in many others, include claims that a whole series of Russian Baltic Germans turned up fighting in the German army.

[91] One object of its ire was Petrograd mayor Tol'stoi, who was appalled by persecution of innocent German and Austrian civilians and several times interceded on their behalf: *Novoe vremia* (August 3, 1914), 4 and 5, and Tol'stoi, *Dnevnik*, II, entries of October 16, 1914, January 8, 1915 and March 26, 1915, 632, 678, and 721.

[92] M.V., "Vil'gelm ili germanskii narod?" *Kievaskaia kopeika* (May 24, 1915), 3.

[93] D.B., "Za chto borotsia Rossiia," *Il'ia Muromets* (November 15, 1915), 2, and S.V., "Kak my izbavimsiia ot nemtsev-kolonistov," (February 28, 1916), 13–15.

[94] For example, "Germanizm," *Sel'skii vestnik* (January 11, 1915), 4; "Vyselenie kolonistov" (April 1, 1915), 4; "Protiv nemetskogo zasil'ia" (June 19, 1915), 4, and "Kolonisty predateli" (June 23, 1915), 3. Relevant issues for 1916 include *Sel'skii vestnik* (January 17, 1916), 1; N. Petrov, "Bor'ba s nemetskim zasiliem" (January 1, 1916), 2, and "Razorenniia shpionskaia gnezda," (September 4, 1916), 3.

Exclude and Expropriate

This heady mix of fears, rivalries, and economic nationalism combined with the mobilizing dynamic of the war to produce radical policies directed against foreign influence on the economy. Historian Eric Lohr has explored these nationalizing campaigns, which began with enemy subjects but soon extended to Russian subjects of "enemy-alien" origin. The first deportations, usually accompanied or followed by sequestration or confiscation of deportees' property, began in October 1914 in areas of the empire under military control. These removals were justified on security grounds: having enemy subjects resident in borderlands posed a military risk.[95] By early 1915, with the worsening popular feelings against Germans, deportations and expropriations expanded from strictly military undertakings to become a more general government project. A series of decrees promulgated between January 11, 1915, and February 8, 1917, largely ended German and Austrian participation in Russian industry, finance, and commerce. The decrees liquidated firms owned entirely by enemy subjects and partnerships with even one enemy-subject partner, as well as enemy-subject shares in Russian joint-stock corporations; some of the liquidated entities and shares were acquired by Russian-owned companies, others by state institutions. In all, Lohr estimates, 1,839 commercial firms and 59 large industrial firms were liquidated or changed hands.[96]

Three decrees of February 2, 1915, promulgated under article 87 of the Fundamental Laws, liquidated enemy-alien land holdings in rural areas; one of these decrees applied only to enemy subjects, but the other two applied to Russian-subject German settlers in a broad swathe of territory near the western borders. Not all settlers, or colonists, of German origin were initially affected; for example, immigrants who had legally taken Russian subjecthood prior to 1880 or who had converted to Orthodoxy prior to 1914 were exempt, as were individuals who had fought for Russia in previous wars as either officers or volunteers.[97] The February decrees provided for "voluntary sale" of lands belonging to the individuals coming under their jurisdiction.

Soon, however, the question of *who* exactly ought to receive these well-cultivated lands became far more pressing. As we have seen, Chief of Staff General Ianushkevich wanted German colonists' lands to be used as

---

[95] Lohr, *Nationalizing the Russian Empire*, 62–66.   [96] Ibid., 66–75, 82.

[97] For fuller details on the provisions of the laws, the colonists exempted from them, and the areas affected, see David G. Rempel, "German Colonists in South Russia during the Great War," *Journal of Modern History* 4, 1 (March 1932), esp. 53–56, 58–61; in practice local officials often ignored the few permitted exceptions.

an incentive to keep Russian soldiers fighting. Others envisioned limiting purchase to individuals of "Russian nationality," with an eye to bolstering the presence of ethnic Russians in the empire's sensitive borderlands. Still others advocated making the lands available to the Peasant Land Bank, to ensure that they would pass exclusively into peasant hands. This latter approach – which seemingly had no relation at all to the decree's stated objective about strengthening state defense – was the one that was adopted, in May 1915.[98]

Suspicions about German colonists' loyalty and proposals to expropriate their land on behalf of the peasantry were mutually reinforcing. In spring 1915, in private correspondence intercepted by the police, one sees numerous references to peasant expectations that at war's end soldiers would be rewarded with land. In May 1915, one A. Griaznov wrote to Agriculture Minister Krivoshein predicting troubles after the war if the government was not prepared to satisfy peasant wishes: "In Rostov on the Don in the bazaars, in front of patriotic pictures, on tram cars, I have heard threats to the government if it does not provide land to the peasants for all their burdens connected with the war. In Chernomorskoi province I hear the same thing." A letter from Samara province, in December 1915, explained, "In the village they nourish hopes that all the land will be parceled out to the peasants. They expected this on the 300th anniversary of the House of Romanov, then for the 100th anniversary of the Fatherland War, and they expect it now at the conclusion of this war."[99] More than one member of the propertied classes worried that if peasant expectations were not met at war's end, they would demand, or simply take, land from the nobility. The tsar should make giving disabled soldiers land taken from German colonists a top priority, A. S. Viazigin wrote to Markov II from Kharkov in 1915: "Otherwise, all the hatred will be directed at the estate owners."[100]

In December of 1915, new and more drastic decrees extended the area of expropriation for Russian subjects far beyond the borderlands to embrace twenty-one provinces of European Russia, while all limits were lifted on expropriation of enemy subjects' land holdings. A last set of

---

[98] Lohr, *Nationalizing the Russian Empire*, 100–02. An article in the respected legal journal *Pravo* offered an extended analysis of the contradictory features of the decrees, including language exempting large land holdings and certain nonpeasant land holdings from liquidation – exceptions the article's author found quite telling in laws ostensibly meant to combat German "dominance": M.D., "Mery 'bor'by s nemetskim zasil'em,'" *Pravo* no. 6 (February 12, 1917), 287–99.

[99] GARF, f. 102, op. 265, d. 1042, "Obzor" of letters (1914–15), ll. 2, 74, 75.

[100] GARF, f. 102, op. 265, d. 1042, "Obzor" of letters (1914–15), ll. 71, 75, and David G. Rempel with Cornelia Rempel Carlson, *A Mennonite Family in Tsarist Russia and the Soviet Union, 1789–1923* (Toronto: University of Toronto Press, 2002), 167–68.

decrees on expropriating rural land holdings was approved in early February 1917, extending the expropriation area for German Russian subjects to almost the entire empire.

Statistics for those affected are incomplete, and since there was a ten to sixteen months' hiatus between compilation of lists of those to be expropriated and actual inception of the process, many farmers listed for expropriation in 1917 ultimately escaped that fate. Even incomplete numbers are not small, however. One scholar estimates that, by February 1917, of the 3.5 million *desiatin* of land slated for alienation, between 500,000 and 600,000 *desiatin* had actually been expropriated. In Lohr's calculation, by the time of the revolution the regime had declared its intention to expropriate land holdings of more than half a million of its citizens.[101] Tens of thousands of German Russians were impoverished by the forced sale of their land at deeply depressed prices, delayed compensation from these sales, and hasty sale of their livestock and equipment at bargain-basement prices. They were then forced to leave their communities and move with their families – at their own expense, like convicts – to new, unfamiliar locales, sometimes being uprooted repeatedly as permissible settlement areas were revised and reduced. Thousands died en route.[102]

One striking feature these anti-German campaigns shared in common with the operations against Jews is how frequently the word "cleansing" is used. Articles in the press, military orders, and private correspondence could all employ it. "Volynia province is almost cleansed of German colonists," *Sel'skii vestnik* told its readers in August 1915.[103] On September 30, 1915, a military order to the administration of the city of Slutsk warned that, in the event of Jewish contact of any kind with the enemy, "the city will be immediately cleansed of Jews."[104]

Russian Germans listed for expropriation frantically hired lawyers and drafted petitions, usually without success. One task of the Special Committee on Fighting German Domination, created by the Council of Ministers in June 1916, was to evaluate such petitions.[105] The committee

---

[101] Rempel, "German Colonists," 62–63; Lohr, *Nationalizing the Russian Empire*, 119–20.
[102] Rempel, "German Colonists," gives the figure of 40 percent fatalities for the more than 110,000 German colonists driven out of the western borderlands (not including the Polish provinces) in 1915 and early 1916. Evictions in the four southern provinces of Bessarabia, Kherson, Tavrida, and Ekaterinoslav, which had the largest population of German colonists– about 489,000 – were on a much more piecemeal basis.
[103] "Vyselenie kolonistov," *Sel'skii vestnik* (August 4, 1915), 3.
[104] GARF, f. 579, op. 1, d. 2014, l. 2.
[105] RGIA, f. 1483, Special Committee on Fighting German Dominance, "Predislovie," l. 2. The formal initiative for creating the committee seems to have come from the emperor: f. 1276, op. 20, d. 113, "Osobyi zhurnal" (July 1916), meeting of 16 May 1916, l. 63.

received a total of 630 petitions from individuals subjected to the decrees of February 2 and December 13, 1915, contending that they did not belong in those categories and should be exempted. It approved a mere seventeen, rejecting all the remainder. It also rejected forty-six of forty-eight petitions from joint-stock companies and business owners asking that their businesses not be liquidated on the basis of the law of July 1, 1915. Among those whose petitions were rejected were the Mennonites of Molochansk district, despite their insistence that they were not Germans, since their ancestors had come to Russia from Holland. This petition enjoyed the backing of the Ministry of the Interior (MVD). Mennonites were legally exempt on religious grounds from conscription into the army, instead being allowed to discharge their service obligations by working as medical orderlies or supplying – and financially supporting – young men to work in state forests; as the MVD noted, the state could ill afford to lose the Mennonites' funding of forest workers.[106] Rooting out "Germans," however, trumped economic logic.

The profiles of the few successful petitioners shed light on what committee members used as criteria for distinguishing who was a genuine, trustworthy Russian. Fairly representative is the biography of one Oskar Berens, a landowner of Kherson province and Russian-born son of a German citizen. Upon reaching legal maturity in 1880, Berens had successfully applied for Russian subjecthood. He was married to a Russian Orthodox woman, had held a variety of responsible positions in local government, and was active in philanthropy. The committee also noted favorably that Berens enjoyed the "confidence of the peasants" and that his sole heir was baptized in the Orthodox faith. Despite this impressive profile, the governor of Bessarabia had recommended rejecting his petition "in view of certain suspicions to the effect that Berens has commented unfavorably on Russian military activities."[107] Unusually, the committee ignored the governor's recommendation and approved Berens's petition, explaining that besides looking at proof of an individual's reliability (*blagonadezhnost'*), a major consideration was whether the petitioner's children were raised in the Orthodox faith, given that they would eventually inherit his land. Similarly, the sixteen other successful petitioners had taken Russian citizenship at least twenty years prior to the

---

[106] RGIA, f. 1483, d. 1, ll. 10–14, 16. Only the intervention of the emperor, to whom the Mennonites also personally petitioned, forced a reexamination of their case, and then only on the basis of their claim to have come from the Netherlands and therefore not to be "Germans." The Forestry Department reported that as of December 1, 1915, it had 4,036 Mennonites at work: RGIA, f. 387, op. 18, 1915, d. 68783, l. 1.

[107] RGIA, f. 1483, d. 1, Report to B. V. Shtiurmer from Trepov, Head of Committee, October 16, 1916, ll. 10–14.

outbreak of the war and were prominently involved in charitable works; most were married to an ethnically Russian woman professing the Orthodox faith. Additionally, several had sons currently serving in the military.[108]

Some Russian Germans considered immigrating to Canada rather than waiting to learn their fate. But leaving one's home and homeland was not a step lightly taken, as a letter of May 2, 1916, intercepted by the police and translated from German, makes poignantly clear. The unsigned letter, sent to one Olga Gofman in Winnipeg, reads in part:

> It's unknown whether we Germans will remain in our fatherland or if we can be moved to Canada. Perhaps they'll send us to Siberia. I love Russia and want to die in Russia, since here every sapling, every little bush is dear to me. Your Canada seems repugnant to me. But if they banish us, then I'll have to pack up and go. Our young people are spilling their blood and dying, and we'll leave Russia with the sense of having fulfilled our duty. Let God's will be done ...[109]

Germans by Faith

In the same way that legal grounds for deporting "German" Russian subjects became more open-ended, the criteria of Germanness also lost more of its objective meaning, at least in the case of Russian Evangelical Christians. Unlike Mennonites, whose ancestors did, in fact, often hail from Germany and who frequently did not speak Russian, many Baptists and Evangelicals were either Slavs (Great Russians, Poles, Ukrainians) or of a national group distinct from Germans, such as Latvians. These individuals therefore came to be categorized as German, and subjected to persecution, on the grounds of their choice of a putatively "German" faith, rather than on the basis of ethnicity or descent.

Suspicions about the allegiance of Russian Baptists and Evangelicals predated the war. Though their numbers were insignificant – not quite 97,000 adherents as of January 1, 1912 – they were active proselytizers, and their congregations had been growing rapidly since the April 1905 edict on religious tolerance.[110] The Orthodox hierarchy's distrust of these sectarians was longstanding, as was its insistence that genuine Russians could not be Protestants: for many clerics, the Orthodox faith

---

[108] It is impossible to determine what other factors may have been at work in these successful petitions; Rempel says his Mennonite family paid bribes to numerous officials in their effort to be classified as Dutch rather than "German": Rempel with Carlson, *A Mennonite Family*, 165–67.

[109] GARF, f. 102, op. 265, d. 1056, "Vyrezki iz pisem, 1916," l. 610.

[110] Figures for these two groups come from Coleman, *Russian Baptists*, 27, and do not include Adventists; judging by continued growth up to the eve of the war, there were probably at least 100,000 such sectarians by July 1914.

was indeed a constitutive element of Russianness. With the outbreak of hostilities, Baptists and Evangelical Christians lost no time in proclaiming their loyalty and participating in war relief. In August 1914 the Petrograd community (*obshchina*) of Baptists pledged to organize and fund an infirmary, declaring their love for the motherland and "burning desire to come to the aid of the government and Red Cross in the cause of caring for the wounded."[111] Such efforts were not enough to mitigate concerns about sectarian loyalties, a problem that was exacerbated by their pacifism. Although many Baptists and Evangelicals served as combat troops during the war, some 370 were prosecuted for refusing to bear arms on religious grounds.[112]

Sectarians contended that Orthodox clerics spearheaded the effort to equate their faith with Germanness and deficiency in patriotism. Certainly, in the August 3, 1915, Duma debate on whether to establish a special Duma committee to fight German domination, it was clerical deputies who insisted on lumping Protestant sectarians together with German colonists. Father Stanislavskii, a deputy from Kharkov province, asserted that part of the cunning German plan to enslave the Slavs was to send preachers to Russia, where they would undermine the people's fighting spirit by luring them into sectarianism. The teachers of the Baptists and "stundists" were the same Germans who were currently ravaging Orthodox places of worship, he alleged, and "we Russian citizens will not permit the trampling of our sacred things in our own country by our fellow countrymen who have been seduced by these German preachers and lost their sense of patriotic duty." Sectarians considered Germany to be their fatherland, and spied for the enemy. He hoped the Duma would ask that all their prayer houses be closed.[113]

A 1915 pamphlet by Bishop Ioann of Eisk, "Spies through Religion," used even more inflammatory language, warning readers not to be fooled

---

[111] Cited in Kandidov, *Sektanstvo i mirovaia voina*, 11–13.
[112] According to figures published in a Tolstoyan religious journal, of the 837 sectarians prosecuted by military courts as of April 1, 1917, for wartime refusal to serve in the military, 114 were Baptists and "stundists" and 256 were Evangelical Christians – that is, 44 percent of the whole: cited ibid., 38–39. There are no figures for the numbers of Baptists and evangelicals who served in the army, though many did so; see Coleman, *Russian Baptists*, 120–21, who notes that, while neither the Baptist or Evangelical movements formally opposed bearing arms, there were serious divisions over this issue among believers.
[113] *GDSO*, IV, 4, sess. 5 (August 3, 1915), cols. 423–25; only the far Right applauded this speech. Russian Orthodox clerics often used the term "stundist" (*shtund*) – borrowed in the 1860s from German Lutherans' name for German Pietists – to refer to all Protestant sects in Russia; see Sergei I. Zhuk, "Making and Unmaking the "Sacred Landscape" of Orthodox Russia – Identity Crisis and Religious Politics in the Ukrainian Provinces of the Late Russian Empire," in Bassin, Ely, and Stockdale, *Space, Place and Power*, 195–218.

by the seeming goodness and sincerity of Baptist sectarians. A spy, in Bishop Ioann's definition, "is a person who hates his Motherland, who despises the Fatherland. He is ready to drink the blood of his own people." But worst of all were spies through religion, who in furtherance of their political calculations "mask their impure goals, their filthy motives, with the Gospels of Lord Jesus Christ." The present war had revealed that Evangelical Christians were just such spies. The bishop warned, "Beware, dear citizens and brothers, of people who serve foreign espionage, Pharisees covering themselves in the holy garb of the Christian religion."[114]

Sectarians tried to counter these charges, in part, by explaining what made them true and loyal Russian subjects. In 1915, Evangelical Christian leader I. S. Prokhanov wrote a long, closely reasoned memo (*zapiska*) asking that the military authorities' persecution of Evangelicals and Baptists be stopped. They were being accused of Germanism and militarism, he said – completely incorrect accusations based on the misapprehension that the German Kaiser funded their movement (he did not). In fact, Prokhanov asserted, they were devoted to the sovereign and faithfully fulfilling their duty to Russia.[115] A false assumption underlay the accusation that Evangelicals and Baptists were German, to the effect that if ethnic Russians profess the same faith as Germans "then that means the Russians cease to be Russian, they have sold themselves and therefore they are traitors." Along this line of thinking, Prokhanov suggested, one would have to conclude that Slavophiles were not Russian patriots, since they had borrowed most of their ideas from German philosophy. Another myth was that Russian Baptists and Evangelicals were German by origin or nationality: in reality, "Russian Evangelical Christians and Baptists are Russian people by blood, upbringing, thoughts, feelings, and in love toward the motherland, Russia."[116]

Prokhanov requested that all the preachers sent into exile or imprisoned be freed and allowed to return, and that the closed prayer houses and *obshchiny* be reopened. Whether his petition elicited any response from the authorities is unclear; such policies were not formally repudiated until the February revolution.[117]

---

[114] Episkop Ioann, *Shpiony ot religii* (Izd. Kubanskogo, vo imia Khrista spasitelia, Otdela Vserossiiskogo Trudovogo Soiuza Khristian-Trezvennikov, 1915), 1–3.
[115] GARF, f. 579, op. 1, d. 2592, "Zapiska Prokhanova I.S., 'O presledovaniiakh evangelskikh i srodnykh im khristian v Rossii vo vremia voiny'" (1915), l. 1.
[116] GARF, f. 579, op. 1, d. 2592, "Zapiska Prokhanova I.S.," ll. 18–20.
[117] Ibid., ll. 1–2. Overall figures for the number of prayer houses closed or sectarians exiled do not appear to exist; policies could also vary by region.

In this climate, looking tough on "Germans" was politically much safer than appearing to defend them. In part to assuage public indignation over German spies and sympathizers, several official committees were organized to further shape policy on Germans in Russia. Although the Committee on Fighting German Dominance created by the Council of Ministers rejected more than 97 percent of the petitions it received, its severity did not save it from criticism. V. M. Purishkevich denounced it in a Duma speech in November 1916, charging that it had become too easy on Germans. The committee, in turn, felt compelled to defend itself by issuing a report on the aggressively anti-German nature of its activities.[118]

Already on August 3, 1915, the State Duma had voted to organize its own "Committee on the Struggle with German Dominance in All Spheres of Russian Life." The debate over creation of this committee illustrates the highly charged mood, including the desire to vent popular wrath against some object other than the army command. Conservatives warned of popular vigilantism along the lines of the Moscow riots, if the Duma was not seen to be doing something about Russian reversals. Several deputies dwelled on the otherness of the German colonists: they lived separately from other Russians, did not speak Russian, and professed a different faith. A few, like Baron Aleksandr F. Meiendorf of Lifland province, did not dispute the idea of forming a committee but cautioned against indiscriminate branding of anyone with a German name as non-Russian and a traitor.[119]

Critics, in turn, labeled the proposal to create the committee a transparent attempt to find scapegoats. Kerenskii, noting that the law of February 1915 did not touch big, privileged landowners, contended that the real intent of the law was to sow discord among the peasantry and thereby "distract the popular masses from those genuinely to blame for the current catastrophe."[120] Miliukov cautioned that violating rights of private property for one group set a dangerous precedent, opening the door for violation of others' property rights as well. Still others put their finger on the economic issues that helped drive these policies: "German dominance" was a simple, demagogic explanation for the systemic problem of Russian underdevelopment, and grabbing German property would not help in the least. A number of deputies noted that the proposed committee transgressed against the sovereign's call for the unity of

---

[118] RGIA, f. 1483, d. 1, l. 15, "Zapiska" of November 19, 1916, by Trepov, and letter of same to Rodzianko of November 1916, ll. 16–20.
[119] *GDSO*, IV, 4, sess. 5 (August 3, 1915), cols. 360–404, 450–71.
[120] Speech by Kerenskii, *GDSO*, IV, 4, sess. 5 (August 3, 1915), cols. 427–28.

all Russians regardless of nationality, faith, or status. Liberal Fedor Rodichev was particularly eloquent on this betrayal of the idea of sacred union: "[T]rying to unite the Russian people with hatred is not the right way to forge unity, our victory must be won only by worthy means."[121]

None of these appeals to reason, decency, or enlightened self-interest slowed formation of the Duma's Committee on the Struggle against German Dominance in Every Sphere of Life: most parties in the Duma were eager to be associated with its activities.[122] In its first weeks of existence the committee endorsed a bill to terminate all special privileges associated with the hereditary estates of the Baltic nobility, a group largely German in its origins. (The bill's unusually broad backing – 205 deputies sponsored its introduction – is telling in its own right.[123]) It also recommended Duma approval for the confiscatory decrees of February and June 1915, which the government had promulgated under article 87 while the legislature was not in session.

Other Internal Enemies

In 1915, organizations with an anti-German agenda were not the only patriotic entities that sprang into being to help combat supposed internal enemies; nor were ethnicity and religion the sole bases for suspicion. If one did not assume that ethnically non-Russians were less loyal than the "core population," one might instead suspect that certain groups were more concerned with advancing their own self-serving agendas than with defending the country. One example comes from the self-styled "Committee of Popular Salvation" (Komitet narodnogo spaseniia), organized in Moscow in September 1915, whose initial twelve-point manifesto asserted that the war was being conducted "on two fronts, against a persistent and skilled external enemy and a no less persistent and skilled

---

[121] Fedor Rodichev, *GDSO*, IV, 4, sess. 5 (August 3, 1915), cols. 413–20.

[122] *Gosudarstvennaia duma. Obzor deiatel'nosti komissii i otdelov. Chetvertyi sozyv. Sess IV. 19 iiulia–3 sentiabria 1915 g.* (Petrograd: Gos. Tipografiia, 1915), 137–40. The committee's thirty-three members included G. V. Skoropadskii, chair; Prince S. P. Mansyrev, vice-chair; A. N. Khvostov, a Right deputy and nephew of A. A. Khvostov, soon to be justice minister; and five Orthodox clerics.

[123] Only the bill on compensating people for losses caused by the war, with 215 sponsors, attracted such widespread support. The committee's report does not allude to the German origins of most Baltic nobles, instead justifying elimination of monopolies on such activities as catching and selling fish in the name of fairness and promoting economic development: "Zakonodatel'noe predlozhenie," August 1, 1915, *Prilozhenie k stenograficheskim otchetam Gos. Dumy. Chetvertyi sozyv. Sess IV. 1915 g.*, no. 15, 1–5; the committee report is in the same volume: "Doklad," August 24, 1915, *Prilozhenie k stenograficheskim otchetam Gos. Dumy. Chetv sozyv. Sess IV. 1915 g.*, no. 47 (k no. 15), 1–2.

internal enemy." Defeating the foreign foe was impossible without first vanquishing the enemy within, which this group identified not on ethnic lines but as any person or entity that did not respect popular sovereignty or had sold out Russian interests (the "Russian press" was the only transgressor named). The manifesto called for immediate appointment of a Supreme Command, to be headed by the improbable combination of Prince G. L'vov, A. I. Guchkov, and Kerenskii.[124] The interest of this rather incoherent text does not lie in any putative impact on policy. Rather, it provides another perspective on the climate of anxiety, anger, and search for culprits that invited a sorting of the population into groups of those who were loyal, and those who were not. Its militarized language, with references to "war on two fronts" and internal "enemies of the people," is also highly representative.

Individuals accused of "profiteering" (*spekulatsiia*) were not subject to expropriation or internal deportation in the way Russian Germans or Jews might be, but as economic conditions worsened they frequently became the object of public wrath and official investigations. The cost of living rose appreciably in 1915, and precipitously in 1916: the price of commodities, other than grain, increased by 94 percent in that year. Added to the problem of inflation were deepening shortages in items of basic necessity.[125] By early 1916, the problem of high prices (*dorogovizna*) and shortages became a dominant theme in public discourse. It was difficult for much of the public to understand the complex factors responsible for soaring costs, or how a country that had been a net exporter of food could be experiencing food shortages. Instead, many people were convinced that hoarders and profiteers were deliberately withholding goods from the market in order to drive up prices. The press reinforced these perceptions by reporting avidly on hidden caches of commodities, and the staggering profits being made on scarce items, as in early 1916 when commercial warehouses in Kiev, Moscow, and elsewhere were found stuffed full of sugar, prompting a spate of editorials about "sugar kings."[126]

"Profiteers" – a term that could cover both manufacturers and retailers – thereby became a subset of the population who were deficient

---

[124] GARF, f. 599, op. 1, d. 2524 (September 8, 1915), "Dispozitsiia No. 1 – Komiteta narodnogo spaseniia," l. 2.

[125] See Gatrell, *Russia's First World War*, 144–46, 248–49, who calculates that by 1916–17 consumption was probably only half its prewar level.

[126] For example, *Russkoe slovo* (January 27, 1916), 3, 4; I. M. Gol'dshtein, "Dorogovizna, sokrytie zapasov i spekulatsiia," *Russkoe slovo* (January 28, 1916), 1; and anon., "Baryshi sakharnykh 'korolei'," *Russkoe slovo* (February 25, 1916), 3; also, "Chem kruche, tem luchshche!" *Gazeta-kopeika* (January 1, 1916), 4.

in patriotism: in a war whose rhetoric was about service and sacrifice, they seemingly sacrificed nothing. Anger over profiteering sometimes meshed with antisemitism, given that so many Jews were involved in trade. But it could equally easily assume class overtones, since big manufacturers and merchants were perceived as growing fat off the war, while most working-class city dwellers were struggling to buy food. Police reports tracking the popular mood in Moscow province in early 1916 show widespread anger at speculators. In the districts of Serpukhov and Podolia, for example, the population blamed the government for high prices but the "attitude toward merchants is positively hostile." In Bogorodoskii district, press exposés about "the speculations of such aristocrats as Count Musin-Pushkin with sugar and State Council member Ofrosimov with shoes for the army provides ample fodder for conversations among the public." Workers there were enraged about shortages and high prices, "especially toward traders, to the extent that serious disorders could erupt for the slightest reason."[127]

By the second half of 1916, as soldiers became more and more agitated by news of inflation and shortages on the home front, military censors reported letters equating speculators with internal enemies. One soldier wrote in August 1916, "It seems to me that before you can dream about victory you must destroy the internal enemies, namely: speculators, merchants and other such harmful egoists who have forgotten the motherland and play into the hands of enemies." An officer charged that, while a husband or son suffered in the front lines, "in the rear his wife, family, mother, sisters, daughters are being robbed by these damned profiteers and internal enemies, who are vastly more dangerous than the external enemy." A soldier from the 43rd Infantry reserve battalion wrote that, if Russia were forced to make a shameful peace it would be the fault of people in the rear, who had created "a rotten organization of traitors and speculators."[128]

For much of 1916, however, continued hopes that a decisive military victory would soon end the war kept these anxieties and discontents from assuming dangerous proportions. The national economic mobilization begun in spring 1915 had corrected the worst shortages in materiel, and the troops were also better fed and clothed. An important boost to morale came from the stunning initial success of General Aleksei

---

[127] GARF, f. 58, op. 5, d. 399, "Moskovsk. Gub. Zhandarsk. Upravlenie (1916), po nabliudeniiu za uezdam Moskovskoi gubernii," ll. 10, 36, 38, 48 (reports on the public mood for January, February, and March 1916).

[128] RGVIA, f. 2003, op. 1, d. 1486, ""Svodka otchetov voennykh tsenzorov shtabov armii" (1916), ll. 186, 226–27.

Fantasies of Treason 209

6.3 "A Letter Home." An artist's rendering of a widely reproduced photograph. Millions of letters passed between the front and home front during the war, attentively monitored by military censors. Political Poster Collection, #RU/SU 338, Courtesy of Hoover Institution Library & Archives, Stanford University.

A. Brusilov's offensive, which opened May 22, 1916, and punched sixty miles through Austrian lines, taking half a million prisoners.[129] Heartened by Russian successes, Romania finally entered the war in August on the Entente side; many hoped that this addition would decisively affect the eastern front. Censorship also meant that most Russians were only dimly aware of massive and devastating rebellions in Russian Turkestan that began in July, evoked by an ill-considered decision to conscript draft-exempt non-Russians there for labor obligations in aid of the military.[130] On July 19, the second anniversary of the

---

[129] Military censorship report of April 1916 for the Southwestern Armies and Kiev Military District, RGVIA, f. 2003, op. 1, d. 1486, ll. 63–64.
[130] Desperate for manpower, the military authorities decided to make use of these mainly Muslim colonial populations as laborers. A subsequent Duma investigation into the

war, newspapers all over the country reflected a renewed optimism: the people's herculean effort to aid the army would result in "victory in the name of Russia's bright future, victory in the name of our motherland's renewal."[131]

But following its brilliant start, the Brusilov offensive concluded indecisively, having cost nearly a million Russian casualties. Romania's offensive turned almost immediately into debacle. By November, with the Russian army dug into new positions for the winter, and dealing with the early onset of bitterly cold weather, many soldiers lost hope that victory was in sight. More and more men were animated by a desire for "peace at any price."[132]

Now, fantasies of treason were increasingly directed to the heart of power. Despite all the energy and expense invested in depicting the patriotism and self-sacrifice of the tsar and his family, many people doubted the loyalty of the German-born empress and her favorites – such as Prime Minister Boris Shtiurmer, a Russian citizen of German descent, and the peasant "holy man" Grigorii Rasputin. In October, Prince Georgii L'vov, head of the Union of Zemstvos, warned Duma president Rodzianko about the widespread belief that "an enemy hand secretly influences the direction of our state affairs."[133] For many ordinary Russians, the large number of senior officials and courtiers with German surnames – which had typified the imperial court and governmental service since the eighteenth century – now assumed sinister meaning.

These dangerous, delegitimizing suspicions burst into the open on November 1, 1916, when Liberal leader Miliukov gave a speech in the Duma listing the many disasters that characterized the government's conduct of the war, pausing repeatedly to ask, "Is this stupidity or is this treason?" At each iteration the crowded chamber shouted in answer

uprising, which cost thousands of lives and devastated the region's economy, was publicly aired in December, deepening the conviction among elites that the regime was simply incapable of handling the war effort: see Daniel Browder, *Turkestan and the Fate of the Russian Empire* (London and New York: Routledge and Curzon, 2003), 1–25, 152–71.

[131] *Rech'* (July 19, 1916), 1–2. A good overview of press coverage is "Vtoraia godovshchina voiny," *Kievlianin'* (July 20, 1916), 4.

[132] After months of insisting on the basically robust (*bodyri*) mood of the troops, military censors for the southwestern front reported a sharp drop in morale in November 1916: RGVIA, f. 2003, op. 1, d. 1486, "Report for November 15–December 15, 1916," l. 231. That this alarming development was common to many sectors of the army as a whole is reinforced by the findings of A. B. Astashov, *Russkii front v 1914–nachale 1917 goda. Voennyi opyt i sovremennost'* (Moscow: Novyi khronograf, 2014), 597–98, 675–76.

[133] Report of the gendarmerie of Moscow province in GARF, f. 58, op. 5, d. 399, l. 187. For an English-language treatment of official depictions of Nicholas during the war, see Wortman, *Scenarios of Power*, II, 510–19.

"Stupidity!" "Treason!" "Both!" Thousands of illicit copies of this speech rapidly circulated all over Russia – often with inflammatory additions to the text – reinforcing concern about traitors at the regime's very core.[134] In his exhaustive study of the wartime images of the imperial family, historian Boris Kolonitskii demonstrates that these fears of treason transcended class, regional, and ideological lines: by the dawn of the New Year, seemingly everyone in Russia doubted the loyalty of the empress and many of the ministers whose appointments she was believed to have secured.[135] A unifying belief that there was treachery at the top constituted a terrible inversion of sacred union.

Conclusions

When publicist Sergei Runin wrote in 1915 that, in a war of nations in arms, "mobilizing morale" was critical to victory, he was stating what seemed by then a self-evident truth.[136] And thanks to the efforts of thousands of writers, journalists, teachers, and others – among them Runin himself – Russia's population had indeed been mobilized behind the war effort, emotionally and imaginatively, to an impressive degree. But national mobilization also had its darker side. Efforts to promote solidarity and sacrifice for the nation's just cause could also evoke efforts to identify and exclude the unworthy; persuading people that defeat would be disastrous stimulated fear and violence as well as patriotic resolve. For Russia, the unintended consequences of national mobilization were devastating.

Russia's adherence to the mobilizing narrative of sacred union was imperfect and inconsistent. The narrative could and did fold new subsets of the population into the patriotic national community, as illustrated by the reimagining of Russia's Poles as loyal Slavic brothers and sisters. In the case of the Fatherland Patriotic Union, it even saw a portion of the far right ready to see Jews as rightful members of the community. But the Russian high command was less than ready to view Jews as loyal Russian citizens or treat them as such. The same press that was instrumental in disseminating the inclusive patriotic narrative was equally important in fanning spymania. And in the State Duma – which relished its new

---

[134] On Miliukov's "stupidity or treason" speech, see Stockdale, *Paul Miliukov and the Quest for a Liberal Russia*, 233–36.
[135] Kolonitskii, *Tragicheskaia erotika*; Kolonitskii notes that most rumors made Alexandra the guilty party, and Nicholas merely a dupe: the image of the "tsar-traitor" was never so widespread as that of the "tsar-fool" (ibid., 240).
[136] Runin, "Sim pobedish' – mobilizatsiia dukha."

popularity as the embodiment of the union of peoples – the majority was nonetheless happy to go after Russia's German population.

The simple need for scapegoats was part of this dynamic. When what was expected to be a short war dragged on with no end in sight, there were obvious political benefits in blaming internal enemies for military misfortune, shortages, rising prices, resumption of the strike movement, and other woes. But wartime policies directed at certain ethnic or religious minorities, or other suspect groups, were profoundly counterproductive. From a purely military perspective, as contemporary critics pointed out, uprooting hundreds of thousands of civilians from war zones complicated the army's retreat in 1915 and hindered its receipt of desperately needed supplies. Encouraging rank-and-file soldiers to believe that whole groups of their fellow citizens were traitors and spies and tolerating – or even sanctioning – soldiers' pillaging of other Russian subjects were not ways to maintain fighting spirit and discipline. And, as William Fuller notes, belief in pervasive treachery robbed people of hope in victory and "made a mockery of personal sacrifice for the Russian cause."[137]

The regime's radical measures against suspect Russian subject groups – including nationalization of private property and internal deportation – were both economically injurious to the war effort and socially destabilizing. Identifying entire population groups as putative or potential traitors had other unintended consequences: it could help consolidate a conscious, national group identity among the accused where such an identity had earlier been weak or inchoate. Individuals lumped together and mistreated by their own government might discover a common national identity that transcended their preexisting class, regional, or political differences.[138]

If these policies were intended to prove the regime's commitment to uncovering internal enemies and fighting until complete victory, they failed miserably. Ultimately, belief in internal treachery and "dark forces" spread to tarnish the imperial family and court. Once Nicholas II lost popular legitimacy, he could not find the necessary support to handle food riots in the capital that turned into political protests. Then Russians found themselves trying to accomplish the impossible: establish a new regime, expand and redefine citizenship, and remobilize support for the nation's war. These efforts are the subject of the next chapter.

---

[137] Sanborn, *Imperial Apocalypse*, 85–86, and Fuller, *Foe Within*, 262.
[138] Lohr, *Nationalizing the Russian Empire*, 164–66, and von Hagen, "The Great War and Mobilization of Ethnicity," 42–45.

7 "For Freedom and the Fatherland"
Shaping Citizens in Revolutionary 1917

> Citizens! Are you prepared to give your strength and, if needed, your life for Freedom, the Motherland, and Brotherhood?
> From the *Appeal* of the Military League, 1917[1]

Shortly after the February revolution ended monarchy in Russia, idealist philosopher Nikolai Berdiaev published an essay avowing that, "The Russian revolution is the most patriotic, the most national, the most popular revolution of all time."[2] Berdiaev's encomium reflected a widespread belief among educated society that the revolution was a popular repudiation of the tsarist regime's sorry conduct of the war. Competent and indubitably patriotic citizens would be able to solve the provisioning crisis, ferret out traitors in responsible positions, and lead the country to victory. Confidence in the new democracy, and happiness with the long-deferred reforms it would promulgate, would bolster national unity and resolve.[3]

On February 27, progressive members of the Duma formed a committee that cobbled together a Provisional Government, which would exercise authority until a Constituent Assembly could be elected and convened. Prince Georgii L'vov, chair of the popular Union of Zemstvos, was selected to head the new government, which quickly promised to honor Russia's commitment to its allies and continue the fight until victory.[4] The Petrograd Soviet of Workers' and Soldiers' Deputies,

---

[1] GARF, f. 579, op. 1, d. 2278, "Vozzvanie Glavnogo Soveta voennoi ligi 'K grazhdanam!'," l. 1.

[2] Quoted in Orlando Figes and Boris Kolonitskii, *Interpreting the Russian Revolution: The Language and Symbols of 1917* (New Haven: Yale University Press, 1999), 163.

[3] On Kadets' tendency to equate the revolution with dedication to winning the war, see William G. Rosenberg, *Liberals in the Russian Revolution, 1917–1921* (Princeton: Princeton University Press, 1974), 64, 94–95. The socialist V. Bazarov surveyed and critiqued such avowals made by members of the Duma's Progressive Bloc: V. Bazarov, "Pervye shagi Russkoi revoliutsii," *Letopis'* (Feb.–Apr. 1917), 380–84.

[4] Duma leaders – particularly President Rodzianko – envisioned an important role for the lower house of the legislature in the new order. However, despite the Duma's wartime popularity, the handful of men who negotiated creation of the new government felt the

established at the same time, was rather more insistent on renouncing annexations and indemnities and more open to the possibility of a negotiated peace; nonetheless, it too was committed to defending "free Russia" from German militarism.[5] The soldier was now a soldier-citizen, proclaimed to be protecting freedom *and* the fatherland. Initially, the great majority of the population shared the commitment to defense. But as the country's economic situation continued to worsen, and violence and disorder spread, the common people's willingness to stay in the war speedily eroded. Trying to rebuild unity, remobilize the home front, and offer new and compelling explanations of why all citizens must continue the fight necessarily consumed much of the new authorities' energies.

These urgent issues claimed others' energies as well. Existing wartime associations, political groups of widely differing views, and hundreds of new organizations and unions that sprang into being all over revolutionary Russia struggled to frame the discussion of the rights and obligations of freshly liberated citizens. Not surprisingly, there were deep differences over what those rights and obligations were, and exactly how they should be fulfilled. And thanks to the virtual elimination of censorship outside the war zones, the people of Russia enjoyed unprecedented opportunities to freely argue their opinions – including demands for a speedy end to the war – and try to mobilize fellow citizens behind them.

New Institutions, New Rights

In the first weeks following the revolution, there were promising signs that Russia was, indeed, reunited and transformed in ways that augured well for the future. Virtually all witnesses attest to an initial euphoria at the relatively bloodless collapse of the old regime (it was not, actually, as bloodless as many imagined).[6] Spontaneous public performances of

---

Duma harbored too many conservative deputies to make its continued existence tenable; it legally ceased to function on February 26. On this line of thinking, see Miliukov, *Vospominaniia*, 456–61. The most exhaustive study of the Duma's role in the February revolution is A. B. Nikolaev, *Revoliutsiia i vlast'. IV Gosudarstvennaia duma 27 fevralia–3 marta 1917 goda* (St. Petersburg: Izdatel'stvo RGPU im. A. I. Gertsena, 2005).

[5] On the Soviet's willingness to support a defensive war effort – the position known as "revolutionary defensism" – see Rex Wade, *The Russian Search for Peace: February–October 1917* (Stanford: Stanford University Press, 1969), 19, 26–32, 46–48.

[6] For example, Ariadna Tyrkova-Williams, a prominent member of the Kadet Party, compared the revolution to Easter in the way it brought everyone together as participants in a "collective miracle" of rebirth: "in the days of early rapture we all believed that this inspiring sense of community would be retained and deepened, that national unity would help us to defend Russia from the Germans and work out a new statehood, strong and free" (Tyrkova-Williams, *From Liberty to Brest-Litovsk: The First Year of the Russian Revolution* [London: Macmillan, 1919], 12–13). On bloodshed during

7.1 Russian soldiers take an oath of loyalty to the country and its new government in March 1917; their original oath pledged loyalty to the person of the tsar. Photo courtesy of Bettmann/Corbis.

unity, celebration of the revolution even by conservatives and one-time monarchists – seemingly everyone donned red ribbons or hoisted a red flag – and generous donations honoring those wounded or killed in the February days were all highly evocative of the early days of the war and the proclamation of a "sacred union" of the nation.[7] Russia's allies immediately recognized the legitimacy of the new Provisional Government and expressed confidence that the new regime would prosecute the

---

the February days – which may have accounted for as many as 1,500 killed and 6,000 wounded – see Orlando Figes, *A People's Tragedy: A History of the Russian Revolution* (New York: Viking Press, 1996), 320–22.

[7] In addition to Figes and Kolonitskii, *Interpreting the Russian Revolution*, important explorations of the festivals and rituals of 1917 include those by Stites, *Revolutionary Dreams* 79–88. B. I. Kolonitskii, *Simvoly vlasti i bor'ba za vlast'. K izucheniiu politicheskoi kul'tury Rossiiskoi revoliutsii 1917 g.* (St. Petersburg; Dmitrii Bulanin, 2001); and Svetlana Malysheva, "Mass Urban Festivals in the Era of War and Revolution, 1914–1922," trans. Hannah Zinn, in Frame, Kolonitskii, Marks, and Stockdale, eds., *Russian Culture in War and Revolution*, Book 2, 99–120. Donations sent just to the Temporary Committee of the Duma to be apportioned among various war-related and revolutionary causes amounted to an astonishing 3,318,448 rubles for the period March 1–April 10: *Pravitel'stvennyi vestnik* (May 14, 1917), 5.

war with renewed vigor. Importantly, the Russian Orthodox Church – the conservatism of its hierarchy notwithstanding – also recognized the new government, on March 7 exhorting the faithful to pray for their new government and drawing up a new oath for soldiers, to replace their old oath to the sovereign. The soldier now swore "on his honor as a citizen" to serve the Russian state to his last drop of blood and to subordinate himself to the Provisional Government until the people's will had been expressed in the Constitutent Assembly.[8]

The Provisional Government insisted that it could not undertake such fundamental reforms as rights to private property and a potential federal structure for the multinational state – these core issues could be determined only by the Constituent Assembly.[9] But certain other pressing concerns could be addressed: in its first whirlwind weeks, with the approval of the Petrograd Soviet, the government passed a raft of new laws and decrees. Poland was promised complete independence, though the meaning of this promise was somewhat ambiguous, given that all of Russian Poland was under German and Austrian occupation. Civil liberties such as freedom of assembly, conscience, and speech were proclaimed. For the Russian Orthodox Church – perhaps as a quid pro quo for its support of the new regime – religious freedom and the separation of church and state meant satisfaction of the longstanding desire to convene a church council (*sobor*) to work out how the church would, in future, govern itself. Political prisoners were amnestied, and the old police force abolished. Workers gained the right to strike. Further confiscation of German colonists' land was put on hold. Equality before the law was proclaimed for all citizens of the empire, regardless of religion, nationality, and social estate.[10] In the army, the general principle of

---

[8] The text of the oath, issued March 7, 1917, is in M. A. Babkin, ed., *Rossiiskoe dukhovenstvo i sverzhenie monarkhii v 1917 gody. Materialy i arkhivnye dokumenty po istorii Russkoi pravoslavnoi tserkvi* (Moscow: Izd-stvo "Indrik," 2006), 407–08. Over the course of 1917, the synod exhorted the faithful to keep supporting Russia's holy war, not only for the sake of "our own narrow happiness and that of our children," but also for the good of all humanity: *Za rodiny, za pravdu Bozhiiu. (Listok no. 18)* (Petrograd: Synodal'naia tipografiia, 1917), 4.

[9] Elections to the all-important Constituent Assembly were not held until November, after the overthrow of the Provisional Government (by then in its third coalition). Admittedly, figuring out how to run Russia's first-ever universal elections with 5 million men at the front and millions of refugees scattered around the country was no easy task, but long delays in promulgating electoral guidelines and fixing a date for voting helped delegitimize the government. A comprehensive study of the elections is Oliver H. Radkey, *Russia Goes to the Polls: The Election to the All-Russian Constituent Assembly, 1917* (Ithaca: Cornell University Press, 1990).

[10] The most detailed discussion of the early legislation of the Provisional Government is V. I. Startsev, *Vnutrenniaia politika Vremennogo pravitel'stva pervogo sostava* (Leningrad: "Nauka," 1980); see also Pipes, *The Russian Revolution*, 298, 320–30.

national equality was embodied by repeal in April 1917 of discriminatory – and preferential – rules regarding conscription and service for national groups. Jews, for example, were no longer prohibited from being officers. Many national minorities pressed for formation of military units on the basis of nationality.[11]

Women also received many of the political and legal rights they had hoped to win eventually through wartime work and sacrifices. In early March the Provisional Government and the Petrograd Soviet proclaimed their adherence to universal suffrage; Russian feminists immediately exerted pressure to ensure that this would include women, who were formally granted the franchise on July 20, 1917. Other decrees issued over the summer enabled women to serve as trial attorneys and as jurors, and gave them equal opportunity and pay in the civil service. Russia's women were now more fully citizens of their country than were the women of any other belligerent state.[12]

Both the Provisional Government and Petrograd Soviet were acutely aware of the role that food shortages and material hardship had played in triggering the revolution. Given the need to ensure the army's fighting spirit, they were especially attentive to the economic concerns of soldiers and their families. They tried to alleviate the hardships that contributed to low morale, as well as earn soldiers' loyalties, by deepening the state commitment to material welfare established by the 1912 military reforms. Soldiers' wages were raised in April 1917, and eligibility for family stipends was significantly broadened to include family members previously excluded.[13] Disabled soldiers were a particular object of concern. A law of April 11, 1917, created substantial supplements to the pensions established by the 1912 law. Within the newly created Ministry of Welfare, a temporary all-union Committee for Aid to Disabled Soldiers was established to work out projects for aiding soldiers and help set up and coordinate the work of comparable local committees.[14] The Committee for Aid planned to publish a journal which would apprise disabled soldiers of programs and benefits, and also develop the population's understanding of the state and society's "obligation to assist

---

[11] Sanborn, *Drafting the Russian Nation*, 80–82.
[12] Richard Stites, *The Women's Liberation Movement in Russia: Feminism, Nihilism, and Bolshevism, 1860–1930* (Princeton: Princeton University Press, 1978), 291–95, and Ruthchild, *Equality and Revolution*, 226–30.
[13] Pyle, "Village Social Relations," 292–99.
[14] The Union of Disabled Soldiers was a Petrograd organization, but extended its reach outside the capital by publishing and distributing a newspaper, *Golos invalida*, from late June: *Russkii invalid* (May 25, 1917), 6, and (June 25, 1917), 4. GARF, f. 6787, op. 1., d. 29, "Postanovlenie Vremennogo pravitel'stva ob uchrezhdenii vremennogo obshchegosudarstvennogo i mestnykh komitetov pomoshchi voenno-uvechnym," ll. 3–5.

7.2 Blinded veterans, led by a Sister of Mercy, demonstrate in support of continuing the war until victory, Petrograd, 1917; the great majority of soldiers did not share their sentiments. Photo courtesy of Bettmann/Corbis.

people who have given to the motherland their health and capacity for work." The Provisional Government was, of course, very happy to receive strong support for itself and the war effort from two new soldiers' organizations, the Union of St. George Cavaliers and the Union of Disabled Soldiers.[15]

These new unions speak to a much larger dynamic at play in revolutionary 1917, the unprecedented formation of new associations – locally and nationwide, some small and others sprawling. The best-known of these new entities were what John Keep calls the mass organizations – the soviets of workers' and soldiers' deputies in the towns, and their rural counterparts, as well as trade unions, factory committees, and militias. These organizations, he notes, "performed a supremely important role as organs of mass mobilization."[16] Other organizations developed to promote national groups' desiderata, professional interests, private property,

---

[15] GARF, f. 6787, op. 1, d. 32, "Proekt postanovleniia ob izdanii zhurnala 'Izvestiia komiteta pomoshchi voennouvechnym,'" l. 1.
[16] John L. H. Keep, *The Russian Revolution: A Study in Mass Mobilization* (London: Weidenfeld & Nicolson, 1976), viii–xi; on factory committees in the capital, including their cultural and educational efforts, see S. A. Smith, *Red Petrograd: Revolution in the Factories, 1917–1918* (Cambridge: Cambridge University Press, 1980), 80–102.

and cultural or religious values.[17] A population that had been mobilized, and had mobilized itself, for the war effort was now mobilizing to attain all manner of interests and goals, many of which had nothing at all to do with the war.

Framing the Patriotic National Discourse

Accompanying new laws and rights were efforts to school new citizens in the meaning and language of citizenship. Diverse parties, organizations, and educational institutions began publishing books and pamphlets, and sponsoring lectures and classes, that explained political and legal concepts to popular audiences. The press of the "Instructors of Moscow University," for example, produced two series of topical pamphlets; the one for popular audiences featured titles such as "What It Means to Be a Citizen" and "Why We Must Beat the Germans."[18] In addition to the commercial press, hundreds of new periodicals – most of them not commercial in nature – also took up these issues, as did existing periodicals of the big public organizations, professional societies and cooperatives, and the Russian Orthodox Church.

Organizations involved in cultural work directed at popular audiences, and especially the all-important army, included the Central Committee of the educational commissions of the Petrograd garrisons, the cultural-educational committee of the Soviet of Soldiers' Deputies in Moscow, wartime patriotic societies such as "For Russia" (which continued its warnings about German domination), and the cultural-educational organs of various political parties. Liberal nationalist Petr Struve launched the "League of Russian Culture," to counter class antagonisms by promoting a sense of common national destiny.[19]

---

[17] In the Ukrainian provinces, for example, banned Prosvita (Enlightenment) Societies, Ukrainian cooperatives, and cultural clubs reemerged throughout the region, many of them spreading nationalist messages: Serhy Yekelchyk, *Ukraine: Birth of a Modern Nation* (Oxford: Oxford University Press, 2007), 67–70. An excellent study of elites' organizations is Matthew Rendle, *Defenders of the Motherland: The Tsarist Elite in Revolutionary Russia* (Oxford: Oxford University Press, 2010).

[18] RGVIA, f. 2003, op. 2, d. 50, "Izdatel'stvo prepodavatelei Moskovskogo universiteta," ll. 24–25; this file lists authors and titles for fourteen popular pamphlets and ten titles in the "Scientific-Political Library."

[19] On enlightenment activities in 1917, see T. N. Zakharova, "Vlianie kul'turnogo faktora na obshchestvennoe soznanie mass v Petrograde v 1917 godu," in O. A. Polivanov and V. I. Startsev, eds., *Revoliutsiia 1917 goda v Rossii. Sbornik nauchnykh statei* (St. Petersburg: Tret'ia Rossiia, 1995), 153–60, and P. V. Volobuev, ed., *1917 god v sud'bakh Rossii i mira. Fevral'skaia revoliutsiia* (Moscow: Institut rossiiskoi istorii RAN, 1997), 218–21. On Struve, see Richard Pipes, *Struve: Liberal on the Right, 1905–1944* (Cambridge, MA: Harvard University Press, 1980), 234–39.

Besides countless articles and lectures devoted to the subject of citizenship, numerous pamphlets appeared on this topic. Most of them identified freedom and equality as the true hallmarks of the citizen. Liberals and moderate socialists were also likely to stress that even members of unpopular groups and privileged classes enjoyed these rights; that freedom was not license; and that citizens were "responsible people."[20] Many were also concerned to pair patriotism and citizenship. A pamphlet by socialist M. Ia. Fenomenov, in the inexpensive series "The Easily Accessible Political Library," warned readers not to buy into the antipatriotic views of many socialist intellectuals. These dreamers could not tell the difference between natural love of one's own fatherland and crude chauvinism of the German variety. In reality, the "tolerant and big-hearted patriotism" of the Russian people, desiring true freedom for all peoples – from the Poles to the Irish – was completely compatible with the brotherhood of peoples preached by the Petrograd Soviet. But freedom had to be defended from outside aggressors: "Patriotism is the sentiment of the free citizen; indifference to the fate of the motherland is the sentiment of the slave."[21]

Newspapers were another important venue for reaching soldier audiences. From March through October 1917 no fewer than 167 military newspapers appeared, about 50 of which were soldiers' papers produced at the front.[22] One new paper was *Soldat-Grazhdanin* (The Soldier-Citizen), a popular daily which the Moscow Soviet of Soldiers' Deputies began publishing shortly after the tsar's abdication. For the soldiers who edited *Soldat-Grazhdanin*, the most crucial issues were consolidation of soldiers' civil and political rights, transformation of the war into a purely defensive one, and persuading fellow soldiers of their civic duty to continue defending the fatherland and freedom.

However, the paper's pages were also full of letters, resolutions, and announcements, sent by activists and individual service people and units in the far-flung Moscow military district, that often expressed more

---

[20] See for example, N. S. Arsen'ev, "O svobodakh i obiazannostiakh grazhdanina" (Moscow, 1917), 4–6; N. N. Pchelin, "Grazhdanin i ego obiazannosti" (Moscow, 1917), 8–9, 11, 14–15; P. V. Gerasimov, "Novyi stroi i prava svobodnykh grazhdan" (Petrograd, 1917), 3, 9; and V. N. Durdenevskii, "Prava i obiazannosti grazhdanina" (Moscow, 1917). The ways different groups understood and employed the languages of citizenship are explored by Figes and Kolonitskii, *Interpreting the Russian Revolution*, 104–26.

[21] M. Ia. Fenomenov, *Russkii patriotizm i bratstvo narodov* (Moscow: Izd. D. Ia. Makovskogo, 1917), 3–5, 20, 26–27.

[22] V. A. Zhuravlev, *Bez very, tsaria i otechestva. Rossiiskaia periodicheskaia pechat' i armiia v marte–oktiabre 1917 goda* (St. Petersburg: Ministerstvo obrazovaniia Rossiiskoi federatsii, 1999), 42–44.

material concerns. These included jobs and pensions for disabled soldiers, as well as the need to increase soldiers' pay and the monthly stipends distributed to soldiers' families; the latter issues, one reader insisted, were just as important as the eight-hour day for workers. In May, soldiers' wives referred to the inadequacy of state aid in urging their fellow *soldatki* to attend organizational meetings, since "we'll achieve nothing if we each try to gain our lawful rights on our own"; soldiers' families were similarly urged by other activists to organize themselves.[23] A resolution by 1,200 reservists demanded that the Petrograd Soviet increase monetary support to soldiers and their families or – if this should prove financially impossible – that it *lower* defense workers' salaries and benefits to the same level as soldiers', since the principle of equality required that the burdens of the war be shared evenly.[24] Whether invoking civic or revolutionary principles, these appeals and resolutions reveal an internalized sense of material benefits owed the country's defenders and their families.

Of course, individuals and subsets of the population could understand the language of citizenship in ways quite distinct from the meaning intended by the authors of instructional articles and pamphlets. Orlando Figes and Boris Kolonitskii have explored how the discourse of human rights and citizenship intertwined with discourses of class among workers. Equality and human dignity had always been important issues for workers. By declaring themselves to be "citizens" and demanding equal rights on this basis, workers were also asserting their class power. In the early stage of the revolution, the language of class was more inclusive, and workers' resolutions spoke of universal rights and the liberation of all people. But, as conditions in Russia worsened, a new class militancy and exclusivity developed. "Where the educated classes spoke of civic rights and duties, the masses took the view that what had taken place was a social revolution in which the old elites were to be the

---

[23] *Soldat-Grazhdanin* (March 15, 1917), 1 (March 22, 1917), 3 (April 28, 1917), 3 (May 6, 1917), 3 (May 13, 1917), 4, and (May 16, 1917), 3. The paper characterized itself as socialist in orientation, supporting a strictly defensive war; no information is available about the unnamed editors, other than their self-identification as "simple, rank-and-file soldier-citizens."

[24] *Soldat-Grazhdanin* (May 28, 1917), 3, 5; the fullest treatment of soldiers' views in 1917, including their growing desire for peace, is Wildman, *The End of the Russian Imperial Army*. In the early 1920s, American veterans demanding adjusted compensation for their service in the world war made a similar appeal to equity and fairness, arguing that conscripted citizen-soldiers were paid $30 per month in wartime while defense workers were receiving the highest wages in American history: Jennifer D. Keene, *Doughboys, the Great War, and the Remaking of America* (Baltimore: Johns Hopkins University Press, 2001), 162–63.

losers and themselves the winners."[25] In the countryside, as Aaron Retish shows in his study of Viatka province, peasants were eager to participate in the new democratic order and welcomed instruction in the practice of citizenship. But they grew disenchanted with elite assumptions about their political backwardness, which turned out to entail continued tutelage and a subordinate status. By summer, peasants were clashing with authorities and demanding "an equal voice as citizens in the political world."[26]

The new freedoms which citizens were urged to defend included the freedom to speak *against* the war. Some people, like Marxist Nikolai Sukhanov, had opposed participation in the war from the outset, but found it difficult to express such views publicly.[27] Others subsequently turned against the war, for a variety of reasons: the belief that its goals had ceased to be just ones, that no victory could make up for its continued horrible costs, or that the humbler classes bore a disproportionate share of the sacrifice.

Thanks to the near absence of censorship outside the military zones in Russia in 1917 – a significant way in which Russia's experience of the war differed sharply from all other belligerents' – the population was now exposed to every conceivable critique of the war, and of the government and society conducting it.[28] Particularly potent were class-based

---

[25] Figes and Kolonitskii, *Interpreting the Russian Revolution*, 104–26. The literature on the creation and evolution of working-class identities is rich; see, for example, Smith, *Red Petrograd*; Diane Koenker, *Moscow Workers and the 1917 Revolution* (Princeton: Princeton University Press, 1981); Diane P. Koenker and William F. Rosenberg, *Strikes and Revolution in Russia, 1917* (Princeton: Princeton University Press, 1989), esp. 179–238; and Porshneva, *Krest'iane, rabochie i soldaty*, 117–74, who sees the war as decisive in transforming workers' mentalities. On the creation of a "plebeian intelligentsia," see Mark D. Steinberg, *Proletarian Imagination: Self, Modernity, and the Sacred in Russia, 1910–1925* (Ithaca: Cornell University Press, 2002), 21–61.

[26] Retish, *Russia's Peasants*, 83–95. For similar findings about peasant political agency in Nizhegorod and Kazan provinces, see Sarah Badcock, "Talking to the People and Shaping Revolution: The Drive for Enlightenment in Revolutionary Russia," *Russian Review* 65 (2006), 617–36.

[27] Nikolai N. Sukhanov, subsequently famous for his seven-volume memoir of the events of 1917, claimed that during the war he was "one of the two or three writers who managed to advocate the antidefensist Zimmerwald position in the legal press." See N. N. Sukhanov, *The Russian Revolution 1917: A Personal Record*, ed., abridged, and trans. by Joel Carmichael (London: Oxford University Press, 1955), 8. Zhuravlev, *Bez very*, 173–215, provides a detailed exploration of publications for soldiers conveying the message that this war (*chuzhaia voina*) was not *theirs*.

[28] In the first weeks of the revolution, "freedom of the press" was fairly ad hoc. According to E. N. Burdzhalov, *Russia's Second Revolution: The February 1917 Uprising in Petrograd*, trans. and ed. by Donald J. Raleigh (Bloomington: Indiana University Press, 1987), 310–13, initially it was press workers who determined what could actually be published (they effectively shut down all publications of the far right, and refused to print *Novoe vremia* until its publisher pledged to the Soviet that it would not publish antirevolutionary

arguments contending that soldiers' sacrifices were wasted on unworthy ends, or denying any meaningful foundation for "national unity" given the opposing interests of the propertied classes and the working masses. For example, the influential Bolshevik newspaper for frontline soldiers, *Okopnaia pravda* (Trench Truth), consistently denounced the imperialist nature of the war and the slaughter of millions of peasants and workers for the interests of Russian and international capital. Its provocative slogan was "The bourgeoisie to the trenches!"[29]

Weak censorship constraints also allowed even more discussion of who was not a loyal member of the national community. Fantastic stories about the treachery of former minister of war Sukhomlinov, Boris Shtiurmer, the imperial family and others – taken as fact – moved from the realm of rumor into print, circulating widely. People were warned to be vigilant about German spies, and in July the Bolsheviks' popularity plummeted, at least temporarily, when a member of the Provisional Government made public allegations about their taking "German gold."[30] The concern with betrayal and disloyalty was not limited to the "unsophisticated masses." "Why is it that in no other people drawn into the war there is so much treason as among the Russians?" lamented Moscow-based historian Iurii Got'e in his diary.[31] Inflammatory language about spies and internal enemies had become so common, Maksim Gorkii ironically observed in June 1917, that "the word 'traitor' is heard just as often as the call 'Waiter!' was heard in the taverns of the old days."[32] Indignation over putative internal enemies further corroded national unity.

---

content). The formal statutes detailing press freedom and abolishing the Chief Administration for Press Affairs – the body primarily responsible for civilian censorship – were promulgated on April 27; the texts are in Robert Browder and Alexander F. Kerensky, *The Russian Provisional Government, 1917: Documents*, 3 vols. (Stanford: Stanford University Press, 1961), vol. I, 228–30.

[29] Wildman, *The End of the Russian Imperial Army*, vol. II, 52–54.

[30] For example, an article by I. O. Landov, "Ukhishchreniia shpionazha," *Voina i mir* (June 13, 1917), 1, warning that "you can't always tell the German who is irreproachably loyal to us from the secret traitor." On the impact in July 1917 of evidence suggesting that Lenin and other Bolsheviks were working for Germany, see Alexander Rabinowitch, *Prelude to Revolution: The Petrograd Bolsheviks and the July 1917 Uprising* (Bloomington: Indiana University Press, 1968), 191–93, 199–200, 218–20, 285–86 n. 72, who concludes that, while the Bolsheviks were indeed taking large sums from the Germans, there is no evidence that Germany influenced Lenin's policies and tactics.

[31] Iurii Got'e, *Time of Troubles: The Diary of Iurii Vladimirovich Got'e, July 8, 1917 to July 23, 1922*, trans., ed. and introduced by Terence Emmons (Princeton: Princeton University Press, 1988), 29, 32.

[32] "Untimely Thoughts," *Novaia zhizn'* no. 61 (June 29, 1917), in Maxim Gorky, *Untimely Thoughts: Essays on Revolution, Culture, and the Bolsheviks, 1917–1918*, trans. Herman Ermolaev (New York: P. S. Eriksson, 1968), 70.

The media free-for-all that was Russia's public space in 1917 was an important factor in the undermining of the army's morale; unfortunately, there were all too many other contributory causes. The abrupt removal of the tsar, and consequent collapse of the old structure of power, accelerated the decline in fighting capacity apparent since fall 1916.[33] The notorious Order No. 1, issued by the Petrograd Soviet at the outset of the revolution, followed by the "Declaration of Soldiers' Rights," played a part in this process. According to their provisions, every military unit was to elect a soldiers' committee that would take charge of all weaponry; soldiers, when off duty, were to enjoy all the rights and freedoms of the citizen. The consequences of these democratizing orders, coupled with the abolition of courts martial and the death penalty, were disastrous: desertions mounted, many officers were forcibly removed by their men, and it became increasingly difficult to enforce orders. By mid April both military and civilian authorities were profoundly concerned about the fighting capacity of Russia's troops. On May 7, Supreme Commander General Alekseev told a Congress of Officers that the "soul of the army" was gone, that too many citizens were not doing their duty to the motherland. That same month, mass mutinies began to occur at the front.[34]

Enlightening a Liberated Citizenry

Not surprisingly, the Provisional Government wished to exert its own influence in shaping the popular understanding of patriotism and citizenship. One innovative means for doing so was its Committee on Social-Political Enlightenment.[35] Shortly after February,

---

[33] On the army's troubled state from mid October 1916, see Astashov, *Russkii front*, 675–712 – who chronicles revolts in several units – and Wildman, *The End of the Russian Imperial Army*, vol. I, 107–15. On the complexities of determining the mood of the army on the basis of soldiers' correspondence, see William G. Rosenberg, "Reading Soldiers' Moods: Russian Military Censorship and the Configuration of Feeling in World War I," *American Historical Review* 119, 3 (June 2014), 714–40.

[34] Order No. 1 was addressed only to soldiers of the Petrograd Military District, but its speedy dissemination at the front effectively made it applicable to the armed forces as a whole. On the impact of these orders see Wildman, *The End of the Russian Imperial Army*, vol. I, 182–90, 332–48, 362–72, and Lincoln, *Passage through Armageddon*, 349–350, 404; the text of Alekseev's speech to the Congress of Officers, May 7, 1917, is in RGVIA, f. 2003, op. 14, d. 7, l. 1. On deep divisions among officers on how best to restore the army's fighting spirit and discipline, see Rendle, *Defenders of the Motherland*, 123–44.

[35] On the new regime's cultural projects, see Daniel Orlovsky, "The Provisional Government and Its Cultural Work," in Abbott Gleason, Peter Kenez, and Richard Stites, eds., *Bolshevik Culture: Experiment and Order in the Russian Revolution* (Bloomington: Indiana University Press, 1985), 39–56; on the committee, see Holquist, *Making War, Forging Revolution*, 3–6, 143–44, 211–17.

a nongovernmental body involved with providing technical assistance for the war effort created the Bureau for Organizing Morale (Biuro organizatsii dukhy); its object was to raise the patriotic consciousness of the revolutionary citizenry. In July, this bureau was renamed the Committee on Social-Political Enlightenment and brought into Aleksandr Kerenskii's newly formed Political Cabinet of the War Minister. Among its members were prominent socialists who supported a defensive war effort shorn of imperialist goals, including Georgii Plekhanov and Soviet executive committee member Vladimir Voitinskii.[36]

A central goal of the committee was to develop popular awareness of the need to defend Russia's new freedom, which meant continuing the "struggle with German militarism." Another goal was to disseminate understanding of unity, discipline, and the defense of spiritual values (*dukhovnye tsennosti*) as "the basic factors of state construction."[37] Besides organizing mass meetings on the theme of "Consciousness and Responsibility," the Committee on Social-Political Enlightenment sponsored free lectures for soldiers on topical issues. It maintained an agitational center, and opened a people's club, with a tearoom and library, which hosted concerts and lectures. From June through September its Agitational Commission ran five series of two-week long courses in "Political Literacy" to train future lecturers – mostly soldiers – on diverse social, political, and cultural topics; some 1,500 would-be agitators attended the courses. In an effort to reach civilians outside the capitals, it opened sixteen branches in the provinces and sent twenty-five lecturers on tour.[38]

The committee's biggest operation was its Literature Commission. The commission tried to keep up with the avalanche of titles appearing on pressing issues of the day, evaluating this literature for content, point of view, and accessibility. Continuing in the tradition of the tsarist Committee on Popular Publications, it then assembled 300,000 mini-libraries (*bibliotechki*) which were distributed at the front and rear. A typical collection contained around twenty titles, with the number of pages and complexity of subject matter growing with the presumed "preparedness" of the intended readers. For example, the collection for the simple soldier included "Why Discipline Is Needed in the People's Army," and "To the Soldier Tired of the War." The collection for the

---

[36] GARF, f. 9505 (Committee on Social-Political Enlightenment), op. 1, d. 1, "Report," l. 4, and f. 1788 (Provisional Government, Ministry of Internal Affairs), op. 1, d. 14, l. 3.
[37] GARF, f. 9505 (Committee on Social-Political Enlightenment), op. 1, d. 1, "Report," l. 4.
[38] GARF, f. 9505, op. 2, d. 2, "Otchety, doklady i plany deiatel'nosti," ll. 18, 30, 38, op. 1, d. 1, l. 6, and op. 2, d. 3, "Tezisy lektury," ll. 21–22.

more sophisticated soldier tackled broader issues, including Gurevich's "Why It Is Necessary to Give Women the Same Rights as Men." Every collection, even the humble assemblage for peasants, included Tatiana Bogdanovich's "Great Days of the Revolution." This pamphlet combined key texts from the February days with a simple narrative featuring the Duma and the "entire people," on the one hand, who were patriotically united to help Russia win the war, versus the tsar and his bad advisers, on the other, who cared more about preserving their power than they did about Russia.[39] In all, the committee's Literature Commission managed to make available to the general population 10 million copies of pamphlets and leaflets in five months' time.[40]

We can gain a sense of the approach of the Committee on Social-Political Enlightenment through the titles of the nearly ninety lectures it sponsored. Political themes included socialism, democracy, the Constituent Assembly, and various parties' programs, as well as several lectures warning against Leninism and "Bolsheviks and Anarchy." Other lectures addressed the land question, workplace rights, national minorities, and the cooperative movement. Several used widespread interest in Russia's newest ally to convey messages about responsible civic behavior, as in "How the American Citizen Is Formed" and "Military Service in America."[41] A complementary cycle of lectures, planned to start in early November, was devoted to *rodinovedenie*, defined as "the most important facts and figures about Russia, her national wealth, her population and culture." The Agitational Commission claimed this subject was of "huge interest" to the population, and particularly to soldiers, noting that lectures on the motherland also contributed to a fundamental goal: "dispersion in the broad masses of basic information on questions of state-mindedness."[42]

The committee also participated in publicizing the "Liberty Loan" (*zaem svobody*), one of the largest and most concerted patriotic

---

[39] T. Bogdanovich, *Velikie dni revoliutsii. 23 fevralia–12 marta 1917 g.* (Petrograd, 1917); GARF, f. 9505, op. 1, d. 7, "Spravka o deiatel'nosti Literaturnoi komissii," ll. 1, 8, 11–13, d. 1, "Polozhenie o komitete," l. 4, and d. 3, "Pis'mo," l. 23.

[40] GARF, f. 9505, op. 1, d. 7, "Spravka o deiatel'nosti Literaturnoi komissii," ll. 1, 8, 11–13, d. 1, "Polozhenie o komitete," l. 4, and d. 3, "Pis'mo," l. 23. In October, the committee submitted an estimate of expenses for one month; of the total 54,145 rubles, the largest expenses were 9,500 spent on automobiles, 5,450 on agitation, 5,400 on artistic undertakings, 5,190 on connections with the provinces, and 16,795 on literature.

[41] GARF, f. 9505, op. 1, d. 4, "Kratkii otchet o deiatel'nosti Agitatsionnoi komissii," ll. 1, 3.

[42] GARF, f. 9505, op. 1, d. 3, "Pis'mo," ll. 12–13, and op. 2, d. 2, "Otchety," l. 18. The commission also had plans for making greater use of films in order to "propagandize healthy political knowledge and historical information."

campaigns of 1917. The Liberty Loan, authorized March 27, 1917, at 5 percent interest, was Russia's seventh domestic loan of the war. The Provisional Government hoped to match or exceed earlier subscription campaigns, since the war effort urgently needed the funds.[43] Moreover, war-loan campaigns, as we have seen, were as much about involving citizens in their country's war effort as they were about raising revenue.

In 1917, as before, propagandizing the loan was a broad-based effort. The Ministry of Finance coordinated efforts to enlist government employees, the clergy, and people working in the financial and commercial sectors on the project. The Soviet of Workers' and Soldiers' Deputies supported the loan and urged "the citizens of free Russia" to follow its example. Clubs and societies formed special groups to popularize the loan. Most of the Russian press took an active part in the campaign, publishing full-page appeals, reporting major loan-related events, and printing weekly subscription totals coming in from all over the country.[44]

The effort to sell the loan featured a revamped patriotic message, as is apparent in the handsome loan posters produced in large quantities. One complex composition, showing a soldier and worker united, melds traditional and more revolutionary motifs – peasant huts and a church with factory smokestacks and a red banner. The slogan similarly joins old and new by saying, "The motherland and freedom are in danger. Give money to the state for the struggle with the enemy." Boris Kustodiev's mature, bearded peasant soldier, standing atop a podium with bayonet in his hands, is the epitome of dignified resolve. The top of the poster reads simply "Liberty Loan," but the inscriptions on the red banners being borne by the marching crowds underline the message that "war until victory" and defense of revolutionary liberty are two sides of the same coin: "Don't let the enemy take away the freedom you've won."[45]

Many cities held a Liberty Loan holiday to energize support. Petrograd's Day of the Liberty Loan, on May 25, 1917, orchestrated by the Union of People in the Arts, mobilized art and artists. Events included a big public meeting at the Mariinskii theater featuring speeches by enlisted men and political luminaries, concerts and shows performed at dozens of indoor and outdoor sites, and a grand parade. The enormous crowds that turned out enjoyed themselves vastly, and the festive event

---

[43] GARF, f. 9505, op. 1, d. 1, l. 5. The classic treatment of Russia's war loans is Apostol, "Credit Operations," 249–52, 263–77; see also Strakhov, "Vnutrennie zaimy v Rossii v pervuiu mirovuiu voinu."

[44] Apostol, "Credit Operations," 271, and *Russkie vedomosti* (June 1, 1917), 4; *Rech'* (June 2, 1917), 4, and (June 22, 1917), 6; and *Den'* (April 8, 1917), 1.

[45] The posters are featured in the excellent catalog by Baburina, *Russkii plakat Pervoi mirovoi voiny*, 109–12, 117–19.

7.3 This poster for the 1917 liberty loan, by artist Boris Kustodiev, links continuing the war with defense of Russia's newly won freedoms. Political Poster Collection, #RU/SU 1225, Courtesy of Hoover Institution Library & Archives, Stanford University

was deemed a terrific success.[46] For Samarkand's Day of the Liberty Loan in July, a special edition newspaper spoke of the need for a new Minin and Pozharskii to emerge from the people and save Russia, just as those heroes had saved the country during the Time of Troubles. It then proceeded to cast Kerenskii as a latter-day Pozharskii and urged every citizen to be like Minin, which meant "supporting comrade Kerenskii" by buying into the loan. The article concluded, "Subscription to the Liberty Loan is a sort of exam one passes to receive the title of 'free citizen.'"[47]

Voronezh held its Day of the Liberty Loan on August 7, by which time Russia's armies were crumbling; its special edition paper reflected the calamitous mood. One article warned "Russia's final hour has arrived!" and counseled citizens to buy shares in the loan if they did not wish to feel the conquerors' lash. Another article made its pitch to a new group of citizens: at a moment when "the motherland faces defeat and betrayal," S. Shestova wrote, women must actively aid their country: "now they are citizens, participants, and organizers of life on a level with men." But what could the ordinary woman do? "She should say to herself, 'I am a daughter of my country, loyal and loving'"– and buy shares in the loan. This was the duty of every citizen, irrespective of class or income.[48]

After a strong start, subscriptions to the Liberty Loan began to falter, slowing irrevocably in July. Some contemporaries, and subsequently some historians, have seen in the disappointing denouement to the Liberty Loan not only a clear sign of popular disillusionment with the war, but also a failure to "pass the exam" of conscious citizenship. But material difficulties also played a major role: citizens experiencing runaway inflation and an imploding economy had reason to fear tying up their money in any long-term investment. One could argue that attracting in such conditions more than 4 billion rubles in subscriptions – an amount nearly double what the biggest previous loan had yielded – was not all that bad a showing.[49]

---

[46] A brief description of the Petrograd celebration is in von Geldern, *Bolshevik Festivals, 1917–1920*, 19–20; and *Rech'* (May 26, 1917), 6, and (May 27, 1917), 6.

[47] "Zaem svobody ili zaem rabstva?" *Den' zaima svobody* (Samarkand, July 1917), 2–3.

[48] M. Shevchenko, "Iz proshlogo voennykh zaimov," and S. Shestova, "Dolg svobodnoi grazhdanki," *Den' zaima svobody. Odnodnevnaia gazeta* (Voronezh, August 7, 1917), 2, 3.

[49] Figures come from *Vestnik vremennogo pravitel'stva*; cited in Browder and Kerensky, eds., *Russian Provisional Government*, vol. II, 490; see also Gatrell, *Russia's First World War*, 201–02, 209. Inflation makes it impossible to determine the relationship of the 1917 figures to those of 1916.

Women Citizen-Soldiers

Russians took part in all manner of stirring new rituals in 1917.[50] But one of the most unique occurred on June 21, 1917, when the citizens of revolutionary Petrograd witnessed the consecration of the standards of a battalion of women soldiers being sent as combatants to the front. Thousands flocked to watch the 300 women – their heads close-cropped, wearing regular army-issue trousers and boots, rifles gleaming – march from their barracks to the great St. Isaac's Cathedral. Among the military and civilian notables waiting to greet the women were Generals Lavr Kornilov and P. A. Polovtsev, Duma president Mikhail Rodzianko, and leaders of various political parties. Two bishops and twelve priests officiated, as the battalion was presented with two icons and a banner sent by Minister of War Aleksandr Kerenskii. Afterwards, enthusiastic soldiers and sailors lifted Commander Mariia Bochkareva on to their shoulders, crowds cheered, orators mounted improvised tribunes to hail the battalion and its head. To the strains of the "Marseillaise," the battalion then marched to Mars Field, to honor the graves of those who had fallen in the first days of the February revolution.[51]

The Women's Battalion of Death (Zhenskii batal'on smerti), as it was called, inspired formation of other companies and battalions of women volunteers in Russia in 1917.[52] The story of these soldiers has much to tell us about changing concepts of patriotism and citizenship in the context of revolution. The February 1917 revolution proclaimed the disparate subjects of the empire to be free and equal citizens, with the duties as well as rights that citizenship entails. Thousands of women

---

[50] New rituals could be crafted around funerals for those who died for the revolution, dedication of new premises and sites, oath-taking, and even voting – something members of proliferating organizations and associations did often in 1917; see Stites, *Revolutionary Dreams*, 79–83, and Kolonitskii, *Simvoly vlasti*, 36–54.

[51] Descriptions come from Bessie Beatty, *The Red Heart of Russia* (New York: The Century Co., 1919), 94–95; Botchkareva, *Yashka*, 189–92; Nina Krylova in Boris Solonevich, *Zhenshchina s vintovkoi. Istoricheskii roman* (Buenos Aires, 1955), 84–87; and *Rech'* (June 22, 1917), 4.

[52] My discussion of the women's battalions is drawn mainly from my article, "'My Death for the Motherland Is Happiness': Women, Patriotism, and Soldiering in Russia's Great War, 1914–1917," *American Historical Review* 109, 1 (February 2004), 78–116. The first scholarly studies of these battalions are by Richard Stites in his seminal work *The Women's Liberation Movement in Russia*, 295–300, and Richard Abraham, "Mariia L. Bochkareva and the Russian Amazons of 1917," in Linda Edmondson, ed., *Women and Society in Russia and the Soviet Union: Selected Papers from the Fourth World Congress for Soviet and East European Studies* (Cambridge: Cambridge University Press, 1992), 124–44; neither of these scholars had access to relevant Soviet archives for their accounts. The fullest treatment is by Laurie Stoff, *They Fought for the Motherland: Russia's Women Soldiers in World War I and the Revolution* (Lawrence: University Press of Kansas, 2006).

"For Freedom and the Fatherland" 231

interpreted this equality to mean that women could and should assume the citizen's right to bear arms.

Close ties exist between citizenship and soldiering in Western culture. Historically, those ties did not work to women's advantage: the belief that citizens should share an "equality of sacrifice," upon which universal conscription was premised, entailed a kind of sacrifice women were prohibited from making.[53] But, because the Great War mobilized populations and demanded their labor and sacrifices on an unprecedented scale, it revised or destabilized a number of gender conventions.[54] As we have seen, Russian feminists – like their counterparts in Europe – believed that women could demonstrate their readiness for full citizenship through patriotic self-sacrifice, and in doing so would ultimately receive the rights they had earned. From the outset of the war, a small number of Russian women had made a still more radical break with their culture's traditional gender roles, by actually taking up arms.[55] Some, such as Mariia Bochkareva, successfully petitioned the authorities for permission to become combat soldiers; many other women had to disguise themselves as men in order to enlist. All told, at least 400 women fought in the imperial Russian army in the Great War.[56] As insignificant as these figures are when compared with the legions of women working

---

[53] George L. Mosse, *The Image of Man: The Creation of Modern Masculinity* (Oxford: Oxford University Press, 1996), esp. 50–55, 107–11, and his *Fallen Soldiers*, 15–33, 65–69; Mosse discusses later challenges to this normative masculinity, but sees it as still dominant on the eve of the Great War. See also Joshua S. Goldstein, *War and Gender: How Gender Shapes the War System and Vice-Versa* (Cambridge: Cambridge University Press, 2001), 251–321.

[54] For the impact of the revolution of 1905 on the development of citizenship rights, see Bradley, "Subjects into Citizens," 1120–23, and Edith W. Clowes, Samuel D. Kassow, and James L. West, eds., *Between Tsar and People: Educated Society and the Quest for Public Identity in Late Imperial Russia* (Princeton: Princeton University Press, 1991). An analysis of the 1905 rhetoric of citizenship as it applied to women is Linda Edmondson, "Women's Rights, Civil Rights and the Debate over Citizenship in the 1905 Revolution," in Edmondson, ed., *Women and Society in Russia*, 77–100.

[55] It is worth noting that the gendering of work roles is not identical from culture to culture, or even from class to class; on women's work in Russian peasant society, see Christine Worobec, "Victims or Actors? Russian Peasant Women and Patriarchy," in Esther Kingston-Mann and Timothy Mixter, eds., *Peasant Economy, Culture, and Politics of European Russia, 1800–1921* (Princeton: Princeton University Press, 1991), 177–206; on factory workers, see Rose L. Glickman, *Russian Factory Women: Workplace and Society, 1880–1914* (Berkeley: University of California Press, 1984); a case study for a profession is Christine Ruane, *Gender, Class, and the Professionalization of Russian City Teachers, 1860–1914* (Pittsburgh: University of Pittsburgh Press, 1994); a concise overview of changes affecting women's work for the period 1861–1917 is Barbara Alpern Engel, "Transformation versus Tradition," in Clements et al, *Russia's Women*, 135–47.

[56] *The Graphic* (London) did not give a source for its figure of 400 women in the Russian army, quoted in *Literary Digest* (June 19, 1915), 1460; Florence Farmborough, an

for Russia's war effort in other capacities, the appearance of armed female soldiers was nonetheless remarkable.[57]

In 1917, revolution deepened the transformations in women's wartime roles already effected by the demands of total war. On April 30, Minister of War Aleksandr Guchkov signed an order instructing all women doctors under 45 years of age to report for military service.[58] On June 13, Minister of War Kerenskii announced the formation of a special commission to look into the feasibility of instituting a military labor obligation for women that would free up men for combat. The commission included representatives from the Union of Women's Democratic Organizations and the All-Russian Women's Union. Significantly, it was these women's organizations that had first raised the question of conscripting women's labor, and they did so by linking service with gender equality. Commission chair O. A. Nekrasova explained the rationale for instituting women's obligatory service in this way:

> The first Provisional Government has acknowledged the civil and political equality of the women of Russia. This equality, which as yet has been realized nowhere in the world on such a scale, lays upon the Russian woman a huge responsibility. Corresponding to equal rights with men there must be equal obligations.[59]

The new emergency precipitated by the army's declining capacity required action and, as so frequently happened in revolutionary Russia, many educated individuals looked to the French revolution for guidance. Leaders of the soviet compared Russia's situation with that of France on the eve of war against Austria in 1792, when the call to defend *la patrie*

Englishwoman who nursed with the Russian Red Cross, maintained that, "A woman soldier, or boy soldier, was no unusual sight in the Russian Army": Farmborough, *With the Armies of the Tsar: A Nurse at the Russian Front in War and Revolution, 1914–1918* (New York: Constable, 1974), 300. See also Stoff, *They Fought for the Motherland*, 30 and 239 n. 32, who suggests a range of 400–1,000 women in the Russian army.

[57] According to Joshua Sanborn, the tsarist military's ideals were both explicitly and implicitly masculine, and the authorities struggled to "insulate the army from feminine contamination": Sanborn, *Drafting the Russian Nation*, esp. 132–33, 146–54, 160. See also two essays by Karen Petrone exploring the gendering of heroism and cowardice, "Masculinity and Heroism in Imperial and Soviet Military-Patriotic Cultures," in Barbara Evans Clements, Rebecca Friedman, and Dan Healy, eds., *Russian Masculinities in History and Culture* (Basingstoke, UK: Palgrave, 2002), 172–93, and "Family, Masculinity, and Heroism."

[58] *Vestnik vremennogo pravitel'stva* (June 14, 1917), 1; six weeks elapsed between the order's signing and its publication.

[59] *Russkii invalid* (June 16, 1917), 1, and (June 17, 1917), 3. While no obligatory military service for women was instituted, an order of August 22 tried to attract women volunteers for noncombat railroad security, to replace male soldiers: RGVIA, f. 2003, op. 2, d. 349, l. 28.

summoned the French citizenry to arms. Explicitly invoking the example of the revolutionary, militia-style army created by the French revolution in Year Two of the Republic, a number of moderate socialists also proposed creation of a volunteer, revolutionary army to bolster – not replace – the existing forces.[60] "New, free Russia" provided a new object of patriotism to replace the discarded object of the tsar. Revolutionary enthusiasm could be used to rekindle the army's resolve to defend both freedom and the fatherland.

Officers and soldiers independently generated a proposal for forming revolutionary shock units, at the Congress of Delegates of the Southwestern Front held May 16, 1917. General Aleksei Brusilov, who became commander in chief on May 27, enthusiastically endorsed the idea of revolutionary units and became one of its main proponents. He also championed extension of the original idea to embrace the rear as well as the front; whereas shock (or "storm") battalions formed at the front would be composed of active troops volunteering from various units, those at the rear would be made up of reservists, officer trainees, and civilian volunteers.[61]

However, it was not feminists, students of the French revolution, or desperate politicians and generals who first conceived of fielding a unit of women soldiers. The women's battalion was the brainchild of Mariia "Yashka" Bochkareva.[62] She had served with distinction since entering the army, being twice wounded and winning a St. George's Cross for valor. She also gradually won acceptance from her fellow soldiers, who gave her the nickname Yashka. When the revolution came in 1917, Yashka greeted it joyously, equating it with freedom for the common people but, as the fighting capacity of the army broke down, she grew alarmed and then indignant. She later claimed that an idea for reversing this disintegration suddenly came to her while on a furlough

---

[60] On the model of the French revolution for creation of revolutionary units, see N. G. Ross, "Popytka sozdaniia Russkoi revoliutsionnoi armii (mai–iiun' 1917 g.)," reprinted in *Novyi chasovoi* no. 1 (1994), 76. The complexities inherent in summoning "the people" to arms in a multinational polity are explored in Mark von Hagen, "The *Levée en masse* from Russian Empire to Soviet Union, 1874–1938," in Moran and Waldron, *The People in Arms*, 159–88. On misuse of the lessons of the French revolution in Russia, see John Keep, "1917: The Tyranny of Paris over Petrograd," *Soviet Studies* 20 (July 1968), 22–45.

[61] RGVIA, f. 2003, op. 2, d. 347, "Formation of Volunteer Battalions, 1917," ll. 2, 17, Brusilov's telegrams of May 16 and May 20, to the Petrograd Soviet and General Staff.

[62] Stoff, *They Fought for the Motherland*, 65–69, 74–77, 91–95, 140–43, details the important role played by the women's movement in general in organizing and supporting these military units. She also questions Bochkareva's claim to have originated the idea of forming a women's military unit, suggesting that such a notion was already in the air.

to Petrograd in early May: form a unit of some 300 women and take them into combat, to "serve as an example to the army and lead the men into battle."[63]

The purpose of the women's battalion, as was the case with *all* volunteer revolutionary units, was to raise the morale of the regular army through heroic, self-disciplined example. Additionally, the first women's battalion, as proposed by Yashka, was explicitly intended to embarrass Russian soldiers into doing their duty. Her proposal caught the imagination of a number of people, including Duma president Rodzianko, who arranged for her to outline her idea to General Brusilov. He, too, liked her idea, which more or less agreed with his thinking on volunteer battalions; several days later, after meetings with the new minister of war Aleksandr Kerenskii, the first "Russian Women's Battalion of Death" was formally approved.[64]

The formidable, even vaguely ridiculous title "Battalion of Death" was not unique to the women's unit. The appellation became popular in May 1917, when Supreme Command first bestowed it on a unit that had solemnly resolved "to defend, to the last drop of blood, young, free Russia," requesting immediate posting to the front wherever the "onslaught of the forces of the revolutionary army might be needed." A month later, on June 17, the eve of the opening of the so-called Kerenskii offensive, the military authorities formally approved the proposal of the All-Russian Military Union that any unit passing such a resolution could be granted the epithet "of death"; members of such a unit sewed a special red-and-black chevron to their sleeves and added the skull-and-crossbones to their banner. A battalion of death was therefore not only intended to be death-dealing on the field of battle, but willing to fight unto death. Its volunteers pledged never to surrender. By October, a total of 106 such units were in existence.[65]

---

[63] Botchkareva, *Yashka*, 56, 72–76, 139–53, and S. V. Drokov, "Organizator Zhenskogo batal'ona smerti," *Voprosy istorii* no. 7 (1993), 164–65.

[64] Botchkareva, *Yashka*, 157–59. *Voina i mir*, a new daily put out under the auspices of the Soviet of Soldiers' Deputies, published numerous pieces highlighting the inspirational role of male *and* female volunteers; for example, "Dobrovol'cheskoe dvizhenie" (June 9, 1917), 3, "Udarnye batal'ony" (July 13, 1917), 4, and "Vysokii patriotizm batal'ona smerti" (August 5, 1917), 2.

[65] *Russkii invalid* (June 24, 1917), 5. The ten-point oath taken by the "revolutionary-citizen" volunteer also stipulated tolerance for comrades' political beliefs, temperance, and adherence to orders; the text is reproduced in *Razlozhenie armii v 1917 godu*, ed. by N. E. Kakurin (Moscow and Leningrad: Gosudarstvennoe izd-vo, 1923), 69–70. I have assembled figures for the number of such units from data in the file "Correspondence on Forming Shock Battalions and Battalions of Death," RGVIA, f. 2003, op. 2, d. 352, ll. 65–69.

"For Freedom and the Fatherland" 235

On May 21, 1917, Yashka publicly appealed for women volunteers at a benefit for wounded soldiers, calling on women "whose hearts are crystal, whose souls are pure," to set an example of self-sacrifice and save Mother Russia. Newspapers carried accounts of the appeal for the "Women's Battalion of Death," and the address where volunteers could sign up.[66] Several days later the All-Russian Women's Congress issued a general appeal to women to enlist, making explicit the connection between citizenship and the duty to serve the country in whatever capacity possible:

Citizenesses!
In this terrible hour, when the dark storm clouds of anarchy, defeat, and economic collapse are gathering over our motherland, when death is foretold for her, *we, women citizens with equal rights*, are obliged to raise our voices, are obliged to unite ... Imperative responsibility and civic duty call upon the Russian woman to support our army's unity of will, to strengthen the falling spirit of our troops [and], having entered into their ranks as volunteers, to transform the passive, standing front into an active, aggressive one.[67]

More than 2,000 women responded to these public appeals, far more than could be accommodated. Not to be deterred, women resolved to organize additional battalions. On June 16, a group of women in Moscow received permission to organize the Moscow Women's Battalion of Death. A committee called "Women for the Fatherland" took charge of this effort. On July 2, in Petrograd, the newly formed Women's Volunteer Committee, under the auspices of yet another new association, the Military League, announced enlistment for the "First Petrograd Women's Battalion" – an entity distinct from Yashka's battalion, which was also based in Petrograd.[68] Women soldiers in Mogilev province and Siberia also asked for permission to organize battalions.[69]

As surprising as the scale of the response was the military authorities' willingness to make use of this outpouring of female patriotism. A confidential July 14 memo of the Chief Administration of the General Staff noted that "women volunteers desiring to enter the regular army are

---

[66] Botchkareva, *Yashka*, 161–62; for example, *Russkii invalid* (May 26, 1917), 4.
[67] The text of the appeal is in *Rech'* (May 28, 1917), 6 (emphasis added).
[68] *Moskovskie vedomosti* (June 17, 1917), 1; *Russkie vedomosti* (July 6, 1917), 4; *Russkii invalid* (July 2, 1917), 3; and Rheta Childe Dorr, *Inside the Russian Revolution* (New York, 1917), 82. Dorr, a war correspondent for the *Evening Mail*, spent several weeks with Bochkareva's battalion; she and Beatty, *The Red Heart of Russia*, provide the most detailed descriptions of the women's battalions by outsiders.
[69] RGVIA, f. 2003, op. 2, d. 28, ch. 2, ll. 60–63; and *Razlozhenie armii*, 70. Tatiana Aleksinskaia, *Zhenshchina v voine i revoliutsii* (Petrograd, 1917), 15, mentions local initiatives in Baku, Ekaterinburg, Mariupol', Minsk, Odessa, Pskov, Riga, Tambov, Tashkent, and Ufa.

appearing in ever greater numbers. In view of this, it appears necessary to undertake further formation [of units]." Eleven women's communication detachments were organized in Kiev, Saratov, and elsewhere, and a women's infantry battalion was organized in Ekaterinodar.[70] Additionally, groups in a number of other cities locally organized women's combat units without even bothering to secure official permission, a form of revolutionary spontaneity the high command found extremely trying.[71] Of course, not all the military high command approved. Several generals, most notably Alekseev and Denikin, opposed creating special revolutionary battalions of any description. As they saw it, civilian volunteers would receive too little training to be of use, while taking good soldiers out of existing frontline units would only hasten the demise of those units' fighting capacity.[72]

Some proponents of the revolutionary army invoked the example of the French revolution specifically as it pertained to women. One example comes from socialist Tatiana Aleksinskaia, who had previously written about her experiences tending the wounded on a medical evacuation train run by the Union of Zemstvos. Her pamphlet *Women in War and Revolution* celebrates the myriad ways in which women citizens of revolutionary France helped to defend their country and the revolution. "The participation of women in the wars of this era remains an example of great courage, revolutionary patriotism, and readiness to sacrifice. Russian women, follow these noble examples!" Aleksinskaia also proposed formation of "one mighty, all-Russian Union of Daughters of the Fatherland" to save the country.[73] Besides seeking to mobilize women's patriotism and capacity for active citizenship, this text legitimates their martial ardor by situating it within the tradition of the French revolution.

These various appeals to women – as full citizens, as daughters of the fatherland, as supporters of the revolution – found an audience. Although the total number of women who signed up for combat duty is

---

[70] RGVIA, f. 2003, op. 2, d. 349, ll. 10–11, 19–20, 42, 47, and f. 29, op. 3, d. 1603, "On Forming Units of Women Volunteers, 21 June–24 December, 1917," ll. 21–22.

[71] The popular illustrated magazine *Niva* featured photographs of women sailors (*zhenshchiny-matrosy*) on October 7, 1917. By early August, the military authorities had transferred responsibility for organizing female units to the Women's Military Union in Petrograd: General Romanovskii to DEGENVERKH, August 11, 1917, RGVIA, f. 2003, op. 2, d. 349, l. 23.

[72] RGVIA, f. 2003, op. 2, d. 347, ll. 11–12, telegram from General Denikin to General Brusilov, 18 May 1917, and l. 18, telegram from Alekseev to Brusilov, 21 May 1917; see also Ross, "Popytka sozdaniia Russkoi revoliutsionnoi armii," 77–78. One might suspect that many generals harbored deep reservations about creating battalions of women soldiers, but the lack of explicit objections is remarkable.

[73] Aleksinskaia, *Zhenshchina v voine i revoliutsii*, 11–12, 14.

7.4 Mariia "Yashka" Bochkareva and soldiers of the first Women's Battalion of Death. In revolutionary 1917, "soldier-citizens" included as many as 6,000 women volunteers. From the Winifred Ramplee-Smith Collection, Courtesy of the Hoover Institution Library & Archives, Stanford University.

impossible to determine, even the partial figures available are surprisingly high. Yashka's battalion, after its initial subscription of 2,000, was speedily whittled down to 300 by its demanding leader. By August 11, the Moscow Battalion of Death had built up to a force of more than 1,000. The Petrograd First Women's Battalion had approximately 1,050 soldiers organized into four companies.[74] It would therefore seem that the very *lowest* figure for women enlisting in combat units was 4,000; given the absence of numbers for other units, the actual figure was probably between 5,500 and 6,500 women, for a period lasting just four months (new enrollments were halted in September).[75]

---

[74] The initial subscription for the Moscow Battalion was 371; large groups of women continued to join up even after the July debacle, as smaller groups of volunteers dropped out on an equally steady basis: RGVIA, f. 3474, op. 2, d. 1, "Dobrovol'tsy," ll. 1–5, 11–31. Figures for the Petrograd Battalion come from the captain of its 3rd Company: Kapitan Shagal, "Zhenskii batal'on," *Voennaia byl'* (Paris) no. 95 (January 1969), 6.

[75] In his report to the British War Office, Bernard Pares said that, as of early August, the All-Russian Central Volunteer Committee knew of some 4,000 female volunteers; cited in Abraham, "Russian Amazons," 131; Beatty, *Red Heart of Russia*, 112, gives the figure

Exactly who joined the women's battalions is a fascinating question. Several contemporary sources depict the battalions as composed primarily of upper-class and educated women, perhaps including a smattering of peasants, the implication being that working-class urban women did not volunteer.[76] Such a depiction would conform to the usual representations of the connection between class identity and patriotism in the Russian revolution. The standard narrative of class suggests that, by summer 1917, as class consciousness and class antagonism grew, support for the war effort was increasingly confined to the upper classes and the bourgeoisie. In Steve Smith's nuanced formulation, although class and national identities in revolutionary Russia were not mutually exclusive, they were highly conflictual; by summer 1917, "the extent to which the political language of nation became utterly discredited in the eyes of workers, soldiers, and peasants is still striking." Another scholar more flatly asserts that the "new civic patriotism did not extend beyond the urban middle classes."[77]

However, the majority of sources show that the women who responded to patriotic appeals to fight represented a wide variety of social estates, classes, and occupations: as important as the language and politics of class identity became over the course of 1917, commitment to the country's defense did not always follow class lines. A set of forms filled out by twenty-two women desiring to join the women's unit in Kiev provides material about age, faith, and level of education. Almost all were aged 18–22, and most were Orthodox, although the group included four Roman Catholics and one Protestant (meaning five of the twenty-two were probably not ethnically Great Russian). Education levels show that the group was by no means exclusively "bourgeois": eight women identified themselves simply as literate (*gramotnaia*) or illiterate (*negramotnaia*).[78]

The variety of social classes represented is captured in the unpublished memoir of Mariia Bocharnikova, a Sister of Mercy who enlisted as a

---

of 5,000 women in combat units. The preliminary order of November 19, 1917, dissolving women's combat units lists 3 battalions and 11 liaison detachments as still in existence, which would represent about 4,300 individuals: RGVIA, f. 2003, op. 3, d. 1603, l. 24. Military records contain no figures for unauthorized women's units, although they complain about their proliferation.

[76] See, for example, "Those Russian Women," *Literary Digest* (September 29, 1917), 51.

[77] S. A. Smith, "Citizenship and the Russian Nation during World War I: A Comment," *Slavic Review* 2 (2000), 329; Figes, *A People's Tragedy*, 412. See also David Mandel, *The Petrograd Workers and the Soviet Seizure of Power* (New York: St. Martin's Press, 1984), 228–29, 239, and Wildman, *The End of the Russian Imperial Army*, vol. I, 374, who asserts that "the patriotic outpourings of cultured society notwithstanding," peasant soldiers had regarded the war as an alien enterprise from the outset.

[78] RGVIA, f. 3474, op. 2, d. 16, ll. 34–56.

soldier in the First Petrograd Battalion. She recalled her first glimpse of new volunteers, still dressed in civilian garb: "Who was not here! The bright sarafans of peasant women, the head-scarves of Sisters of Mercy, factory workers in multicolored print dresses, the elegant gowns of young ladies from society, the humble attire of city workers, maids, nannies..."[79]

Women, like men, volunteered to fight for different reasons, and combinations of reasons. Petitions, memoirs, and newspaper accounts show that love of and loyalty to the *patria* – state patriotism in its most conventional sense – might be joined with a desire for adventure, glory, and honor, or the thirst to be free of the confines and burdens of a woman's wartime life. Volunteers of diverse social origins told American journalist Bessie Beatty they joined "because they believed that the honor and even the existence of Russia were at stake and nothing but a great human sacrifice could save her," while others said they came because "anything was better than the dreary drudgery and the drearier waiting of life as they lived it."[80] Some women spoke of compassion for their "brothers," the soldiers who had already suffered for years and needed their help.[81]

It is difficult to gauge the degree to which these women soldiers believed they were demonstrating women's fitness in principle to be combatants, as opposed to acting on the belief that in a moment of national peril women were able to fight. Certainly, many prominent feminists and women radicals welcomed the women's battalions on the former grounds. On August 2, 1917, at the opening of the All-Russian Women's Military Congress, the "grandmother of the revolution," Socialist-Revolutionary Ekaterina Breshko-Breshkovskaia, approvingly linked these armed women with Russia's female revolutionary tradition.[82] Writing two decades after the event, Nina Krylova, a junior

---

[79] Bakhmeteff Archive of Russian and East European Culture, Columbia University, New York (hereafter, BAR), Bocharnikova Papers, "V zhenskom batal'one smerti," 2. Bocharnikova, unsuccessful in her pre-1917 efforts to enlist, became a Sister of Mercy; a friend telegraphed her about formation of women's battalions, and she received her superior's permission to volunteer.

[80] RGVIA, f. 3474, op. 2, d. 11, ll. 12, 36, 39, 59, and Beatty, *Red Heart of Russia*, 101. An analysis of the phenomenon of mass volunteering in Britain in the Great War is W. J. Reader, *At Duty's Call: A Study in Obsolete Patriotism* (Manchester: University of Manchester Press, 1988).

[81] Dorr, *Inside the Russian Revolution*, 56–57, 71; Solonevich, *Zhenshchina s vintovkoi*, 67; petition from K. M. Otto, in RGVIA, f. 2003, op. 2, d. 28, chast' 2, l. 28.

[82] On feminist attitudes toward the women soldiers, see Stites, *The Women's Liberation Movement*, 298–99, and Linda Edmondson, *Feminism in Russia, 1900–1917* (Stanford: Stanford University Press, 1984), 167–68. Emmeline Pankhurst's favorable opinion of the Women's Battalion is related in Abraham, "Mariia L. Bocharnikova," 128–29. On Breshko-Breshkovskaia, see *Moskovskie vedomosti* (August 2, 1917), 2; *Rech'* (August 3, 1917), 3, and BAR, Bocharnikova Papers, "V zhenskom batalon'e," 7.

officer in Yashka's Battalion of Death, insisted on the women soldiers' feminist orientation: "Each of us felt ourselves not just a Russian woman defending her own country (as every she-wolf defends her den), but also a representative of half the population of the whole planet, taking an exam to prove that even in military matters a woman can be a worthy soldier."[83]

Not all Russian women supported the women's battalions. Some undoubtedly felt that women engaging in organized violence, even for a noble cause, was unseemly or contrary to the essential feminine nature, following the view that woman's role is to create life, not take it.[84] As Richard Stites notes, explicit condemnation of the women's battalions typically stemmed from opposition to the war in general, or to the battalions' role in continuing the hostilities. Among the former was the prominent Bolshevik feminist Aleksandra Kollontai, who denounced the imperialist government's exploitation of these misguided women. Less ideologically inspired were many soldiers' wives and urban working-class women who had simply had enough of grueling work schedules, material hardships, and personal loss. They wanted an end to the war and were angry with anyone or anything that prolonged it.[85]

The inspirational role of the women's battalions worked better among enthusiastic civilians at the rear than it did at the front. The first Women's Battalion of Death was heavily publicized, newspapers described women soldiers as "valiant heroines" (*doblestnye geroiny*), and the public responded generously to calls for donations on their behalf.[86] A letter of June 23 to the Moscow Women's Battalion of Death from the patriotic society "For Russia" extended enthusiastic greetings to these "sister-citizens" (*sestry grazhdanki*), declaring that "Heroic epochs in the life of peoples create heroic hearts ... Let your example and your sacred, noble resolve inspire the cowardly, fortify the wavering, and create a common, irreversible upsurge for the struggle with our immemorial enemy until final victory." Fundraisers for the battalions and solemn

---

[83] Solonevich, *Zhenshchina s vintovkoi*, 94; see also Sofiia Zarechnaia, "Amazonki velikoi voiny," *Zhenskoe delo* (July 15, 1917), 16.

[84] An argument that sees the putative incompatibility between dealing death and giving life as one common to Western culture is Nancy Huston, "The Matrix of War: Mothers and Heroes," in Susan Rubin Suleiman, ed., *The Female Body in Western Culture* (Cambridge, MA: Harvard University Press, 1986), 119–36.

[85] Stites, *The Women's Liberation Movement*, 297–98; for pacifist and socialist criticism, see Melancon, *The Socialist Revolutionaries and the Russian Anti-War Movement*. Shagal, "Zhenskii batal'on," 7–8, suggests a generational factor in public attitudes: "old women cried and blessed us; others, primarily workers, cursed us and spat in our direction."

[86] *Russkii invalid* (July 2, 1917), 3.

"For Freedom and the Fatherland" 241

public rituals, such as the July 2 blessing of a banner given to the Moscow Women's Battalion by the Union of St. George Cavaliers, were made the basis for mass patriotic rallies.[87]

Unfortunately, among regular soldiers these women in uniform were more likely to be objects of ridicule, resentment, or outright hostility. When they arrived to join the 172nd Division of the Tenth Army at the front in early July, their unit now approximately 300-strong, Yashka's women soldiers were booed and harassed. "Why did you come here?" they were asked. "You want to fight? We want peace! We have had enough fighting!" The rank and file understood that women soldiers were at the front to compel men to go on the offensive. Understandably, the effort to shame the troops could also affront them.[88]

On July 7 an offensive in support of the stalled Kerenskii offensive was launched along the western front; the Women's Battalion of Death took part, in an operation near Smorgon. Some two hundred prisoners were taken and the operation was deemed a success, but the gains were short-lived: the refusal of other units to relieve them at the appointed time meant the women and their fellow volunteers were forced to retreat. By the end of the operation, on July 11, the Women's Battalion had suffered approximately thirty-six casualties, at least two of them fatal.[89] Most contemporary accounts report the women's discipline and courage, but their example failed to inspire most of their fellow soldiers.[90]

---

[87] RGVIA, f. 3474, op. 2, d. 11, l. 4; *Russkie vedomosti* (July 3, 1917), 6. *Niva* no. 26 (1917), 895, linked patriotism, citizenship, and manly courage in its salute to the Battalion of Death's participation in battle: "In a terrible, troubled hour Russian woman manfully [*muzhestvenno*] raised her head and entered the ranks of the frontline soldiers. Let this be an example, a high example of patriotism, a persuasive example of civic spirit."

[88] Botchkareva, *Yashka*, 193–95, and Solonevich, *Zhenshchina s vintovkoi*, 95–101. See, for example, Viktor Shklovsky, *A Sentimental Journey: Memoirs, 1917–1922*, trans. Richard Sheldon (Ithaca, NY: Cornell University Press, 1970), 23, 30, who regarded women's battalions as "thought up expressly as an insult to the front."

[89] Botchkareva, *Yashka*, estimates losses of fifty women dead or wounded, 209–19; Senin, on the basis of archival material, estimates two dead, thirty-three wounded, and two lost in action: "Zhenskie batal'ony," 180; Dorr, *Inside the Russian Revolution*, 73–75, names two women killed and reports speaking with thirty-one wounded after the engagement, saying she did not speak with the more seriously injured. A history of the offensive is Louise Erwin Heenan, *Russian Democracy's Fatal Blunder: The Summer Offensive of 1917* (New York: Praeger, 1987).

[90] Quoted in Dorr, *Inside the Russian Revolution*, 75. General Anton Denikin put the blame squarely on the regular, male soldiers: *Ocherki russkoi smuty*, vol. I (Paris, 1922), issue 1, 136; one Siberian commander's favorable appraisal of the battalion's performance is reported in *Rech'* (August 2, 1917), 3. See also *Novoe vremia* (July 11, 1917), 2; "Boevoe kreshchenie zhenskogo batal'ona," *Voina i mir* (July 19, 1917), 2; and Farmborough, *With the Armies of the Tsar*, 304–05, who heard mixed stories, according to which some women bravely attacked while others panicked.

Thereafter, as the Kerenskii offensive turned into a rout, the women's determination to keep fighting provoked more and more hostility among men consumed by the desire for peace. The reputation of Yashka's battalion's among rank-and-file soldiers was further compromised by her well-known association with General Lavr Kornilov, who became Supreme Commander on July 29, 1917, and who shared her desire to reimpose strict discipline in the army. After Kornilov's abortive attempt to suppress the Petrograd Soviet in late August, the soldiers of Yashka's battalion were regarded as counterrevolutionary "Kornilovites," and threatened with death by their fellow soldiers.[91] Its position having become untenable, the battalion was moved to an inactive sector.[92] In September 1917 the high command halted further enlistment of women.[93]

By mid September, it seemed Russia was on the brink of catastrophe. The failed Kornilov rebellion further poisoned relations between officers and the rank and file in the army, as well as deepening class and political divisions in the rear. Just as ominously, disorders were engulfing more and more of the country. A revealing snapshot of the chaotic conditions comes from the "Overview of the Press" for September 13–29, compiled for the Provisional Government by the Committee on Social-Political Enlightenment: "In various papers, there is news of pogroms in Kiev and Odessa, disorders in Bakhmut, development of pillaging in Bessarabia province; in Petrograd; there have been calls for pogroms against Jews ... In Benderakh, a third day of pogroms. Soldiers rob and attack the population, Cossacks have been sent in ... In Astrakhan, exchanges of gunfire continue. In Azov, food riots."[94]

---

[91] Regular soldiers also beat or killed men who wanted to keep fighting: Botchkareva, *Yashka*, 230–36, 240–42, and Heenan, *Russian Democracy's Fatal Blunder*, 118–19.

[92] There are discrepancies in the sources concerning the battalion's fate. Botchkareva, *Yashka*, 242–43, 254–57, says the battalion was still functioning when the Bolsheviks seized power; Nina Krylova, in Solonevich, *Zhenshchina s vintovkoi*, 148–50, says the battalion broke itself up before that date, with some of its members joining other women's battalions.

[93] A September 7 memo from the Stavka Committee on Formation of Revolutionary Battalions to General Staff stated that women were still coming frequently to volunteer for battalions and asked where to direct them: RGVIA, f. 2003, op. 2, d. 349, l. 32. The Military Council's decision of November 30, 1917, to disband women's combat units was promulgated on January 10, 1918, as Order No. 22 of Glavnoe upravlenie general'nogo shtaba: RGVIA, f. 2003, op. 2, d. 349, ll. 66–67.

[94] GARF, f. 9505, op. 2, d. 8, "Kratkii obzor pechati" (September 13–October 24), ll. 6–13; Bakhmut is in Ekaterinoslav province, part of present-day Ukraine. Focusing on the Volga province of Saratov, Donald J. Raleigh, *Experiencing Russia's Civil War: Politics, Society, and Popular Culture in Saratov, 1917–1922* (Princeton: Princeton University Press, 2002), 29–34, adds a general "impulse toward localism," including Russia's breakdown into local economic units, to the list of woes afflicting the nation by summer 1917.

"For Freedom and the Fatherland" 243

All this information was published in the press and accessible to the public, contributing to the climate of fear.

These were the conditions in which the Bolshevik leadership planned and implemented their overthrow of the "bourgeois" Provisional Government. As historians have noted, participation in the events of October 24–25 in Petrograd was relatively low on both sides, especially when compared to the mass nature of the February revolution.[95] One group that did defend the beleaguered Provisional Government was a unit of women soldiers.

On October 24, the 2nd Company of the First Petrograd Women's Battalion – a unit of 139 soldiers – was hastily dispatched to help defend the palace, along with Cossack units and several groups of cadets from area military academies. Apparently the women were among the last to give up, on the evening of October 25, most of the other defenders having melted away due to the lack of promised reinforcements and provisions.[96] In the early hours of the morning, the women soldiers were arrested but soon released; most returned the next day to their camp.[97]

Then, women soldiers faced the same difficulties confronting all Russia's soldiers during the chaotic demobilization process that began on November 10, 1917. There were no formal provisions for these suddenly unemployed soldiers, no apparatus to ease the transition to civilian life amid conditions of economic collapse.[98] In some instances, women fared better than their male counterparts – in Petrograd, at least, the patriotic organizations that had supported female units turned to finding them temporary lodging, food, and civilian clothes.[99]

---

[95] A detailed description of the seizure of power is Alexander Rabinowitch, *The Bolsheviks Come to Power* (New York: W. W. Norton, 1976), 242–304. Perhaps a total of 30,000 people, for both sides, participated; on debates over the numbers, see Figes, *A People's Tragedy*, 492–96.

[96] Accounts by defenders include BAR, Bocharnikova Papers, "V zhenskom batal'one," 23–27, and Aleksandr Sinegub, "Zashchita Zimnego dvortsa," *Arkhiv Russkoi revoliutsii* no. 4 (Berlin, 1922), 121–97; see also Meriel Buchanan *Petrograd: The City of Trouble, 1914–1918* (London, 1918), 196–97, and Sir Alfred Knox, *With the Russian Army, 1914–1917*, vol. II (New York, 1921), 705–11.

[97] BAR, Bocharnikova Papers, "V zhenskom batal'one," 26–30; Shagal, "Zhenskii batal'on." 9; and Knox, *With the Russian Army*, vol. II, 711–14, who asked the British ambassador to request the women soldiers' immediate release. Rumors concerning rape and mistreatment were apparently incorrect: Beatty, *Red Heart of Russia*, 216.

[98] The demobilization process began with the November 10th decree, releasing soldiers of the 1899 call-up into the reserves; a more general demobilization was worked out in an order of December 21: S. N. Bazarov, "Demobilizatsiia russkoi armii," *Voenno-istoricheskii zhurnal* (1998) no. 2, 27–37.

[99] Shagal, "Zhenskii batal'on," 10, mentions receiving help from the Petrograd Committee of Public Safety and the Red Cross; BAR, Bocharnikova Papers, "V zhenskom batalon'e," 36–42, refers to help from women's organizations; see also Stoff, *They Fought for the Motherland*, 160–61. We have no way of determining the eventual fate of most of the 5,000 or more women who entered combat units in Russia's Great War. Some joined the anti-Bolshevik forces in the Russian civil war, usually as Sisters of

Lacking provisions at the front and unwilling to wait any longer, hundreds of thousands of men deserted en masse, taking their weapons with them and terrorizing the civilian population. On November 27, the chief of staff of the southwestern front, Lieutenant General N. N. Stogov, warned of a potentially "terrible outcome, when a disorganized, starving army moves into the rear and destroys its own fatherland."[100]

Conclusions

In August 1917, a disillusioned soldier wrote to the Central Executive Committee of Soviets, accusing it of continuing a war that was not in Russia's interests: "you lie about freedom and things like that... You want to turn the country into a wasteland. You're taking the bread away from our wives, the bread they earned with their tears. You are enemies of the people! Down with all of you! I am a soldier, and I love my God and my homeland. You are traitors to Russia. You have betrayed Russia to England and France!" Also in August, a group of soldiers warned the same body: "if you defend the interests of the capitalists, then Russia is lost. We'll strangle all the capitalists and you with them. Hold on to the peasant soldier and make a speedy peace – that's the only way to save Russia."[101] It would be hard to imagine an understanding of the relationship between war, patriotism, and revolution further from the one articulated by Nikolai Berdiaev in March 1917. By August 1917, as the army unraveled and violent disorders spread across Russia, it seemed clear that the "national" revolution and the war as a patriotic project were no longer conjoined for the majority of the citizenry. Exploring the process of this uncoupling – and important exceptions to it – has been a central goal of this chapter.

> Mercy rather than as soldiers; others joined the Red Army, mainly in non-combat roles. On women in the Soviet military during the civil war see Elizabeth A. Wood, *The Baba and the Comrade. Gender and Politics in Revolutionary Russia* (Bloomington, 1997), 52–57 and Sanborn, *Drafting the Russian Nation*, 153–58. Battalion founder Yashka Bochkareva organized a women's paramedic unit in Siberia under White leader Admiral Kolchak. Following Kolchak's defeat, she was arrested by agents of the *cheka* (special police), tried as an enemy of the workers' regime, and shot on May 16, 1920. She was 30 years old. The published transcript of Bochkareva's final interrogation is "'Moi batal'on neostramit Rossii...' Okonchatel'nyi protokol doprosa Marii Bochkarevoi," *Rodina* no. 8–9 (1993), 78–81.
>
> [100] Bazarov, "Demobilizatsiia," 30–31, 34, writes that by January 1918 "armed banditry and pseudo-revolutionary violence had assumed the scale of a national catastrophe." Sanborn, *Imperial Apocalypse*, 221–34, notes the devastating impact of radicalized, deserting soldiers from mid July 1914.
>
> [101] Letters to the Central Executive Committee of Soviet from a soldier at the front, August 9, 1917, and from the soldiers' committee of the 129th Bessarabian Infantry (received August 5, 1917), in Mark D. Steinberg, *Voices of Revolution, 1917*, documents trans. by Marian Schwartz (New Haven: Yale University Press, 2001), 214–15 and 207.

Not surprisingly, the unexpected overthrow of the imperial regime in February–March 1917 was both liberating and destabilizing. It seemed, briefly, that the national unity of July 1914 was restored. The new democratic authorities declared age-old inequalities of social estate, class, ethnicity, and religion legally null and void. Revolution brought new freedoms, and the rights various subordinate population groups had hoped to secure through their service and sacrifice in the nation's war. Jubilant crowds celebrated, orators declaimed the meaning of these great events from every podium and street corner, and people made use of their freedom of speech and association to advance and defend their goals. Discarding tsarist-era institutions, the revolutionary citizenry created thousands of new organizations and networks – ranging from political parties to consumer cooperatives, professionally based unions to military leagues to new aid societies. In doing so, they were able to draw upon the mobilizing and publicistic skills they had developed during two and a half years of war.

For many of these groups, along with the Provisional Government, defining or redefining the nature of Russia's war and citizens' role in the war effort was a priority. Dozens of new periodicals, hundreds of pamphlets produced in enormous print runs, and thousands of agitational speakers sought to enlighten civilians and above all soldiers on the topics of revolutionary patriotism; the obligations of conscious and active citizenship, as well as the rights owed citizens; and the need to defend newly democratic Russia and to renounce annexations and indemnities. And, because the Great War had transformed even the rural mass of the population into avid consumers of the press, these exhortations and explanations had potentially vast audiences.

But national unity was short-lived. Fissures opened along numerous preexisting fault lines, with class tensions assuming particular importance. It was not necessarily the case that peasants and workers could not understand "state needs" or did not love their country – though frustrated elites increasingly blamed these alleged deficiencies. Different sectors of the population did not always employ the languages of nation and citizenship in the same way, or share identical priorities for what "new, free Russia" should be. Humble citizens were economically less able to ride out ever worsening inflation and shortages, while the unhappy connection between continuing war until victory and delaying much-desired reforms fed popular war-weariness and class mistrust. An army that had sustained perhaps 9 million casualties was losing its will to keep fighting.[102]

---

[102] The total of 8,737,300, drawn from *Rossiia v mirovoi voine 1914–1918 goda (v tsifrakh)*, 4–5, is deceptively precise, and includes approximately 775,400 killed in action and 3,343,900 captured. It is better understood as a very rough estimate, since statistics

Plummeting discipline and morale in the army also inspired a new manifestation of patriotic citizenship: the formation of revolutionary battalions that enrolled not only 50,000 male volunteers, but more than 5,000 women as well. The phenomenon of thousands of women volunteering for combat in 1917 can be understood in part as the revolution's extension of the mobilization of the population effected by the war. Radically democratizing Russia, and beginning the process of extending to women full political rights and equality before the law, the revolution created the legal, symbolic, and moral grounds upon which newly minted women citizens could become citizen-soldiers. The movement's transcendence of class and social estate also reminds us that class conflict and class identity, as important as they became, existed alongside and sometimes yielded to other, powerful loyalties.

Another complicating dynamic in revolutionary 1917 was the near absence of civilian censorship. The population of Russia was exposed to critiques of the war and of the government conducting it, as well as to profoundly disheartening stories on riots, crime, internal enemies, and shortages, to a degree unmatched by any other combatant population in the Great War. Deteriorating conditions, and unfiltered press coverage of them, helped corrode the new government's credibility as well as popular resolve to continue the fight to the end. Small wonder, then, that control of the press was on Lenin's mind when the Bolsheviks seized power in Petrograd on October 24–25. Besides speedily issuing decrees on peace and land, on October 27 the new regime ordered the closer of all "counterrevolutionary" publications. Over the course of the next year, as civil war spread, all independent periodicals – socialist ones included – eventually suffered the same fate.[103] One lesson learned in Russia's Great War was the danger posed by a free press in wartime.

---

on Russian military casualties are incomplete and highly disputed; see, for example, A. E. Stepanov, "Obshchie demograficheskie poteri naseleniia Rossii v period Pervoi mirovoi voiny," in V. Malkov, ed., *Pervaia mirovaia voina. Prolog XX veka* (Moscow: Nauka, 1998), 474–84, who estimates 10.7 million military casualties (3 million of which were deaths) by the *end* of 1917, for approximate losses of 60 percent in the armed forces.

[103] Alexander Rabinowitch, *The Bolsheviks in Power: The First Year of Soviet Power in Petrograd* (Bloomington: Indiana University Press, 2007), 22–25, 46–47, 316–17, 374–76; a number of publications critical of the Bolsheviks managed to survive up to the first anniversary of October. On the fate of Russia's largest commercial publication, see A. G. Mendeleev, *Zhizn' gazety "Russkoe slovo." Izdatel' sotrudniki* (Moscow: ROSSPEN, 2001), 33–37; a consistent critic of the Bolsheviks and enjoying a daily circulation in excess of 1.2 million in 1917, the Moscow-based *Russkoe slovo* was closed briefly on October 26, and then permanently on November 26, 1917; *Pravda* and *Izvestiia* were installed in its buildings.

Conclusion

> It is an unprecedented event in world history when a numerous people, which considers itself a great people ... has in eight months dug itself a grave with its own hands. It follows that the very idea of a Russian power, a Russian nation, was a mirage, a bluff, that this only seemed to be so and was never a reality.
>
> Iurii Got'e, November 16, 1917

Moscow-based historian Iurii Got'e was 44 years old when he began keeping a diary in summer 1917, recording in it the anger, shame, and grief he felt at the unraveling of his beloved country. Chronicling social dissolution, the breakdown of the army, and seeming public indifference to impending defeat, his entries return again and again to the absence of national feeling. On July 16, 1917, he wrote that the fall of Russia as a great and unified power was due to its own inadequacies, namely the "complete atrophy of a sense of patriotism, motherland, common solidarity, and *union sacrée.*" Ten days later he remarked the resemblance between the Time of Troubles and 1917, doubting, however, that there would be a new "Minin and Pozharskii" to save the country.[1] On January 1, 1918, describing the peace negotiations with Germany being conducted by the Bolshevik government, he wrote that they were selling Russia out, but continued, "And why shouldn't they sell? After all, there is no nation in Russia, nor is there a people."[2]

Writing hundreds of miles north of Moscow, in the Tot'ma district of Vologda province, peasant farmer A. A. Zamaraev recorded similarly despairing feelings in his diary. He wrote on July 20, "The army has disgraced itself and the motherland; it's become disgusting to look at the soldier."[3] On October 26, he said of the Bolshevik seizure of power, "I pity poor Russia, all tormented and ruined. Turmoil and anarchy everywhere." On February 15, 1918, reflecting on the renewed German advance, he wrote "The death of Russia. Germans in Petrograd. Ukraine has separated.

---

[1] Got'e, *Time of Troubles*, 28, 42. [2] Ibid., 95, 114.
[3] Morozov and Reshetnikov, eds., *Dnevnik totemskogo krest'ianina*, 165.

Finland is independent. The Japanese are in Siberia." And finally, on March 1, "A shameful, terrible peace has been concluded ..."[4]

It is easy to understand how the calamitous implosion of the Russian war effort, internal unity, and order could strike some contemporaries as sorry proof of a Russian deficit in national feeling. This was particularly true in that Russians were not aware that, in every combatant country, the various versions of sacred union were virtually defunct by 1917. They did not know about the mass mutinies that rocked the French army in spring of that year – a very well-kept secret – or the strikes and shortages that compelled a number of governments to try to remobilize their populations behind the war.[5] They therefore viewed Russia's inability to sustain the fight to the end as truly exceptional, deepening the sense that they as a people had been found wanting, and that Russia itself, in contrast to the more "advanced" states that were its allies and foes, did not constitute a nation.

And as Zamaraev and Got'e's diary entries suggest, the unraveling of the imperial state posed further agonizing questions about what constituted "Russia." Over the course of 1917, in conditions of growing anarchy and economic freefall, national movements radicalized in the borderlands. Then, defeat brought with it a fundamental reconfiguration – and truncation – of Russian space.[6] The new Soviet government formally concluded a separate peace with Germany and the other members of the Quadruple Alliance on March 3, 1918. The terms were harsh. By provision of the Treaty of Brest-Litovsk, Russia lost 1.2 million square miles of territory and an estimated 60 million inhabitants. It acknowledged the independence of Ukraine – which had already signed its own separate peace in February 1918 – as

---

[4] Ibid., 182, 185.
[5] Leonard V. Smith, *Between Mutiny and Obedience: The Case of the French Mutiny* (Princeton: Princeton University Press, 1994). On falling morale and antiwar sentiments among other belligerents, see John Horne, "Remobilizing for 'Total War': France and Britain, 1917–1918," in Horne, ed., *State, Society, and Mobilization in Europe*, 195–211, and Roger Chickering, *Imperial Germany and the Great War, 1914–1918*, 3rd edn. (Cambridge: Cambridge University Press, 2014), 153, who states that "the *Burgfrieden* did not endure" into 1917. In similar vein, Flood, *France 1914–1918*, 180, asserts that the French *union sacrée* was dead by 1916. Another study suggests that the *union sacrée* was destroyed in 1917 by Georges Clemenceau's exclusionary "second mobilization" of the home front: Smith, Audoin-Rouzeau and Becker, *France and the Great War, 1914–1918*, 114–16. The point here is that the erosion of national unity and the wartime political truce was not a uniquely Russian experience, but more nearly a universal one.
[6] For an overview of nationalist movements in the borderlands in 1917–21, see Jeremy Smith, *Red Nations: The Nationalities Experience in and after the USSR* (Cambridge: Cambridge University Press, 2013), 17–53, who notes that in the borderlands, as in the center, class and nation could represent competing demands.

Conclusion 249

well as Finland and Poland. The Baltic area and Transcaucasia also ceased to be part of Russia.[7]

Self-avowedly "nationally minded" Russian groups and parties, of course, condemned the peace of Brest-Litovsk as disastrous for the country, as well as a shameful betrayal of its allies.[8] But most socialists (and for that matter, many Bolsheviks) also saw the peace as betrayal, of the revolution or the country; Menshevik leader Fedor Dan charged that Lenin's government, in return for aiding the German conquest of Ukraine, had been granted "the most august permission of the Kaiser" to rule over the remnants of Russia.[9] Widespread outrage virtually ensured that localized opposition to the Bolsheviks would escalate into full-blown civil war.[10] Most of Siberia and all of Russian Central Asia, as well as areas in the Russian north, southern Russia, and the Volga region ceased to be under the control of the Bolshevik-headed Russian state. Warlords emerged in Siberia, Ukraine, and elsewhere, adding their undisciplined forces to the violent mix of Red, White, Black, and Green armies, or simply preying on local populations; several million people perished in these conflicts. Epidemic diseases and starvation wiped out even more people as the economy collapsed.[11] Russia in 1918–21 was

---

[7] For provisions of the treaty, see the classic treatment by John W. Wheeler-Bennett, *Brest-Litovsk: The Forgotten Peace, March 1918* (New York: W. Morrow, 1939), 270–75, 345–46; terms were renegotiated in August 1918, at which time Germany added a claim for 6 billion marks as compensation for losses caused by Russia.

[8] See, for example, Rosenberg, *Liberals in the Russian Revolution*, 288–89, 318–20.

[9] Quoted in Vladimir N. Brovkin, *The Mensheviks after October: Socialist Opposition and the Rise of the Bolshevik Dictatorship* (Ithaca: Cornell University Press, 1987), 128. A detailed overview of workers' and socialists' responses to the proposed separate peace – both the version initially accepted by Lenin and Trotsky on February 19, and the final, harsher version signed March 3 – is Rabinowitch, *The Bolsheviks in Power*, 161–209. On the Socialist Revolutionaries, see Scott B. Smith, *Captives of Revolution: The Socialist Revolutionaries and the Bolshevik Dictatorship, 1918–1923* (Pittsburgh: University of Pittsburgh Press, 2011), 2–42, who notes their rather exceptional employment of both the language of class and the language of nationhood in trying to make sense of events.

[10] Porshneva's detailed discussion of popular reaction to the Brest peace includes analysis of telegrams sent to the Fourth, Extraordinary Congress of Soviets in March 1918: 54 percent of telegrams denounced the peace, with 76 percent of these objections coming from local soviets of workers', soldiers', and peasants' deputies. See Porshneva, *Krest'iane, rabochie i soldaty*, 240–53. Similarly, eyewitness Viktor Shklovsky mordantly noted, "Before signing the Treaty of Brest Litovsk, the Bolsheviks sent telegrams to all the major soviets to ask whether they should sign the treaty. They all answered no ... The treaty was signed. Evidently the Bolsheviks had inquired out of curiosity": Shklovsky, *Sentimental Journey*, 141.

[11] On costs of the civil war, see Evan Mawdsley, *The Russian Civil War*, 2nd edn. (Edinburgh: Birlinn, 2000), 285–88, who offers estimates of 7–10 million deaths and a drop in national income in 1920 to 40 percent of what it had been in 1913. An especially terrifying picture is provided by the case study of the Urals in Narskii, *Zhizn' v katastrofe*,

not simply a postimperial rump of its former self; it was, as Joshua Sanborn rightly argues, a failed state.[12]

The war, and the revolution it launched, therefore had a shattering impact on the Russian state as well as the Russian empire. But as horrendous as these effects were, they do not preclude the war also having played a significant role in emergence of the modern Russian nation. Wars, as many scholars note, frequently make nations – or remake them – changing forms of governance and economic practices, altering social relationships, forging new identities. In mobilizing populations at the state's behest, they can also nationalize them.[13]

As the first total war, the Great War engendered an unprecedented mobilization of human and economic resources.[14] The Russian public rose to the challenge. Some 15 million men marched off to fight, while millions of other citizens organized relief networks, donated money and goods, helped plow one another's fields, submitted to labor requisitions, subscribed to the war loans, and volunteered in a myriad of ways. The imperial government, unable to handle the war's huge demands on its own, had to allow and to fund (albeit grudgingly, at times) a degree of national associational activity and public initiative such as it had never before countenanced. In effect, the war accelerated the process of imagining, articulating, and enacting an encompassing national community across the vast space of the Russian land mass.

Constructing "Sacred Union"

Patriotic narratives helped limn this nation at war. I have used the term "sacred union" – one of several ways Russians referred to the internal

---

one section of which is subtitled "The Scale of the Catastrophe: From Freedom to Cannibalism," 32–167.
[12] Sanborn, *Imperial Apocalypse*, 239–40, 247–53.
[13] For example, von Hagen, "The Great War and the Mobilization of Ethnicity," 34–50, and Eric Lohr, "War Nationalism," in Lohr et al., eds., *The Empire and Nationalism at War*, 91–107, who makes a provocative case for theories viewing nationalism as the product of an "event," such as war or state collapse, rather than the result of long-term developments. In the field of American history, different scholars identify different wars as nationally formative; see, for example, James McPherson, *The War that Forged a Nation: Why the Civil War Still Matters* (Oxford: Oxford University Press, 2015), 1–14.
[14] A helpful overview of debate on the meaning of the term "total war" is Stig Forster, "Introduction," in Roger Chickering and Stig Forster, eds., *Great War, Total War: Combat and Mobilization on the Western Front, 1914–1918* (Cambridge: Cambridge University Press, 2000), 1–15; most definitions encompass the idea that large-scale industrialized warfare requires the labor and support of civilians on the home front: in the Great War, "More than ever before, whole nations became integrated fighting units" (ibid., 7).

unity and political truce declared at start of the war – as a shorthand expression for the dominant patriotic narrative constructed in July and August 1914. Sacred union translated into a highly inclusive vision of the nation: all classes and social estates, all faiths and nationalities, were characterized as part of the national patriotic community and devoted to defending its integrity and wellbeing. Sacred union also stressed the defensive and just nature of Russia's war, one enjoying God's support, thus legitimizing the conflict and sanctifying the sacrifices required of the population. A national identity based on a shared past and territory, and loyalty to it, rather than on ethnicity, faith, or descent, was not only more inclusive but also essentially modern.

Some variants of the wartime patriotic narrative held that the war had revealed the true essence of the Russian people, whether this was understood as the people's age-old devotion to tsar and country or its more recently developed civic maturity. But the war was also perceived as transformative: raising consciousness, burning away the dross of internal enmity or materialism, ending Russians' thrall to demon drink. In this way, sacred union could accommodate even formerly suspect population groups, such as disaffected Poles or urban proletarians, as well as widely different understandings of what postwar Russia should be. For a multinational, multiconfessional empire with deep political differences and yawning class divides, the flexibility and promise of the patriotic narrative were crucial. And, if one subscribes to the understanding of "nationhood" as a concept that is accommodating as well as exclusionary – as Alon Confino and other students of nationalism suggest – the wartime patriotic narrative underlines the potential for such a diverse polity to be meaningfully a "nation."[15]

One function of the narrative was to help unite the population *against* the external foe. Drawing on widespread popular resentment of Germans and Germany, various thinkers, media organs, and patriotic societies generated literature demonizing the enemy as barbaric, stoking anger over German economic dominance, and sowing fears of espionage. However, many central themes of the patriotic narrative were positive, meant to instill pride and inspire people with a sense of whom and what they were fighting *for*. Besides praising the virtues and loyalty of all Russians – in the broad, nonethnic sense of the word (*rossiiskii*) – the

---

[15] Alon Confino, *The Nation as Local Metaphor: Wurttemberg, Imperial Germany, and National Memory, 1871–1918* (Chapel Hill: University of North Carolina Press, 1997), 4; exploring how multiple German states became a single German nation after 1871, he notes that "the striking potential of nationhood to integrate diverse and frequently hostile groups is forgotten too easily."

narrative drew on previous triumphs over aggressors, celebrating heroes such as Minin and Pozharskii, and the union of tsar and people in the 1812 Fatherland War. It also honored heroes of the present conflict, among them Kuz'ma Kriuchkov, Stefan Veremchuk, and, later, Yashka Bochkareva. In this way, the patriotic narrative drew images and sustenance from a proud past even as it looked forward to a better future. This interweaving of shared past and future sacrifice for the nation, putatively undertaken voluntarily by a people, is the very stuff of modern nationhood.

Rousing patriotic narratives cannot mobilize a nation unless they are widely diffused. Postwar critiques notwithstanding, the imperial government, commercial publishers, and civil society worked to disseminate narratives and imagery of sacred union on an unprecedented scale. Dozens of new war-related periodicals came into existence. Nongovernmental organizations and for-profit publishers produced pamphlets and entire book series about the war effort, tailored for varied and diverse audiences. War-related images and material objects – posters and woodcuts, portraits and flags, postcards and badges and maps – were produced on a huge scale, widely distributed, and eagerly purchased. They aided people in picturing not just battles and leaders, but the far-flung national community that was engaged in this struggle, at the front and on the home front. Lectures, readings, and slide shows on the war were organized in cities and towns, but also in the countryside by cooperatives, zemstvos, and village teachers. The imperial government made sizeable investments in publishing and distributing mass-edition pamphlets aimed at popular audiences, as well as pumping money into *Sel'skii vestnik*, a daily newspaper aimed at the rural population.

The Russian Orthodox Church, which represented a vast institutional network as well as a community of faith, augmented these various efforts. It disseminated patriotic messages by means of regular prayers for the war effort and Russia's fallen, through the sermons and talks of parish priests and army chaplains, by instruction and outreach in some 40,000 parish schools, and through its many publications, including the new daily paper for the parish, *Prikhodskii listok*. Rituals of commemoration, services of thanksgiving for military successes, local pilgrimages, and the national day of prayer for victory all helped sanctify the nation's just war and the sacrifices its sons and daughters brought to "the altar of the fatherland."

I suggest that the enormous project of war relief was a significant component of the narrative of sacred union, and thereby of the national self-imagination. In mobilizing the civilian population, it cut across gender, class, and confessional divides. The work of relief embodied in deeds the rhetoric about a uniquely giving nation, as well as demonstrating the loyalty – and competence – of the citizenry. Because it involved so much of the population, extending into the smallest hamlets and affecting many national minorities, war relief made social patriotism not just an all-Russian phenomenon, but a grass-roots one. The scale of need called into being new aid networks: more than 1,350 institutions in the Union of Cities and Union of Zemstvos, hundreds of Tatiana Committees and cooperatives, hundreds of committees organized by and for national minorities, and many thousands of Russian Orthodox parish guardianship councils. Vibrant and expanding associational networks, in tackling war-generated problems across the empire, were also helping stitch together the Russian national community itself. They united thousands of local communities spatially, tangibly, and imaginatively.

In Russia, as in all the belligerent states, various interest groups worked mightily to shape the patriotic discourse along lines they could approve. The diversity of voices and values meant that versions of the patriotic narrative disseminated by state authorities or particular political orientations were not always consonant with the variants crafted by other groups. The church, not surprisingly, tended to construct "Russianness" most narrowly, often equating it with Russian Orthodox Christianity. This perspective left tens of millions of non-Orthodox Russian citizens on the margins of, or outside, the national community, thereby undercutting the inclusive narrative of the secular authorities. The central government could send out contradictory messages, proclaiming all Russian subjects to be patriots, while subsidizing far-right newspapers that were bashing "traitorous" Jews and liberals by mid 1915. But we should not mistake contestations over the meaning and content of patriotism, and what membership in the national community entailed, for an absence of powerful, shared themes and myths. And most of the population had ample incentive to buy into the broad themes of sacred union, since proving one's patriotism laid a basis for various groups to accrue political capital, or try to enhance their claims to full inclusion in the nation.

Subjects into Citizens

In their comparison of the experience of the war in Paris, London, and Berlin, Jay Winter and Jean-Louis Robert point out that the meaning of citizenship in all three cities broadened to include provision for populations especially hard hit by the war, such as the families of soldiers: "Entitlement rights expanded in wartime, once more linking urban citizenship to the nation under siege."[16] And just as the war broadened the material benefits of citizenship, it could also expand the boundaries of citizenship, to more fully include women, those who did not own property, or other politically marginal populations, as Nicoletta Gullace demonstrates was the case for Britain, and Jennifer Keene and others argue was true in the United States.[17]

The experience of the Great War in Russia similarly affected understandings of citizenship. Already in 1912, the law entitling the families of soldiers mobilized in wartime to a monthly stipend, irrespective of financial need, essentially created a new right of citizenship. During the war, aid grew to encompass other material benefits for soldiers' families, assistance for wounded and disabled soldiers, and relief for millions of war refugees. Importantly, widely disseminated literature about these material provisions and appeals to the population to give and to volunteer were often couched in the language of civic duty, represented as what was *owed* by the state and the people to fellow citizens who defended the nation or suffered due to the nation's war.

Rhetorically, the language of sacrifice and the language of citizenship became enmeshed, solidifying the understanding of the reciprocal relationship of duty and rights. Leaders in the public organizations, progressive political parties, national minority groups, and the women's movement explicitly drew this connection, anticipating a postwar expansion of rights thanks to the population's patriotic service and sacrifice. Anecdotal evidence suggests that ordinary Russians were also internalizing these new rights of citizenship, as evidenced by the demands of soldiers' wives (*soldatki*) and the insistence of peasant deputies to the State Duma, in 1916, that peasant soldiers' defense of the motherland should win all peasants full equality before the law.

However, as every belligerent state discovered, even the most successful national mobilization can have unintended consequences. In Russia, there were many. One consequence of national mobilization was to heighten or create a non-Russian national consciousness on the part of national minorities. This was particularly the case among Ukrainians and

---

[16] Jay Winter and Jean-Louis Robert, eds., *Capital Cities at War: Paris, London, Berlin, 1914–1919*, vol. I (Cambridge: Cambridge University Press, 1997), 550.

[17] Gullace, "*The Blood of Our Sons*," 184–98; Keene, *Doughboys, the Great War, and the Remaking of America*, who concentrates on the forging of a new social contract for the citizen-soldier; and Kimberly Jensen, "Women, Citizenship, and Civic Sacrifice: Engendering Patriotism in the First World War," in John Bodnar, ed., *Bonds of Affection: Americans Define Their Patriotism* (Princeton: Princeton University Press, 1996), 139–59, who examines how women active in the war effort focused on the social contract of citizenship to make their claims for increased civic participation and equality.

certain refugee populations, as Mark von Hagen and Peter Gatrell have shown, contributing to centrifugal and even separatist currents in 1917. Whipping up anti-German sentiment produced three days of devastating rioting in Moscow in 1915, in addition to radical – and costly – nationalizing economic policies directed at both enemy aliens and Russia's own Germans. Hysteria about internal enemies contributed not only to the army's mistreatment of the Jewish population in the war zone but also, subsequently, to delegitimizing doubts about the patriotism of the imperial family and court.

The Revolutionary Nation

When bread riots erupted in Petrograd in February 1917, the delegitimization of the dynasty was so complete that not even elites would rally to its defense. The Provisional Government and Petrograd Soviet speedily granted many of the liberties and civil rights that Russians had dreamed of winning through their patriotic wartime service. War aims were redefined to reject annexations and indemnities. Changes were also effected in patriotic narratives: the triadic formula of faith, tsar and fatherland was discarded, and a joined pair – "freedom and the fatherland" or "the motherland and the revolution" – became the precious objects of defense. Unhappily, initial unity around the new formulas and confidence in the new authorities eroded with shocking speed. Many factors contributed to this erosion, including unrealized expectations of immediate material improvements – another unintended consequence of wartime national mobilization. Russia, like every combatant state, had basically promised its citizens that victory would bring not only a better world order, but also palpable benefits to offset the terrible costs of the war; since it turned out that no recompense could possibly be commensurate with all the losses sustained, when war ended and demobilization began, even victorious powers could find themselves contending with angry and disillusioned citizens (some of whom still had guns in their hands).[18] But in Russia, and Russia alone, revolutionary regime change unleashed these great expectations long before an end to the war was in sight.

[18] A thoughtful exploration of demobilization and the disappointment of "great expectations" is Stéphane Audoin-Rouzeau and Annette Becker, *14–18: Understanding the Great War*, trans. Catherine Temerson (New York: Hill and Wang, 2000), 159–71. On the Italian experience, see Walter J. Adamson, "The Impact of World War I on Italian Political Culture," in Roshwald and Stites, eds., *European Culture in the Great War*, 308–29; on Germany, see Richard Bessel, "Mobilization and De-Mobilization in Germany, 1916–1919," in Horne, ed., *State, Society, and Mobilization*, 212–22.

Moreover, the near absence of civilian censorship from March to November in 1917 – another important way in which Russia's wartime experience differed from that of other combatants – allowed heated debate over the war, the meaning of patriotism, and the duties and rights of the newly liberated citizenry. The authorities were almost powerless to prevent dissemination of narratives that undercut soldiers' willingness to fight by depicting the war as unjust and its burdens unfairly distributed, or suggesting that imminent world proletarian revolution meant the imperialist war would soon be over anyway. In these conditions, for many humble Russians, loyalty to the motherland was gradually uncoupled from any perceived need to keep fighting and dying until "victory."

Weariness with fighting and dying did not translate into peace; in withdrawing from the Great War, Russia was already devolving into civil war. For another three years, both the Bolsheviks and their opponents battled for the loyalties of the population, casting themselves as legitimate leaders and stewards of this inchoate Russian fatherland. They sought to devise symbols, slogans, and heroic myths to appeal to the population (or their own followers) and, especially, to remobilize them to fight. For all their differences, Whites and Reds both appealed to love of country and things held "sacred" by the members of the national community.

The anti-Bolshevik forces considered themselves the true Russian patriots, but nonetheless struggled to propagate an attractive patriotic narrative. Internal divisions and lack of a coherent and agreed-upon political program hampered them profoundly, making it difficult to generate positive, unifying themes. What became the main slogan of the Whites in southern Russia, "Russia, one and indivisible," did not have the appeal of "sacred union": it was less flexible and more backward-looking, lacking the fulfillment of subaltern groups' aspirations implied in the wartime patriotic narrative. Peasants could not be sure of keeping the lands they had acquired, minorities could not be sure of equal rights and cultural autonomy, and Jews could expect humiliation and violence. The Whites' strongest appeal was religious, representing themselves as defenders of Orthodoxy and the restorers of "Holy Russia," versus Russia's betrayers, the atheist Bolsheviks (or "Jew-Bolsheviks"), bought and paid for with "German gold." The Orthodox Church not only strongly supported the Whites but also provided them the means of communicating with millions of believers.[19]

---

[19] On anti-Bolshevik views and propaganda, see Paul F. Robinson, "Always with Honour: The Code of White Russian Officers," *Canadian Slavonic Papers* 41, 2 (1999), 121–41;

Conclusion

When Georgii Plekhanov, founding father of Russian Marxism, supported Russia's war effort in 1914, repudiating the Communist Manifesto's famous claim that "the worker has no fatherland," Lenin had savagely attacked this "chauvinism." Once in power, however, the Bolsheviks proved willing to use tropes familiar from pre-October patriotic narratives. On February 21, 1918, as the German army resumed its offensive in Russia, the Soviet of People's Commissars issued Lenin's decree "The Socialist Fatherland Is in Danger!" It summoned workers and peasants to revolutionary defense of the country, declaring that it was their "sacred duty" to defend the Republic of Soviets against the bourgeois-imperialist German hordes. Point eight of the decree played chillingly to continuing fears about enemies within, stipulating that "Enemy agents, profiteers, marauders, hooligans, counterrevolutionary agitators, and German spies are to be shot on the spot."[20]

Bolshevik propaganda drew on national feeling by emphasizing the Whites' subordination to their imperialist foreign allies; White generals were depicted as snarling dogs, their leashes held by figures representing the United States, France, and Britain. The Soviet government again cast itself as the true defender of Russia's independence during the Soviet–Polish war. In May 1920, invading Polish armies captured Kiev, regarded by many Russians as the birthplace of their culture. Newspapers called upon the population to join the army and "defend the fatherland" from the Polish aggressors. Cartoons in the famed ROSTA windows in Moscow depicted a Polish officer devouring a peasant woman (*baba*). According to Orlando Figes, the Bolsheviks were stunned by the strength of the public response. Some 14,000 officers joined the Red Army to fight the Poles, thousands of civilians volunteered for war work, and there were mass patriotic demonstrations. Grigorii Zinoviev, head of Petrograd's soviet executive committee, admitted, "We never thought Russia had so many patriots."[21]

Peter Kenez, *The Birth of the Propaganda State: Soviet Methods of Mass Mobilization, 1917–1929* (Cambridge: Cambridge University Press, 1985), 63–69; and Oleg Riabov, "The Symbol of "Mother Russia" across Two Epochs: From the First World War to the Civil War," in Frame, Kolonitskii, Marks, and Stockdale, eds., *Russian Culture in War and Revolution*, 91–96.

[20] Plekhanov, *O voine*, 23–27, and V. I. Lenin, *Collected Works*, vol. XXVII (Moscow: Progress Publishers, 1965), 30–33.

[21] On civil war depictions of the Whites, see Victoria Bonnell, *Iconography of Power: Soviet Political Posters under Lenin and Stalin* (Berkeley: University of California Press, 1997), 194–99; Figes, *A People's Tragedy*, 697–700. ROSTA (Rossiiskoe telegraficheskoe agentstvo) was the acronym of the renamed Petrograd Telegraph Agency; it became famous for the cutting-edge graphic illustrations of leading news items that it displayed in the windows of its Moscow headquarters.

Postwar "Demobilization"

Many of the mobilizing techniques and tropes employed in the Great War outlived the years of armed struggle. The endurance of certain themes reminds us, yet again, of continuities between the late imperial and Soviet regimes. To take but one example, Amir Weiner has influentially argued that the idea of "purification of the nation" was a revolutionary and Bolshevik project, which became even more violent, ethnicized, and indiscriminate thanks to the Second World War.[22] But themes of purification and cleansing are apparent in Russia's Great War, with its hunt for spies and internal enemies – who needed to be "unmasked" – its rhetorical or physical exclusion of population groups, and the narratives of transformation or irredeemability. The very phrase "enemy of the people," so evocative of the Stalinist terror, dates from the Great War.[23]

Ideas of citizenship provide a complex illustration of continuity and rupture. On the one hand, Soviet citizenship as laid out in the 1918 constitution represented a radical departure from post-1905 trends in Russian citizenship practice. By deliberately depriving whole subgroups of the population of citizenship rights on the basis of their class origins or putative anti-Soviet behavior, Eric Lohr notes, the new regime created "an extreme form of 'obligations only' subject status not seen since the era of serfdom."[24] But, as Golfo Alexopolous demonstrates in her study of outcasts' petitions to be reinstated in the community of citizens, the ideal of mutual reciprocity between state and citizen remained. Many people had internalized the belief, powerfully disseminated in the Great War, that loyal service and sacrifice for the state earned one political rights of citizenship *and* access to the material benefits that the state owed its citizens. By highlighting community service and voluntarism as proof of worthiness for full citizenship, many of these outcasts' petitions also remind us of wartime depictions of citizens as active and contributory.[25]

---

[22] According to Weiner, in the Soviet Union, the creation of a pure and harmonious socialist society came to entail violent "excision" or cleansing of alien elements from the body politic: Weiner, *Making Sense of War*, esp. 24, 38, 145–49.

[23] On the Stalinist use of the term "enemy of the people," which she calls "*the* signature phrase of the terror," see Wendy Z. Goldman, *Inventing the Enemy: Denunciation and Terror in Stalin's Russia* (Cambridge: Campbridge University Press, 2011), 73–78.

[24] See Lohr, *Russian Citizenship*, 132–79, who nonetheless argues that Bolshevik citizenship policy was not simply a return to old-regime subjecthood.

[25] Alexopoulos, *Stalin's Outcasts*, 2–11, 135–57; by the time of the first five-year plan, deprivation of rights of citizenship brought with it a host of other deprivations, often including loss of employment, housing, and access to education. Emphasis in these petitions on involvement in community service is also reminiscent of the same insistence in wartime petitions by Russian Germans that they were, indeed, "Russian."

In 1936, the so-called Stalin Constitution ended the practice of excluding categories of the population from enjoyment of these rights and benefits, returning – at least on paper – to a more egalitarian and uniform conception of citizenship. However massively these constitutional rights were subsequently violated, they were nonetheless much prized by the Soviet citizenry.

In the 1920s, internationalist themes predominated over national ones, as the Soviet regime set about rebuilding the shattered economy and worked to create a socialist society and culture. Soviet Russia, in striking contrast to other former combatants of the Great War, turned its back on formal commemoration of a war that Lenin had descried as "imperialist." National projects for honoring and memorializing the service of soldiers of this war were permanently shelved: no holiday would be created, no monuments or museums to them built. The special fraternal cemeteries that had already been created would suffer the common fate of all cemeteries in the Soviet Union in the 1920s and 1930s, falling into disuse and disrepair. The Soviet authorities instead devoted themselves to creating a myth of the revolution and civil war. But, as Karen Petrone shows in her study of Soviet memory of the Great War, the marginalization of the First World War in Soviet culture does not signify "an absence of memory or the failure of Russians to see the war as a compelling human struggle."[26] Increasingly, the state would celebrate many of the same attributes of the people that had been identified in First World War patriotic discouse: staunch bravery, heroism, love of the motherland, and willingness to sacrifice oneself on its behalf. Only the quality of compassionate generosity seems to have disappeared.[27]

In the mid 1930s, there was a much more explicit return to celebration of the heroic, prerevolutionary national past. As David Brandenberger and other scholars have shown, facing an ever more threatening international climate, and the consequent need for popular mobilization, the regime began to deploy Russian national heroes, imagery, and myths "to popularize the reigning Marxist-Leninist ideology." In the Great Patriotic War, this rehabilitation of the national past was even more pronounced. The seventeenth-century heroes Minin and Pozharskii,

---

[26] Petrone, *The Great War in Russian Memory*, 5–6, 272–91. On Soviet construction of the memory of October 1917, see Frederick C. Corney, *Telling October: Memory and the Making of the Bolshevik Revolution* (Ithaca: Cornell University Press, 2004).

[27] From 1919, the Soviet state increasingly monopolized provision of social welfare, leaving no space for the kind of private and public organizations that were so important in generating and distributing aid in the Great War; on this process, see David L. Hoffmann, *Cultivating the Masses: Modern State Practices and Soviet Socialism, 1914–1939* (Ithaca: Cornell University Press, 2011), 48–69.

frequently pointed to in the Great War as exemplars of Russian patriotic initiative and sacrifice, figured in the Soviet pantheon of heroes.[28]

In sum, mass production and consumption of narratives of a united and inclusive Russian nation require that we rethink old representations of wartime patriotism as mainly an elite and urban phenomenon. Patriotic narratives were spread through print media, graphic images, spoken discourse, and material objects. They were also spread through and by vast networks of war relief, which in helping compatriots suffering from the war also allowed millions of aid workers, volunteers, and donors to enact their patriotism, demonstrating it in deeds. No less meaningfully, patriotic narratives were disseminated and performed across the country in rituals honoring and memorializing soldiers and heroes.

While we can rarely know exactly how ordinary people interpreted these narratives and rituals, they did offer an appealing picture of an inclusive, far-flung Russian national community worthy of defense. We do know that tens of millions of people mobilized in this total war regarded it as transformative, believing that they and their country had been changed fundamentally and that the postwar order would reflect that. It is thus quite possible to conclude that, for Russia, as for other states, the war experience helped consolidate in the population a sense of membership in a great national community. Many of the perceived contours and attributes of that national community – and related understandings of the rights owed the loyal citizens who constituted it – would outlive the war and civil war and be worked into Soviet renderings of Russian national identity.

---

[28] Brandenberger, *National Bolshevism*, 118–19, 135, 144–45, 151.

Select Bibliography

Archival Sources

Bakhmeteff Archive of Russian and East European Culture, Columbia University, New York

Mariia Bocharnikova, "V zhenskom batalon'e smerti" (unpublished memoir)

Gosudarstvennyi Arkhiv Rossiiskoi Federatsii (GARF), Moscow

f. 58, Gendarme Administration of Moscow Province
f. 63, Moscow Okhrana
ff. 102 and 102 OO, Department of Police
f. 116, Union of the Russian People
f. 117, Union of Archangel Michael
f. 523, Constitutional Democratic Party
f. 579, P. N. Miliukov
f. 601, Nicholas II
f. 1467, Extraordinary Investigative Commission
f. 1788, Provisional Government, Ministry of Internal Affairs
f. 6281, First World War Collection of the Academy of Science
f. 6787, Provisional Government, Ministry of State Welfare
f. 6834, Special Commission on the Arts
f. 9505, Central Committee on Social-Political Enlightenment, 1917

Hoover Institution Archives on War, Revolution, and Peace, Stanford, CA

World War I Poster Collection

Library of Congress, Photography and Graphics Division, Washington, DC

Lot 5452, "Russian War Loan Postcards, 1915–16"
Lot 6540, "Red Cross Stamps"

Lot 8812, "Red Cross Photographs, Training Camp, First Petrograd Women's Battalion," 1917

Rossiiskii Gosudarstvennyi Istoricheskii Arkhiv (RGIA)

f. 560, Ministry of Finance
f. 776, Chief Administration for Affairs of the Press
f. 796, Chancellery of the Holy Synod
f. 797, Chancellery of the Chief Procurator
f. 800, Printing Office of the Holy Synod
f. 1276, Council of Ministers
f. 1405, Ministry of Justice
f. 1483, Committee on Fighting German Domination

Rossiiskii Gosudarstvennyi Voenno-istoricheskii Arkhiv (RGVIA), Moscow

f. 29, Chancellery of the War Ministry
f. 401, Military-Scientific Committee, General Staff
f. 1343, Staff of the Petrograd Military District
f. 2000, Chief Administration of the General Staff
f. 2003, Staff of the Supreme Commander (Stavka)
f. 2005, Military-Political and Civil Administration of the Supreme Command
f. 3474, Moscow Women's Battalion of Death
f. 12651, Chief Administration of the Russian Society of the Red Cross
f. 16070, Aleksandrovskii Committee for the Wounded
f. 16280, Skobelev Committee
f. 16325, Alekseevskii Committee, 1905–1917

Russian Newspapers and Periodicals

Den'
Derevenskaia gazeta
Dobrovolets'
Gazeta-kopeika
Izvestiia komiteta Vserossiiskogo soiuza gorodov
Kievlianin'
Letopis'
Letopis' voiny
Lukomor'e
Narodnoe obrazovanie
Niva
Novoe vremia
Prikhodskii listok
Prizrenie i blagotvoritel'nost' v Rossii
Rech'

Select Bibliography 263

Russkaia mysl'
Russkoe bogatstvo
Russkoe slovo
Russkie vedomosti
Russkie zapiski
Russkii invalid
Sel'skii vestnik
Sovremennik
Soldat-Grazhdanin
Vestnik Krasnogo kresta
Voina
Voina i evrei
Voina i mir
Zhenskii vestnik
Zhenskoe delo

Published Primary Sources

Abramowicz, Hirsz. *Profiles of a Lost World: Memoirs of East European Jewish Life before World War II*, trans. Eva Zeitlin Dobkin, eds. Dina Abramowicz and Jeffrey Shandler. Detroit: Wayne State University Press, 1999.
Alekseev, V. P. *Svobodnyi grazhdanin i ego prava*. Moscow: Narodnaia biblioteka, 1917.
Aleksinskaia, Tatiana. *Zhenshchina v voine i revoliutsii*. Petrograd, 1917.
Alexinsky [Aleksinskaia], Tatiana. *With the Russian Wounded*, trans. Gilbert Cannan. London: T. Fischer Unwin, Ltd., 1916.
Anfimov, A. M., ed. *Krest'ianskoe dvizhenie v Rossii v gody Pervoi mirovoi voiny. Iul' 1914 g.–fevral' 1917 g. Sbornik dokumentov*. Moscow and Leningrad: Izd. "Nauka," 1965.
Ansky, S. *The Enemy at His Pleasure: A Journey through the Jewish Pale of Settlement in World War I*, ed. and trans. Joachim Neugroschel. New York: Henry Holt and Co., 2002.
Arsenev, N. S. *O svobode i obiazannostiakh grazhdanina*. Moscow, 1917.
Averbakh, O. I. *Zakonodatel'nye akty, vyzvannye voinoiu 1914 goda*. Vilnius, 1915.
Baburina, N. I. *Russkoi plakat Pervoi mirovoi voiny*. Moscow: Firma "Iskusstvo i kul'tura," 1992.
Beatty, Bessie. *The Red Heart of Russia*. New York: Century Co., 1919.
Belov, Vadim. *Evrei i poliaki na voine. Vpechatlenie ofitsera-uchastnika*. Petrograd: Izd-o "Biblioteka Velikoi voiny," 1915.
Bochkarev, V. N. *Chto chitat' o voine*. Moscow: Moskovskoe obshchestvo narodnykh universitetov, 1915.
Bogdanovich, T. *Velikie dni revoliutsii. 23 fevralia–12 marta 1917 g.* Petrograd, 1917.
Bonch-Bruevich, M. D. *Vsia vlast' sovetam. Voennye memuary*. Moscow: Voennoe izdatel'stvo ministerstva oborony SSSR, 1964.
Botchkareva, Maria. *Yashka: My Life as Peasant, Soldier, and Exile. As Set Down by Isaac Don Levine*. New York: Frederick A. Stokes Co., 1919.
Britnieva, Mary. *One Woman's Story*. London: Arthur Barker, 1934.

Select Bibliography

Browder, Robert and Alexander F. Kerensky, eds. *The Russian Provisional Government, 1917: Documents.* 3 vols. Stanford: Stanford University Press, 1961.

Brusianin, V. V. *Voina, zhenshchiny i deti.* Moscow: Mlechnyi put', 1917.

Brusilov, A. *A Soldier's Notebook, 1914–1918.* London: Macmillan, 1930.

Buchanan, Meriel. *Petrograd: The City of Trouble, 1914–1918.* London: C. Scribner's Sons, 1918.

Chego zhdet Rossiia ot voiny. Sbornik statei. Petrograd: Kn-vo "Prometei," 1915.

Cherniavsky, Michael. *Prologue to Revolution: Notes of A. N. Iakhontov on the Secret Meetings of the Council of Ministers, 1915.* Englewood Cliffs, NJ: Prentice-Hall, 1967.

Danilov, Iu. N. *Rossiia v mirovoi voine, 1914–1915 gg.* Berlin: Slovo, 1924.

Denikin, A. I. *The Russian Turmoil. Memoirs: Military, Social, and Political.* London: Hutchinson and Co., n.d.

Farmborough, Florence. *A Nurse at the Russian Front: A Diary 1914–1918.* London: Constable, 1974.

Fedorchenko, Sof'ia. *Narod na voine.* Kiev: Tip. Vserossiiskogo zemskogo soiuza, 1917.

Fenomenov, M. Ia. *Russkii patriotizm i bratstvo narodov.* Moscow: Izd. D. Ia. Makovskogo, 1917.

Gessen, I. V. *V dvukh vekakh. Zhiznennyi put'.* Berlin: Speer and Schmidt, 1937.

Gippius, Z. N. *Stikhi. Dnevnik, 1911–1921.* Berlin: Slovo, 1924.

Glinka, Ia. V. *Odinnadtsat' let v gosudarstvennoi dume. 1906–1917. Dnevnik i vospominaniia.* Moscow: Novoe literaturnoe obozrenie, 2001.

Golovine, N. N. *The Russian Army in the World War.* New Haven: Yale University Press, 1931.

Gorets, Evgenii. *Izmenniki i predateli Rossii.* Moscow: Sytina, 1917.

Gorky, Maxim. *Untimely Thoughts: Essays on Revolution, Culture, and the Bolsheviks, 1917–1918,* trans. Herman Ermolaev. New York: P. S. Eriksson, 1968.

Gosudarstvennaia duma. Stenograficheskie otchety, IV. St. Petersburg, 1914–17.

Gourko [Gurko], Basil. *Memories and Impressions of War and Revolution in Russia, 1914–1917.* London: John Murray, 1918.

Grave, B. B., ed. *Burzhuaziia nakanune Fevral'skoi revoliutsii.* Moscow, 1927.

Grigorov, I. *Soldatskaia pamiatka. (Chto soldaty dali Rossii i chto oni dolzhny poluchit').* Moscow: Narodopravstvo, 1917.

Gruzenberg, O. O. *Yesterday: Memoirs of a Russian-Jewish Lawyer,* trans. Tatiana Tipton. Berkeley: University of California Press, 1981.

Gurko, V. I. *Features and Figures of the Past: Government and Opinion in the Reign of Nicholas II,* trans. by Laura Matveev. Stanford: Stanford University Press, 1939.

Episkop Ioann. *Shpiony ot religii.* N.p.: Izd. Kubanskogo, vo imia Khrista spasitelia, Otdela Vserossiiskogo Trudovogo Soiuza Khristian-Trezvennikov, 1915.

"Iz 'Chernoi knigi' rossiiskogo evreistva. Materialy dlia istorii voiny 1914–1915 g." In *Evreiskaia starina. Sbornik statei za 1917–1918 gody,* vol. X. Petrograd, 1918, 195–296.

The Jews in the Eastern War Zone. New York: American Jewish Committee, 1916.

Kerensky, Alexander F. *The Catastrophe: Kerensky's Own Story of the Russian Revolution.* New York: D. Appleton and Co., 1927.

Select Bibliography

Kir'ianov, Iu. I., ed. *Pravye partii. Dokumenty i materialy*, vol. II, *1911–1917 gg.* Moscow: ROSSPEN, 1998.
Kornilov, A. A. "Vospominaniia," *Voprosy istorii*, nos. 8, 9 and 10 (1994): 112–28, 112–22, 122–34.
Krasnyi arkhiv, 106 vols. Moscow, 1923–41.
Kratkyi obzor deiatel'nosti Vse-rossiiskogo zemskogo soiuza na zapadnom fronte, 1915–1977 gg. Moscow, 1918.
Kratkii otcherk deiatel'nosti Vserossiiskogo zemskogo soiuza. Moscow, 1916.
Kul'chitskii, Rotmistr. *Sovety molodomu ofitseru*, 6th edn. Kharkov, 1917.
Lemke, Mikhail Konstantinovich. *250 dnei v tsarskoi stavke. (25 sent. 1915–2 iulia 1916.)* Petrograd: Gos. Izdatel'stvo, 1920.
Mansyrev, Kn. S. "Moi vospominaniia o gosudarstvennoi dume." *Istorik i sovremennik (Berlin)*, 3 (1922), 3–44.
Nemetskoe zasil'e i pravila 2 fevralia 1915 g. Moscow: Tip. A. I. Mamontova, 1915.
Martov, Iu. O. *Proletariat i natsional'naia oborona*. Petrograd, 1917.
Mikhailov, D. *Krasnyi krest i sestry miloserdiia v Rossii i za-granitsei*. Petrograd and Kiev: Knigoizdatel'stvo "Sotrudnik," 1914.
Miliukov, P. N. *Taktika fraktsii narodnoi svobody vo vremia voiny*. Petrograd, 1916.
"Tseli voiny." *Ezhegodnik gazety Rech' na 1916 g.* Petrograd, 1916.
Vospominaniia (1859–1917), reprint. Moscow: Politizdat, 1991.
Nashi vragi. Obzor deistvii chrezvychainoi sledstvennoi komissii. Petrograd, 1916.
Nikitin, Evgenii. *Velikaia voina i dukhovnoe vozrozhdenie Rossii.* Moscow: Izdanie komissii po organizatsii obshche obrazovatel'nykh chtenii dlia fabrichno-zavodskikh rabochikh goroda Moskvy, 1915.
Nol'de, Baron B. E. *Dalekoe i blizkoe. Istoricheskie ocherki.* Paris: Izd-vo "Sovremennye zapiski," 1930.
Obolenskii, V. A. *Moia zhizn', moi sovremenniki*. Paris: YMCA Press, 1988.
Obzor deiatel'nosti Obshchestva "Samodeiatel'naia Rossiia" za 1915 god. Petrograd, 1916.
Orlov, A. S. *Kooperatsiia v Rossii nakanune i vovremia voiny*, 2nd edn. Moscow: Izdanie "Pechat T-va I. N. Kushnerev i Ko.," 1917.
Os'kin, D. P. *Zapiski soldata*. Moscow: Izd. Federatsiia, 1929.
Osobyi zhurnal soveta ministrov (1914–1916). Moscow: ROSSPEN, 2008.
Otchet Soveta o deiatel'nosti "Obshchestva 1914 goda" za 1915-i god. Moscow, 1916.
Paleologue, Maurice. *An Ambassador's Memoirs*, trans. F. A. Holt, 3rd edn., 3 vols. London: Hutchinson and Co., 1924.
Plekhanov, G. V. *O voine*. Petrograd, 1915.
Purishkevich, V. M. *Tribuna. Rechi V. M. Purishkevicha (stenogrammy) v Gosudarstvennoi dume vo vremia voine.* Petrograd, n.d.
Rabochee dvizhenie v Petrograde v 1912–1917 gg. Dokumenty i materialy. Leningrad: Lenizdat, 1958.
Razlozhenie armii v 1917 godu, ed. by N. E. Kakurin. Moscow and Leningrad: Gosudarstvennoe izd-vo, 1923.
Rossiia v mirovoi voine 1914–1918 godov (v tsifrakh). Moscow: Tsentral'noe statisticheskoe upravlenie, 1925.
Rozanov, Vasilii V. *Voina 1914 goda i russkoe vozrozhdenie*. Petrograd: Tip. Tv-a A. S. Suvorina, 1915.

Runin, Sergei. *Dve sestry – Rossiia i Pol'sha, "Otkliki,"* issue 3. Petrograd, 1915.

Sim pobedish' – mobilizatsiia dukha, Otkliki. Politicheskii zhurnal-fel'etony, reprint of article of July 10, 1915. Petrograd, 1916.

Runkevich, S. G. *Velikaia otechestvennaia voina i tserkovnaia zhizn'*. Petrograd, 1916.

Shavel'skii, Otets Georgii. *Vospominaniia. Poslednego protopresvitera russkoi armii i flota*, 2 vols. New York: Izd. imeni Chekhova, 1954.

Shchegolev, P. E., ed. *Padenie tsarskogo rezhima*, 7 vols. Moscow, 1924–27.

Shelokhaev, V. V., ed. *Partiia sotsialistov-revoliutsionerov. Dokumenty i materialy, 1900–1922 gg*, 3 vols. Moscow: ROSSPEN, 1996–97.

ed. *Partii demokraticheskikh reform, Mirnogo obnovleniia, Progressistov. Dokumenty i materialy, 1906–1916 gg*. Moscow: ROSSPEN, 2002.

Shklovskii, Viktor. *A Sentimental Journey: Memoirs, 1917–1922*, trans. Richard Sheldon. Ithaca: Cornell University Press, 1970.

Shulgin, V. V. *The Years: Memoirs of a Member of the Russian Duma, 1906–1917*, trans. Tanya Davis. New York: Hippocrene Books, 1984.

Sputnik voiny. Sbornik vozzvanii, rechei i prikazov po voprosov voiny. Kiev: Tip. A. I. Grosman, 1917.

Steinberg, Mark D., ed. *Voices of Revolution, 1917*, documents trans. by Marian Schwartz. New Haven: Yale University Press, 2001.

Stenograficheskie otchety zasedanii XI S"ezda upolnomochennykh ob"edinennykh dvorianskikh obshchetv. Moscow, 1915.

Stepun, Fedor A. *Iz pisem praporshchika artillerista*. Moscow: Zadruga, 1918.

Struve, Petr. "Istoricheskii smysl' Russkoi revoliutsii i natsional'nye zadachi." In *Iz glubiny. Sbornik statei o russkoi revoliutsii*. Moscow and Petrograd: Kn-va "Russkaia mysl'," 1918, 235–50.

Sukhanov, N. *Nashi levye gruppy i voina*, 3rd edn. Petrograd: Tip. E. M. Malakhovskogo, 1916.

The Russian Revolution 1917: A Personal Record, ed., abridged, and trans. by Joel Carmichael. London: Oxford University Press, 1955.

Thompson, Donald C. *Blood Stained Russia*. New York: Leslie-Judge Company, 1918.

Tikhomirov, D. I. *Velikaia voina Rossii za svobodu i ob"edinenie slavian. Sbornik statei dlia shkolnik i narodnykh bibliotek*. Moscow: Biblioteka dlia semei i shkoly, 1914.

Trubetskoi, Kn. E. N. *Otechestvennaia voina i ee dukhovnaia smysl'*. Moscow: Tip. T-va I. D. Sytina, 1915.

Velikaia revoliutsiia i krizis patriotizma. N.p., 1919.

Tyrkova-Williams, Ariadna. *From Liberty to Brest-Litovsk: The First Year of the Russian Revolution*. London: Macmillan, 1919.

Velikaia voina v obrazakh i kartinakh, 6th edn, ed. Iv. Lazarevskii. Moscow, 1916.

Voina i derevnia. Kazan: Tsentral'naia tipografiia, 1915.

Voina i derevnia. Petrograd: Tip. "Sel'skogo Vestnika," 1916.

Vrangel', N. N. *Dni skorbi. Dnevnik 1914–1915 godov*, ed. A. A. Murashov. St. Petersburg: Zhurnal Neva, 2001.

Vserossiiskii zemskii soiuz. *Obzor deiatel'nosti glavnogo komiteta, 1 avgusta 1914 g.–1 fevralia 1915 g*. Moscow, 1915.

Select Bibliography 267

Za rodinu, za pravdu Bozhiiu. Petrograd: Synodal'naia tipografiia, 1917.
Zakhareva, Lidiia. *Dnevnik sestry miloserdiia. Na peredovykh pozitsiakh.* Petrograd: Izd. Biblioteka "Velikoi voiny," 1915.
Zamaraev, A. A. *Dnevnik totemskogo krest'ianina A. S. Zamaraeva, 1906–1922 gody*, ed. by V. V. Morozov and N. I. Reshetnikov. Moscow: Rossiiskaia akademiia nauk, 1995.

Secondary Sources

Anderson, Benedict. *Imagined Communities: Reflections on the Origin and Spread of Nationalism*, 2nd edn. New York: Verso, 1991.
Apostol, Paul N. "Credit Operations." In Alexander M. Michelson et al., *Russian Public Finance during the War*. New Haven: Yale University Press, 1928, 233–336
Astashov, A. B. *Russkii front v 1914–nachale 1917 goda. Voennyi opyt i sovremennost'*. Moscow: Novyi khronograf, 2014.
Audoin-Rouzeau, Stéphane and Annette Becker. *14–18: Understanding the Great War*, trans. Catherine Temerson. New York: Hill and Wang, 2000.
Babkin, M. A. *Dukhoventsvo russkoi pravoslavnoi tserkvi i sverzhenie monarkhii. (Nachalo XX v.–konets 1917 g.)*. Moscow: Gosudarstvennaia publichnaia istoricheskaia biblioteka Rossii, 2007.
 Sviashchenstvo i tsarstvo. (Rossiia, nachalo XX v.–1918 g.) Issledovaniia i materialy. Moscow: Izdatel'stvo "INDRIK," 2011.
Badcock, Sarah. "Talking to the People and Shaping Revolution: The Drive for Enlightenment in Revolutionary Russia." *Russian Review* 65 (2006): 617–36.
 "Women, Protest, and Revolution: Soldiers' Wives in Russia during 1917." *International Review of Social History* 49 (2004): 47–70.
Bakhturina, A. Iu. *Okhrainy Rossiiskoi imperii. Gosudarstvennoe upravlenie i natsional'naia politika v gody Pervoi mirovoi voiny (1914–1917 gg.)*. Moscow: ROSSPEN, 2004.
Belogurova, T. A. *Russkaia periodicheskaia pechat' i problemy vnutrennei zhizni strany v gody Pervoi mirovoi voiny (1914–fevral' 1917)*. Smolensk: Gody, 2005.
Berezhnoi, A. F. *Russkaia legal'naia pechat' v gody Pervoi mirovoi voiny*. Leningrad: Leningradskii gosudarstvennyi universitet, 1975.
Billing, Michael. *Banal Nationalism*. London: Sage, 1995.
Bobroff, Ronald. "Devolution in Wartime: Sergei D. Sazonov and the Future of Poland, 1910–1916." *International History Review* (2000): 505–28.
Bonnell, Victoria. *Iconography of Power: Soviet Political Posters under Lenin and Stalin*. Berkeley: University of California Press, 1997.
Bradley, Joseph. "Subjects into Citizens: Societies, Civil Society, and Autocracy in Tsarist Russia." *American Historical Review* 107, 4 (October 2002): 1094–1123.
Brandenberger, David. *National Bolshevism: Stalinist Mass Culture and the Formation of Modern Russian National Identity, 1931–1956*. Cambridge, MA: Harvard University Press, 2002.

Brooks, Jeffrey. *When Russia Learned to Read: Literacy and Popular Literature, 1861–1917*. Princeton: Princeton University Press, 1985.

Brubaker, Rogers. "In the Name of the Nation: Reflections on Nationalism and Patriotism." In Philip Abbott, ed., *The Many Faces of Patriotism*. Lanham, MD: Rowman & Littlefield, 2007, 37–51.

Burbank, Jane. "An Imperial Rights Regime: Law and Citizenship in the Russian Empire." *Kritika* 7 (2006): 397–431.

Russian Peasants Go to Court: Legal Culture in the Countryside, 1905–1917. Bloomington: Indiana University Press, 2004.

Capozzola, Christopher. *Uncle Sam Wants You: World War I and the Making of the Modern American Citizen*. New York: Oxford University Press, 2008.

Chermenskii, E. D. *IV Gosudarstvennaia duma i sverzhenie tsarizma v Rossii*. Moscow: Mysl', 1976.

Chulos, Chris J. "Orthodox Identity at Russian Holy Places." In Chris J. Chulos and Timo Piirainen, eds., *The Fall of an Empire, the Birth of a Nation: National Identities in Russia*. Burlington, VT: Ashgate, 2000, 28–50.

Cohen, Aaron. *Imagining the Unimaginable: World War, Modern Art, and the Politics of Public Culture in Russia, 1914–1917*. Lincoln: University of Nebraska Press, 2008.

Coleman, Heather J. *Russian Baptists and Spiritual Revolution, 1905–1929*. Bloomington: Indiana University Press, 2005.

Colley, Linda. *Britons: Forging the Nation, 1707–1837*. New Haven: Yale University Press, 1992.

Confino, Alon. *The Nation as a Local Metaphor: Wurttemberg, Imperial Germany, and National Memory, 1871–1918*. Chapel Hill: University of North Carolina Press, 1997.

Cornwall, Mark. *The Undermining of Austria-Hungary: The Battle for Hearts and Minds*. Cambridge: Cambridge University Press, 2000.

Crews, Robert D. *For Prophet and Tsar: Islam and Empire in Russia and Central Asia*. Cambridge, MA: Harvard University Press, 2006.

Cunningham, Hugh. "The Language of Patriotism, 1750–1914." *History Workshop Journal* 12 (1981): 8–33.

Curtiss, John S. *Church and State in Russia: The Last Years of the Empire, 1900–1917*. New York: Octagon Books, 1965.

Dagger, Richard. "Republican Citizenship." In Engin F. Isin and Bryan S. Turner, eds., *Handbook of Citizenship Studies*. London: Sage, 2002, 145–58.

Daly, Jonathan W. *The Watchful State: Security Police and Opposition in Russia, 1906–1917*. DeKalb: Northern Illinois University Press, 2004.

Dekel-Chen, Jonathan, David Gaunt, Natan M. Meir, and Israel Bartal, eds. *Anti-Jewish Violence: Rethinking the Pogrom in East European History*. Bloomington: Indiana University Press, 2011.

Diakin, V. S. *Russkaia burzhuaziia i tsarizm v gody Pervoi mirovoi voiny, 1914–1917*. Leningrad: Nauka, 1967.

Natsional'nyi vopros vo vnutrennei politike tsarizma (XIX–nachalo XX vv.). St. Petersburg: LISS, 1998.

Dumova, N. G. *Kadetskaia partiia v period Pervoi mirovoi voiny i Fevral'skoi revoliutsii*. Moscow: Nauka, 1988.

Engel, Barbara Alpern. "Not by Bread Alone: Subsistence Riots in Russia during World War I." *Journal of Modern History* 69, 4 (December 1997): 696–721.
Engelstein, Laura. "'A Belgium of Our Own': The Sack of Russian Kalisz, August 1914." *Kritika* 10, 3 (Summer 2009): 441–73.
Fel'shtinskii, Iurii. *Krushenie mirovoi revoliutsii. Brestskii mir.* Moscow: Terra, 1991.
Figes, Orlando. *A People's Tragedy: A History of the Russian Revolution.* New York: Viking Press, 1996.
Figes, Orlando and Boris Kolonitskii. *Interpreting the Russian Revolution: The Language and Symbols of 1917.* New Haven: Yale University Press, 1999.
Flood, P. J. *France 1914–1918: Public Opinion and the War Effort.* New York: St. Martin's Press, 1990.
Frame, Murray, Boris Kolonitskii, Steven G. Marks, and Melissa K. Stockdale, eds. *Russian Culture in War and Revolution, 1914–1922, Book 1, Popular Culture, the Arts, and Institutions; Book 2, Political Culture, Identities, Mentalities, and Memory.* Bloomington: Slavica, 2014.
Frankel, Jonathan. *Crisis, Revolution, and Russian Jews.* Cambridge: Cambridge University Press, 2009.
Fuller, William C. Jr. *The Foe Within: Fantasies of Treason and the End of Imperial Russia.* Ithaca: Cornell University Press, 2006.
Galili i Garcia, Ziva. "Origins of Revolutionary Defensism: I. G. Tseretelli and the 'Siberian Zimmerwaldists.'" *Slavic Review* 41 (Sep. 1982): 454–76.
Gatrell, Peter. *Russia's First World War: A Social and Economic History.* Harlow, UK: Pearson Education, 2005.
A Whole Empire Walking: Refugees in Russia during World War I. Bloomington: Indiana University Press, 1999.
Gaudin, Corinne. "Circulation and Production of News and Rumor in Rural Russia during World War I." In Frame, Kolonitskii, Marks, and Stockdale, eds., *Russian Culture in War and Revolution, 1914–1922, Book 2, Political Culture, Identities, Mentalities, and Memory*, 55–72.
Gillis, John R., ed. *Commemorations: The Politics of National Identity.* Princeton: Princeton University Press, 1994.
Gleason, William. "The All-Russian Union of Zemstvos and World War I." In T. Emmons and W. Vucinich, eds., *The Zemstva in Russia: An Experiment in Local Self-Government.* Cambridge, MA: Harvard University Press, 1982, 365–82.
Grave, B. *K istorii klassovoi bor'by v Rossii v gody imperialisticheskoi voiny. Iiul' 1914–fevral' 1917 g.* Moscow, 1926.
Gregory, Adrian. *The Last Great War: British Society and the First World War.* Cambridge: Cambridge University Press, 2008.
Gronsky, Paul P. and Nicholas J. Astrov, *The War and the Russian Government.* New Haven: Yale University Press, 1929.
Gullace, Nicoletta F. *"The Blood if Our Sons." Men, Women, and the Renegotiation of British Citizenship During the Great War.* New York: Palgrave Macmillan, 2002.
Hamm, Michael. "Liberal Politics in Wartime Russia: An Analysis of the Progressive Bloc." *Slavic Review* 53 (1974): 453–68.

Hasegawa, Tsuyoshi. *The February Revolution: Petrograd, 1917*. Seattle: University of Washington Press, 1981.
Hedda, Jennifer. *His Kingdom Come: Orthodox Pastorship and Social Activism in Revolutionary Russia*. DeKalb: Northern Illinois University Press, 2008.
Heenan, Louise C. *Russian Democracy's Fateful Blunder: The Summer Offensive of 1917*. New York: Praeger, 1987.
Heretz, Leonid. *Russia on the Eve of Modernity: Popular Religion and Traditional Culture under the Last Tsars*. Cambridge: Cambridge University Press, 2008.
Herrlinger, Page. *Working Souls: Russian Orthodoxy and Factory Labor in St. Petersburg, 1881–1917*. Bloomington: Slavica, 2007.
Hickey, Michael C. "Discourses of Public Identity and Liberalism in the February Revolution: Smolensk, Spring 1917." *Russian Review* 55 (1996): 615–37.
Hirsch, Francine. *Empire of Nations: Ethnographic Knowledge and the Making of the Soviet Union*. Ithaca: Cornell University Press, 2005.
Hobsbawm, E. J. *Nations and Nationalism since 1780: Programme, Myth, Reality*. Cambridge: Cambridge University Press, 1990.
Hoffmann, David L. *Cultivating the Masses: Modern State Practices and Soviet Socialism, 1914–1939*. Ithaca: Cornell University Press, 2011.
Hoffmann, David L. and Yanni Kotsonis, eds. *Russian Modernity: Politics, Knowledge, Practices*. New York: St. Martin's Press, 2000.
Holquist, Peter. "Anti-Soviet *Svodki* from the Civil War: Surveillance as a Shared Feature of Russian Political Culture." *Russian Review* 56 (Jul. 1997): 445–50.
"'Information Is the Alpha and Omega of Our Work': Bolshevik Surveillance in Its Pan-European Context." *Journal of Modern History* 69, 3 (1997): 415–50.
Making War, Forging Revolution: Russia's Continuum of Crisis, 1914–1921. Cambridge, MA: Harvard University Press, 2002.
Horak, Stephen M. *The First Treaty of World War I: Ukraine's Treaty with the Central Powers of February 9, 1918*. New York: Columbia University Press, 1988.
Horne, John, ed. *State, Society and Mobilization in Europe during the First World War*. Cambridge: Cambridge University Press, 1997.
Hosking, Geoffrey. *Russia: People and Empire, 1552–1917*. Cambridge, MA: Harvard University Press, 1997.
Ivanova, Iu. I. *Khrabreishie iz prekrasnykh. Zhenshchiny Rossii v voinakh*. Mascow: ROSSPEN, 2002.
Jahn, Hubertus J. *Patriotic Culture in Russia during World War I*. Ithaca: Cornell University Press, 1995.
Kaiser, Robert J. *The Geography of Nationalism in Russia and the USSR*. Princeton: Princeton University Press, 1994.
Kandidov, B. *Sektanstvo i mirovaia voina*. Moscow: Ateist, 1930.
Kappeler, Andreas. *The Russian Empire: A Multiethnic History*, trans. Alfred Clayton. Harlow, UK: Pearson Education, Ltd., 2001.
Keep, John L. H. *The Russian Revolution. A Study in Mass Mobilization*. London: Weidenfeld & Nicolson, 1976.

Kenez, Peter. *The Birth of the Propaganda State: Soviet Methods of Mass Mobilization, 1917–1929*. Cambridge: Cambridge University Press, 1985.
Kenworthy, Scott. "The Mobilization of Piety: Monasticism and the Great War in Russia, 1914–1916." *Jahrbucher fur Geschichte Osteuropas* 52 (2004): 388–401.
Khasbulatova, O. A. *Opyt i traditsii zhenskogo dvizheniia v Rossii (1860–1917)*. Ivanovo: Ivanovskii gosudarstvennyi universitet, 1994.
Kir'ianov, Iu. I. *Pravye partii v Rossii, 1906–1917*. Moscow: ROSSPEN, 2001.
Kohn, Stanislas. *The Cost of the War to Russia: The Vital Statistics of European Russia during the World War, 1914–1917*. New Haven, 1932.
Kolonitskii, Boris. *Simvoly vlasti i bor'ba za vlast'. K izucheniiu politicheskoi kul'tury Rossiiskoi revoliutsii 1917 g*. St. Petersburg: Dmitrii Bulanin, 2001.
Tragicheskaia erotika. Obrazy imperatorskoi sem'i v Pervoi mirovoi voine. St. Petersburg: Novoe literaturnoe obozrenie, 2010.
Kotkov, V. M. *Sotsial'no-kul'turnaia deiatel'nost' v armii*. St. Petersburg, 2000.
Kotsiubinskii, D. A. *Russkii natsionalizm v nachale XX stoletiia. Rozhdenie i gibel' ideologii Vserossiiskogo natsional'nogo soiuza*. Moscow: ROSSPEN, 2001.
Kotsonis, Yanni. "'Face-to Face': The State, the Individual, and the Citizen in Russian Taxation, 1863–1917." *Slavic Review* 63 (2004): 221–46.
States of Obligation: Taxes and Citizenship in the Russian Empire and Early Soviet Republic. Toronto: University of Toronto Press, 2014.
Lieven, D. C. B. "Dilemmas of Empire, 1850–1918: Power, Territory, Identity." *Journal of Contemporary History* 34, 2 (1999): 163–200.
"Pro-Germans and Russian Foreign Policy 1890–1914." *International History Review* 2 (1980): 34–53.
Lieven, Dominic. *Russia Against Napoleon*. New York: Penguin Books, 2009.
Lih, Lars. *Bread and Authority in Russia, 1914–1921*. Berkeley: University of California Press, 1990.
Lincoln, W. Bruce. *Passage through Armageddon: The Russians in War and Revolution, 1914–1918*. Oxford: Oxford University Press, 1994.
Lindenmeyr, Adele. *Poverty Is Not a Vice: Charity, Society, and the State in Imperial Russia*. Princeton: Princeton University Press, 1996.
Liulevicius, Vejas Gabriel. *War Land on the Eastern Front.: Culture, National Identity, and German Occupation in World War I*. Cambridge: Cambridge University Press, 2000.
Lohr, Eric. *Nationalizing the Russian Empire: The Campaign against Enemy Aliens during World War I*. Cambridge, MA: Harvard University Press, 2003.
"Patriotic Violence and the State: The Moscow Riots of May 1915." *Kritika* 4 (Summer 2003): 607–26.
"The Russian Army and the Jews: Mass Deportations, Hostages, and Violence during World War I." *Russian Review* 60 (2001): 404–19.
Russian Citizenship: From Empire to Soviet Union. Cambridge, MA: Harvard University Press, 2012.
Lowe, Heinz-Dietrich. *The Tsars and the Jews: Reform, Reaction and Anti-Semitism in Imperial Russia, 1772–1917*. Chur, Switzerland: Harwood Academic Publishers, 1993.

Makhonina, S. Ia. "Russkaia legal'naia zhurnalistika XX v. (1905–fevral' 1917) (Opyt sistemnogo issledovaniia)." In B. I. Esin, ed., *Iz istorii russkoi zhurnalistiki nachala XX veka*. Moscow: Izd. Moskovskogo universiteta, 1984, 5–49.

Malkov, V. L., ed. *Pervaia mirovaia voina. Prolog XX veka*. Moscow: Nauka, 1998.

Martin, Terry. *The Affirmative Action Empire: Nations and Nationalism in the Soviet Union, 1923–1939*. Ithaca: Cornell University Press, 2001.

McReynolds, Louise. *The News under Russia's Old Regime: The Development of a Mass Circulation Press*. Princeton: Princeton University Press, 1991.

Melancon, Michael. *The Socialist Revolutionaries and the Russian Anti-War Movement, 1914–1917*. Columbus: Ohio State University Press, 1990.

Meyer, Alfred G. "The Impact of World War I on Russian Women's Lives." In Barbara Evans Clements, Barbara Alpern Engel, and Christine D. Worobec, eds., *Russia's Women: Accommodation, Resistance, Transformation*. Berkeley: University of California Press, 1991, 208–24.

Milne, Lesley. "Novyi Satyrikon, 1914–1918: The Patriotic Laughter of the Russian Liberal Intelligentsia during the First World War and the Revolution." *Slavonic and East European Review* 84, 4 (2006): 639–65.

Minakov, V. P. *Obshchestvenno-pedagogicheskoe dvizhenie v Rossii v gody Pervoi mirovoi voiny*. Voronezh: IMMIF, 2003.

Monger, David. *Patriotism and Propaganda in First World War Britain*. Liverpool: Liverpool University Press, 2012.

Moran, Daniel and Arthur Waldron, eds. *The People in Arms: Military Myth and National Mobilization since the French Revolution*. Cambridge: Cambridge University Press, 2003.

Narskii, I. V. *Revoliutsionery "sprava." Chernosotentsy na Urale v 1905–1916 gg. (Materialy k issledovaniiu "russkosti.")*. Ekaterinburg: Cricket, 1994.

Zhizn' v katastrofe. Budni naseleniia Urala v 1917–1922 gg. Moscow: ROSSPEN, 2001.

Nikolaev, A. B. *Revoliutsiia i vlast'. IV Gosudarstvennaia duma 27 fevral 3 marta 1917 goda*. (St. Petersburg: Izdatel'stvo RGPU im. A. I. Gertsena, 2005.

Norris, Stephen M. *A War of Images: Russian Popular Prints, Wartime Culture, and National Identity, 1812–1945*. DeKalb: Northern Illinois University Press, 2006.

Orlovsky, Daniel. "The Provisional Government and Its Cultural Work." In Abbott Gleason, Peter Kenez, and Richard Stites, eds., *Bolshevik Culture: Experiment and Order in the Russian Revolution*. Bloomington: Indiana University Press, 1985, 39–56.

Pearson, Raymond. *The Russian Moderates and the Crisis of Tsarism, 1914–1917*. London: Barnes & Noble, 1977.

Peregudova, Z. I. *Politicheskii sysk Rossii (1880–1917)*. Moscow: ROSSPEN, 2000.

Petrone, Karen. "Family, Masculinity, and Heroism in Russian War Posters." In Billie Melman, ed., *Borderlines: Genders and Identities in War and Peace, 1870–1930*. New York: Routledge, 1998, 95–119.

Select Bibliography

The Great War in Russian Memory. Bloomington: Indiana University Press, 2011.

Petrovsky-Shtern, Yohanan. *Jews in the Russian Army, 1827–1917: Drafted into Modernity*. Cambridge: Cambridge University Press, 2009.

Pipes, Richard. *The Russian Revolution*. New York: Knopf, 1990.

Struve: Liberal on the Right, 1905–1944. Cambridge, MA: Harvard University Press, 1980.

Pisarenko, I. S. et al. *Blagotvoritel'nye organizatsii kaluzhskoi gubernii v gody Pervoi mirovoi voiny*. Kaluga, 2001.

Plokhy, Serhii. *Ukraine and Russia: Representations of the Past*. Toronto: University of Toronto Press, 2008.

Polner, T. I., V. Obolenskii, and S. Turn, eds. *Russian Local Government during the War and the Union of Zemstvos*. New Haven: Yale University Press, 1930.

Porshneva, O. S. *Krest'iane, rabochie i soldaty Rossii nakanune i v gody Pervoi mirovoi voiny*. Moscow: ROSSPEN, 2004.

Prusin, Alexander V. *The Lands Between: Conflict in the East European Borderlands, 1870–1992*. Oxford: Oxford University Press, 2010.

Pyle, Emily E. "Village Social Relations and the Reception of Soldiers' Family Aid Policies in Russia, 1912–1921," Ph.D. diss., University of Chicago, 1997.

Rabinowitch, Alexander. *The Bolsheviks Come to Power*. New York: W. W. Norton, 1976.

The Bolsheviks in Power: The First Year of Soviet Power in Petrograd. Bloomington: Indiana University Press, 2007.

Prelude to Revolution. The Petrograd Bolsheviks and the July 1917 Uprising. Bloomington: Indiana University Press, 1991.

Read, Christopher. *From Tsar to Soviets: The Russian People and Their Revolution, 1917–1921*. Oxford: Oxford University Press, 1996.

Rendle, Matthew. *Defenders of the Motherland: The Tsarist Elite in Revolutionary Russia*. Oxford: Oxford University Press, 2010.

Retish, Aaron B. *Russia's Peasants in Revolution and Civil War: Citizenship, Identity, and the Creation of the Soviet State, 1914–1922*. Cambridge: Cambridge University Press, 2008.

Reynolds, Michael A. *Shattering Empires. The Clash and Collapse of the Ottoman and Russian Empires, 1908–1918*. Cambridge: Cambridge University Press, 2011.

Rosenberg, William G. *Liberals in the Russian Revolution, 1917–1921*. Princeton: Princeton University Press, 1974.

"Reading Soldiers' Moods: Russian Military Censorship and the Configuration of Feeling in World War." *American Historical Review* 119 (June 2014): 714–40.

Roshwald, Aviel. *The Endurance of Nationalism: Ancient Roots and Modern Dilemmas*. Cambridge: Cambridge University Press, 2006.

Ethnic Nationalism and the Fall of Empires: Central Europe, Russia, and the Middle East, 1914–1923. London: Routledge, 2001.

Ruthchild, Rochelle Goldberg. *Equality and Revolution: Women's Rights in the Russian Empire, 1905–1917*. Pittsburgh: University of Pittsburgh Press, 2010.

Rutman, R. E. *Rossiia v period Pervoi mirovoi voiny i Fevral'skoi burzhuazno-demokraticheskoi revoliutsii.* Leningrad, 1975.
Sanborn, Joshua. *Drafting the Russian Nation: Military Conscription, Total War, and Mass Politics, 1905–1925.* DeKalb: Northern Illinois University Press, 2003.
Imperial Apocalypse: The Great War and the Destruction of the Russian Empire. New York: Oxford University Press, 2014.
"The Mobilization of 1914 and the Question of the Russian Nation: A Re-examination," *Slavic Review* 59, 2 (Summer 2000): 267–89.
Senin, A. S. "Armeiskoe dukhovenstvo Rossii v Pervuiu mirovuiu voinu." *Voprosy istorii* no. 10 (1990): 159–65.
Seregny, Scott. J. "Zemstvos, Peasants, and Citizenship: The Russian Adult Education Movement and World War I." *Slavic Review* 59, 2 (Summer 2000): 290–315.
Shevzov, Vera. *Russian Orthodoxy on the Eve of the Revolution.* Oxford: Oxford University Press, 2004.
Siegelbaum, Lewis H. *The Politics of Industrial Mobilization in Russia, 1914–1917: A Study of the War-Industry Committees.* London: Macmillan, 1983.
Smirnov, N. et al. *Rossiia i Pervaia mirovaia voina. (Materialy mezhdunarodnogo nauchnogo kollokviuma).* St. Petersburg: Izd. "Dmitrii Bulanin," 1999.
Smith, C. Jay Jr. *The Russian Struggle for Power, 1914–1917: A Study of Russian Foreign Policy during the First World War.* New York: Philosophical Library, 1957.
Smith, Jeremy. *Red Nations: The Nationalities Experience in and after the USSR.* Cambridge: Cambridge University Press, 2013.
Smith, John T. "Russian Military Censorship during the First World War." *Revolutionary Russia* 14 (June 2001): 71–95.
Smith, Leonard V., Stephane Audoin-Rouzeau, and Annette Becker. *France and the Great War, 1914–1918,* French sections trans. Helen McPhail. Cambridge: Cambridge University Press, 2003.
Smith, S. A. "Citizenship and the Russian Nation during World War I: A Comment." *Slavic Review* 59, 2 (2000):316–29.
Red Petrograd: Revolution in the Factories, 1917–1918. Cambridge: Cambridge University Press, 1983.
Startsev, V. *Vnutrenniaia politika Vremennogo pravitel'stva. Pervogo sostava.* Leningrad, "Nauka," 1980.
Steinberg, Mark D. *Proletarian Imagination: Self, Modernity, and the Sacred in Russia, 1900–1925.* Ithaca: Cornell University Press, 2002.
Steinwedel, Charles. "To Make a Difference: The Category of Ethnicity in Late Imperial Russian Politics, 1861–1917." In Hoffmann and Kotsonis, eds., *Russian Modernity,* 67–86.
Stepanov, A. E. "Obshchie demograficheskie poteri naseleniia Rossii v period Pervoi mirovoi voiny." In V. Malkov, ed., *Pervaia mirovaia voina. Prolog XX veka.* Moscow: Nauka, 1998, 474–84.
Stites, Richard. "Days and Nights in Wartime Russia: Cultural Life, 1914–1917." In Aviel Roshwald and Richard Stites, eds., *European Culture in the Great War: The Arts, Entertainment, and Propaganda, 1914–1918.* Cambridge: Cambridge University Press, 1999, 8–31.

Revolutionary Dreams: Utopian Vision and Experimental Life in the Russian Revolution. New York: Oxford University Press, 1989.

Stockdale, Melissa K. "'My Death for the Motherland Is Happiness': Women, Patriotism, and Soldiering in Russia's Great War, 1914–1917." *American Historical Review* 109 (February 2004): 78–116.

—— *Paul Miliukov and the Quest for a Liberal Russia, 1880–1918*. Ithaca: Cornell University Press, 1997.

—— "Russian Liberals and the Contours of Patriotism in the Great War." In V. V. Shelokhaev, ed., *Russkii liberalizm. Istoricheskie sud'by i perspektivy*. Moscow: ROSSPEN, 1999, 283–92.

—— "United in Gratitude: Honoring Soldiers and Defining the Nation in World War I Russia." *Kritika* 7, 3 (Summer 2006): 459–85.

—— "What Is a Fatherland? Changing Notions of Duties, Rights, and Belonging in Russia." In Mark Bassin, Christopher Ely, and Melissa K. Stockdale, eds., *Space, Place, and Power in Russia: Essays in the New Spatial History*. DeKalb: Northern Illinois University Press, 2010, 23–48.

Stoff, Laurie S. *They Fought for the Motherland. Russia's Women Soldiers in World War I and Revolution*. Lawrence: University Press of Kansas, 2006.

Stone, Norman. *The Eastern Front, 1914–1917*. London: Penguin, 1975.

Sudavtsov, N. A. "Zemstvo v gody Pervoi mirovoi voiny." In A. P. Korelin, N. G. Koroleva, and L. F. Pisar'kova, eds., *Zemskoe samoupravlenie v Rossii, 1864–1918, Book 2, 1905–1918*. Moscow: Nauka, 2005, 237–316.

Suny, Ronald Grigor and Terry Martin, eds. *A State of Nations: Empire and Nation Making in the Age of Lenin and Stalin*. New York: Oxford University Press, 2001.

Tiutiukin, S. V. *Voina, mir, revoliutsiia. Ideinaia bor'ba v rabochem dvizhenii Rossii 1914–1917 gg*. Moscow: Izd. "Mysl'," 1972.

Tsimbaev, K. N. "Pravoslavnaia tserkov' i gosudarstvennye iubilei imperatorskoi Rossii." *Otechestvennaia istoriia* no. 6 (2005): 42–51.

Tumanova, A. S. *Obshchestvennye organizatsii i russkaia publika v nachale XX veka*. Moscow: Novyi khronograf, 2008.

—— *Obshchestvennye orgnizatsii Rossii v gody Pervoi mirovoi voiny (1914–fevral' 1917 g.)*. Moscow: ROSSPEN, 2014.

Tuminez, Astrid S. *Russian Nationalism since 1856: Ideology and the Making of Foreign Policy*. Lanham, MD: Rowman & Littlefield, 2000.

Ul'ianova, G. N. *Blagotvoritel'nost' v Rossiiskoi imperii. XIX–nachalo XX veka*. Moscow: Nauka, 2005.

Verhey, Jeffrey. *The Spirit of 1914: Militarism, Myth and Mobilization in Germany*. Cambridge: Cambridge University Press, 2000.

von Hagen, Mark. "The Great War and the Mobilization of Ethnicity." In Barnett R. Rubin and Jack Snyder, eds., *Post-Soviet Political Order: Conflict and State-Building*. London and New York: Routledge, 1998, 34–57.

—— *War in a European Borderland: Occupations and Occupation Plans in Galicia and Ukraine, 1914–1918*. Seattle and London: University of Washington Press, 2007.

Wade, Rex. *The Russian Revolution, 1917*, 2nd edn. Cambridge: Cambridge University Press, 2005.

The Russian Search for Peace: February–October, 1917. Stanford: Stanford University Press, 1969.
Weeks, Theodore R. *From Assimilation to Antisemitism: The "Jewish Question" in Poland, 1850–1914*. DeKalb: Northern Illinois University Press, 2006.
Nation and State in Late Imperial Russia: Nationalism and Russification on the Western Frontier, 1863–1914. DeKalb: Northern Illinois University Press, 1996.
Welch, David. *Germany, Propaganda and Total War, 1914–1918: The Sins of Omission*. New Brunswick, NJ: Rutgers University Press, 2000.
Werth, Paul W. *The Tsar's Foreign Faiths: Toleration and the Fate of Religious Freedom in Imperial Russia*. Oxford: Oxford University Press, 2014.
Wheeler-Bennett, John W. *Brest-Litovsk: The Forgotten Peace, March 1918*. New York: W. Morrow, 1939.
Wildman, Allan K. *The End of the Russian Imperial Army*, 2 vols. Princeton: Princeton University Press, 1980, 1987.
Winter, Jay. *Sites of Memory, Sites of Mourning: The Great War in European Cultural History*. Cambridge: Cambridge University Press, 1995.
Winter, Jay and Jean-Louis Robert, eds. *Capital Cities at War: Paris, London, Berlin, 1914–1919*, vol. I. Cambridge: Cambridge University Press, 1997.
Wood, Elizabeth A. *The Baba and the Comrade: Gender and Politics in Revolutionary Russia*. Bloomington: Indiana University Press, 1997.
Wortman, Richard. *Scenarios of Power: Myth and Ceremony in Russian Monarchy*, vol. II, *From Alexander II to the Abdication of Nicholas II*. Princeton: Princeton University Press, 2000.
Yekelchyk, Serhy. *Ukraine: Birth of a Modern Nation*. Oxford: Oxford University Press, 2007.
Youngblood, Denise. *Russian War Films: On the Cinema Front, 1914–2005*. Lawrence: University of Kansas Press, 2007.
Zhuravlev, V. A. *Bez very, tsaria i otechestva. Rossiiskaia periodicheskaia pechat' i armiia v marte–oktiabre 1917 g*. St. Petersburg: Ministerstvo obrazovanniia Rossiiskoi federatsii, 1999.

Index

1812 Fatherland War, 35–37, 54, 108, 118, 133, 145–46, 158–59, 161, see also Second Fatherland War
1905 revolution, 4, 106

Aleksandrovskii Committee for the Wounded, 109
Alekseev, General Mikhail, 71, 236
  interest in propaganda efforts, 52
Alekseevskii Committee, 109
Aleksei Nikolaevich Romanov, 54
Alexander I, 18, 37
Alexandra Fedorovna, Empress, 18–20, 124
  as traitor, 210
All-Russian Day of Prayer, 82–83
Anderson, Benedict, 3, 10, 85
Ansky, S. (Rappaport), 9, 177, 186
antisemitism, 99, 176–77, 184, 208
anti-war sentiment, 3, 39, 41–42, 104, 210, 214, 222–23, 240, 242, 257
Antonii, Archbishop of Kharkov, 93, 100
Arkhangelsk, 145
Armenians, 30, 110, 112
arrests, of revolutionary activists, 42
associations, 107, 109–10, 118–19, 131, 146, 169, 187–88, 192–93, 254
Astashev, Aleksandr, 6
Astrakhan, 151, 189
Atrocities, Extraordinary Investigative Commission, 49–52
  1917, 214, 218–19, 232, 245, 251
Austrians, 33, 70, 72, 195

Baku, 17, 119
Baptists, 100
Black Hundreds, see Right Parties
Bloody Sunday, 1905, 21
Bochkareva, Mariia "Yashka", 1, 13, 233–35, 237, 242, 244
Bolsheviks, 42, 74, 223, 226, 240, 246, 257
  anti-Bolshevik forces, 257

Bonch-Bruevich, General M. D., 169
borderlands, 111, 157, 189, 198, 249
  ethnic composition of population, 153
Brandenburger, David, 3
Brest-Litovsk, Treaty of, 250
Brusilov, General Aleksei A., 2, 209, 233–34
Burbank, Jane, 12

Capozolla, Christopher, 129
censorship, 38–42, 214
  1917, 209, 214, 222–23
  military, 80
  and Jews, 157–58
chaplains, 69, 91–93
charitable associations 108–12, 117, 130, 260
Chelnokov, Mikhail V., 116
Chernigov, 95
Chief Administration for Affairs of the Press, 40, 52
Chkhenkeli, A. I., 128
cinema, 74, 152, 159
  for propaganda, 47–48
  in Germany, 48
citizens, 7, 88, 119–20, 140, 162, 185, 187, 203, 219–20, 229
  appeals to, 106, 148, 235–36
  as subscribers to war loans, 82
citizen soldiers, 140, 165, 214, 220, 230, 246
citizenship, 140–41, 231, 254–55, 259–60
  broadening of, 255
  definitions of, 11–12 see also, language of citizenship
  Soviet, 260
  war relief as duty of, 129
citizenship rights, 7, 128, 161–64, 259–60
  aid to soldiers' families, 142–44
  earning of, 139
  and women, 126, 231, 235
civic duty, 115, 221, 229, 235, 255

civil war, 257–58
class, 30, 57, 107, 133, 137, 212, 221, 238, 242, 252
cleansing, 167, 181, 195, 200, 259
clergy, Russian Orthodox, 77, 79, 81, 88, 94–95, 101, 203
 political investigations into, 104
Colley, Linda, 5
commemoration, 35–36, 140, 145, 158, 160, 260
Committee of Elizaveta Fedorovna, 109–10
Committee of Popular Salvation, 206
Committee on Popular Publications, 53, 142
Committee on Social-Political Enlightenment, 224–27
community, 81, 147, 161, 214
 "imagined" national, 3
 national minorities, 121
 national-religious, 89
 sense of belonging, 138
Constantinople, 54, 99
Constitutional Democratic Party (Kadets), 25, 128, 178, 213
continuum of crisis, 6
cooperatives, 118–19, 226, 253
Cossacks, 17, 243
 and anti-Jewish violence, 178
 images of, 48, 67
Council of Ministers, 49
 and abolition of Jewish Pale of Settlement, 182–83
 and rights of national minorities, 172
 expenditures, 36
 on land for soldiers, 156
 on soldiers, 144

Dan, Fedor, 250
Danilov, General Iurii, 2, 116
Declaration of Soldiers' Rights, 224
demobilization, 243, 249
Denikin, General Anton, 2, 45, 236, 241
deportations, of Germans 198–202
Dolina, Maria I., patriotic concerts, 131, 136
Duma deputies, 24, 42, 162–63, 185, 206
duty,
 as component of patriotism, 63
 of the citizen, 95, 193

economic nationalism, 191
Ekaterinburg, 94
elites, 3
Elizaveta Fedorovna, Grand Duchess, 149

enemies of the people, 207, 244, 259
equal rights, 127, 163, 165, 188, 221, 232, 257
 and women, 127, 231, 235
Evangelical Christians, as "Germans," 100, 202, 204
Extraordinary Investigation Commission, see Atrocities, Extraordinary Investigation Committee

"faith, tsar and fatherland," 16, 37, 57, 75, 85, 97, 147
Far Right, All-Russian Congress of Monarchists (November 1915), 189–90
fatherland (otechestvo),
 definition of, 11
Fatherland Patriotic Union, 188, 191
feminists, 123, 126, 217, 239
film, see cinema
flags, 15, 19, 30–31, 130, 160
"For Russia", 219, 240
fraternal cemeteries, see war cemeteries
Free Economic Society, 119
French revolution, as model, 233, 236
Fridman, Niftel, 25

Galicia, 54, 98–99, 177
Gatrell, Peter, 6, 120
gender roles, 231–32
 women, 122–23, 126, 240
generosity, as Russian national characteristic, 137, 254
German colonists, 197–98, 216
 press depictions of, 58
German dominance, 54, 73, 98, 193–95, 219
 popular belief in, 103
German Dominance, Special Committees on Fighting, 201, 205–6
Germans, anti-German sentiment, 49, 104, 191, 197, 210, 252
Golovin, General Nikolai N., 2, 32
Golubev, I. Ia., 23
Goremykin, Ivan L., 24
 Duma speech praising Poles (1915), 172
Gorkii, Maksim, 184, 223
Got'e, Iurii, 223, 248
Great Retreat, 38, 69, 182
Great Russian (russkii), 4, 59, 73, 100, 128, 157, 199, 238

heroes, 63, 87, 155–56, 240, 261
 as element of national myth, 66
 efforts to publicize, 69

failure to publicize, 45
fallen soldiers, 147
hero-martyrs, 66, 72, 147
Kriuchkov, Koz'ma, 67
Nesterov, P. N., 68
perpetuating memory of, 148
Oleg Konstantinovich, Prince, 68
privileges and benefits for, 150–52
publicizing heroes and their deeds, 150–52
Sisters of Mercy, 69
women, 240
high command, fear of politics, 45, 48, 155, 178, 211, 236
history, awareness of and teaching, 3, 36
Hobsbawm, Eric, 10
Holquist, Peter, 6, 164
Holy Rus', 162
Holy Russia, 257
Holy Synod, 78, 93
prewar problems, 77
war-related proclamations, 75
Holy War, 24, 35, 98, 105
First World War as holy war, 53
Second World War as, 75

Ianushkevich, General N. N., 2, 191
antisemitism of, 182, 186
icons, 17, 19, 230
inflation, 34, 137, 207
inorodtsy, definition, 25
"internal enemies," 101, 167, 189, 207–8, 223
Iusupov, Prince F. F., Governor General of Moscow, 195
Ivanova, Rimma M., 126

Jahn, Hubertus F., 3, 130
Jewish Pale of Settlement, ad hoc abolition of, 183
Jews, 118, 176–77, 186, 188, 190, 200
and war relief, 121
as soldiers, 158, 185
differential treatment of Jewish heroes, 157–58
expulsions (1915), 157–58, 179
in Duma, 25, 185–86
patriotism of, 30, 112
relations with Poles, 177
self-defense efforts, 183–85
taken hostage by Russian military, 179
"just war," 16, 24, 27, 73
depictions of Russia's war as, 21, 43, 53–54, 57

Kaiser Wilhelm II, images of, 97
Kalisz, atrocities in, 48, 50
Kaluga, 136
Kazan, 24, 36
Kerenskii, Aleksandr, 26, 205, 207, 229–30
Kharkov, 93, 101, 145
Kiev, 30, 68, 119, 124, 236, 258
Kir'ianov, Iu. I., 41
Kishkin, N. M., 121
Kolonitskii, Boris, 6, 211
Kornilov, General Lavr, 242
Kovno province, expulsion of Jews (1915), 181
Kriuchkov, Koz'ma, 68
Krivoshein, Aleksandr V., Minister of Agriculture, 55, 156, 183
Krivtsov, Aleksei N., 49
Kursk, 26, 95, 114
Kutuzov, Field Marshal Mikhail I., 17

labor strikes (July 1914), 17, 42
Ladies' Committees, 110, 122, 129
land,
as reward for St. George Cavaliers, 154–56
expropriations, 198, 200
land for soldiers, Ianushkevich proposal (1915), 154–56
language of citizenship, 107, 139, 185, 219, 221, 255
language of class, 221–22, 238, 250
language of sacrifice, 96, 105, 139, 255
Latvia and Latvians, 24, 33, 120, 169
leaflets, patriotic, 93
League of Equal Rights for Women, 127
letters, 8, 39, 202
from soldiers, 138, 147, 177, 208–9, 224, 244
for soldiers, 87–88, 92, 119, 137, 226
literature for soldiers, 51–53, 88, 92, 101, 142–44, 147, 225–26
Lohr, Eric, 6, 12, 198
L'vov, Georgii, 210, 213

Maklakov, Vasilii, 162
Manifesto to Poles (August 1, 1914), 171
Mansyrev, Prince S. P., 127, 193
maps, 10, 36, 64, 86
wartime demand for, 53
Markov II, Nikolai, 26, 118, 185
martyrs, 162, see also heroes
meaning of the war, Mass organizations, 1917, 37, 53, 56–57, 93–94, 96–99, 219–20, 227
medals, 32, 35

280 Index

memorializing fallen soldiers,
   functions of, 147–48
   in other belligerent countries, 145, 148
Memory, 37, 148, 260
Mennonites, 121, 141, 201
Miasoedev, Sergei N., 102, 168
military clergy, see chaplains, military
Military League (1917), 235
military reforms of 1912, law on aid to
     soldiers' families, 141–42, 144
military service, 7, 141, 201, 203, 217
   and citizenship rights, 162
   as citizen's sacred duty, 91
   evasion of, 116
military zones, 39
Miliukov, Pavel N., 5, 8, 25, 129, 205
   and defense of national minorities, 185
   "treason or stupidity" speech, 210–11
Minin and Pozharskii, 28, 62, 229, 260
Ministry of Agriculture, 154
Ministry of Finance, 227
Ministry of Internal Affairs, 36, 61, 71, 201
mobility, geographic and social, 3, 183
mobilization,
   civilian self-mobilization, 16, 106, 119, 127
   consequences of, 211, 256
   home front, symbiosis of state and private efforts, 74
   military, 16–17, 31–33, 46
   of expectations, 4, 139, 256
   posters, 63
   techniques of, 46
mobilization of morale, 45, 211
monarchist parties, see Right Parties
monasteries and monastics, 79, 85
   contributions to the war effort, 79–80
   criticisms of, 80–81
morale, 129, 224–25, 234
   1916, 210
   army, 217, 245–46
   clerical efforts to raise, 88, 94
Moscow, 22, 28, 31, 219–20, 226
   anti-German pogroms, 1914, 193
   censorship, 41
   imperial family's visit, 1914, 22
   merchants, 119, 128
   military mobilization, 33
   Moscow Women's Battalion of Death, 235
   Municipal Guardianship of the Poor, 117
   riots, 1915, 195
   zemstvos, 113
Mosse, George, 145

motherland (rodina), 54, 115, 137, 142, 153, 204, 226
   definition of, 11
   love of, 21, 27, 56–57, 70, 156
   national characteristic, 72
Muslims, 24, 59, 120, 163, 209
myth of war enthusiasm, 31
myths, 5, 72, 108, 260

narratives, 3, 5, 17, 21, 42–43, 46, 76, 99, 140, 211, 254
   heroic, 3, 108
   of heroism, 73
Narskii, Igor, 6
nation and nationhood, 4, 11, 140, 248, 251–52
national anthem, 19, 30, 36, 160, 194
national community, 46, 86, 105, 116, 137–39, 141, 143, 150, 156, 251, 253
   exclusion from, 7, 144, 157, 190–91
   foundations of, 148
   membership in, 58, 66, 89, 100, 158, 161, 182, 186–87, 191, 223
national consciousness, 3, 129, 138, 255
national holiday, in honor of those who shed their blood for Russia, 158–61
national identities, 85, 120, 161, 212
national landscape, 183
national minorities, loyalty of, 176
Nationalist Party, 25
Nekrasova, O. A., 232
Nemirovich-Danchenko, V. I., 15
networks, 105, 107–8, 110, 114–15, 138, 253
Nicholas II, 18, 35, 44, 53, 144, 152, 211
Nikolai Nikolaevich, Grand Duke, 82, 156, 168, 179
Nizhnyi Novgorod, 189
nobles, associations, 118
Novgorod, 103, 145
nurses, see Sisters of Mercy

Obolenskii, V. A., 18
Octobrists, 25 see Zemstvo-Octobrists
Odessa, 30, 33, 41, 242
Order of St. George, see St. George Cavaliers
Orenburg, 32
Orlov, Grigorii, 187

Palace Square, St. Petersburg, 19, 21
Pale of Settlement, 176, 182–83
Paleologue, Maurice, 18
pamphlets, 35, 51, 166

Index

1917, 226
  mass editions of, 69, 71
  on aid to soldiers' families, 143
  on memorialization, 147
  published by Orthodox Chruch, 88
parades, 15, 29, 36, 152, 159
Pares, Bernard, 34
parishes,
  guardianship councils, 80–81, 89
  numbers of, 80
  schools, 76, 86
patriotic culture, 3, 52
  war relief as component of, 137
patriotic demonstrations, 28–30, 33, 42, 57, 194, 241, 258
patriotic exemplars, clergy as, 95
patriotic exhibits,
  traveling St. George exhibit, 1916, 151
patriotic shows (spektakly), 88, 130–31
patriotic societies, 69, 130, 187–88, 193, 206–7, 235, 240
patriotism,
  and political capital, 120, 128–29
  and revolution, 213, 220, 233, 236, 244
  and violence, 31, 194
  as profitable, 64
  definitions of, 10–11
patriots, 204, 257
  characteristics of, 57–58
Peasant Land Bank, 154
peasants, 3, 31, 52, 72, 126
  and citizenship rights, 162–64
  expectations of land for service, 154–56, 199
  interest in news of war, 55, 245
  and war relief, 134
"people's war," 21, 121, 133
periodicals, 21, 40, 59
  closed by authorities, 40
  for soldiers, 55, 177, 197
    1917, 220, 223
      Soldat-Grazhdanin (The Soldier-Citizen), 221
  new, 9
  wartime, 21
Perm, 32
Peshekhonov, A., 27
petitions, 184, 259
  for aid for soldiers' families, 143
  from expropriated Russian Germans, 200–1
Petrograd Soviet of Workers and Soldiers' Deputies, 213–14, 217, 227, 242
Petrone, Karen, 6

philanthropic associations, see charitable' associations
pilgrimage, imperial family's trip to Moscow as, 54
pilgrimages, 82
Pitirim, Metropolitan, and Jews, 100
Plekhanov, Georgii, 60, 225, 258
pogroms, 178, 193, 242
Poland, 39, 155, 170, 216
Poles, 25–26, 111, 177, 191
  1918, 258
  included in patriotic narrative, 170–75
  prewar distrust of, 170
police, 17, 103, 167, 216
  and demonstrations, 30
Polish Legions, 173
political capital, 139
political truce, 15, see also sacred union
Polivanov, A. A., Minister of War, 176
Poltava, 94, 145
popular piety, 78
Porshneva, O. S., 3
posters, 62, 131, 227
POWs, 82, 114, 136
  alleged German mistreatment of, 51
Pravda, 42
press, 9, 13, 27, 30, 40, 43, 48–49, 56, 126, 207, 211, 240, 245
  and anti-German feeling, 60–61, 195–97
  and war-loan campaigns, 62, 227
  coverage of war relief, 118, 121, 134, 137
  "Day of the Press," 130
  government subsidies to, 60–61
  Right-wing, YY, 58–60, 222
  Ukrainian, 40
  workers', 61
print media, 3
Progressive Bloc, 190
prohibition of alcohol, 34–35
Prokhanov, I. S., 204
propaganda, 48, 225–27
  institutions of, 45, 52
  mass-edition pamphlets, 55
  Russian use of, 46
Provisional Government, 215–18, 223, 224, 227, 243
public lectures, 39, 62, 184, 219, 225–26
public mood, 31, 33, 208, 210
public organizations, 113–16, 118
  critics of, 116
Purishkevich, Vladimir M., 23, 173, 205
  and Jews, 188
Pyle, Emily E., 141

Index

Red Cross, Russian Society of, 79, 109, 113, 123–24, 169
refugee relief, as source of national solidarity, 120, 184
refugees, 80, 111, 115, 182, 184
regeneration through war, 98
religious services, non-Orthodox, 28
Retish, Aaron B., 3, 6
Right parties, 26, 61, 188–91
riots, draft, 32, 41
rituals, 10, 18, 43, 82–83, 91, 105, 125
   1917, 230, 241
   for schoolchildren, 87
   of political reconciliation, 23
Rodzianko, Mikhail, 23, 234
rossiiskii, 4
Rostov on the Don, 199
Runin, Sergei, 173, 211
rural sentiment, 31, 104
Russian nation, inclusive defintions of, 74
Russian Orthodox Church, 75–76, 105, 137, 216
   memorialization, 82, 145–46
   prayers, 28, 82
   Prikhodskii listok (Parish News), 89–91
Russkii rabochii (Russian Worker), 61
Russo-Japanese war, 16, 32, 108, 154
Ruzskii, General N. V., 146

sacred duty, 114–15, 258
sacred union, 21, 72, 107, 128, 140, 148, 187, 211, 215, 249, 252
   and access to citizenship rights, 128
   components of, 17, 121
   depictions of, 74
   familial images of, 27, 64–66, 111–12, 173
   generosity as component of, 129
   including national minorities, 27, 111–12, 169
   Orthodox Church's version of, 99, 105
   violations of, 60, 185, 206
sacrifice, 2, 16, 37, 45, 54, 58, 66, 138–40, 145, 156, 160–61, 185, 212, 231
   as component of Russian national character, 72
   as proof of patriotism, 138
   see also, language of
Samarkand, 229
Sanborn, Joshua, 6, 32, 251
Sazonov, Sergei D., Minister of Foreign Affairs, 24, 156
scapegoats, 167, 205, 212
Schools and the war, 53, 86, 89, 160

Second Fatherland War, 6, 38, 57, 69, 148
sectarians, 78, 100, 202–4
Sel'skii vestnik (Rural Herald), 55–58, 143, 186
Seregny, Scott, 6
Sevastopol, 110
Shavel'skii, Father Georgii, 69, 91, 97
Shishkina-Iavein, Poliksena, 127
Shtiurmer, Boris, 210, 223
Siberia, 1, 76, 115, 235, 250
Sisters of Mercy, 68, 123–26
   becoming soldiers, 239
   memorialized, 82
   negative images of, 126
   numbers of, 123, 125
   social composition of, 124
Skobelev, General Mikhail D., 47
Smolensk, 35
Social Democrats, 26–27, 190
social patriotism, 107, 122, 254
Society for Aid to Soldiers and Their Families, 106, 109
Society for Remembrance, 146–49
   membership in, 148
Society of 1914, 193
soldiers, 87, 125, 143, 164–65, 212, 239, 248
   disabled, 109, 146, 217–18
   honoring soldiers, 88, 146–48, 158–61
   on Jews, 138
   religious-patriotic conversations with, 93–94
   surrendering and desertion, 52, 144, 157, 224, 244 see also, literature for soldiers
soldiers' oath, 91, 94, 215–16
soldiers' wives (soldatki), 41, 141, 143–44, 221, 255
Sologub, Fedor, 131, 184
speculators, as unpatriotic, 207–8
spies, 197, 203, 223, 258
   through religion, 204
spymania, 167–69, 178
   in other combatant states, 167
St. George Cavaliers, 150–54, 218
   Committee for, 150–51
   Sisters of Mercy as, 126
St. Petersburg Telegraph Agency, 21, 29, 113
State Council, 23
State Duma, 29, 102, 107, 172, 176, 188, 190, 203, 210–13, 215, 226
   and aid to soldiers' families, 141–42
   and bill on rights of peasants, 162–64

Index

and defense of Jews (1915), 185–86
Committee on the Struggle with German Dominance, 205–6
in propaganda, 55
Jewish deputies, 184
July 26, 1914, meeting of, 23–27
popular confidence in, 102, 185
sessions (1915), 57, 186
stenographic reports, 9
Stavropol, 101
strikes, political, 41
Struve, Petr, 219
subjects and subjecthood, 12, 107, 162, 190, 198, 259
definition of, 11–12
Sukhanov, Nikolai, 222
Sukhomlinov, V. A., Minister of War, 102, 168

Tambov, 2, 155, 235
Tatars, 87, 112
Tatiana Nikolaevna, Grand Duchess, 124
Tatiana Committee, 110–12
Tikhanovich-Savitskii, Nestor N., 189
Time of Troubles, 190, 229
Tol'stoi, Count Ivan I., 17, 133, 171, 184
critiques of nationality policy, 169
Tomsk, 32
total war, 46, 140, 232, 251
traitors, 95, 102, 145, 166, 177, 184, 190, 212, 223, 244, 257
Trubetskoi, Prince Evgenii, 98, 185
Trudovik Party, 26
Turkestan, 152, 209
Turkey, depictions of, 51, 54

Ufa, 36, 83
Ukrainian national consciousness, 4
Ukraine and Ukrainians, 30, 40, 72, 184, 219, 249
as disloyal, 190
Union of Archangel Michael, 187
Union of Cities, 121, 128
donations to, 136
founding, 114
fundraising, 131
membership in, 115
Union of Russian People, 30, 59, 61
Union of Tsar and People, 15, 18, 23, 43, 57
Union of Zemstvos, 53, 113–16, 136, 213
founding, 113–14
union sacrée, see sacred union

United Russia, 15
United States, citizens and the war, 129, 221, 226
unity, 27, 31, 43, 88, 111, 181, 185, 187–88, 205, 215, 225, 256

valorization, see heroes
Verhey, Jeffrey, 13, 31
Vermechuk, Stefan, 69–73
Vladimir, 85
Vladivostok, 115
Voina i evrei (The War and Jews), 185
Volga, 151
Volga region, 189, 250
Vologda, 33, 134
voluntary associations,
on the eve of the war, 107–8
proliferation of in 1917, 218–19
volunteers, 81, 95, 115, 119, 123, 129
for military service, 233–34, 239
women, 237
Volynia, 69
von Hagen, Mark, 4
Voronezh, 229
Vrangel', Baron Nikolai N., 1, 40, 56, 112, 171

war as opportunity, 76–77, 86, 120, 128
war as transformative, 4, 35, 44, 119–20, 138, 191, 251–52
war cemeteries, 145–46, 149, 260
war loans, 81–82
campaigns, 61–66, 226–29
function of, 66
Liberty Loan, 229
war memorials, 147
designs, 149
function of, 145
local, 85
war relief, 7, 87, 108–9, 117, 131, 143
and business community, 119, 128
and national minorities, 120–21, 128, 203
donations, 44, 115, 133
by professional associations, 119
Russian Orthodox Church, 79
fundraising strategies, 129–33
Jewish Committee for the Relief of Victims of War, 184
Polish, 120, 172, see also volunteers
Warsaw, 171, 179
Winter Palace, 30
defense of (1917), 243

women, 5, 13, 41, 49, 82, 115, 126–28, 226
  as citizens, 217, 229, 235
  see also gender roles
  new wartime occupations, 121–22
  soldiers, 230, 231, 237, 239–40
  war relief, 122–28, 130
women's battalions, in combat, 241–44
Women's Mutual Aid Society, 117
workers, 19, 60–61, 192, 208, 238
  and war relief, 133
  as patriots, 63
  attitude toward war, 27, 240
  patriotism of, 30, 65

Yashka, see Mariia "Yashka" Bochkareva

Zamaraev, A. A., 33, 134, 249
Zemstvo-Octobrists, 25–26
Zweig, Stefan, 1